In Memory of

Dr. Kristin
Fedders
1966-2006

THE COLLECTING CULTURES SERIES
Edited by Susan M. Pearce

Other titles in the series:
Collecting in a Consumer Society by Russell W. Belk

ON COLLECTING

*An investigation into collecting
in the European tradition*

Susan M. Pearce

London and New York

First published 1995
by Routledge
11 New Fetter Lane, London EC4P 4EE

Simultaneously published in the USA and Canada
by Routledge
29 West 35th Street, New York, NY 10001

First published in paperback 1999

Typeset in Stempel Garamond by
The Florence Group, Stoodleigh, Devon

Printed and bound in Great Britain by
T J International Ltd, Padstow, Cornwall

British Library Cataloguing in Publication Data
A catalogue record for this book is available from the British Library

Library of Congress Cataloguing in Publication Data
Pearce, Susan M.
On Collecting : An investigation into collecting in the European
tradition / Susan M. Pearce.
p. cm. — (Collecting cultures)
Includes bibliographical references and index.
1. Collectors and collecting—Europe—History. I. Title.
II. Series.
AM342.P43 1995
069.5'094—dc20 94-35151

ISBN 0–415–07560–2 (hbk)
ISBN 0–415–07561–0 (pbk)

CONTENTS

———— ·◆· ————

— Contents —

SERIES EDITOR'S PREFACE

Nearly one in every three people in North America collects something, and this figure is unlikely to be very different for most of northern and large parts of southern Europe. Some 30 per cent of this population are therefore willing to define themselves as collectors, and to see collecting as a significant element in their lives. 'Collecting' is difficult to define (and its scope is an important issue which the books in this series address), but clearly the gathering together of chosen objects for purposes regarded as special is of great importance, as a social phenomenon, as a focus of personal emotion and as an economic force.

In the past, the study of collecting has concentrated upon the content of collections, usually viewed from the perspective of a traditional discipline such as the History of Art, Geology or Archaeology. In this, of course, study was in line with characteristic modernist approaches to understanding, of which the disciplines themselves were also a major part. New work in the field has opened up new and fruitful ideas which are concerned with collecting as a process in itself, and with the nature of collecting as part of our effort to construct an intelligible world-view.

Collecting seen from this angle will be the topic of the volumes of this series. The books will explore issues like: the social context of collecting in both the historical long term and the medium term of single lives; the relationship of collecting to consumption; and the ways in which collecting can contribute to the creation of identity in areas like the dimensions of time, space and gender. Particular studies will draw also on debates concerning the nature of material culture and our response to it, and the nature of the museum as the institution concerned with collecting.

Collecting lies near to the hearts of many of us, and close also to our social mind and our ability to understand ourselves and the world we live in. This series is the first to explore this significant and fascinating area of human experience. Objects are our other selves; the better we understand them, the closer we come to self-knowledge.

Susan M. Pearce

PLATES

——— •◆• ———

FIGURES

——— •◆• ———

PREFACE

——— •◆• ———

A book of this kind is a long time in the making and draws on a wide range of sources. I have been engaged with collectors and collections over a period of some thirty years and much of what I have absorbed has gone into the writing of this book. The book also draws heavily on three very important projects into the nature of collecting which have been mounted over the recent years – the Odyssey Project organised at the University of Utah in the USA, the People's Show Project in Britain and the Leicester University Contemporary Collecting Project carried out throughout Britain. All of these will be published in appropriate detail elsewhere, but information and concepts drawn from them inform this book. I should like to record my debt to Russell Belk and his colleagues in Utah, Peter Jenkinson and many museum colleagues across the English Midlands and Sarah Wheeler who acted as my Research Assistant for the Contemporary Collecting Project.

This book is cast in the form of a broadly based investigation into the nature of the collecting process, in one specific tradition; that of Europeans, including both those living in Europe today and those of European descent elsewhere in the world. I have deliberately cast my net wide, in the belief that collecting is a more significant social phenomenon than has usually been supposed, and one which has suffered in its investigation from over-narrow cultural assumptions.

The reasons why I have chosen to write from a European perspective are set out in detail in the early part of the book. Suffice it to say here that the work of Fernand Braudel seems to offer a way of approaching the ancient philosophical dilemma of historical determinism as against individual free-dom of action by combining the notion of organic historical continuity with that of a more immediate social and individual process. This notion helps us to understand a specific complex and long-term practice like that which we see as accumulating and collecting in the European tradition.

A large number of individuals have contributed particular pieces of information. Singling out names is always difficult, but I should like to record my thanks to Janet Dugdale, Emma Chaplin, Fiona Spiers, Lorna Mackenzie, Sarah Harbidge, Liz Sobell, Alex Bounia, Philip Butler, Angela Kellie, Stuart Sale, Charlotte Matthews, Paul Kiddy, Peter Woodhead, Victoria Barlow, Elizabeth Austin, Helen Sykes, Dan Hillier, Marcia Wallace, Eliza Towlson, Alan Brodie, John Carman, Victoria Knapman,

Jeanne Cannizzo, Deirdre Figueiredo, Paul Hyman, Joanna Mattingley, Kathy Elliot, Gillian White and Margaret Blake. To all these and others too numerous to mention, I am grateful.

I wish to record my best thanks to Madeline Lowe, to Ann Sarson who turned a handwritten manuscript into a word-processed text, and to Jim Roberts who produced all the figures. Finally, as always, my thanks go to Mac, my husband.

Leicester, May 1994

NOTE TO THE PAPERBACK EDITION

I am grateful to Routledge for providing the opportunity for this book to appear in a paperback form, so that it can be more generally accessible. Since it first came out in 1995, I have been able to complete and publish the Leicester University Contemporary Collecting Project, which presents the evidence and conclusions drawn from a substantial survey of collecting habits in Britain (*Collecting in Contemporary Practice*, Sage 1998). This does not change the ideas expressed in this book, but does give the detailed material which fed into some of the suggestions here (see p. 12). Similarly, a publishing project entitled *The Collector's Voice* (Vols 1–4, Scolar Press; Vols 1 and 2 to appear 1999) is aimed at offering the texts of collectors' own views of their activities, from the earliest times to AD 2000. This will provide in accessible and edited form the authored statements which run parallel to the discussion in this book.

Collecting seems likely to remain an important social phenomenon as the millennium comes and goes. It represents one of the fundamental ways in which people use material culture to construct their identities and their social roles. The collecting process is now well-established as a topic in the academic field, and this printing of *On Collecting* is offered in the hope of stimulating further interest and study.

Leicester, December 1998

ACNOWLEDGEMENTS

—— •◆• ——

Acknowledgement is made for permission to use the following quotations:

Extract from *Cold Comfort Farm* (1956) by Stella Gibbons reprinted by permission of Curtis Brown Limited; extract from *A Family Affair* (1972) by Michael Innes reprinted by permission of A. P. Watt on behalf of J. I. M. Stewarts; excerpt from *Aristotle: Prior and Posterior Analytics* (1964) by J. Warrington by permission of Everyman's Library; excerpt from *Aristotle on the Art of Poetry* (1920) ed. I. Bywater by permission of Oxford University Press; excerpt from p. 101, lines 3152–9, 3152–70 of *Beowulf* (1953) ed. and trans. D. Wright reproduced by permission of Penguin Books; extract from *Between the Acts* (1942) by Virginia Woolf with thanks to the Hogarth Press; extract from pp. 128–9 of *The Cloud of Unknowing* (1961) trans. C. Wotters reproduced by permission of Penguin Books; excerpt from *Common Culture* (1990) by P. Willis by permission of the Open University Press; excerpt from *The English as Collectors* (1972) by L. Herrmann by kind permission of the author; excerpt from *The Frogs* (1970) by Aristophanes ed. R. Lattimore through correspondence with Hodder & Stoughton; excerpt from *The Gnostic Gospels* (1982) by E. Pagels by permission of Weidenfeld & Nicolson; excerpt from *The Human Condition* (1959) by H. Arendt by permission of the University of Chicago Press; excerpt from *Letters of Cicero to his Friends* (1978) ed. D. Bailey by permission of Penguin Books; excerpt from *The Name of the Rose* (1983) by Umberto Eco by permission of Martin Secker and Warburg Ltd; extract from p. 315 of *Chronicles of the Crusades* (1963) by Geoffroide Villehardouin and Jean, Lord of Joinville, trans. and ed. M. Shaw by permission of Penguin Books; excerpt from *The New Golden Land* (1975) by H. Honour by permission of Allen Lane and Peters, Fraser and Dunlop; quotations from the words of collectors in the People's Show by kind permission of Walsall Museum & Art Gallery; excerpt from *The Politics of Aristotle* (1959) ed. H. W. C. David by permission of Oxford University Press; excerpt from *The Sacred Grove* (1970) by D. Ripley by permission of William Heinemann Ltd, through A. M. Heath Ltd; excerpt from *The Streets of Pimlico* (1983) by A. N. Wilson by permission of Martin Secker and Warburg through A. M. Heath Ltd; excerpt from *Something Fresh* (1967) by P. G. Wodehouse by permission of Random House; excerpt from *Utz* (1988) by B. Chatwin by permission of Random House.

PART I

COLLECTING PROCESSES

CHAPTER ONE

COLLECTING PROCESSES

—— •◆• ——

'Now my hobby,' said the [nerve] specialist, 'is the collecting of [Egyptian] scarabs. Why should you not collect scarabs? Some scarabei bear inscriptions having references to places, as, for instance, "Memphis is mighty for ever".'

Mr Peters' scorn changed suddenly to active interest.

'Have you got one like that?'

'Like – ?'

'A scarab boosting Memphis. It's my home town.'

'I think it possible that some other Memphis was alluded to.'

'There isn't any other except the one in Tennessee,' said Mr Peters patriotically.

Gradually Peters came to love his scarabs with that love passing the love of women which only collectors know.

Something Fresh (Woodhouse 1967: 40–1)

INTRODUCTION

This book is about the European face of that curious human activity which we call collecting, and which, as a curtain-raiser, may be described as the gathering together and setting aside of selected objects. Our relationship with the material world of things is crucial to our lives because without them our lives could not happen, and collecting is a fundamentally significant aspect of this complex and fascinating relationship. There is a need to open up the study of collecting to a range of interpretations, and to bring investigations of its significance into the mainstream, as part of our under-standing of social life as a whole. Local and limited studies of elements in collecting practice must always inform the broader interpretative picture, but they are meaningless – or at any rate mean much less – if, like collec-tions themselves, they cannot be seen as part of a programme in which the overall significance is somehow more than the sum of the individual parts.

Broadly based interpretations face considerable difficulties of their own. Some exponents of the recent or current orthodoxy have been suspicious of ideas like broad historical trends and the power of cultural and social traditions in the long term, especially where European affairs are concerned, because such notions (like all notions) are open to political misuse. But, whether we like it or not, we are all situated in a historical sequence of cause and effect, and the world can show a range of such sequences, of which European history is one, which have their own particular and continuing character. It behoves us, then, to investigate this tradition and, particularly, to examine one of its most salient characteristics: its capacity to create special accumulations of significant material objects.

This book is not a history of European collections, although, as we shall see, a historical perspective is essential to our understanding; nor is it a history of museums or the museum movement although, again, the notion of the museum has a significant place. Still less is it an analysis of the importance of collected material from the perspectives of particular disciplines: I shall not be concerned to trace how certain collections have added to our understanding of Rembrandt the painter or what role Cycladic figures may have played in local prehistoric religion; or at any rate I shall not try to do this in the traditional sense. Rather, this is an investigation into collecting as a set of things which people do, as an aspect of individual and social practice which is important in public and private life as a means of constructing the way in which we relate to the material world and so build up our own lives. It is essentially an investigation into an aspect of human experience.

These bold statements raise more questions than they answer. In particular, they provoke three questions: what is our relationship with the material world in general; what particular part of that relationship counts as 'collecting' in any useful sense; and how can we study collections and collecting in ways which are likely to shine light on the nature of the experience which they embody?

This chapter will grapple with these questions, and concludes by describing a triple perspective on the nature of collecting which will structure the rest of the book. But in order to understand whence these questions arise and how some answers to them may be given, we need to look first at the critical tradition.

THE CRITICAL TRADITION: CURIOUS LITERATURE

The notion of collecting as a field of human activity and therefore as a proper field for study is still young, but just as collecting itself as a self-conscious activity runs back at least to the curiosity collections of the sixteenth century and has continued to this day, so the literature about collecting has a similarly lengthy pedigree. 'Curious' is a word which has come down in the world and, from describing serious intellectual engagement, it came to be the traditional term in the book trade for pornographic books and drawings. As we shall see, the explanations offered for the collecting process have taken similar twists and turns. We need to gain a purchase on past perspectives in order to see how the present study has emerged and where it is heading (Figure 1.1).

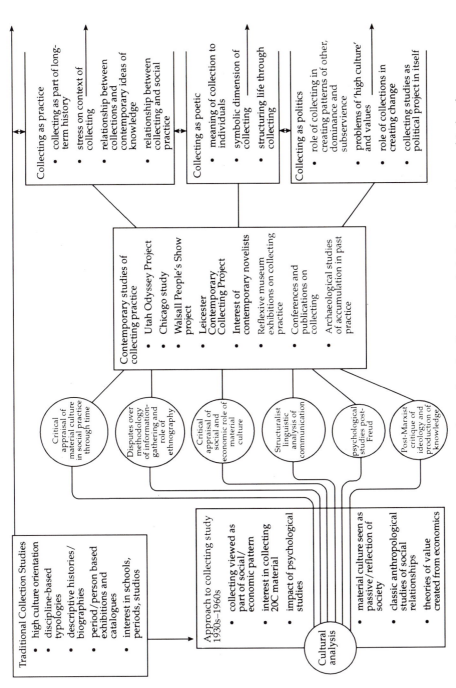

Traditional Collection Studies

- high culture orientation
- discipline-based typologies
- descriptive histories / biographies
- period / person based exhibitions and catalogues
- interest in schools, periods, studios

Approach to collecting study 1930s–1960s

- collecting viewed as part of social / economic pattern
- interest in collecting 20C material
- impact of psychological studies
- material culture seen as passive / reflection of society
- classic anthropological studies of social relationships
- theories of value created from economics

Cultural analysis

Critical appraisal of material culture in social practice through time

Disputes over methodology of information-gathering and role of ethnography

Critical appraisal of social and economic role of material culture

Structuralist linguistic analysis of communication

psychological studies post-Freud

Post-Marxist critique of ideology and production of knowledge

Contemporary studies of collecting practice

- Utah Odyssey Project
- Chicago study
- Walsall People's Show project
- Leicester Contemporary Collecting Project
- Interest of contemporary novelists
- Reflexive museum exhibitions on collecting practice
- Conferences and publications on collecting
- Archaeological studies of accumulation in past practice

Collecting as practice

- collecting as part of long-term history
- stress on context of collecting
- relationship between collections and contemporary ideas of knowledge
- relationship between collecting and social practice

Collecting as poetic

- meaning of collection to individuals
- symbolic dimension of collecting
- structuring life through collecting

Collecting as politics

- role of collecting in creating patterns of other, dominance and subservience
- problems of 'high culture' and values
- role of collections in creating change
- collecting studies as political project in itself

Figure 1.1 Past perspectives in the study of collecting and their relationship to this book

Traditional collection studies have always, and still do, concentrate on that material perceived as 'high culture', and its intellectual coherence is derived from the place it occupies in what gradually, in modernist Europe, emerges as the main disciplines – very broadly those of natural science, academic history, archaeology, anthropology and the history of art (which includes what museums frequently call decorative or applied art). It is true that the study of physical material in the sixteenth, seventeenth and early eighteenth centuries did a great deal to establish the parameters of these disciplines as recognised fields of study, but it is also true that work within them has concentrated upon the meaning of individual items or groups of collected material rather than upon the significance of the collecting process. Attention concentrated upon typologies and taxonomies, and an interest in periods, schools and studios. It finds its typical expression in exhibitions and catalogues which concentrate on these topics.

Equally characteristic, too, is the production of a very considerable volume of published work about individual collections and collectors, and similar studies of the history of public or semi-public collections, and of the history of the world's great museums. Typically this work has been cast in a biographical and anecdotal mode. At its (all-too-common) worst it is soft, and sentimental in the poorest sense, while at its best it is part of the historiographical tradition which aimed at the narration of successive events, accurately detailed from contemporary sources. In tracing the history of collections, contemporary lists, annotated catalogues and related material like sale bills are of course primary evidence. Like the catalogues, these writings offer an indispensable source of material for the student of collecting, although they themselves are written from a limited point of view.

During the middle third of the century the bundle of attitudes and critical stances which can be loosely lumped together under the 'cultural analysis' title began to gather strength, drawing in large part upon Marx and Freud and on the early generations of their commentators. With this was linked a developing sense of local community, which similarly had nineteenth-century roots in the work of collectors like Hazelius and his imitators (Kavanagh 1990: 13–21), and which saw conscious efforts to collect what would now be called the material evidence of popular culture. In line with contemporary ideas, material culture in general was seen as the passive reflection of social action, and in economic ideas as receiving its value from the forces of production rather than consumption. Social relationships were seen in the style of classic anthropological studies in terms of prestige hierarchies, and collecting took its place as a factor in the creation of social position in which objective values were taken for granted.

In only one aspect of developing cultural analysis was collecting viewed as a process of significance in its own right. This occurred among the classic psychologists, who tended to concentrate on the first two syllables of the word 'analysis' rather than on its whole import. Freud's original biological drive model (most accessible in the 1963 edition of his collected works) was elaborated by Jones (1950), Abraham (1927) and Fenichel (1945). These writers were concerned to show a continuity between childhood experiences and adult personality, and especially between the anal-erotic stage of infant sexual pleasure, which relates to sphincter control, to the production of faeces viewed as product creation symbolic of all future productive acts, and also to toilet-training and its attendant struggle with adults, and the adult traits like obstinacy, orderliness and parsimony.

Jones made what he saw as the link between all this and collecting quite specific, when he wrote of:

> the refusal to give and the desire to gather, . . . collect, and hoard. All collectors are anal-erotics, and the objects collected are nearly always typical copro-symbols: thus, money, coins (apart from current ones), stamps, eggs, butterflies . . . books, and even worthless things like pins, old newspapers, etc. . . . A more deifying manifestation of the same complex is the great affection that may be displayed for various symbolic objects. Not to speak of the fond care that may be lavished on a given collection – a trait of obvious value in the custodians of museums and libraries.
>
> (Jones 1950: 430)

Abraham developed this by making a correspondence between collecting and erotic activity in general:

> [the] excessive value he [the collector] places on the object he collects corresponds completely to the lover's overestimate of his sexual object. A passion for collecting is frequently a direct surrogate for a sexual desire . . . a bachelor's keenness for collecting often diminishes after he has married.
>
> (Abraham 1927: 67)

Fenichel pursues the relationship between success and failure in toilet-training and later attitudes to personal success. Anal conflicts include fear of loss and enjoyment of an erogenous pleasure and these may be displaced on to collecting as:

> A patient with the hobby of excerpting everything he read and arranging the excerpts in different files enjoyed in so doing (a) an anal-erotic pleasure: what he read represented food; his files represented the faeces, into which the food had been turned by him; he liked to look at his faeces and to admire his 'productivity'; (b) reassurance: the filing system was supposed to prove that he had things 'under control'.
>
> (Fenichel 1945: 383)

Lerner (1961) put these suggestions to an experimental test. He

7

constructed a list of twenty-two 'anally-connotative' words, matched these with a similar list of neutral words, and put the whole group to fifteen stamp-collectors and to a control group of fifteen non-collectors. The resulting data suggested that the collectors did differ from the others in their perceptions about the anal and neutral words, in ways which might show the validity of the anal-character concept, the notion of sublimation and the relationship of this to the collecting habit.

Rather like the parallel, if less well-developed, view which sees collecting as the masturbatory pursuit of solitary pleasures, these notions have now entered into the bloodstream of certainly the popular view of collecting. As late as 1968 Baudrillard, in his effort to distinguish between 'collecting' and 'accumulating' or 'hoarding', could say:

> Le strade inférieur est celui de l'accumulation de matières: entasse-
> ment de vieux papiers, stockage de nourriture – à mi-chemin entre
> l'introjection orale et la retention anale – puis l'accumulation sérielle
> d'objets identiques. La collection, elle, émerge vers la culture . . . sans
> cesser de renvoyer les uns aux autres, ils incluent dans ce jeu une
> extériorité sociale, des relations humaines.
>
> (Baudrillard 1968: 147–8)

> The most basic level is the accumulation of materials: e.g. the hoarding
> of old papers, stockpiling of food – midway between oral introjection
> and anal retention – then [comes] the serial accumulation of identical
> objects. Collecting tends towards the cultural . . . while maintaining
> their own interrelation, they [i.e. the collected objects] introduce social
> exteriority, human relations, into the process.
>
> (Baudrillard 1968: 147–8)

As a serious attempt to explain the social phenomenon of collecting as a whole, the notion of anal retention is best taken with a dose of salts. With its concentration on a sexuality divorced from social practice and the personality as a whole, it can offer only a fatally limited account of human motive. But it did for collecting what early psychology did in all areas of experience – it forced us to come to terms with the undoubted fact that our feelings and actions have an interior or underside quite different from that presented to the world.

As cultural analysis gathered strength through the 1960s to the 1990s (Olmsted 1991) a range of crucial critical paradigms emerged and these can be described briefly. The impact of structuralist and linguistic thought – particularly in relation to the analysis of human communication through words, myths, the organisation of human relationships, and objects – offered ways of understanding the links between these things in the context of the crucial distinction between metonymy and metaphor (or signifier and signified) (see Hawkes 1977). This has links with the post-Marx critique of ideology and the production of knowledge; the critique that is often described as post-structuralist or post-modernist. The parentage of the movement is complex, but includes much of what is often called 'the new French thought' embodied by writers like Foucault, Lacan and Derrida (Fekete 1984) with its broadly structuralist base, and its post-structuralist Marxist and post-Marxist notions about the nature of power and the workings of ideology, which, we cannot now avoid seeing, permeate all human activity. An important strand in this endeavour has been in the area of gender studies and of the power-broking relationships between men and women. This work has influenced all study in the humanities, particularly that concerned with literature in the broadest sense (see Eagleton 1983), a study which has many affinities with that of material culture and collecting.

In economic discourse, consumption is traditionally regarded, in Adam Smith's words, as 'the sole end and purpose of all production' (1937: 625), and this remains the thrust of the discipline, in spite of Veblen's (1899) ground-breaking work. But Veblen's work has fed into the developing field of social studies, particularly that concerned with the role of material culture in human affairs. Writing from a background in anthropology, Douglas and Isherwood in their book *The World of Goods* (1978) began to approach the question of why people buy goods. In showing that purchasing choices would be seen as cultural experiences with real meaning, they brought about a significant shift from a predominantly social to a predominantly cultural perspective.

Within sociology, Baudrillard (1981, 1983) emerged as the key figure in the effort to create a theory of material culture in relation to consumption and commodity and neo-Marxist notions of the capitalist society. As Campbell puts it:

> This he attempts by drawing upon semiotics and focusing on the 'commodity sign' rather than the commodity. He argues that, in capitalist societies, consumption should be understood as a process in which only the signs attached to goods are actually consumed. Baudrillard's work involves a meeting of Marxist thought with semiotic analysis such that Marx's distinction between use and exchange value is linked to the analysis of commodities as signs. Hence the theory of the commodity sign and the claim that, in modern capitalist society, commodities are not valued for their use but understood as possessing a meaning which is determined by their position in a self-referential system of signifiers.
>
> (Campbell 1991: 61–3)

But by far the most important book in the new wave of consumption studies is Bourdieu's (1984) *Distinction: A Social Critique of the Judgement of Taste*. Bourdieu stresses the hierarchical character of modern society and the centrality of consumption practices upon which the hierarchy is based.

Bourdieu sees material possessions as representing the individual's possession of symbolic and cultural capital and the way in which taste can be displayed. Not all possess this capital to the same extent, since each has his 'habitus' or personal cultural inheritance which limits his ability to move up the social hierarchy. As a critique of value creation Bourdieu's work is illuminating, but he is less strong in relation to the subjective or inward motives of object consumers.

We would expect this to be the forte of the latter-day psychologists, but here we are largely disappointed. There are some signs that contemporary psychologists are heeding Kassarjian's (1982) plea that cultural values should not be neglected in the study of consumption, and the work of Csikszentmihalyi and Rochberg-Halton (1981) shows how the cognitive concerns of the new generation of psychologists can be linked with appreciations of cultural orientations which are central to the interests of historians and social scientists. However, much work in psychology still looks to discern one all-embracing and specific explanation for human action, although sex has been successively replaced by inauthenticity, loss of identity and loss of contact, and now helplessness and fear of dependence. A recent study by Werner Muesterberger (1994) takes the view that collecting is a quest for comfort and reassurance, an observation which would be difficult to challenge because it is so broad and all-embracing, but which leaves much actual collecting process out of the account. Beyond this, however, are the broad-ranging analyses of the philosophy of mind – particularly those of John Searle (e.g. 1992) – which criticise cognitive stances in a favour of an approach which emphasises the centrality of consciousness to any account of mental functioning, an approach which has obvious implications for a view of our relationship to the physical word.

Meanwhile, the archaeologists – whose discipline involves material culture and collecting *par excellence* – had set about absorbing what was emerging in all the fields just described, prompted by an article by Peter Ucko on the significance of penis sheaths (Ucko 1969). While there is a limit to what can be got out of a penis sheath, the result, in the hands of scholars like Renfrew (1984), Hodder (1986), Shanks (1987) and Shanks and Tilly (1987) has been the development of an understanding of material culture in society which stresses the active role objects play in relation to social configuration and the process of social change (see Appadurai 1986a). Objects are seen as essentially cultural, and capable of engaging in a cultural dialogue with human individuals from which social changes will emerge. To this is linked a perception of the need to account both for long-term changes or developments without relying either on an unacceptable determinism or an equally unacceptable ahistoricism of the kind which emerges in some post-structuralist writers. However 'true' or 'false' it may be, history clearly does affect the present. Fernand Braudel has emerged as the most significant contributor to this debate.

Finally, we have the contemporary heightened sense of the difficulties of methodology and of the gathering of the raw data upon which all these essays in social understanding depend. In part, this had to do with our increasing understanding of the reflexive nature of knowledge, and consequently of the flawed character of all our investigative efforts; points which have been made with great eloquence by Clifford (1988) and Clifford and Marcus (1986). These and related difficulties have been developed in the work of Martyn Hammersley (e.g. 1992) in his explorations into the nature and value of ethnography and case-studies. The tensions inherent in both quantitative and qualitative social studies, and those between these two, will not easily be resolved and the debate will continue.

If all this effort had to be summed up in one sentence relevant to the present study, it would be that we are now concerned to develop critical approaches which will enable us to see life as process and practice; to see it not so much in terms of a set of given ideas and values or as a body of applied knowledge, but rather as a group of things which people do and which have various constraints and outcomes. As we would expect, this has been translated into a number of studies designed to tell us why and how people collect.

Ideas about the relationship between people and goods were taken further by the investigation carried out by Csikszentmihalyi and Rochberg-Halton (1981) into the household objects considered to be special by a sample of typical American families living in Chicago, and the reasons they give for interacting with these objects. They offered a number of important suggestions, including the way in which objects are tokens of remembrance, respect and love, and most interestingly the way in which

> homes [where] objects are signs of warm symbolic ties between family members are different from homes in which such meanings are absent. Families that lack shared positive emotional meanings live in a barren symbolic environment. The houses they inhabit and the objects they own are material things – having no other value – to be used and consumed. In such homes children grow up concerned with the safety of their own selves, with little psychic energy left over to care for others. Their goals, like the goals of their fathers, are bent on the achievement of terminal rewards, on the immediate gratification of needs conditioned by the consumer culture.
>
> (Csikszentmihalyi and Rochberg-Halton 1981: 242)

The fact that collecting is itself a form of consumption has been picked up by Russell Belk and his colleagues, all of whom have taken part in the Consumer Behaviour Odyssey project. The Odyssey was a transcontinental interdisciplinary research project undertaken in 1986 by a team of researchers across North America, and was intended to explore the relationship between consumption phenomena and fundamental consumer behaviour. As the project progressed, it developed much interesting information about the collecting habits of contemporary North Americans which have enabled Belk and his colleagues to formulate some significant analyses of the nature of the collecting process (and which, as we have seen, shows a distinct recent and contemporary tendency to turn the relationship the other way).

In 1993–4 the Leicester Collecting Project in contemporary Britain was carried out. It involved the random distribution of 1,500 questionnaires, followed up by a series of interviews designed to plump out this quantitative information with qualitative studies. The return rate from the questionnaires was over 60 per cent, an excellent reply rate, and the project has added considerably to our understanding of collecting processes (Pearce forthcoming 1996).

Linked with these research endeavours is the People's Show Project, first launched at Walsall Museum, Britain by Peter Jenkinson in 1990. This involved the mounting of an exhibition composed entirely of collections created by local people. The original show created much media attention which focused on collecting, and it has been followed up by further People's Shows at Walsall and at a very broad range of other museums throughout Britain. It has been a major museum phenomenon of the 1990s and has been matched by an equally significant sequence of reflexive museum exhibitions, which concentrate upon collecting practice and the ways in which this has helped to shape understanding. Important here have been the *Museum Europa* exhibition at Copenhagen (National Museums of Denmark 1991) and shows at the Victoria and Albert Museum in the contemporary design galleries.

Parallel to this have been the important studies produced by Krysztof Pomian (1990), Oliver Impey and Arthur Macgregor (1985) and the *Journal of the History of Collections* which Impey and Macgregor edit. The volume edited by Elsner and Cardinal (1994) has brought together a number of important essays. Conference and publication, those twin hallmarks of academic endeavour, have now become marked features of the new critical interest in collecting. In 1992 Sheila Campbell, curator of the Malcove Collection, University of Toronto, organised a conference 'Private Collector/ Public Museum' which looked at the relationship between these two collecting modes. The Department of Museum Studies at Leicester University organised a conference on museum issues in material culture theory (Pearce 1989) and has since produced a number of relevant publications (Kavanagh 1991; Pearce 1992). Influential, also, have been studies on hoarding and accumulating produced from a prehistoric perspective, particularly that published by Richard Bradley (1990): his analysis of the social practices which lie behind accumulation have a more than prehistoric relevance.

One further manifestation of the contemporary interest in collecting as social practice is worth mentioning, and this is the quite amazing extent to which collecting now appears as a major theme in what we might call serious fiction. To be sure, the accumulation of material is a standard human pre-occupation here as elsewhere, and our relationship to this world's goods is one of the major themes of European nineteenth-century fiction in general, as it was of nineteenth-century society: we need only recall the examples of Balzac's *Cousin Pons* and James' *The Spoils of Poynton* (1963). But it is surely no accident that two of the most influential avant-garde twentieth-century novels – one, Joyce's *Finnegans Wake* (1939), written at the end of the first third of the century, and the other, Eco's *Foucault's Pendulum* (1990) written towards its end – both take us, in their first few pages, into the museum and to the contemplation of collections on show, thus prompting fundamental questions about the nature of value and knowledge.

The theme was taken up in a series of novels in which the act of collecting defines characters or parts of the story, or provides an all-embracing simile. This is true of Fowles' *The Collector* published in 1967, Moore's *The Great Victorian Collection* (1975), Chatwin's *Utz* (1988), elements in Byatt's (1990) *Possession* and Lively's (1979) *A Treasure in Stone*, together with a number of others which have made a lesser mark. It is an interesting facet of contemporary culture which needs a full-length study to do it justice. It certainly signals a willingness on the part of the writing and reading public to see collecting as an adequate metaphor for large parts of experience.

Armed with this overview of the critical tradition, we can move to two themes which underlie much of it: what material things are like and how we relate to them.

OUR RELATIONSHIP WITH THE MATERIAL WORLD: IN THE NATURE OF THINGS

The material world, that is, the world outside each individual, may be defined as including the whole of humankind's physical environment, embracing the landscape, the air which is manipulated by flesh into song and speech, the animals and plants off which humans live and the prepared meals which come from them, our own bodies and those of other human beings. All of these are raw material capable of organisation into the kind of cultural construct which we call human society. James Deetz has put this in a famous phrase:

> Material culture is that segment of man's physical environment which is purposely shaped by him according to culturally dictated plans.
>
> (Deetz 1977: 7)

This broad material context should not be lost from sight, but a study devoted to the collection of objects must restrict itself to that area of the material world which we usually refer to when we talk of accumulating; that is, to the area of discrete materials, for which 'object' or 'thing' or 'piece' is our usual word, meaning an item which can, perhaps with some difficulty, be lifted up from its immediate surroundings and moved somewhere else. Specimens from the natural world fulfil this basic criterion as much as human-made things, and they too are perpetually constructed and reconstructed into the cultural whole. As I have argued elsewhere (Pearce 1992: 30–1), it is clear that the acquisition of a natural-history specimen involves selection according to contemporary principles, detachment from the natural context, and organisation into some kind of relationship (many are possible) with other, or different, material. This classification process transforms a 'natural' piece into a humanly defined object, that is, an artefact, and collections of natural history can be discussed in material culture terms just as can those of more obviously 'human' workmanship.

Concentrated work since the mid-1980s on the nature of material culture, particularly material culture in the more limited sense defined here, and our relationship with it (e.g. Hodder 1986; Miller 1987; Pearce 1992) has given us some important insights. It is clear that the ability to make things and the ability to say things – two closely intertwined facilities – stand at the root of human culture. There are differences between the discourse of language and of material culture and one of the most important of these is that, like ourselves but unlike words, objects have a brutally physical existence, each occupying its own place in time and space. This means that objects, again unlike words, always retain an intrinsic link with the original context from which they came because they are always stuff of its stuff no matter how much they may be repeatedly reinterpreted. It also means that objects, unlike sounds, are capable of being possessed and hence, of course, of being accumulated, stored and collected.

Nevertheless, material culture and language have two important attributes in common. Both mean something to their own societies; words and objects are pointless if they do not carry intelligible meaning. Similarly, neither can carry meaning alone; a word only has meaning in relation to other words amongst which it will be embedded through socially meaningful organisation, and equally an object only has meaning in relation to, or in juxtaposition with, other objects. Objects are, therefore, socially meaningful, but their meaning is produced by arranging them in sets, both mentally and physically.

Given this fact of interdependence we can see three perspectives within which objects operate socially. Firstly, objects may be considered as artefacts, that is, as lumps of the physical (natural) world transformed into artefacts by social process (culture). Study here can embrace a wide range of statistical and locational analyses, and also methods of scientific characterisation (e.g. petrology, metallurgy and metallography) and technological analysis. More fundamentally, the study of objects as artefacts links up with a functionalist perspective to show how material culture operates synchronically in society. So, for example, a group of objects on a living-room mantelpiece can be analysed in ways which yield information about their fabric, decoration and construction. They can also be perceived as performing a range of functions (Figure 1.2) which help to keep our society in being: they help to maintain the production system of manufacture and purchase, they play a role in our family lives, they are a means by which social prestige can be maintained, and one of them will tell us what time of day it is.

Secondly, objects may be considered as signs and symbols, creating categories and transmitting messages which can be read. This involves treating object sets as texts, to be interpreted by applying to material culture the concepts developed by semiologists and structuralists for the analysis of language. This, too, treats society synchronically. So, for example, we

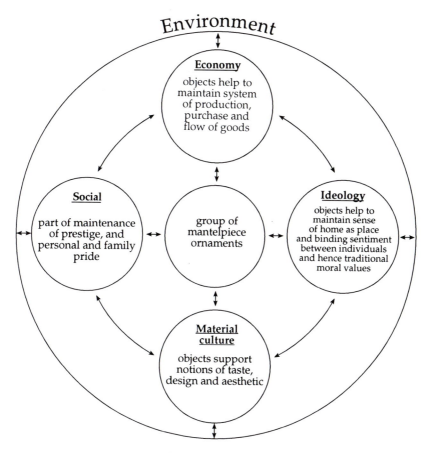

Figure 1.2 Functionalist analysis of mantelpiece ornaments

candlestick	potted plant		soap		biscuit barrel
china bowl	sugar bowl		tin Elastoplast		wine glasses
clock	:	coffee jar	:	toothpaste	:	fruit bowl
china bowl	china pig		shampoo		wine glasses
candlestick	flour jar		washing powder		biscuit barrel

Figure 1.3 Relationships between typical lines of objects on mantel-piece, kitchen shelf, bathroom shelf and dining-room sideboard

might regard a typical (that is, socially acceptable) line-up of objects on a living-room mantelpiece as a material culture set which forms an integrated, organically related, or metonymic, unity and see this as contrasted with, but equal, equivalent or metaphorical too, the rows of objects on the principal kitchen shelf, bathroom shelf and dining-room sideboard (Figure 1.3). These categories do have real social meaning. We would be genuinely taken aback if we saw a half-empty baked bean tin on the living-room shelf and immediately would begin to formulate censures or excuses, depending upon our nature and our relationship to the owner of the tin. In another, but equally important, way we see the triple relationship of clock flanked by two candlesticks in the living room as somehow seemly and suitable, while the unbalanced line-up in the bathroom does not bother us. The four categories of shelf objects are playing their part in structuring our individual and social lives, and they do this by both constructing and reflecting the broad pattern along the lines suggested by the structuralist plot given in Figure 1.4.

Thirdly, objects may be studied as meaning: that is, as things to which both individuals and societies attach differing moral and economic values as a result of their historical experience, both personal and communal. In modern Britain the contents of our homes permeate our lives to such an extent that the history of their manufacture and design involves a study of the history of our class structure, of our view of the relationships between the sexes, of taste and fashion and so on. It is this historical detail which plays a large part in shaping the content of each individual component of the artefact sets and the way in which the sets are formed. It is for historical reasons that some designs strike us as classic or chic, and others as dowdy or common. It is this approach to objects which is the most familiar and it finds its expression in written historical narratives, which usually take a chronological form.

The interdependence of all these analytical modes is obvious. All societies make and use things which help them to stay alive in their own environments, but not everything which they make, like many of the ornaments, has an

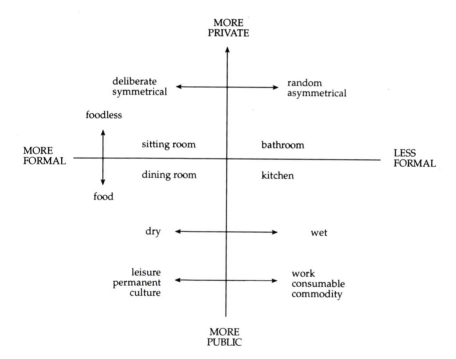

deliberately displayed	:	randomly gathered
symmetrical	:	asymmetrical
more formal	:	less formal
public	:	private
individual culture	:	standard commodity
permanent	:	consumable
domestic leisure	:	domestic work
foodless	:	food
dry	:	wet

MORE
PRIVATE

deliberate symmetrical ⟷ random asymmetrical

foodless

MORE
FORMAL

sitting room   bathroom

dining room   kitchen

LESS
FORMAL

food

dry ⟷ wet

leisure permanent culture ⟷ work consumable commodity

MORE
PUBLIC

Figure 1.4 Binary pairs drawn from the lines of objects on shelves, and the structuralist plot which they produce

obvious utilitarian purpose. All societies need to use objects to help create the social categories without which organised life would fall apart, so functionalist and structuralist analyses support and illumine each other. The content of each specific social system, however, is made more intelligible by historical study. A number of difficulties can be urged against all the approaches to the interpretation of objects described here (see Pearce 1992: 144–91). Among other things, they all share the objection that they are essentially subjective, a charge which does not take us very far because it is one to which all forms of understanding are vulnerable, to a greater or lesser extent.

To put the problem another way, they depend upon our ability to recognise social norms, a difficult feat in the anti-positivist climate of the day. 'Social norms' is one way of describing what we might otherwise call 'accepted values' or 'proper behaviour'; that is, the cluster of ideological constraints, the rules of dominance and suppression which underpin any social surface and which are visible to anybody who looks at any method of social analysis provided he is looking at it in these terms. All three kinds of analysis derive their intelligibility from the way in which they can recognise what are, from this point of view, essentially ideological relationships, and shed light on how they have developed and how they interreact.

But 'society' only exists through its individual members, and each individual will have a complicated relationship with his society's 'accepted values' and ideas of 'proper behaviour'. He will understand (probably very well) what these ideas and values are, but he may wish to modify, strengthen or abandon them. It is this tension, of course, which creates that process of steadily developing change which we call history. This brings us to a further important point. Objects play their own part in perpetuating ideological structures and creating individual natures, even though the European tradition – with its perceived fundamental duality between active, understanding human subject and passive, inert object (meaning the entire material world) – has made us reluctant to admit this. As Arendt has put it:

> The things of the world have the function of stabilizing human life, and their objectivity lies in the fact that . . . men, their ever-changing nature notwithstanding, can retrieve their sameness, that is, their identity, by being related to the same chair and the same table. In other words, against the subjectivity of men stands the objectivity of the man-made world rather than the sublime indifference of an untouched nature . . . Without a world between men and nature, there is eternal movement, but no objectivity.
>
> (Arendt 1958: 137)

Objects are not inert or passive; they help us to give shape to our identities and purpose to our lives. We engage with them in a complex interactive or behavioural dance in the course of which the weight of significance which they carry affects what we think and feel and how we act. This both

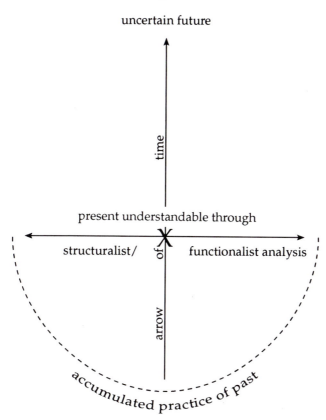

X Point of individual consciousness

Figure 1.5 Organic relationship between the individual in a present which can be understood in functionalist/structuralist terms, the accumulated practice of the past and the process of time into an uncertain future

contributes to the stability of social structures and to that of our own lives, and adds its mite to the accumulation of mental shifts which we call social change. We can observe this happening to ourselves when we walk down any high street and look in the shop windows.

The whole complex process which makes up our real lives in a material world can be expressed along the lines shown in Figure 1.5. Here the individual stands at the crux where the present – to be analysed in semiotic and functionalist terms, themselves two aspects of experienced reality with all its ideological character – is transected by the arrow of historical time, which comes bringing the weight of the past with it. The individual responds to the past and the present, and to his own inclinations, and the aggregated result of all this is the uncertain future into which we all move. What we must never forget is that all this happens in the real world of concrete material, actual possession and the enjoyment of real goods.

What is true of all objects as such is equally true of those groups of objects which we call collections. They, too, as collective entities as well as in terms of their individual components, have histories which can be traced, and are susceptible to analysis, which, viewed from the appropriate perspective, will reveal the very important part they play in the construction of power and prestige and the manifestation of superiority. They, too, are active carriers of meaning, and have a very large share in the creation of individual personality and the way lives are shaped. They, too, like all objects, hold meaning only in so far as they relate to other meaningful objects, for significance rests in the web of relationships which is physically inherent in each thing. All objects are part of sets, often more than one set at a time, but collections are sets in a particular sense, which marks them off from other kinds of object sets, and it is the nature of this perceived difference which we must now explore.

WHAT IS A COLLECTION? CHOICE PIECES

Down the years the notion of 'the collection' has attracted a number of shots at definition and, although definition-making is a grey business at best, with each effort open to a range of niggling objections based on individual examples, definitions are a useful way of gaining a purchase on how the subject has been perceived. In 1932, Durost, one of the earliest writers on the subject, offered:

> A collection is basically determined by the nature of the value assigned to the objects, or ideas possessed. If the predominant value of an object or idea for the person possessing it is intrinsic, i.e., if it is valued primarily for use, or purpose, or aesthetically pleasing quality, or other value inherent in the object or accruing to it by whatever circumstances of custom, training, or habit, it is not a collection. If the predominant value is representative or representational, i.e., if said object or idea is valued chiefly for the relation it bears to some other object or idea, or objects, or ideas, such as being one of a series, part of a whole, a specimen of a class, then it is the subject of a collection.
>
> (Durost 1932: 10)

This homes in on the idea that collections are essentially composed of objects which bear an intrinsic relationship to each other in a sequential or representative sense, rather than each being valued for its own qualities.

Durost seems to have had in mind typical serial collections like those of cigarette cards or butterflies, and his definition excludes accumulations which cover objects with obvious qualities of their own, such as pictures.

Some writers have been much exercised over possible distinctions between 'collecting', 'accumulating' and 'hoarding', pulling into the argument examples of misers from both literature and life. Belk quotes the example (1988: 139) of a 70-year-old man who had accumulated three garages full of miscellaneous goods and was facing pressure to discard the things so that his family would not be faced with the burden of coping with them after his death. There is the further specific problem that the word 'hoard' is used in one sense in general speech in relation to somebody who finds it difficult to throw anything away, and in archaeological language to mean a deposition of clear social and perhaps individual significance, even if we are seldom sure what that purpose was.

The usual distinction drawn between 'collector' and 'miser/accumulator/hoarder' is that the collector has a 'rational' purpose in mind which the other does not. The difficulty with this is that the psychological drives between the two are by no means as clear-cut as the use of different words would suggest. Equally, as the collecting literature makes abundantly clear, collections seldom begin in a deliberate way. Characteristically, a woman suddenly realises that the items of Victorian jewellery she inherited from various great aunts, lingering at the back of a drawer, constitute an interesting group of material, and then she may set out to look for similar pieces. Objects, in other words, may spend time as part of a miscellaneous, or even miserly, accumulation before their potential collectionhood is perceived.

This brings us to definitions which stress the subjective side of the collecting process. Aristides offers:

> collection . . . [is] 'an obsession organized.' One of the distinctions between possessing and collecting is that the latter implies order, system, perhaps completion. The pure collector's interest is not bounded by the intrinsic worth of the objects of his desire; whatever they cost, he must have them.
>
> (Aristides 1988: 330)

This recognises the collecting drive very well, but still looks to include the kind of systematic element which Durost stressed. Belk and his colleagues have arrived at the following: 'We take collecting to be the selective, active, and longitudinal acquisition, possession and disposition of an interrelated set of differentiated objects (material things, ideas, beings, or experiences) that contribute to and derive extraordinary meaning from the entity (the collection) that this set is perceived to constitute' (Belk *et al.* 1990: 8). This makes the significant point that the collection is somehow more than the sum of its parts, and it substitutes the idea of 'systematic' for that of 'interrelated', which is an improvement.

Alsop has offered a refreshingly simple approach. He says: 'To collect is to gather objects belonging to a particular category the collector happens to fancy . . . and a collection is what has been gathered' (Alsop 1982: 70). This is, in effect, to say that a collection is what a collector thinks it is: a very open approach to definition, and one which forms an appropriate point at which to pick up the notion of sets, discussed a moment ago, and to endeavour to come closer, not to outcomes – which Alsop and the others concentrate upon – but to collecting processes. We can best put the question very concretely. In an ordinary household, do we – or do we not – feel that the rows of objects on the living-room mantelpiece and the kitchen and bathroom shelves are collections in any significant sense of that word, and why?

Let us consider the three groups of objects as social ideas, frozen thoughts and feelings, all of which have been created deliberately by our society and the individuals in it in order to give themselves the chance of living what is locally considered to be a decent life, and which will then help to convey this idea of decency to the next generation of children. We can express this notion by adding a column to Figure 1.3 (Figure 1.6) where the four dots signify that the object sets are not a one-to-one reflection of the natural world but an inscription upon it, a social metaphor conceived in relation to it, and where the double dots show that each of the sets is regarded as socially distinct, that is metaphorical to the others. It is immediately apparent that the degree of 'necessity' or purely utilitarian value is equally present or absent in each case. The need to clean our teeth in the bathroom is as much of a social construct as the need to look at admired things in the living room, and one which is much less deep-seated. On the other hand we cannot argue that, in any fundamental sense, the living-room set has been chosen in a different and less functionally orientated way than the bathroom set, because it too is intended to work in our lives. And yet, we feel that kitchen and bathroom goods are 'only' utilitarian, that they are consumables and as such occupy a lowly place in our regard. Mantelpiece ornaments, by contrast, carry not a greater weight of social

the world	candlestick	potted plant	soap
of available	china bowl	sugar bowl	tin Elastoplast
material	: : clock :	coffee jar	: toothpaste
culture and			
possible	china bowl	china pig	shampoo
constructs	candlestick	flour jar	washing powder

Figure 1.6 Metaphorical relationship of lines of objects to the 'natural' world

meaning but a weight of more greatly regarded social meaning, and it is this that can be seen to bring them closer to some of our notions of what constitutes a collection. They are, in some way, 'on display'; they have been chosen deliberately from a range of possible material, and they encourage questions about their intrinsic aesthetic or craftsmanship values.

However, our emotional categories are not distinct. What seems to one person to be simply an attractive row of jars on the kitchen shelf may to another person be the nucleus of an important containers collection. This impulse applies equally to soap wrappers or squeezed out tubes of tooth-paste. Here we would not talk about intrinsic values, except to notice their absence; what we do recognise is the same process of selection at work. Through these deliberately naïve examples we are beginning to see that the notion of the special object set we call a collection is bound up with ideas – not about intention and purpose of the objects themselves as such, since we social animals do everything with intention of one sort or another – but about the deliberate intention to create a group of material perceived by its possessor to be lifted out of the common purposes of daily life and to be appropriate to carry a significant investment of thought and feeling, and so also of time, trouble and resource.

The selection process clearly lies at the heart of collecting. This can most easily be examined by employing some of the simple semiotic ideas first advanced by Saussure in the early years of this century (Figure 1.7), because these show the link between the world of potential collection objects, that is, the ordinary world of things organised into sets, and the creation of the collection. The left-hand half of the figure shows the *langue* of the given society, in which the potential material culture, available to it from its history and physical resources, is structured according to the agreed categories within the society. Out comes that society's *parole*, that is, actual material objects organised into meaningful sets, the bathroom goods, the *batterie de cuisine*, the cars, and so on. Also here is the natural world, itself brought into the material communication system at work here through its incorporation by naming and speculation into the world of human society. These things, already deeply cultured, are the raw material for collections. They enter the collecting *langue* where they are reworked according to the structuring notions of the individual collector, and out come the objects rearranged into a multitude of different sets, each of which is a collection.

There are many, wide-ranging structuring notions which may animate any given collector. They include the notion of creating interrelated series of the kind described by Durost, but they also include feelings which relate more to the life-cycle of the collector than to the nature of the collected objects, and all points in between. It becomes clear that one reason why some think of the mantelpiece material as a more of a collection than the bathroom material is that when we see it on its shelf it has already been through a selection process of the kind described here. It has already

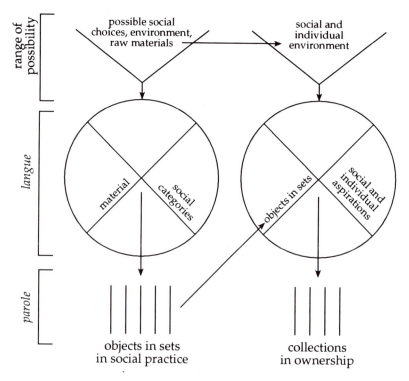

Figure 1.7 Relationship between object sets in social practice and the collecting process, put in terms of Saussurian semiotics

been selected out and set apart from the ordinary consuming processes of life to which toothpaste or curry powder are normally subject. They will only achieve its status if they are chosen to do so.

One way of describing this quality of separateness or 'set-apart' is to say that collection objects have passed from the profane – the secular world of mundane, ordinary commodity – to the sacred, taken to be extraordinary, special and capable of generating reverence (Belk *et al.* 1988). This seems to be a key characteristic of collections, which will show its round of facets as this book proceeds. The fundamental statement of how things become sacred – that is, how they are transformed by sacrifice – was made by Hubert and Mauss in 1974. The act of sacrifice, they say, changes the nature of the thing being sacrificed, and makes it holy: the sacrifice passes by way of death from life to eternity, a fact of life which is both uplifting and sad. This is the central paradox of all collected pieces. They are wrenched out of their own true contexts and become dead to their living time and space in order that they may be given an immortality within the collection. They cease to be living goods working in the world and become reified thoughts and feelings, carefully kept by conscious preservation. They are made to withdraw from daily life in order to enable another order of life to come about.

This capacity to achieve sacredness through death by collecting explains some of the feelings which cluster about collected objects. They can, quite frequently, carry the smell of things embalmed in darkness, poor faded ghosts which now can only see the living but not reach them. Their tone of sadness is strengthened by that vein of strained feeling which runs through much European sentiment, mawkish and morbid. But they also draw strength from the apparently universal human feeling – which achieves, of course, a particular intensity in Christian imagination – that only by death can new understandings and the hope of a correct relationship with the eternal come about. Collecting, also, is one way in which we hope to understand the world around us, and reconcile ourselves to our places within it. A collection may be, in some sort, a tomb, but our responses to it establish our own lives; in collecting, as in all other rites of funeral and sacrifice, death is for the living.

So far we have concentrated upon the collectors' side of the story, but objects too have their biographies. If the sacred-making process of selection expresses the subjective or psychological needs of the collector, we have to ask how it is that certain objects attract the selection process and others do not, and this brings us to questions of perceived value and how value is created. These are large issues which will absorb our attention in Part Four of this book, but it is helpful to make a start on them here. Kopytoff (1986) has explored the way in which 'the production of commodities is a cultural and cognitive process: commodities must be not only materials produced as things, but also culturally marked as being a certain kind of thing' (p. 64). He uses the idea of the cultural biography of things to suggest what the career of an object has been, what roles it has performed during the course of its social life and how it has taken its various places in patterns of exchange.

If we taken an object like a rabbet plane (Plate 1) – made about 1910 and intended to enable a joiner to produce the elaborate wooden mouldings the age required for skirting-boards, picture rails and the like – we can see what a various life it has led. The plane began as a member of a very clear-cut set, that of the group of planes required to make all the various moulded shapes, but this was not a collection: it is the kind of group which shares with garden equipment or any tools of a trade a notion of value through usefulness long appreciated which belongs in a different room of our mental lives.

In the year following the First World War, this kind of home decoration became unfashionable and uneconomic, and so the plane faced its first life crisis. At this point it might have been thrown away as useless, but it was kept, probably for sentimental reasons, together with the kind of hoarding

Plate 1 Rabbet plane for creating elaborate wooden mouldings for house fittings and furniture. One of a set of similar planes, each of which would produce a different moulding. Made about 1910.
(photo: University of Leicester)

instinct which finds it difficult to abandon anything of potential use. It was now entering a phase of what we might call 'passive collection', and here it remained until after the Second World War. Somewhere around this time it will have become an object of interest to those who were beginning deliberately to gather material relating to dying crafts. It will have acquired a social and therefore a financial value, and may well have passed through a round of collectables fairs and antique shops before finding a place in an 'important' (that is, large and well-presented) collection. From here, the next and final step is into the collection of a respected, probably public, museum, where the sacredness of collection becomes a kind of immortality. We see that the same object can exist in a number of situations, or social discourses, through the (often lengthy) course of its physical life, and may therefore figure in a number of interpretative patterns, as it attracts different notions of value and significance: some 'public' or generally accepted, and others private and subjective.

When we put this value creation together with notions of selection to create the sacred, and the intensely subjective and inward structuring which gives form to the selection process, it becomes clear that how and why objects arrive in collections, and perhaps leave them again is very complex and has to do with the subtle interaction of social custom, individual quirk and the glow of meaning which shines out of the object itself. We are dealing with human hearts and minds and with the objects which they respond to. We must, therefore, expect all the muddle and confusion which surround all aspects of life on earth and all doings of those inconsistent, moody and untameable creatures we call human individuals. Our collected possessions lie close to our hearts and, like our hearts they remain, in the last analysis, mysterious.

We can, however, pick out a number of key points which have a bearing on the notion of a collection. Collections are sets of objects, and, like all other sets of objects, they are an act of the imagination, part corporate and part individual, a metaphor intended to create meanings which help to make individual identity and each individual's view of the world. Collections are gathered together for purposes which are seen by their possessors as lifting them away from the world of common commodities into one of special significance, one for which 'sacred' seems the right word. Collections occupy a particular position in the processes by which value is created, because value is, to a considerable extent, a creation of the imagination rather than of need; and in the play of the imagination the objects themselves are powerful actors.

The outcome of the collecting process may have all kinds of characters. The imaginative link which holds material together may be purely personal or may engage the wider world. The collection may declare an outward value or it may be valueless in other than the subjective sense. It may live amongst other goods, so that its special nature is apparent only to its owner's eye; or it may occupy a special place of its own. It may be a private accumulation or the public act of a central authority; it may be a large group of important pieces in a formal setting, or it may be a small heap at the back of a cupboard. In all this, the motives behind the accumulation are more important than its content. There are very many sorts of collection and to have too tight or prescriptive a view is wrong and unhelpful in an effort to understand how they have and do operate. In this book the collection net will be deliberately cast wide in order to aid interpretation. 'Choice' is at the heart of the collecting process; a word which expresses its special dual nature as selection and as the allotment of value, whatever form this value may take.

THE SHAPE OF THIS STUDY

Bearing in mind the thrust of recent and contemporary debate already described, and the emergence of collecting study as a field of discourse in its own right, three parameters of analysis emerge. These are collecting in practice in the historical long term, collecting as part of the poetic through which individuals define themselves, and collecting as an aspect of the contemporary (and future) politics of value and social structure.

Collecting as practice

The study of collecting in social practice is intended to tease out an understanding of how communities develop strategies which enable them to bring together the accumulating possibilities of objects and other social structures – like family relationships, notions of surplus and prestige, and religious practices – in order to maintain the social pattern and project it into the future. Such a study needs chronological depth if it is to offer the best insights into how things work, and it is most satisfactory if it can be limited to one tradition, where the pattern of organic growth over time can be investigated. For this book, the European tradition has been chosen (taken to include the traditions of those people now living in Europe and those of European descent now living elsewhere in the world). There are two reasons for this choice: the nature of the evidence available to us and the nature of the European tradition itself.

The first reason is relatively straightforward. In spite of much work carried out into the role of material culture by anthropologists working among non-European people, it is nevertheless true that we know a great deal more about how Europeans, past and present, have made and used accumulations of objects than we do about how this has been done in other traditions. This is true in the naïve sense that more historical and information-gathering study has been expended on European material goods. It is also true that the tradition of interpretation of material culture is European, whether this has involved psychological and social studies about past and contemporary collecting or cultural and critical studies about the social role of objects inside or outside the European tradition. Whether we like it or not, the analyst of material culture has no choice but to write in the light of a Euro-centred mentality.

The second reason, the nature of the European tradition, probably underlies the first, for it hinges on the notion that Europeans have thought more about the nature of objects because, in a fundamental sense, objects and their accumulation loom larger and are treated differently in the European tradition than in other traditions. This needs considerable care for it goes without saying that all societies, without any exceptions known to us, use objects as they do language: to construct their social lives.

Nevertheless, the most cursory glance at European society today, and at the European history which brought it to birth, shows unmistakably how a huge investment of social capital (words not chosen casually) has been put into the production and use of material goods, in contrast to other traditions in the world.

Study of a number of non-European traditions is beginning to supply evidence which suggests that they embody a different view of the material world, which is part and parcel of a cluster of views embracing not only objects but also ideas of personal identity and social appropriateness (see also Lach 1994). Belk has shown that materialism, defined as the importance a consumer attaches to worldly possessions, is not a universal human trait, although a relatively normal one among those of European culture. Studies carried out by Wallendorf and Arnold found Americans to be significantly more possessive than Nigerians, although the growth in a Third World consumer culture shows Third World nations aspiring to Western consumption patterns at a much faster pace than their economic growth (Belk 1992: 50).

Marriott (1976) and Vaidyanathan (1989) have both argued that, compared with Western notions about the self, Indian notions are less individualistic and less likely to see the self in Cartesian terms as both subject and object. Belk notes that 'even the notion of actively extending self through possessions seems too proactive to apply in India', and, 'more aggregate levels of self, especially family self also appear to be more dominant in India. Since Hindu traditional belief emphasises renouncing material desires . . . this too would seem to make a consolidation of Indian extended self via possessions problematic.' We should, however, note that the traditional beliefs of Christianity (Mehta and Belk 1991: 399) are here exactly the same. Clearly, many substantial studies remain to be written which take up these ideas and those ideas surrounding non-European aesthetic traditions such as those of India (Goswamy 1991) and of Japan (Yamaguchi 1991). Nevertheless, the lines of divergence seem to be unmistakable.

The European relationship to the material world appears to be intimately bound up with two of the distinguishing features of the European tradition. The first of these is its willingness to view the world of matter as external and 'objective' to the knowing human subject, a notion fundamental to modern European philosophy since Descartes; the second – which is in a sense this scientific notion of matter as objective and available for study turned into social institution – is the concentration on the production of goods which we variously call capitalism or industrialisation. As Kopytoff, in a discussion of Braudel's work, has put it:

the development in early modern Europe of a range of new institutions shaped what might be called a new exchange technology and this, in turn, led to the explosion of commoditization that was at the root of capitalism. The extensive commoditization we associate with capitalism is thus not a feature of capitalism per se, but of the exchange technology that, historically, was associated with it and that set dramatically wider limits to maximum feasible commoditization.

(Kopytoff 1986: 72)

This book has, therefore, been written from a particular perspective. I believe that, in order to get to grips with collecting in social practice, it is necessary to analyse specific social practices in some detail; for this, some temporal and spatial limits must be set, and it is more satisfactory if these show the internal coherence associated with the study of a single tradition – defined as a self-reflecting communal state of mind based on perceived inherited cultural unities like languages, ideas of right and wrong, decent behaviour and notions of value and quality – among which views of the proper role of the material world are very significant. The tradition which, *par excellence*, has shown most interest in material goods is that of Europe, where, as we have seen, it may be said that the difference between Europe and others is not just one of degree, but also of kind, and is part and parcel of the scientific and industrial or capitalist outlook which characterises European society.

But the book embodies two additional contentions. Firstly, it seems likely that the peculiarly European view of the material world has its roots in prehistory, and here the investigative techniques of anthropology are particularly helpful in enabling us to discern social practice. Secondly, although specific economic and social attitudes to the world of goods have been produced by the European tradition *and* have helped to sustain it, study has tended to concentrate on the first of these propositions rather than on the second. Here, I shall concentrate on the second and show how European attitudes to the accumulation of goods have helped the system to continue developing along its characteristic trajectory, both in terms of social relationships and in terms of the kinds of individuals involved in it.

I shall hope to show that, in one broad geographical area of the world, there is a linear and organic (though not necessarily inevitable) connection between prehistoric hoarding and the contemporary institution of collecting, both inside and outside museums, and between what we can see of the mind-set operating in ancient times and that of contemporary collectors. For this reason, this book takes a much longer historical view than is usual in studies about collections – which generally begin somewhere around the fifteenth-century European Renaissance – and a much wider view of what it is helpful to see as a collection, following the broad definition arrived at in the previous section and setting this in context. This book will concentrate on trying to understand how it is that objects work for Europeans, and why, pre-eminently, Europeans say it with things, and Part Two will analyse European collecting practice of the long term.

Notions like the reality of long-term cultural traditions, and of the link between language and culture – both of which are developed in Part Two – are emerging from a period of unpopularity among archaeologists as the idea of cultural continuity, never doubted by linguists and historians, gains ground against ideas of limited social interaction which could reduce intrinsic cultural similarity to merely similar answers to similar problems. In the same way, it is helpful to combine the insights of sociology, whether of Foucault or of social anthropologists, which can recognise community types (for example, complex states or classical epistemes) with the notion of historical continuity as a way of understanding what we seem to observe. Probably an unwillingness to think in terms of organic cultural distinctiveness and continuity – particularly where European history is concerned – was a natural reaction among archaeologists whose formative years were spent disentangling intellectual ideas from the uses to which they had been put in Germany, Russia and elsewhere; but we are now ready, as Europeans, to look at the social anthropology of ourselves.

Collecting as poetics

The poetics of collecting is principally concerned with how individuals experience the process of collecting in their own lives, how they report on their relationship to it and how this can be analysed by the investigator. It is concerned with the meaning of collecting to the collectors themselves, how it affects their lives, and how, cumulatively, the sum of individual collecting habits interacts with social practice. The symbolic nature of collecting can only operate through individuals for whom things are symbolic, and it is this imaginative scope that I shall be concerned to examine.

'Poetics' is a word that stands at the source of the European effort to understand and assess creative activity, and as such it is acquiring a respectable pedigree in contemporary critique (see Clifford 1988; Karp and Levine 1991). It is worth glancing briefly at this source. Gilbert Murray, when discussing Aristotle's *Poetics*, says 'the words *poêsis*, *poêtês* mean originally "making" and "maker"' (Murray 1920: 6) and continues: 'another difficult word which constantly recurs in the *Poetics* is *prattein* or *praxis*'. These words are, of course, cognate with the English word 'practice', the use of which in this book I have just discussed. Murray continues, '*praxis* is generally translated "to act" or "action". But *prattein*, like our "do" also has an intransitive meaning "to fare" either well or ill . . . . It shows [men's] experiences or fortunes rather than merely their deeds. Aristotle can use the passive of *prattein* for things "done" or "gone through"' (1920: 10). *Praxis* is another word much used in contemporary critique, and together these terms give the sense of individual creative power which can show how an individual experiences the world both as actor and acted upon. In material culture terms, the imaginative effort to assemble a collection shows exactly this.

'Poetic' is a European word for a European thing. The notion of the essential self, acting and suffering, seems to lie at the heart of European consciousness as it does of ancient and modern European poetic diction: viewed in these terms, the Romantic movement was essentially a particularly powerful restatement of long-continuing predispositions. The notion of the individual is characteristically expressed in forms of 'fiction', a word which also descends from 'to make'. Viewed in this light, the collecting process is a form of fiction through which imaginative constructions can be expressed. And, like the use of language in fiction, objects in collections can be used in a range of poetics, to give us 'formal' or 'classic' statements with beginnings, middles and ends, 'stream of consciousness' productions, bits of slang, and so on, according to the view and capacity of the collecting individual, who is using objects, like language, to create and project the image of himself and how he sees the world.

The analysis of this image-making can be approached in a number of ways. In 1992 I distinguished three approaches to collecting which embody three possible individual relationships to the object world; these I described as the souvenir, fetishistic and systematic modes of collecting (Pearce 1992: 68–88). In souvenir collecting, the individual creates a romantic life-history by selecting and arranging personal memorial material to create what, in the light of what has just been said, might be called an object autobiography, where the objects are at the service of the autobiographer. In fetishistic collecting, the objects are dominant and the collector responds to his obsessive need by gathering as many items as possible: here, in contrast to souvenir collecting, the objects are allowed to create the self. In systematic collection, an ostensibly intellectual rationale is followed, and the intention is to collect complete sets which will demonstrate understanding achieved. Many collections will, of course, operate in all these modes at the same time: a Cranberry glass collection will carry a set completion potential, it will embody memories of times and places and will delight the heart of its fetishistic possessor. But each collecting mode sums up a different individual relationship to the material world.

In this book, I take a different point of departure. We all, as individuals, create our identities through a range of relationships: to ourselves, to our fellows and to the dimensions of time and space. European individuals seem to do this through a European poetic with many forms of fictional discourse; probably both the notion of such a poetic and the urge to analyse it are parts of the same tradition. How this poetic works in relation to the world of collected objects is what I discuss in Part Three.

Collecting as politics

'Politics', like *praxis*/'practice' and 'poetic', is a word which casts a long shadow. It is a dynamic word, expressing both the exercise of power, particularly that kind of all embracing cultural power which we call ideology, and the capacity to negotiate change. If practice shows us what kinds of meanings objects and collections have been given in social tradition, and poetics tells us how individuals have worked within and through these institutions to make meaning for themselves, a discussion of the politics of collecting brings these two together to show why and how collected objects are subject to different valuations and the importance which this has. Politics asks questions like: By whom and how are collecting values recognised? What is the ideal career of a collection? and How does our judgement of material change?

These questions involve understanding the parameters of object valuation as these have emerged into the modernist, and post-modern, tradition. They are linked with ideas of distance, and with the discourses which create a successive range of Others in relation to a perpetually reductive Us: in the European tradition, this element in its material construction is essential and all-pervasive. The complex operations of the modern market represent the intersection of community values and individual values, themselves tied to areas like the relationship between culture and commodity. It is here that collections are achieved and change is created.

Part Four is devoted to a discussion of these issues. It will look at the ways in which collecting has contributed to the creation of patterns of dominance, but also, and more optimistically, to the ways in which collecting can be an assertive force for change.

CONCLUSION

This book, then, is framed as an investigation into European collecting as experience. Collecting and collections are part of our dynamic relationship with the material world. Object groupings, like all other social constructs, are born from the essentially mysterious workings of the communal and individual imagination, sanctified by social custom but capable of growth and change. But for an object group to count as a 'collection', whichever of a range of words may appear suitable for this activity and its outcome through time, it must have been created as a special accumulation, intended at some point in time to fulfil a particular social and psychic role, and considered by the collector's society to be appropriate for this role, a view which, however, the collections themselves will actively influence.

The three aspects of collecting – practice, poetics and politics – are an organic whole, the internal relationships of which can be expressed in Figure 1.8, itself a version of Figure 1.5 which expresses relationships within the material world in general. The historical arrow brings with it to the contemporary stage the weight of European collecting practice as this has developed over the long term. The individual, represented by a cross, stands

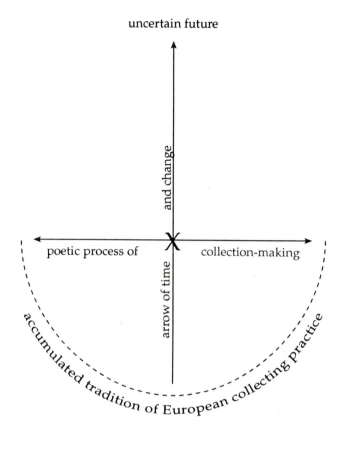

uncertain future

poetic process of

collection-making

and change

arrow of time

accumulated tradition of European collecting practice

X point of individual consciousness

Figure 1.8 Organic relationship between collecting practice in the long term, individual collecting poetic and the politics of value and change

at the crux of past and present and creates his collection in terms of the tension between these two and of his individual poetic response. It is through this process that values are reinterpreted in the political interplay of individuals and society, and the historical arrow is taken forward into the changing future.

A number of words are commonly used to describe various attributes of the collecting process, but, as we have seen, the effort to formulate precise definitions of words that usually crop up in the discussions of collections – like 'hoard', 'treasure', 'accumulation' and 'collection' – are not very helpful, in spite of the ink that has been spilt over them, for each of them tends to highlight one aspect of object-gathering at the expense of others, and each may merge into another, depending upon personal moods and the conjunction of circumstances. I shall, therefore, throughout this book, use all these various terms as seems appropriate in particular circumstances, especially in those areas of discussion where they have traditionally been used – for example, 'hoards' in prehistory or 'treasure' in relation to medieval accumulations – without according to them any particular weight or significance, but regarding them simply as useful words to use in respect of the different aspects of a long-term human preoccupation. Many aspects of the nature of collecting will be pondered upon at greater length as this book develops. What I have tried to do in the three main parts of this book is to describe one constellation of human experience by naming some of the stars and by plotting the emergence of the picture. There is no progression or hierarchy between the elements of the discussion, for no star is more important than its companions; and, like collecting, the figure in the night sky, though deeply embedded in our awareness, does not exist outside the particular point in time and space on which our imaginations stand; meaningful assemblages of objects, like the Seven Stars of our vision, are inscriptions on the darkness.

PART II

COLLECTING IN PRACTICE

CHAPTER TWO

THEMES AND PARAMETERS

First we have to state the subject-matter of our inquiry: it is demonstration, i.e. demonstrative science. Next we must define (1) a premise, (2) a term, (3) a syllogism, (4) the nature of a perfect and of an imperfect syllogism; and after that (5) the inclusion or non-inclusion of one term in another as a [*sic*] in a whole, and what we mean by predicting one term of all (or of none) of another.

Aristotle, *Prior Analytics* (Warrington 1964: 3)

EUROPEAN COLLECTING: THE HEART OF THE MATTER

We have seen in the previous chapter that the accumulation of objects into groups that can usefully be called collections is one of our characteristic ways of organising the meaning which we call social practice, and that our intention in this book is to analyse the meanings and implications of one particular collecting tradition, that of Europe. As I have said, sensible limits must be set to any study and it is as well if these have the kind of internal coherence which an integrated subject gives. It helps if this subject is well documented in some historical depth, as is the case with Europe. But more importantly, and more interestingly than this, it seems possible that, as we shall see, there may be features at the root of the European tradition which are of their own kind, and which have helped to define and create the peculiarly intense relationship which Europeans have towards the production and accumulation of goods, including those goods which might reasonably be said to belong to other people. But in what sense 'Europe' exists, and to what extent it, or anywhere else, can have a collecting (or any other) 'tradition' – especially if that tradition is seen to be genuinely formative and of deep duration – are taxing issues which must be faced.

In one sense Europe is easy to define: it is a smallish peninsula with a smaller peninsula to the north and various groups of offshore islands, situated on the extreme north-western edge of the planet's main land mass. It is clearly bounded on three sides by the sea. The fourth, the eastern, side is more problematic, and, however boundaries are drawn up, necessarily embraces a grey area where Europe meets 'the East'; but broad linguistic and cultural considerations, as we shall see, suggest that the traditional boundary in the plains around the line of the Don and the Volga makes a kind of sense. 'Europe', however, includes not only the majority of those now living and who have always lived within this area, but also those born of 'European' descent who live everywhere else in the world, particularly in Northern and Southern America, and the lands of the Pacific. Difficulties in defining the eastern frontier geo-culturally, together with the need to take into account the people of European descent has frequently promoted the use of the word 'Western' instead of European, a word intended to include Western Europe and North America.

'Western' is an emotive word used in ways which far transcend physical limits. Hall (in Hall and Gieben 1992: 276–8) has argued that the West (to use his term) is a historical not a geographical construct, and that by 'Western' we mean a particular type of 'modern' society which therefore enables us to define 'Western' and 'non-Western', and to do so by drawing on a contrasting set of images which contains, along with notions like urban: rural, also ideas about good and bad (although the relationship of this pair to the other pairs is far from clear). Notions of 'Western' therefore constitute an ideology against which people and places can be defined.

All this is true in its way, but from the point of view of anthropological enquiry, particularly that which is able to draw upon considerable historic and prehistoric depth, it appears as defining effects rather than causes. Notions of Westernism, in this sense, do not much pre-date the sixteenth century, and by then Europeans had been conscious of their own corporate identity for some time, chiefly through exploring their relationship with the Islamic world. Hulme speaks of 'the consolidation of an ideological identity through the testing of [Europe's] eastern frontiers prior to the adventure of Atlantic exploration . . . a symbolic end to that process could be considered Pius III's 1458 identification of Europe with Christendom' (Hulme 1986: 84). This was, indeed, as Hulme says, an end not a beginning. As Roberts notes, 'The word "Europeans" seems to appear for the first time in an eighth century reference to Charles Martel's victory (over Islamic forces) at Tours' (Roberts 1985: 122). We need a deep perspective to approach questions about the history of European society which need answering, conspicuously that of why Europe, alone of all the world's societies, has achieved that qualitatively different state known as 'modern industrial society', with all the economic, social and political developments which these three words usually imply, and – the particular theme of this book – how all this relates to notions about material culture.

Gordon Childe expressed the problem with characteristic bluntness when he said:

> The history of Europe poses two fundamental questions that prehistoric archaeology should be able to answer. Four to five thousand

years ago the natives of Europe were on precisely the same level, as far as equipment and economic organization are concerned, as the natives of eastern North America – a very similar environment – were on only 400 years ago and as some native tribes in New Guinea are on today. Why then did they not remain illiterate Stone Age barbarians as the Red Indians and the Papuans did? On an answer to this first question prehistorians are agreed: the proximity of Egypt and Mesopotamia. In the Nile valley and the Tigris–Euphrates delta alone could be created the economic and political organization necessary to get a metallurgical industry started. But this answer at once raises the second question: How could European barbarians outstrip their Oriental masters as they have done?

(Childe 1958: 7)

We may not relish the terms in which the problems are put, but they still remain important questions, to which answers are needed.

A number of well-recognised and well-considered themes are clearly important: we might single out the developing ideals of classical humanism, of Christian charity and equality, of self-governing communities connected by relationships of representation and consent, and of rational scientific thought and experiment. All these are massive topics upon which the very finest of scholarship has been lavished, but this scholarship has, on the whole, tended to overlook one very significant characteristic. Along with its favoured geophysical situation which supplies it with food, timber and metals in some abundance, and with the hopes and practices just mentioned, European society holds another long-term characteristic which has been just as fateful: it seems to involve a distinctive relationship with the material world, and with the world of objects: manufactured, used and collected.

This has been abundantly clear during the last two hundred years or so, as industrialisation, one of the key features of modern society, has spread across the continent. Industrialisation is a number of things, but one of its clearest characteristics is an immense proliferation of material goods. It is of the essence of the capitalist system – part of the cluster of modernist European features – to produce goods in order to stimulate acquisition, and so the production of more goods, in a cycle of which the most visible manifestations are the contents of shops and homes, including the collected material within those homes. The mass-producing and consumer society did not suddenly spring into being in Lancashire, Yorkshire and the English Midlands around 1780, although these, no doubt, are its location in the forces of the middle range. Its roots run back into prehistory, as Childe suggested, and in the following chapter we shall try to suggest some long-abiding features of European society which have an intimate role in our dynamic relationship with the world of collectable objects.

But first, we must bring this prehistoric common inheritance into sharper focus, and in so doing face the thorny subjects of culture and its transmission. Since 1786, when Sir William Jones realised that Sanskrit, Greek and Latin, and perhaps Gothic, Celtic and Old Persian also, all 'sprang from a common source, which, perhaps, no longer exists' (Jones 1786), few scholars have doubted that almost all the European languages, and a number in central Asia and northern and central India, belong to a common family to be called Indo-European, that this language family probably had a common ancestor, and that the ancestral language may well have been spoken in the area somewhere between the eastern Mediterranean, the Black Sea and the Caspian (although there are a number of alternate views). Finally, and more generally, it seems to be true that languages only spread in the mouths of actual speakers. Such a process can be seen from a number of points of view, and various language diffusion models can be suggested and defended, which require smaller or larger numbers of 'native' speakers, account for locally attested linguistic situations and so on (see Renfrew 1987 and references there). But put very baldly, it seems to be true that now, and for a significantly long time, most people living in geographical Europe (and some beyond it) – apart from recent arrivals who define themselves differently – speak, at root, a common language.

The question is, is this not only literally true, but also true in the metaphorical sense in which we talk of 'speaking the same language', an interestingly instructive phrase which shows our instinctive assumption that language and culture are the same thing? In other words, when did this situation happen, did it involve a specific kind of culture as well as of language and how important was this for the future course of European society? The great majority of Indo-European scholars hold that what can be deduced about the vocabulary of Primitive or Proto-Indo-European suggests that the culture of its bearers included specific society practices to be discussed in the next chapter, together with a hierarchical society – perhaps divided into the three classes of priests, warriors and peasants – which was reflected by a similar structure of gods, and a poetic tradition which concentrated upon the figure of the hero (Benveniste 1969). Features which seem to fit with this in the archaeological record, particularly the relatively sudden appearance across much of the language territory of the rich, individual barrow burials which look like those of heroes and chiefs, suggest that the relevant social changes took place around the beginning of the third millennium BC. Henceforward, in spite of various 'Old European' survivals (Hamp 1979) the nature of European society and the course of its history has possessed a character after its own kind, indelibly marked with essentially Indo-European institutions and traditions.

This, the classic view, has been attacked recently by Renfrew (1987) who has argued that 'the spread of farming was responsible for the initial dispersal of the Indo-European languages in Europe' (p. 159), a process usually reckoned to have happened as a series of local transformations of the 'early farming package' (p. 158) during the sixth and fifth millennia BC. The ensuing Neolithic peasant communities do not look 'Indo-European', and Renfrew accounts for this by proposing that language and culture should not be viewed as a simple equation, particularly when all kinds of inherited prejudices are involved in our interpretation of both. On the contrary: societies develop as the result of complex re-actions, internal and external, and the broad cultural similarity of many (but not all) European groups from around the sixth millennium BC can be explained by supposing that they all had to grapple with broadly similar circumstances. Renfrew, however, is forced to admit that specific items of vocabulary are shared across much of the Indo-European language family, and that the distinct possibility that there is a close correspondence in early verse forms across archaic Irish, Vedic Sanskrit and Homeric Greek, may be showing us different facets of essentially the same culture (pp. 259–61).

For the purposes of the argument in this book, it does not greatly matter whether European customs have a unity because similar circumstances in many places, crossing with each other, have created the similar mind-sets which we see unfolding in the historical progression, or whether this similarity should be attributed to some shared, language-based, ancestral thoughts and feelings about what society should be like. I incline towards the traditional view when modified and refined by contemporary archaeological theory. What matters here is the notion that we can recognise a significant body of society practice which has shaped the minds and lives of most people (whatever their 'ethnic' roots) living within a specific geographical area, that of Europe, and their descendants elsewhere, over a period of some four millennia – a body of practice which has distinctive, indeed (viewed in a world context) peculiar characteristics, which have given it its particular flavour and influence, a particularity which has much to do with the view of materiality which it involves. I shall call this body of practice 'European', a term to be interpreted (primarily) culturally and linguistically.

I will leave the last word with Indo-European scholars who have identified the verse forms just referred to, the poetic formulaic phrases which seem to be part of the most ancient Indo-European tradition we can see, and to have been preserved independently in subsequently separate languages. The most famous of these, presented as a formula in Vedic Sanskrit and Homeric Greek, is 'imperishable fame' (Watkins 1982: 104), a phrase which seems to sum up the essential character of much typically European thought and effort, particularly that of the European upper and, eventually, middle class, who have for millennia seen themselves as linked by the same presumptions about what language expresses, by the same approaches to family organisation and, successively, by classical aspirations, Christian practices and modernist ideas about knowledge – the European class which has, broadly speaking, commanded the collecting of material goods.

PARADIGMS OF STUDY

Given this field of reference, a number of paradigms of study – approaches to the structuring of the discussion – present themselves, drawn from the major disciplines concerned with the nature of human society. What follows is perforce selective, and those ideas which seem to illustrate best how societies behave in relation to the accumulation of objects have been chosen (even though this is always a hazardous procedure because, since no society can exist without the accumulation of material, all social theory must, one way or another, take it into account). However, undaunted by this undoubted truth, the reader will find it helpful to take a closer look at the way in which social anthropologists have discerned some basic social types behind the plethora of actual human societies; how modern critical theory – drawing on Marx but developed in France by Foucault and his followers, viewing these social types within the context of European history – has seen how each constitutes its own mode of relationships within the historical sequence; and how the notions of the French Annales historians, especially Fernand Braudel, offer an approach to fitting the whole together in a way which shows us how to develop our analysis of the special peculiarities of the European tradition.

Classifying actual human societies into a small number of broad types has been a European preoccupation since Aristotle and has been continued in modern times by writers like Arnold Toynbee (Hodder 1991), Gordon Childe (1958), Karl Polanyi (Renfrew 1984) and a range of influential anthropologists and archaeologists. Such an approach has obvious drawbacks. For historical and other reasons, 'pure' social types seldom exist (although they do sometimes), and therefore the erection of the notion of types into Toynbee-like superstructures should be avoided. The existence of a given type at a given time and place does not suppose either a determined past or a determined future. Nor, it should go without saying, should one type be regarded necessarily as either socially 'primitive' or as morally 'different'. Nevertheless, it is striking that, broadly speaking, all these social analyses have tended to throw up very similar categories, or, to put it another way, there is a long tradition that to divide human communities into four or five major types is a useful way of singling out and comparing their distinctive characteristics.

The broad types are usually given labels like hunter-gatherers, peasant farmers, chiefdoms/aristocracies, palace/temple states, complex states and modern industrial states. Figure 2.1 sets out some examples of actual societies and the salient characteristics by which the types can be recognised.

	Hunter-gatherers	Peasant farmers	Chiefdoms/aristocracies	Palaces/temples	Complex states	Modern industrial states
	e.g. Inuit, European Palaeolithic, Mesolithic, some American Indians	e.g. European Neolithic, some Africans, American Indians	e.g. European Bronze Age, Iron Age, Polynesia, European post-Roman	e.g. Mycenae, Shang, Maya, medieval feudal states	Rome, later China, 16C and 17C Europe	18C, 19C, 20C Europe, USA, modern Japan
Some characteristics	personal qualities important, reciprocity exchange, no professionals, sex sometimes fairly uninhibited, shamans, basic building, some oral literature, no 'high' art	'big men' emerge, reciprocity exchange, no professionals, marriage customs designed to produce healthy, legitimate children, fertility cults, solid building, little art or literature	chief/king, 'birth' important, chief controls redistributive exchange, professional craftsmen, war bands, gods and goddesses, epic verse, ornamental work, earth and stone building	king/god, highly stratified society, re-distributive economy, written records, army, priestly hierarchy, palace complex, royal tombs, literature, 'high' art	'the state' embodied in ruler, market exchange, middle class, professional army, state religion and personal beliefs, moral philosophy, civic building, wide range of arts	the state = the people, very complex, market economy, taxes, social stratification but social movement, factory-based mass production
Technology	human power and dogs	human, traction animals, some pyro-technology	human, animal, elaborate pyro-technology often	human, animal, pyro-technology	human, animal, pyro-technology, wind, water	steam, electricity, nuclear, complex pyro-technology

Figure 2.1 Types of human communities and their salient characteristics

The line between chiefdoms/aristocracies and palace/temple states is dotted because the two have a range of essential features in common, and here it is possible that the second does indeed represent a developed version of the first (although there is no *necessity* for the first to become the second). It will be seen that the characteristics of each type ramify through all the important human activities and that these characteristics extend to the available technology and to the typical material products. It would, of course, be a vulgar error to suppose that the available level of technology and material culture in any sense acted as a determining factor – and still less as a curb – on social development. Each society is an organic whole in which all parts integrate to create its own unique flavour, and it is as a part of this holistic creation that technology and material culture exercise their own potency.

This potency can work in a number of ways, each appropriate to its particular social type. The economist Karl Polanyi and those who have developed his ideas (Renfrew 1984) distinguish three main modes in which goods are exchanged, 'reciprocity', 'redistribution' and 'market exchange', each of which has its own suite of social characteristics and is a part of each of the broad social types. Reduced to their essentials these can be expressed in the diagrams shown in Figure 2.2. Reciprocal exchange supposes a relationship of equality or symmetry between the exchanging parties, who meet face to face and conduct their own barter independently of any outside force. The transaction may happen anywhere, at the home place of one or the other or at some traditional spot between, and it may happen at any time, although some traditional moment may be favoured. This sort of exchange is characteristic of small-scale hunter-gatherer and farming communities. It is clear that the collecting of objects in such societies will also be on a small scale and will be widely dispersed among the adult population. Very few things, perhaps only those greatly treasured, will be retained in such ownership for long: most will circulate freely around the community.

Very different are redistributive societies. Here the relationship is unequal or asymmetrical in that the flow of goods is into one central institution and out to individuals. Material goods are collected into one place, where is concentrated the physical store, the retainers who protect it, the ritual which legitimates the system and the person of the ruler who serves as the focus for all this economic and psychic activity. The social relationship here is of tribute and dependency, and in such societies the economic system is usually one aspect of a very highly structured hierarchy into which birth, land tenure, production and distribution, and spiritual power are embedded as an organic whole. Since such societies are urgently in need of fine objects with which to emphasise visual distinctions of birth and hierarchy, and to enact impressive rituals, they will also feature a tradition of fine craftsmanship. This will have to be supported by the acquisition of

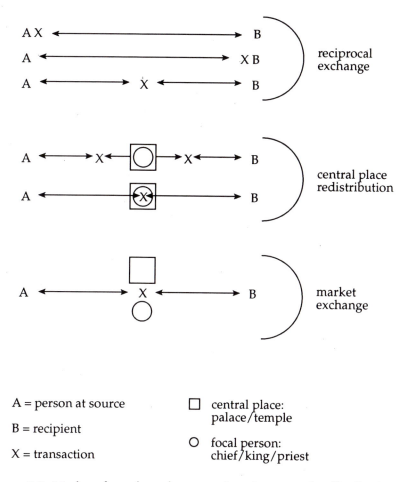

A = person at source

B = recipient

X = transaction

□ central place:
palace/temple

○ focal person:
chief/king/priest

Figure 2.2 Modes of goods exchange: reciprocity, central redistribution
and market exchange

valuable material, and the maintenance of expensive craftsmen who must
be kept in bed and board throughout their lives by the contributions of
the rest, and who may well form part of the central retinue. All this is the
characteristic nature of chiefdoms, aristocracies and palace/temple states,
and Figure 2.1 shows an idealised version of what such societies are like.
Clearly such societies are ideally placed to achieve large accumulated
collections of particularly prized objects in the central repository and to
maintain this repository as a sacred trust as long as the society itself shall
survive.

Market exchange shares some features with both reciprocal and redistribution exchange. A central authority is essential to provide the legal and

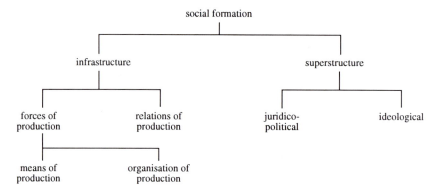

Figure 2.3 Marxist analysis of social interactions (after Renfrew 1984: 250)

physical security without which a market cannot function, and this author-ity will (at least in part) maintain itself through the toll which it takes in levies and dues. In order to be effective, markets must meet regularly, and they must happen at a known central location. On the other hand, they depend upon a multitude of small-scale, detailed and frequently person-to-person transactions in which lineage and ritual standing – although not always wholly insignificant – nevertheless matter less than the ability to pay the going price, itself a product partly of central interference and partly of the multiplicity of previous exchanges. It is clear that in these, the complex and modern societies, emphasis is going to be placed on the quan-tities of goods available as well as their qualities. It is also clear that we have conditions in which the accumulation of collected material will be a possibility across a broad spectrum of the population, irrespective of per-sonal origins but reflecting some measure of immediate economic success.

Social analysts since Marx and Engels have viewed the progress of human society in a model which broadly conforms to the succession just described, particularly in its later stages. In his *Capital: A Critique of the Political Economy* (1951) Marx produced an analysis which broke down the whole of a social complex into a number of interacting components, and their relationships have been conveniently tabulated by Renfrew (1984: 250) (Figure 2.3). It is generally held that Marx assigned the primary role to the economic infrastructure, and in 1894 Engels made this clear:

> What we understand by the economic relations, which we regard as the determining basis of the history of society, is the manner and method by which men in a given society produce their means of subsistence, and exchange the products among themselves (in so far as division of labour exists) . . . It is not that the economic situation is cause, solely active, while everything else is only passive effect.

There is, rather, interaction on the basis of economic necessity, which *ultimately* always asserts itself.

(Renfrew 1984: 250)

Each of the social types distinguished so far in terms of their social and economic characters can be discussed in the light of this analysis, in ways which reveal the prime importance of the production, exchange and accumulation of material culture, and the effect which this has had upon the creation of thoughts and feelings (that is, on the political and ideological superstructure).

This kind of paradigmatic approach to historical understanding has been taken considerably further by a range of contemporary post-Marxist and post-structuralist thinkers like Chomsky, Barthes, Derrida and, above all, Foucault (see also papers by Taborsky 1982, 1985). In *The Archaeology of Knowledge* (1974) Foucault defines the epistemes as the unconscious but productive set of relations within which knowledge is produced and local rationality defined (Foucault 1974: 191), and he distinguishes three major epistemes, the Renaissance, the classical and the modern. Foucault's writing elsewhere suggests that these should be preceded by a medieval or feudal episteme, expressed in characteristic terms on the basis of ideas about feudalism (which was, historically speaking, fundamentally a *French* society whose ideas were carried in the lingua franca) set out by classic French historians of the earlier generation like Marc Bloch. For Bloch it was the 'bonds of interdependence between men, which, more than anything else, gave the feudal structure its special character' (1965: xxi). As Foucault sees it, an important part of this special character was the period's view of the material, spatial world:

in the Middle Ages there was a hierarchic ensemble of places: sacred places and profane places; protected places and open, exposed places; urban places and rural places (all these concern the real life of men). In cosmological theory, there were the supercelestial places, as opposed to celestial, and the celestial place was in its turn opposed to the terrestrial place. There were places where things had been put because they had been violently displaced, and then on the contrary places where things found their natural ground and stability. It was this complete hierarchy, this opposition, this intersection of places that constituted what could very roughly be called medieval space: the space of emplacement.

(Foucault 1986: 22–7)

The feudal episteme would embrace an interdependent hierarchy of time, space and the cosmos, centred upon God and man, in which the essence of knowledge was an experience of unity at the heart of oppositions.

For Foucault the basic characteristic of the Renaissance episteme was

49

the notion that the resemblances between things constitute the ways in which they can be brought into relationships, and so interpreted in a web which comprehended the earth and stars. Hooper-Greenhill (1992: 14) discusses Foucault's four forms of interpretation which reveal the similitude of things: *convenientia* which indicates the adjacency of things; *aemulatio* which retains the principle of adjacency but allows that this may operate at a distance; *analogy*, a complicated superimposition of these two; and the play of *sympathies* which turn things in the direction of natural sympathies, as flowers turn to the sun. As Hooper-Greenhill says, 'Resemblance, sameness, links and relationships are a basic structure of knowing. To know is to understand how the things of the world are the same, however different they may look' (1992: 14).

The classical episteme shifted knowledge into ordered structures, arrived at through observation and measurement, that allowed the creation of hierarchical series, and so that classic outcome of classical knowledge, the classificatory table (Foucault 1970: 74). Knowledge now depended upon the recognition of differences, not similarities, upon which could be constructed sequences of relations expressing fine shades and degrees of difference, the process which we recognise as the creation of taxonomies. This supposes, of course, the existence of objective knowing in which fine differences are discovered to have existed always and not just 'seen' at some particular point in time, and rests on the assumption that such knowledge is capable of true verification.

The modern episteme began for Foucault at the end of the eighteenth century (1970: 217), although in terms of our relationship with the material world, particularly as this is experienced by collectors, this is probably several decades too early, and might be better regarded as beginning around the middle of the nineteenth century. Foucault described the change:

> the general area of knowledge was no longer that of identities and of differences, that of non-quantitative orders, that of a universal characterisation, of a general toxonomia, of a non-measurable mathesis, but an area made up of organic structures, that is, of internal relations between elements whose totality forms a 'function'.
>
> (1970: 218)

As Hooper-Greenhill puts it:

> Things are no longer simple visual pieces to be moved about on a board of one-level hierarchies, but are understood as organic structures, with a variety of different relationships to each other, some at one level and some at another. The organising principles of the new three-dimensional space are analogy and succession.
>
> (1992: 17)

The implications of Foucault's work, and that of some of his contemporaries, particularly Foucault's understanding of the modern episteme, have themselves helped to create the climate of ideas which is often described as post-modern, a word with its own complex history in contemporary thought, but which is a useful way of describing the climate of ideas that developed around 1960 and which constitute a sufficiently clean departure from the preceding modern period (roughly 1850–1960) to justify a term of its own. The epistemological stress on organic relationships, following the collapse of eighteenth-century classificatory knowledge, opened the door to an analysis of the nature of organic relationships, and this then began to reveal their arbitrary and essentially inorganic nature: the fabric of human societies and individual lives become merely a series of *ad hoc* inventions which in turn produce what passes for 'objective' knowledge in each generation, that is, the sequence of epistemes already identified.

As Foucault puts it in one of his later writings:

> We are in the epoch of simultaneity; we are in the epoch of juxtaposition, the epoch of the near and far, of the side-by-side, of the dispersed. We are at a moment, I believe, when our experience of the world is less than that of a long life developing through time than that of a network that connects points and intersects with its own skein.

(Foucault 1986: 24)

God, meaning and knowledge, we are now invited to understand, are merely each society looking into its own bathroom mirror, and moreover doing so afresh each morning, carrying nothing over from the days before: a proposition which may work in theory but never does so in practice.

It must be said that the ideas of contemporary French thinkers about the nature of knowledge and its successive historical manifestations are not as new or startling revelations as they are sometimes said to be. The nature of knowledge and of human thought has been a European preoccupation since at least Locke in the late seventeenth century; no one has ever taken a clearer view of the arbitrariness of social authority than Hobbes, writing a little earlier; and a wealth of historians, writing in French, German and English over the past two centuries (or near enough), have expended much scholarship and talent in developing our ideas about how past people thought and felt. The phases in European thought and feeling which they have broadly agreed to identify are very much the same as those which Foucault isolates as possessing individual and identifiable epistemes. What contemporary thinkers have done is to recast all this into their own language and, putting it all together, to press it to its logical (if the word may be allowed) deconstructive conclusion, one which matches the rootlessness of the post-modern world.

The three main models, then, presented here – the anthropological analysis of social types and the role of material culture within them, Marxist ideas about the relationship between material production and consumption and ideology, and contemporary notions about successive European approaches to the creation of knowledge, particularly in relation to the material world – give us a framework within which to analyse how successive generations of Europeans have carried out the accumulation and collection of objects. What is needed now is a fourth model, a diachronic model which will bind these successive synchronic analyses together into a coherent sequence which expresses the fact that what concerns us is happening in a relatively small geographical space, among people who are descended culturally from each other in every sense and who see themselves as part of a living tradition with a past and a future – ideas which, as we shall see, are frequently very important to collectors.

If such a diachronic model is to be helpful (and not merely chronic in the most demotic sense), it should be as simple and as flexible as possible. The best is that devised by the French *Annales* school of historians, developed originally by, among others, Marc Bloch whose work on feudal society has already been mentioned, and in the second generation principally by Fernand Braudel (Bintliff 1991b: 4–8). The *Annales* paradigm suggests that historical time is dominated by three chief groups of processes which mould societies, and which operate simultaneously but at different wavelengths in time. What we observe at any given moment is the result of interaction between these three processes. The three processes are the Long Term/Structures of Long Duration (*Longue Durée*), the Medium Term/Forces (*Conjonctures*) and the Short Term/Events (*Evénements*) (Figure 2.4). The Long Term includes geophysical constraints, the cultural traditions of peoples and civilisations, relatively stable technologies and world-views (*mentalités*). The Medium Term embraces social and economic history, demographic cycles, the particular history of eras and regions, and again *mentalités*: these would include Foucault's successive epistemes. The Short Term takes in individual histories and the detailed narrative of particular events.

The difficulties the actual writing of such history pose to the working historian notwithstanding this structural history is, as Bintliff justly says, a landmark with inexhaustible potential for reconciling in a single methodology the general and the particular, the event and the millennial trend, the individual and society (1991b: 8). It offers a framework within which it is possible to get some purchase on the process of social change.

EUROPEAN SEQUENCES

If the social types set out in Figure 2.1 – with the economic and material characteristics which we have just discussed – are now set into a historical sequence, it becomes apparent that this is one way of viewing the history

HISTORY OF EVENTS	SHORT TERM EVENEMENTS
	Narrative, Political History; Events; Individuals.

STRUCTURAL HISTORY	MEDIUM TERM CONJONCTURES
	Social, Economic History; Economic, Agrarian, Demographic Cycles; History of eras, regions, societies; World-views, ideologies, (*mentalités*).

LONG TERM STRUCTURES OF THE 'LONGUE DUREE'

Geohistory: 'enabling and constraining'; History of civilisations, peoples; Stable technologies, world-views (*mentalités*).

Figure 2.4 The *Annales* paradigm (after Bintliff 1991b, Figure 1.2)

of European society chronologically from its earliest beginnings to the present day, the only part of the world which has been through the complete sequence up to post-modern industrial society under, so to speak, its own steam. There is broad agreement among prehistorians that the original European hunter-gatherer communities were superseded by communities of peasant farmers around 5000 BC (in very broad terms). By around 2000 BC we can perceive a broadly trans-European patchwork of chiefdoms, which in some southern Europe societies developed the characteristics of palace states. Each of these has its own characteristic flavour, but all seem to be intimately linked to the centralised exchange of exotic goods and the fine pieces which could be made from them: bronze, gold and amber in the earlier phase conveniently called the Bronze Age, and bronze, gold, amber, silver and various forms of glass in the following Iron Age.

By AD 100 the three southern peninsulas, Italy, Iberia and the Balkans, the land west of the Rhine and two-thirds of the island of Britain had become part of the Roman complex state with its market economy. Throughout the Roman centuries the peoples beyond the Rhine and the Danube seem to have continued to live classic chiefdom lives, and when the Roman empire collapsed through their external and its own internal pressures, they re-established such communities in the west and south (except the Balkans) in the societies we know as the Germanic successor states. These show their mixed inheritance. Much of their tone and colour, and clearly much of how they liked to see themselves, reflects their chiefly or aristocratic nature, but they also aspired to some of the complex institutions which the Roman past had had. This part of their enterprise failed, partly as a response to fresh onslaughts of chiefdom peoples from Scandinavia, and the result was what we know as feudal Europe. It will be obvious how well, in broad terms, the idealised chiefdom/palace state described in Figure 2.1 provides a model for feudal society.

Through processes which have been traced many times, this society transformed itself first into the complex market economy states of late medieval and Renaissance/early modern Europe, and then into fully modern states following the scientific, commercial, political and industrial revolutions of the late seventeenth and eighteenth centuries. The particular economic and cultural conditions of the second half of the twentieth century are, arguably, different enough to what has gone before to justify the title 'post-modern' as a means of demarcating this period from its predecessors.

We can now draw together the threads of the discussion and present the results in Figure 2.5. What is described here as the Archaic phase begins with the earliest European traditions, linguistically and culturally, which we can see, and embraces prehistoric traditions of accumulation and their successors in the early medieval world. All these societies can be described as chiefdoms, and the social framework within which they worked represents the mentalities of the long term, in Braudel's phrase, which have been crucial to the nature of European object accumulation, and European society, ever since. For reasons largely to do with the available sources of information, but also in part the character of the societies involved, much of the material discussed here will be drawn from central and northern Europe.

The Archaic phase also includes Classical institutions, that is, elements of collecting practice as these developed in the Mediterranean world of Greece, Greater Greece, and the Roman Empire, and it is important to remember that these, although by the full-blown Roman empire part of the workings of a complex state, nevertheless share in that mind-set of the long term which has already emerged into view. Gradually, with a good many false starts, northern and Mediterranean traditions finally fused in the Christian, feudal states of the full medieval world, as these began to appear around 1050–1100. It was within these that Foucault saw his feudal episteme as operating. Accumulating traditions in these communities, as we shall see, gather up all that has gone before and transmit it into what is usually identified as the world of the Renaissance. The Renaissance is where most discussions of collecting begin, but to do so is to fail to understand

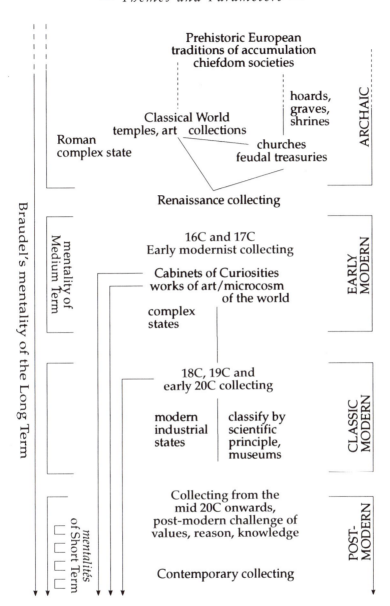

Figure 2.5 The European historical sequence

some fundamentals about the tradition of collecting within which the people of the Renaissance operated, and so to fail to appreciate why they thought and acted as they did. Part Two has been written partially to correct the balance and to offer a broader context for subsequent collecting. Therefore, Archaic themes are treated at some length.

In terms of appreciation of the material world (as perhaps with other things), the collectors of the earlier fifteenth century behaved as much like their predecessors as their successors, and the new episteme, to use Foucault's term, works in the collecting world of the sixteenth and seventeenth centuries, with its early modernist approach to understanding paralleled by the developing complexity of its political and economic structures. By the early eighteenth century this modernist world had moved into its classic phase, backed by a new understanding created by the scientific epistemology developed at the end of the seventeenth century, and by a corresponding density of social, political, technological and ultimately (especially in Western Europe) industrial institutions. The phase of classic modernism embraces both Foucault's classical episteme of the eighteenth century, with its emphasis on classification, and his modern episteme of the nineteenth/early twentieth century with its emphasis on total organic function, because these are essentially successive subsets of the same mental frame.

The post-modern phase runs from about 1960, and is the phase in which we find ourselves today. Post-modern collecting practice, like post-modern society in general, draws (more than it might care to admit) on what has gone before, but views itself through a counter-episteme concerned to subvert previously perceived relationships and realities. Correspondingly, as we shall see, it is the meeting ground – or even the middle ground – where come together overt traditional practices of the Long Term now much enriched by modernist developments, the largely covert nature and needs of the individual, themselves also a part-product of the same tradition, and the place where social values and individual values intersect to bring about change.

The two last topics will concern us in Parts Two and Three. We are now ready to analyse the component parts of the sequence set out in the chart (Figure 2.5) in order to gain an idea of how each phase collected objects, why it did so and how this process modulated through time. Both Figures 2.4 and 2.5 should be borne in mind throughout the following pages. We shall be interested in questions like: what were the circumstances surrounding the formation of collections, what did they contain, what were the outward reasons for their formation (including the typical intellectual ideas of the time) and what have been the typical institutions and physical arrangements in which the collections have been embedded? We shall start by looking first at the structures of the Archaic phase.

CHAPTER THREE

ARCHAIC THEMES OF THE LONG TERM

———— •◆• ————

Upon the headland the Geats erected a broad, high tumulus, plainly visible to distant seamen. In ten days they completed the building of the hero's beacon. Round his ashes they built the finest vault that their most skilful men could devise. Within the barrow they placed collars, brooches, and all the trappings which they had plundered from the treasure-hoard. They buried the gold and left that princely treasure to the keeping of earth. So the Geats who had shared his hall mourned the death of their lord, and said that of all kings he was the gentlest and most gracious of men, the kindest to his people and the most desirous of renown.

Beowulf (Wright 1953: 101)

I swear by Almighty God that I will well and truly try and true deliverance make between our Sovereign Lord the King and the Prisoner at the Bar whom I shall have in charge and a true verdict give according to the evidence.

Jurors' oath in a trial for murder

Poynton, in the south of England, was this lady's established, or rather her disestablished home, having recently passed into the possession of her son. There had been in the first place the exquisite old house itself. Then there had been her husband's sympathy and generosity, his knowledge and love, their perfect accord and beautiful life together, twenty-six years of planning and seeking, a long, sunny harvest of taste and curiosity. Lastly, she never denied, there had been her personal gift, the genius, the passion, the patience of the collector. Mr Gereth had left things in a way that made the girl marvel. The house and its contents had been treated as a single splendid object; everything was to go straight to his son, and his widow was to have a maintenance and a cottage in another county. No account whatever had been taken of her relation to her treasures, of the passion with which she had waited for them, worked for them, picked them over, made them worthy of each other and the house, watched them, loved them, lived with them.

(James 1963: 11–13)

INTRODUCTION

Some of the themes to be identified here, especially those to do with approaches to kinship, marriage and inheritance, and with ideas of the sacred in the broadest sense, come from the ancient past but pervade the frame of our social lives to this day. In order to achieve as good a grip as possible on this elusive material, I have concentrated upon the northern Europeans, drawing on both technically prehistoric (i.e. pre-Roman) and technically historic (i.e. post-Roman) material to make my points. This partiality, made necessary by the nature of the evidence, should not obscure the point already made, that the traditions of the southern Europeans also seem to have partaken of these broad themes. Mediterranean themes, classical and then Christian, will form the topic of the next chapter.

HOARDS, GRAVES AND SHRINES

The accumulation of objects, first principally of stone and then of metal, witnessed by finds of burials and other deposits, is one of the most striking features of ancient society in northern and central Europe, as it appears in the archaeological record over a period of some five millennia from roughly 4000 BC. During the earlier part of this period, traditionally the prehistoric Neolithic and Bronze Ages, roughly from 4000–700 BC the finds come from what are traditionally called graves or hoards, and to a certain extent they have their broad equivalents in the three south European peninsulas of Iberia, Italy and the Balkans. Around the early part of the first millennium BC, or roughly the beginning of the traditional later prehistoric Iron Age, we begin to see a general tendency towards the establishment of sacred buildings for which 'shrine' or 'temple' are our usual terms, with which deposits of valuable goods begin to be associated although they are still put in with the dead or deposited separately. Throughout much of Europe, but not the area north of the Danube and east of the Rhine, the centuries either side of AD 1 saw the local communities being brought politically and economically into the Roman Empire, although how much effect this had upon the hearts and minds of many of those concerned is unclear. As strength drained from the Imperial system in the west around AD 400, its place was taken by a series of Migration period or early medieval Germanic lords from beyond its frontiers whose traditions were essentially prehistoric, and for whom the desire to gather rich grave goods and hoards was very significant. This summary needs to be fleshed out with more discussion: first of the Neolithic and Bronze Age material, then of the Iron Age material, and finally of that of the early medieval heroic world.

Much ink has been spilt in the endeavour to understand the accumulations of material goods, which loom so large in the archaeological record for the central and northern European Neolithic and Bronze Ages (Bradley 1987, 1988, 1990; Levy 1982; Pearce 1983; Coles and Harding 1979). Indeed, like totemism in anthropology, the ways in which this material has been understood is in many aspects an index of how archaeology has itself developed as a discipline. Attention in central Europe has generally been directed towards the identification and classification of the types within each find, in order to create interlocking chronological sequences for each particular region. In Britain, the stress has been upon the ways in which stone was worked and circulated, and bronze was circulated, stored and reused. In Scandinavia, interest has concentrated upon the contexts of the finds and there has been a greater willingness to view the material as 'votive' or 'ritual', that is, to assess its importance across the range of social process.

Recent and contemporary work brings these three traditions together. Evidence collected together by Bradley (1990) shows that across northern Europe generally in the Neolithic, stone axes, sometimes with other material like amber, were ceremonially deposited around the major monuments of the time, the communal tombs and enclosures, in the earth and in watery situations like bogs. Knowledge of copper, gold and bronze metal and metallurgy developed in central and northern Europe from around 2300 BC and from that time until around 700 BC the record shows a complex sequence of metal deposits. Chronological studies based on metal typology are still fundamental in order to show us groups of material which seem to be broadly contemporary and to put these into chronological bands. Once this has been done, however, the finds can be analysed according to their character and this produces interesting results.

Figures 3.1, 3.2 and 3.3 show how this has been done for the multiple deposit finds for south-western Britain during the conventional later Early Bronze Age, the Middle Bronze Age and the early part of the Late Bronze Age (Pearce 1983). A review of the material as a whole suggested that the finds could be usefully analysed on the basis of their content if this was broken down into weapons (mainly daggers, spearheads, swords and related equipment like chapes); personal ornaments of either bronze or gold; domestic or craft equipment like awls and knives; and finds associated with smithing activity, like moulds, ingots, casting waste and scrap metal. It became clear that axes could either form deposits on their own or be associated with all of the other categories. A similar review suggested that the immediate context of the material could best be analysed in terms of graves, that is, associated with human remains; closed finds, that is, evidently intentionally deposited as a group (although not necessarily all at the same time); and scatters, that is, material which was mixed with household rubbish and was probably not a hoard at all in any useful sense. A view of the wider context of the find would relate it to the broader themes of land use.

This analysis shows that in south-west Britain during the later Early

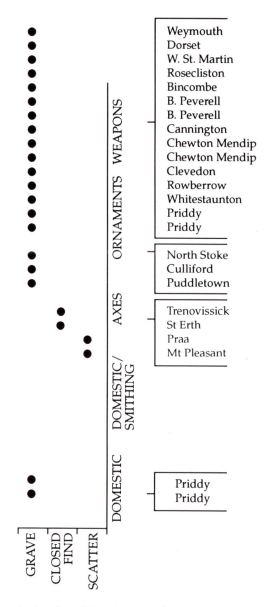

Figure 3.1 Analysis of multiple bronze finds of the late Early Bronze Age in south-west Britain (after Pearce 1983: Figure 5.9)

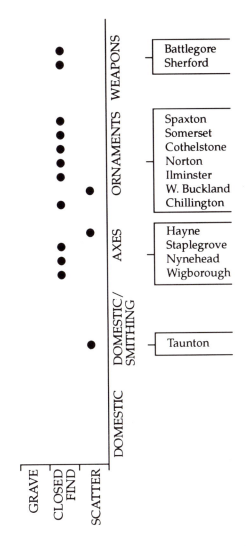

Figure 3.2 Analysis of multiple bronze finds of the Middle Bronze Age in south-west Britain (after Pearce 1983: Figure 5.13)

Bronze Age, weapons buried with the dead are a characteristic find, but that sometimes craft tools were also used as grave goods. Axe hoards were buried, and occasionally axes turn up in what look like ordinary working contexts, like that from the site of South Cadbury hill fort. During the Middle Bronze Age we can see that grave finds drop almost, but not quite, out of sight and that closed finds featuring axes and bronze ornaments are very characteristic. In the early Late Bronze Age we still see axe hoards

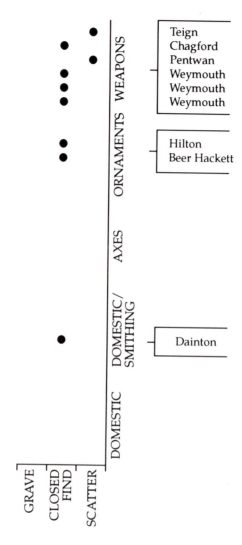

Figure 3.3 Analysis of multiple bronze finds of the early part of the Late Bronze Age in south-west Britain (after Pearce 1983: Figure 5.24)

and hoards of gold ornaments, various scatters, and some weapons buried in graves, but weapon hoards are now conspicuous, and many of them have come from wet sites like pools, rivers and bogs. To complete the picture, the later Late Bronze Age multiple finds from the south-west are shown in Figure 3.4. The metal is much more plentiful and in some ways more complex, but the picture is broadly the same.

Throughout this broad sweep, we can see that some multiple finds seem

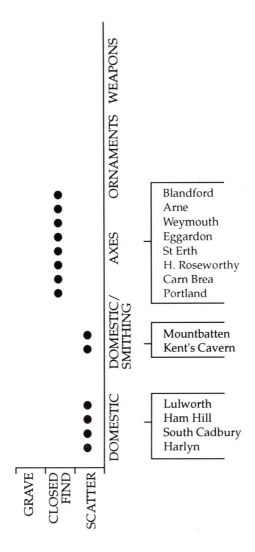

Figure 3.4 Analysis of multiple bronze finds of the later Late Bronze Age in south-west Britain (after Pearce 1983: Figure 5.32)

to be genuinely utilitarian in the most ordinary sense, and not part of any active cycle of accumulation and dispersal. Some metal, especially in the early phase (but never entirely absent), was laid in graves; some was buried in circumstances which do not make it clear whether the material was regarded as lost, or whether it could be used as a 'bank deposit'; and some was lost to human kind by way of water. What is true of south-western Bronze Age Britain is true – very broadly and with an infinity of local transformations – throughout contemporary central and northern Europe, and to a certain extent in southern Europe also (Figure 3.5).

Viewing this long Neolithic/Bronze Age tradition with a wide-angled lens rather than a microscope, and selecting those aspects which are most relevant to the history of object accumulation in Europe, we can see that the broad sweep was something like this. The notion of accumulating stone axes stretches back to the beginnings of a Neolithic lifestyle based on land clearance and agriculture, for which the axes were essential. In order to make this possible, long-range systems of exchange had to be developed which would get the axes from the areas of suitable stone where they were made to the social centres and other places where they were distributed and used. Such systems would necessarily involve the network of obligation which is characteristic of gift exchange. The final deposit of axes as ritual offerings to unseen powers, whatever imagery these were clad in, served to endorse the social system and legitimatise the prestige of those who took a leading role in the organisation. With only relatively minor changes, this sentence is amazingly applicable to any phase in the history of European collecting.

The axe-accumulating tradition, first translated into copper and then bronze, remained significant generally until the end of the Bronze Age, and must reflect complex social structure. But in the early bronze-using phase this tradition is paralleled by another which concentrates upon the deposition of weapons – usually daggers, together sometimes with gold and amber – in graves where single individuals are buried, either as inhumations or cremations. It is this single grave tradition, and its social implications which suggest the importance of princely lineages and all that accompanies them, which is traditionally associated with the spread of Indo-European speakers across the continent. If this is true, though, it seems clear that essentially they added on a particular strand to what was already an ancient tradition of object accumulation. Europe became what it may already have been, or was on the road to becoming – a mosaic of many small chiefdoms, rising occasionally, as in Greece, or perhaps Spain, to full-scale palace states or something close to it, and sometimes as in Britain around 1200 BC, showing fewer signs of centralised organisation. Everywhere, however we seem to see relatively small-scale communities dependent upon the psychic and economic power of a ruling blood-line which maintained its authority through control of redistributive gift exchange and the ability to accumulate the correct offerings, and so kept its grip on fields and herds and labour tribute.

Soon after c. 1000 BC the record shows us that the practice of throwing metal into wet sites, always an aspect of the tradition, became very much more significant (Torbrügge 1971). The metalwork is mostly weapons and their accompaniments, ornaments, and specially prestigious pieces like sheet-metal cauldrons which, judging by the later tradition of oral

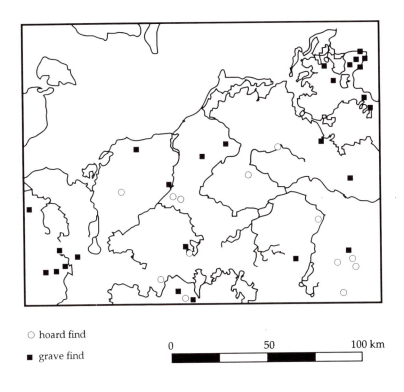

○ hoard find

■ grave find

0   50   100 km

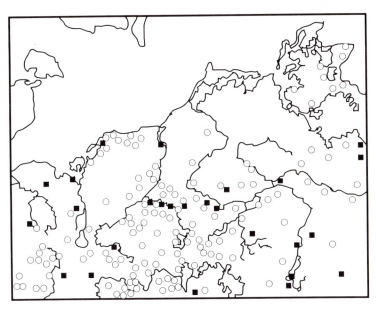

Figure 3.5 The changing relationship between metal objects in graves and hoard finds in north-east Germany in Period 2 and Period 3 of the Early Bronze Age (after Schubart 1972)

literature, would have played a part in the feasting of warriors. The water finds are very significant, but they must not obscure the fact that some material (in some cases perhaps the same material) is still associated with the dead, or that hoards in which axes, tools, bronze or gold and ornaments figure largely are still deposited in the ground sometimes in circumstances which suggest that they are votive offerings.

The same broad pattern continues after the technological and social change which marks the beginning of the later prehistoric Iron Age. The practice of throwing fine metalwork – especially that connected with war – into water continues. So does the practice of burying hoards: of gold ornaments; of the iron bars known as currency bars, and in the pre-Roman Iron Age latest phases, of coins. In parallel, and at some times much more conspicuously than at others, we see graves richly stocked with valuable objects.

At the same time through the centuries of later prehistory, we can begin to see the earthwork enclosures, hill forts in their later phases, which are best interpreted as the political and economic centres of the chiefs upon whom the networks of gift accumulation and exchange depended (or upon which they depended), and sometimes the development of built shrines to emphasise the quality of some (but only some) of the holy places. These shrines are sometimes situated within hill forts (Cunliffe 1978: 321, 322) in Britain and within broadly comparable earthwork enclosures in continental Europe, like those in the Late Iron Age in the Upper Danube region, and in the Celto-Ligerian *oppida* of Entremont and Roguepertuse. These last may have been influenced by the temple-building tradition of the Mediterranean world, but this only serves to underline the broad similarities within the accumulating tradition south, north and north-west of the Alps.

The tradition of hoards and rich graves continues, as archaeology and literature show us, during the Roman period beyond the frontiers of the Empire and into the early medieval heroic world. Beside the large numbers of scantily equipped graves, showing a very wide variety of funeral customs, and the smaller number of upper-class burials equipped with swords and jewellery, we see a few burial mounds, like those of Sutton Hoo (Suffolk), Vendel, Upsala and Valsgärde (Sweden) dating around 600 AD and Jelling and Oseberg (Sweden) around 900 AD, of immensely impressive size and magnificence, matched, where these survive, by the richness of their grave goods.

The great gold hoard from Hoen in eastern Norway, discovered in 1834, the largest gold hoard in Scandinavia, was deposited probably just before AD 900, and so stands chronologically towards the end of this northern tradition. It brings many of the threads together. It contained a large gold necklace, a late Roman cameo in a Migration period gold mount, a Frankish trefoil brooch, gold ornaments and a number of coins. This hoard has been variously interpreted, and Greig regarded it as being a single Danegeld payment extracted from the Abbey of St Denis sometime during the raids of 845–926 (Greig 1964: 122). However, fragments of high-quality decorated late-Roman glass vessel were found in a field not far from the Hoen discovery. The vase had been repaired locally in the early medieval period judging by its gold reinforcements, and is believed to come from a burial, presumably a princely one. The relationship between this burial and the later deposition of the gold hoard, wherever its contents come from, can scarcely be coincidental. Equally, the hoard came from marshland. This is likely to be a part of its significance, and it links it with the well-known series of Scandinavian weapon hoards deposited in bogs during the fourth century AD, and the diversification of objects hoarded and sites chosen for broadly similar hoards in the fifth and sixth centuries (Hines 1989).

At the end of the epic poem, *Beowulf*, which seems to have reached the form in which we have it today in about 750 AD, Beowulf fights a dragon which guards a quantity of gold in what seems to be a burial mound. Beowulf kills the dragon but receives his own death wound and dies gazing on the treasure which has cost him his life (Wright 1953). In the Volsunga cycle (Morris 1962), assumed to date from much the same period as *Beowulf* or a little later, we have the same twin motifs. Sigurd, the Volsung hero, fights the dragon Fafnir in his underground lair and wins a hoard that could fill an otter skin up to the measure: it consists of gold, golden rings, weapons and a golden coat of mail, and Sigurd is able to carry it away in two chests. When at the end of the story, Gunnar, Sigurd's sworn brother dies, the secret of the hoard dies with him. In the German version of the cycle, the *Nibelungenlied*, believed to have taken its known form around AD 1200 but drawing on traditions which certainly go back to the early medieval period, Siegfried (the southern equivalent of Sigurd), wins the Nibelung's treasure, kept in this poem in a cavern (Hatto 1969: 27–8). The treasure passes by marriage to Siegfried's wife Kriemhild, but it is stolen from her by Hagen, Siegfried's murderer, who hides it by sinking it in the Rhine, and dies, rather than reveal its whereabouts (Vestergaard 1987).

In these epic stories we approach the imaginative heart of the early northern world, and they seem to tell us three things about the qualities of buried gold, notions not contradicted by the evidence of archaeology. Firstly, no clear distinction seems to be made between burial in earth and burial by water: Hagen marks the spot where the gold is sunk in the same way that an earth burial place would be noted. Secondly, where earth deposition is involved, it is usually not clear whether or not a human burial accompanies the treasure. Both Beowulf's dragon and Fafnir seem to be guarding barrows, and both beasts may have been thought of as the dead man. The dragon's gold goes back into the barrow with Beowulf, when he is buried in his turn. We feel that the power of the other world hangs about the gold by water and earth, whether or not it actually accompanies a body, and sense the continuity with a tradition long-established. Finally, we understand that the gold is dead in more ways than one. Beowulf anticipates that the dragon will be his doom, and the gold itself is cursed: we are told 'for the princes who placed their treasure there had pronounced a solemn curse on it which was to last until Doomsday' (Wright 1953: 99). Sigurd's treasure is similarly doom-laden: 'then the dwarf went into a hollow of the rocks and cried out, that the gold ring, yea, and all the gold withal should be the bane of every man who should claim it hereafter' (Morris 1962: 130).

There are two hints in *Beowulf* that this is, at least in part, because hoarded-away treasure is useless treasure. After Beowulf's death we are told that 'things had not gone well with the dragon which had wrongfully kept the treasure hidden in the barrow' (Wright 1957: 99). At Beowulf's funeral, where the same treasure was put in his barrow, we are told 'they buried the gold and left that princely treasure to the keeping of the earth where it yet remains, as useless to men as it was before' (p. 101). This sentiment may have something to do with the Christian colour which has been cast over the essentially pagan world of the poem, but we sense throughout the stories that hoarded gold is rightly used among men by giving it away in an exchange which itself stands on the threshold between the worlds; if it is devoted to the Otherworld it takes on the dangerous character of that world and the man who hugs it to himself is doomed to tragedy. He has not used the gold properly as a bridge between two worlds but has stranded himself fatefully in the gulf between the two.

We seem, then, to see in the chiefdoms of ancient Europe, three long-abiding and interlinked material-based traditions. Valuable goods, particularly of metal, are required in the ordinary utilitarian occupations of daily life and as society gradually gathers in complexity, these technological demands become themselves more complex in self-feeding spiral. The demands have to be provided for by the conversions of food surpluses into material goods through networks of exchange centred upon rulers in their strongholds, who are in a position to accumulate and help others to accumulate what we see as hoards. Partly in order to maintain sensitive social equilibriums and partly to underpin the cosmological structures through which the world is understood, a significant proportion of this wealth is withdrawn from circulation, by way of earth or water, or sometimes through reservation in a sacred place, but often in circumstances which include acknowledgement to the mighty dead. The gold work and the other precious things are themselves luminous with power. If they are used well, either in this world to create social relationships, or as acts of corporate dedication to the Otherworld, they are forces for good; but if they are abused, they are dangerous.

QUESTIONS OF GIVE AND TAKE

The giving and receiving of gifts is one of the standard ways across the human family of creating social relationships, and as such has been documented in some of the classics of anthropological literature (Mauss 1925; Meillet 1907; and now Derrida 1992). Leach (1982) has expressed the notions of indebtedness and power which gift exchange embodies in the set of equations shown in Figure 3.6. These show that the obligations which gift indebtedness is held to involve constitute social relationship. The payment of debt, the transfer of the gift, is the concrete manifestation of the relationship, and its nature defines the nature of the relationship. If the gift exchange is reciprocal or equal, then the relationship is one of equality or symmetry; if it is one-way only, or unequal in value, then the relationship is asymmetrical, and manifests a power flow from the 'higher' to the 'lower'. Also, as Leach points out (1982: 159) each statement is reversible. Every social relationship entails a state of indebtedness, just as every state of indebtedness entails a social relationship.

Leach also points out that the left-hand side of the chart has to do with 'economic' relationships, with what a Marxist might think of as the economic structure of the means of production and its control through the excesses of power. If the left-hand column is read by itself, downwards, it gives, in its own terms, a reasonable analysis of economic relations in modern industrial (or any other) society, and corresponds to the left-hand side of Figure 2.3. The right-hand column sets out the social relationships between, for example, employers and employees, and subjects and governments, and represents roughly the right-hand side of Figure 2.3. It seems clear that what we have here is best regarded as an interlocking equivalence in which the trends of production of the goods, the ways of the accumulation and dispersal of the goods, the people concerned and the gifts themselves, are all active participants.

state of indebtedness	=	social relationship
payment of debt	=	manifestation of relationship
nature of payment	=	nature of relationship
reciprocal equal payments	=	equality of status; absence of power flow either way
asymmetrical patterns	=	inequality of status; power flow from 'higher' to 'lower'

Figure 3.6 Gift exchange as indebtedness and power (after Leach 1982: 169)

Gift exchange, with all that this implies for production and collection, ramifies through European society, historically and spatially, as it does through all others, and this principle holds good notwithstanding the fact that, over recent centuries, the gift exchange of goods has transmuted to a considerable (although, as we shall see, by no means total) extent into the exchange of money. As Leach has shown, money exchanges are inseparable from the web of obligation, esteem and status which are inseparable from all exchange systems (Leach 1982: 162–4). Gift exchange, we may say, is the principle behind the range of distribution systems which we have already identified as typical of the various social types. It is, fundamentally, the way in which material culture expresses and upholds social structures.

The notion of an interdependent system of mutual exchange appears across the European family of languages, and at an early enough stage to suggest that, as we would expect, it was a prime social mechanism in the archaic chiefdoms just discussed. As Watkins has shown, the root *do* means 'give' in most Indo-European languages but 'take' in Hittite, German *nehmen* is 'take' but Greek *nemo* is 'give', 'apportion'; English 'give' is cognate with Irish *gaibid*, 'takes'. The general notions of the semantics of the root *dap* group themselves around the idea of gift-giving: Latin *daps* means 'sacred bouquet offered to the gods', but *damnum* (from *dapnom*) means 'damage entailing liability'. In Irish, the word for poetry, the highest gift of all which – given by poet to patron – conveys immortality and is matched by largesse bestowed, is *dain*, the cognate of Indic *danam* and Latin *donum*, 'gift'. The title of Mauss's classic work on the whole notion of reciprocal gifts is *Essai sur le don* (Watkins 1982: 105).

The imagination of the early medieval world (both Germanic and later Scandinavian or 'Viking') was dazzled by the notion that heroic deeds are matched by splendid objects, that the 'imperishable fame' of the hero which shall be sung of to the end of the world – in the phrase which stands at the roots of recorded European consciousness (Watkins 1982: 104) – shall be met with 'honourable gifts', a phrase which, as we shall see, may occupy a similar crucial place in the imaginations of those who used it. Splendid gifts were given from one man to another, sometimes from man to the gods, and sometimes from man to a dead hero. All of these forms stand within long-continuing traditions which constituted the earliest medieval society in ways which it itself believed were at its heart, and all require analysis.

We can come closest to experiencing what the splendid objects were by considering the goods placed in the royal ship burial at Sutton Hoo, with its sword, shield and helmet, dishes, ceremonial drinking horns and gold, enamelled purse filled with gold coins, and by matching these with the description of warriors in *The Ruin* poem:

There once many a man
moon-glad, gold-bright, of gleams garnished,
flushed with wine-pride, flashing war-gear,
gazed on wrought gemstones, on gold, on silver,
on wealth held and hoarded, on light-filled amber

(Alexander 1966: 30–1)

We understand that human happiness could go no further.

The objects themselves, as we know from epic verse and from archaeology, were sometimes heirlooms, as apparently were some of the Sutton Hoo pieces. The technical skills required in their manufacture are of a very high order and presuppose the maintenance by princely families of suites of specialised metal smiths and jewellers, just as the materials and objects themselves, like the Frankish and Byzantine pieces at Sutton Hoo, presuppose extensive, but not necessarily intensive, trading links. We see a classic, chiefly redistributive economy centred upon god-descended princely families and their immediate retainers, who live together in the royal hall, where the objects themselves are hoarded and distributed, and where everything of importance takes place. The royal hoard is constantly depleted as presentations are made, and can only be replenished by constant warfare against similar royal houses; political fortunes, therefore, ebb and flow with the ability to attract substantial numbers of warriors and keep them fed, watered and rewarded, and consequently power is in a perpetual state of spiral, either up or down.

In this kind of community, therefore, together with kin, 'honourable gifts' constituted perhaps the most significant social bond. Markey has shown that the word for such gifts in *Beowulf* (Old Saxon), *methom*, derives from an inherited Germanic **maipm*, which occurs in appropriate forms in some (but not all) early Germanic languages, and was 'the term *par excellence* of gift/exchange' in the early medieval Germanic world, a term which formed part of the language of epic and the primitive economy of heroic society 'but hardly anywhere in active use by the ninth century' (Markey 1990: 351). Markey suggests that **maipm* 'unambiguously points to an underlying **moi-t-mo*, pre-Primitive Germanic **moitm-*' (p. 353), a usage which might take us back into at least the later centuries BC. The word *methom*, especially in *Beowulf*, is particularly associated with *gemæric* as the context for gift exchange (*maéne* still carries the idea of 'well-endowed' in its modern English descendant as, for example, in our phrase 'a man of means'). In *Beowulf gemaene* means something like 'dutifully, honourably, given' and Markey (p. 355) suggests that this reflects a pre-Primitive Germanic **moitmos gho-moinis*, which we may render as 'honourable gift exchange'. Markey notes that this corresponds approximately to a Common Italic **donom da-/do*, and suggests that here we have tracked down a formula of early Northern European poetic diction which encapsulates a crucial social practice, like that represented by the culturally akin 'imperishable fame'. The recorded practices of Migration-age princes, therefore, throw their light backwards into prehistory, as well as casting their shadow before.

What this light shows us becomes clearer when we consider two other words which also belong with notions of 'reward', *mizdo* and *laun*. As Benveniste has shown, *mizdo*, while ultimately related to *maipm*, meant 'worldly reward' while *laun* meant 'providential' or 'heavenly reward' and as such had a gathering tendency to be used in Christian contexts. Markey sets out the potential relationship between the three words in an interesting paragraph which deserves quoting in full:

> Now, if, as seems highly likely, *laun* originally defined providential, divine reward/treasure in opposition to *mizdo* (and congeners) as the expression of secular reward/treasure, payment gained by contest, conquest, or work, then where does *maipm* fit into this continuum and what, if any was its relationship to *laun* on the one hand and or its formal sibling *mizdo* on the other hand? Then too, in addition to the exigencies of a conversion literature as outlined above, why did *maipm* vanish? Why, too on its deathbed in that literature, was it so readily ambiguous (both secular and divine) and unable to make a transition to one pole (*laun*) or the other (*mizdo*). We suggest that, as the original expression for courtly gift/exchange within the *communitas*, *maipm* occupied a pivotal position midway between totally {+secular/–divine} and totally {–secular/+divine}, indeed just as the princeps as communal leader (Goth *piudans*) and addressee of the *maipm* ritual occupied the same position:
>
> | *laun* | *maipm* | *mizdo* |
> |---|---|---|
> | + divine | + – divine | – divine |
> | – secular | + – secular | – divine |
> | – secular | + – secular | + secular |
>
> (Markey 1990: 352)

We can conclude that *maipm*, honourable gifts and the weapons, helmets and ornaments of gold and jewels inseparable from the idea, stood at the critical threshold between two worlds, and that the act of exchange between prince and follower constituted a rite which acknowledged and confirmed mutual obligations, a character which collected material was long to maintain.

Gradually, as the economic structure of the early medieval world developed into the more complex states of later medieval and early modern Europe, the relationships embodied in the notion of *mizdo* – payment for work and the market exchange of consumables for cash – became the dominant social paradigm; this is, indeed, one way of expressing the whole economic and social development which can be crudely lumped under the word 'capitalism'. But throughout, the idea that gifts are separate from this world has not left us; gifts, whoever they are between, retain something of the sacred and culturally embedded character of *maipm*.

The implications of the idea of gift exchange in relation to the accumulation of objects and the rites of obligation which they represent is an important skein in the arguments which relate to European material history, and the theme could be traced without difficulty through medieval court and parish customs, and beyond into our own times. A glance in any high-street shop window around Christmas time will show the contemporary and local system of culturally embedded gift exchange operating at full swing, involving us in all the characteristic social practices and their implications. Christmas presents are given to close family and in some circumstances to friends, but the cut-off points are difficult to determine and then to establish. We feel considerable embarrassment if we are presented with a gift and do not have one to offer in return; many women, in fact, hold a few suitably wrapped objects in reserve to give as 'emergency presents' if necessary.

Men do not usually bother, and this is because Christmas gift exchange is articulated differently between the sexes. A woman, usually the wife and mother, frequently buys for all the family, certainly the males, although it is not her name which will appear on the label as the giver. If this system breaks down, it is not conducive to harmony after Christmas lunch. Women friends usually exchange gifts, but with men this is rare. Our inherited social system requires women to take a greater interest in the whole process as a part of their domestic and home-making role, and hence the lesser interest manufacturers have shown in providing a suitable male gift and our standard lament, 'It's so difficult to find presents for men'. But more recently, manufacturers have spotted this as an exploitable gap in the market and hence the effort to persuade men that they need male bath salts and all the rest, given advertising launches as 'Gifts for Men'.

Choice of gift is equally difficult, for presents must be individually chosen to fit their recipient but must not suppose an unbecoming degree of intimacy. They must be 'right' if they are not to disappoint. In nineteenth-century Europe, for example, the gifts which a woman could properly receive from any man not a member of her family were limited to flowers, sweets and the 'right' kind of book, usually innocuous verse. The value of the gift is related to similar deep concerns, even though, unlike commercial exchanges, it's 'the thought that counts'. We are still clear that seniors give more valuable presents to juniors than the juniors return, and to do otherwise is a social gaffe. Friends are at pains to give each other presents of equal value, and this is likely to have been achieved originally by a mildly awkward conversation in which the norms of the relationship are arrived at. The relative value of Christmas gifts exchanged between husband and wife will express the highly complex network of dependence and authority which binds these two together. Each such gift requires pages of social analysis or serious fiction to do its meaning justice.

More points could be made, and these the readers will fill in for themselves. Enough has been said to show that gift-giving is still for us a very significant social practice, which touches our gender, our kinship system, our relationships of power and dependence, our ideas about good taste in a very concrete social situation, and, of course, the enormous implications of all these things in the wider economic world of production and demand. It is also very important to note here that personal presents are one of the principal ways in which, in the modern world, collections are started and increased. The demands of time, trouble and money in assembling a set of Christmas presents for distribution are considerable, but every twelve months we struggle with the gift-wrapping and the presentation boxes in order to fulfil our exchange obligations and the relationships which they both express and uphold; and in this we are doing, in essence, what our ancestors have done as far back as we can see.

OATHS AND ORDEALS: MATERIAL EVIDENCE

The work of a number of linguists, and particularly of Thomas Markey, has given us a significant insight into the nature of European society which has a bearing on the matter in hand, and this revolves around its fundamental orientation as an oath/ordeal organisation rather than as a totem/tabu organisation, regarded by an anthropological consensus as two basic sociocultural types which are found in complementary distribution and seldom overlap. Totemism has been the subject of such intense anthropological speculation that the history of it as an idea is more or less the history of anthropology as such, and Markey gives a helpful summary of this history in his 1985 paper. He suggests:

A simple yet suitably broad and generally acceptable, working definition of totemism might well assume the following form. Totemism is the realisation of a particular, but generally mystical (or otherwise numinous), relationship between the members of a given social (typically kinship) unit and a natural object or group of objects (e.g. heavenly body, a plant, animal, or mineral or even meteorological phenomena) with which that unit is usually characteristically associated and from which it derives its name . . .

But perhaps the most significant attribute of totemism is that it consists in a projection of mental attitudes on natural objects. However, that very projection, that very bridging, which asserts a continuity between culture on the one hand and nature on the other hand, is never subjected to experimental validation, nor could it be, and even if it were attempted it would defy such validation. A certain fish is, for example, equated with or classified as moral, boars with/as brave, diamonds with/as ethical, and so on. But what probative test is there to demonstrate that boars are brave and diamonds are ethical? This is metaphorical thinking and a 'symbolic' logic of equal but opposite (e.g. left vs. right, male vs. female) that classifies by sentiment rather than function.

(1985: 180–1)

Markey goes on to draw attention to the fact that:

Systemically totemism is normally, perhaps even naturally, correlated with tabu. Tabu confers corrective significance on totemism; it is the police force of totemism and its boundary condition. The correlation of totemism with tabu, an undeniable empirical fact for the vast majority of totemizing cultures, gives rise to what we here term the *totem/tabu* or *t/t*-paradigm

(1985: 181)

Clearly, it is the mystical/numinous character of totem and tabu which provides its psychic energy and defines the kind of world outlook which such a paradigm society is likely to have. Bertrand Russell has defined mysticism as possessed of four hallmark properties:

1) it invokes intuition alone and rejects discursive logic; 2) it is holistic rather than atomistic and isomorphically correlates all differences as integrated parts of a larger whole, of a cosmology, of a *Weltanschauung* entitled the Universe; 3) it denies Time and claims to play itself out in an all-embracing synchronic present with no meaningful past and little predictive future (other than the dire consequences of breaking a tabu, hence the policing/governing nature of tabu as a correlative of totemism); and 4) it views evil as mere (personified) appearance: there are only problems and no counter-examples in a world of mysticism devoid of principled, propositional or analytic and experimental logic. The probative basis of totemism is necessarily experiential, not experimental, logic.

(Markey 1985: 181–2, drawing on Russell 1917: 1–31)

Totem/tabu societies, therefore, will have no interest in tests of validity, the rational link between cause and effect, or action and consequence, or the nature of historical sequence. They will see the world as an undivided unity in which each fraction is part of the wholeness of things, perceiving no dualities, whether between man and the natural world, man and matter, word and object, or right and wrong, other than as a matter of sacred transgression.

The data embedded in the *Human Relations Area Files* held at the

University of Michigan suggests that the complementary paradigm to totem/tabu should be that of oath/ordeal and, as a matter of social and historical fact, it is to this paradigm that European society, past and present, seems to belong, some cultural admixture notwithstanding. Like totem/tabu, oath/ordeal possesses its own kind of logic in the structure of oath, guaranteed by its own cosmological sanctions embodied in ordeal. Here, oath is defined as 'a formal invocation to gods/men to witness the contested validity of acts or intentions'. Characteristically, oaths adopt a formula, which carries the legitimatising weight of precedent, and are uttered in special places and at special times, in relation especially to the adjudication of guilt and innocence. The total familiarity with which we ourselves hear utterances like 'I swear I am innocent', or 'I swear before almighty God that what I say shall be the truth, the whole truth and nothing but the truth' bear witness (*sic*) to the mind-set of which these phrases are a part, and there is abundant evidence for such practices in the European past.

Oaths are frequently validated by ordeal, like the medieval trials by fire, water or earth, which lasted in Britain well into the seventeenth century as a way of testing witches. In continental Europe there is evidence that particular ordeals, like the ordeal of hot iron, were associated with particular social classes, documented at length by no less a scholar than Grimm (1899: 567–86). The use of riddles as tests, and the performance of feats in order to achieve offices like kingship, are too well-known to need any labouring. By far the commonest ordeal in European society, however, is that of the duel, of ritual single combat, sometimes to the death, which in a range of variants runs back as far as we can see, and which in specialised sections of central European society, like the clubs at some of the German universities, has scarcely yet come to an end. Here either a champion acting on behalf of his community, or an individual acting on his own behalf, offers to prove upon his body the truth of the assertions which have been made. We still know perfectly well what is meant by phrases like 'throwing down the gauntlet' or 'settling the matter by fair fight'.

The oath/ordeal paradigm involves the notion of individual rights and responsibilities, since only a single person can perform oaths and ordeals, and the corresponding notion of the rest, who hear, see and judge. It requires a recognition that events happen in temporal sequence which has a bearing on how they can be seen to relate to each other: the strong system of tenses which Indo-European languages characteristically possess has often been noticed, and is an integral part of the mental process. It sets up a dichotomy between word and object, between man and the material world, which rejects the notions of the unity of all things in favour of a sense of separations which hinge on pairs like true : false, supported by previous events : unsupported, proven by successful defence/ordeal : unproven, genuine : deceitful, innocent : guilty, and so on (Chandler *et al.* 1993). It carries the seeds of a potential development of moral and social

Totem/Tabu		Oath/Ordeal	
	+ = present, — = absent, > = more, < = less		
+	divine intervention/tabu	+	divine intervention/ordeal
—	applies to individual only	+	applies to individual only
—	word/object dichotomy	+	word/object dichotomy
+	causal/—descriptive naming	—	causal/+descriptive naming
—	Searlean intentionality	+	Searlean intentionality
+	metaphorical etymology of	—	metaphorical etymology of
	so-called intentional terms 'lying,		so-called intentional terms 'lying',
	telling the truth' etc.		'telling the truth', etc.
	outside-inward spiritual expression		inside-outward spiritual expression
—	sacer/sanctus distinction	+	sacer/sanctus distinction
+	emphasis on numinous	—	emphasis on numinous
—	propositional	+	propositional
>	iconography in ritual	<	iconography in ritual
—	law by precedent	+	law by precedent
+	historicity/—history	—	historicity/+history
>	economy by status	<	economy by status
	low social stratification		high social stratification
<	jurisdictional hierarchy	>	jurisdictional hierarchy
>	tribalistic	<	tribalistic
>	synecdochic	<	synecdochic

Figure 3.7 The oath/ordeal and totem/tabu paradigms (after Markey 1985: 189)

philosophy, logic and scientific experiment, analytical history and, most significantly for our present purposes, a particular relationship to the material world, which is regarded as 'other' and therefore as a fit arena for the exercise of the analytic qualities just described.

In all this, the oath/ordeal paradigm differs radically from the totem/tabu paradigm, and the distinctive features of each can be usefully set out in tabulation form (Figure 3.7). Fundamentally, the two paradigms represent different ideas about the sacred. For totem/tabu societies, all is numinous, diffused with the same divine. For oath/ordeal societies, the sacred is divided into *sacer*, that which is charged with the presence of the divine, and *sanctus*, that which is cut off from mortals. This is a concept impossible to totem/tabu which sees nothing divided from anything else, and in consequence expects an uninterrupted continuity between nature and society, the divine and the world, and appreciation of the numinous is a collective experience. In oath/ordeal societies, by contrast, the sense of dichotomy is fundamental and the experience of both essentially individual.

GENEALOGIES: *COUSINAGE, DANGEREUX VOISINAGE*

In 1982 Leach wrote: 'When you read anything that any anthropologist has written on the topic of kinship be on your guard. The argument may not mean what you think; the author himself may not have understood what he is saying' (1982: 137–8). When this awful warning is linked with the difficulties of reconstructing what kinship systems may have been like in the remote past and linking this with more recent and contemporary situations, and with the undoubted fact that non-anthropologists usually find the whole subject arid and unhelpful, it will be seen that in this section I have set myself an uphill task. I have done this, because, in spite of all the thronging difficulties, the fact remains that how a society sees its pattern of marriage and family relationships creates an essential part of its social character, and there are reasons for thinking that the broadly European system has, and for a long time has had, special characteristics, particularly as these affect the property-owning and collecting classes, which have played a significant role in defining long-term *mentalités*, especially in relationship to notions about the material world.

The most comprehensive study of European kinship is that produced by Friedrich (1966) who was able to draw on a long tradition of previous study (e.g. Crossland 1959; Thieme 1953) and on criticism by social anthropologists like Goody (1959) who warned that proto-historical studies are too often encumbered by the incorporation of discarded hypotheses of social anthropology as part of their academic tradition. Friedrich brought together both a large body of European data drawn from textual and linguistic study and theories of kinship semantics drawn from social anthropology, and has used these to suggest what can be determined about early European kinship in relation to immediate blood relationships, the extended family and the relationships through marriage.

Friedrich suggests that across the European language family the words for blood-kin suggest a general and early recognition of the relationship set out in Figure 3.8. Similarly, the words for relations through marriage, that is affines or (as we say) in-laws, suggest the broad existence of eight special terms, of which five were normally used by a woman when speaking of her husband's close blood relatives (Figure 3.9). From this Friedrich infers that the terms imply that on marriage the girl removed to the familial group of her husband's father and this matches other early textual evidence which shows a great concentration of power in the father's hands, giving us an extended family of patriarchal type. Further evidence allows the suggestion that quite often the patriarchal family formed a physical household and associated field rights held by the father, where everybody lived (patrilocal) and descent was reckoned in the male line (patrilinear) (1966: 14–23). All this produces a system which is deeply familiar to modern English men and women, especially if their appreciation of it has been sharpened by a taste for Victorian novels. Each of us would be wholly unsurprised if, on drawing his or her own immediate family tree, it looked very much like that shown in Figure 3.10, and the same is broadly true of any modern European from Cork to Moscow, or from Sydney to New York.

pHtrwos
father's brother
HG/R/5

pHte:r
father
HG/R/9

maHte:r
mother
HG/R/11

awyos
mother's brother 3
mother's father 2

bhraHte:r
brother
HG/R/10

sweso:r
sister
HG/R/10

swHnws
son
HG/R/7

dhwgHte:r
daughter
HG/R/9

nepot
grandchild 4
sister's child 2
sibling's son 4

HG = found in Homeric Greek
R = found in the Rigvedas
2–11 = number of Indo-European language stocks in which term found
H = laryngeal/mid-central vowel sound

Figure 3.8 Proto-Indo-European terms for blood-kin (after Friedrich 1966: 7)

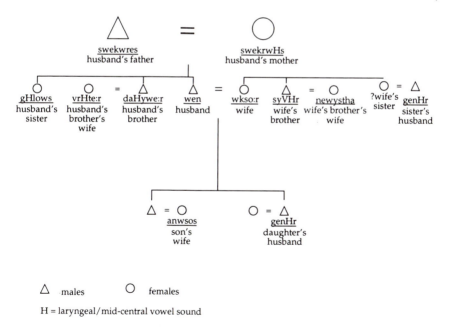

△ males   ○ females

H = laryngeal/mid-central vowel sound

Figure 3.9 Proto-Indo-European terms for affines (after Friedrich 1966: 15)

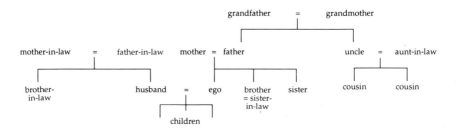

Figure 3.10 Typical modern English family tree

Europeans are not the only society in the world organised in terms of this sort of structure, but it is probably fair to say that such structures are relatively unusual. To quote Leach again:

> In a great many social systems the only fully legitimate marriages are those in which the bride and bridegroom are not only already kin but kin of a specific category such as, say, that which includes the relationship mother's brother's daughter/father's sister's son. The rules are formally protected by supposedly powerful religious taboos, breach of which will result in supernatural punishment for all concerned.
>
> (Leach 1982: 144)

In these social systems, in other words, marriage between cousins of one kind or another is regarded as desirable. This gives us the sort of family tree set out in Figure 3.11, which relates to no actual society and is ludicrously over-simplified but in its general shape serves to show how unfamiliar this system is to the European mind, and how different are some of its implications to those to which Europeans are accustomed.

Before we explore these implications, some problems must be faced. Language has a complex relationship to life and norms are not necessarily

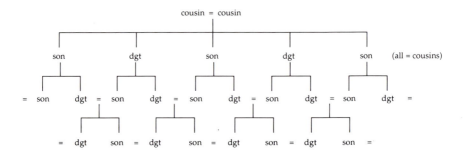

Figure 3.11 Much simplified sketch of one approach to a cross-cousin marriage system

normal; in other words in real day-to-day living all sorts of special arrangements have to be made which are at odds with the desirable pattern. We are
discussing not so much how communities actually are, as how they think they
ought to be. This relates to another important point. It is generally the upper
reaches of a hierarchical society which feel most heavily the social pressure
to 'do the right thing', and where, therefore, we are likely to find the kinship
norms and their implications weighing most heavily. The tendency in early
European kinship to underplay the significance or desirability of cousin
marriage, or even to forbid it, became in the hands of the Catholic church (in
part for good reasons of its own to do with encouraging legacies) a definite
ban on marriage within the prohibited degrees of cousinhood, which during
the eleventh and twelfth centuries were interpreted as extending through
seven generations. No doubt this was generally ignored at village level. But
when Henry I of England wished to marry two of his illegitimate daughters
to Hugh FitzGervais and William Warenne the relevant pedigrees were
submitted to Anselm, Archbishop of Canterbury, and Ivo, Bishop of
Chartres. It became clear that the women and the two men shared a common
ancestor (Figure 3.12) even though nobody could then name him and so the
marriages were forbidden (Southern 1959: 82–3).

In the same way, during the eighteenth and nineteenth centuries it was
the European landed classes and higher bourgeoisie who were expected to
contract only fully legal marriages, perhaps to establish a patrilocal home,
to make a clear distinction between legitimate and illegitimate children, and

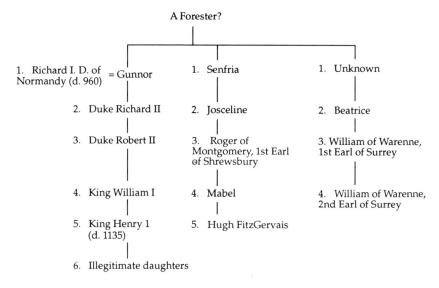

Figure 3.12 Pedigree of Henry I of England, Hugh FitzGervais and
William of Warenne (after Southern 1959: 83)

to bequeath their property correctly. The consequences of this are, of course, the stuff of family history, both real and fictional. Further down the social scale, things seem to have been different. To take an immediate, and not at all flippant example as many men can testify, the old English working class tended to be matrilocal rather than patrilocal, in that the newly married couple often moved in with the wife's mother, who exercised power because she was the husband's mother-in-law, a situation reflected in a whole class of bitter music-hall humour. Here, however, it is the habits of the property-owning and collecting classes with which we are most concerned.

This raises another crucial question. Intimately tied with kinship arrangements are arrangements for the transmission of property and this has been the topic of intense discussion (for example Goody *et al.* 1976; Macfarlane 1978). In theory there is no reason why a system like the European one should not be linked with a broad division of property between all the children of a marriage, perhaps in a variety of proportions. Something of this kind seems to have operated at various points in the historical past where we have evidence, and still strikes a chord with many people as the 'fair' way to behave. The difficulty, however, is that, given the non-cousin marriage system, property passed out to children indiscriminately is likely to seep away into the hands of affines rather than stay within the main family stem, which will then be much weakened. This has been countered by a distinct tendency to create a single heir, usually that classic European figure, the heir-at-law, male, legitimate and first-born.

This arrangement carries the consequence of cutting out all younger sons and daughters, and although the usual expectation has been that something will be done for them, this may have been relatively little. However, the position of women within the system is much more complex than this and the range of local customary variants should not blind us to the fact that property was frequently attached to women, sometimes as brides and often as widows. As Goody puts it:

> While women suffered many disabilities the role of merry widow (and later of the gay divorcée) was nevertheless distinctive of certain groups of European societies, as Chaucer's Wyf of Bath reminds us . . . With regard to succession, many situations in European history turn on the possibility of women succeeding to office, both to the paramountcy (monarchy) and at subsidiary levels. The question of female succession to office is linked to the inheritance of land, and that in turn to the transmission of immovables; both possibilities are potentially available as options because of the fact that women share in male (or rather conjugal) property . . . These then are some of the broad features that distinguish European systems.
>
> (Goody 1976: 11–13)

82

No matter how much European women may have been dispossessed or excluded (and of course they have been), we should not forget that this has been in tandem with a certain recognition of legal, social and individual rights which may, at any rate, have been claimable by some women in some circumstances, usually, again, among the better endowed classes. Just as it is no accident that the framework of European culture has created particular individual and political systems, so it is not accidental that the same framework should also have produced the high medieval notions of courtly love and the successive women's movements, from at the least the 1770/1780s, which are also an aspect of rational, modernist understanding. One consequence of this has been to create a peculiarly European kind of eroticism in which women occupy a confused position between 'object' and 'partner', visible across literature in historical depth and art over the modernist centuries. This, as we shall see, has had its own kind of impact upon the relationship between material collecting and the making of gender.

All these varied arrangements may in part account for the extremely confused approach to marriage and kinship which we actually find when we look at specific historical societies at particular times and places across the sweep of European history. It is also possible that different or older traditions of kinship may be playing a part at various points throughout this historical sequence. The point here is not the many variations or deviations which may be played on the theme, but the theme itself, that is, an approach to marriage, inheritance and kinship which is identifiably European, now and in the past. This pattern has played an important part in social navigation and it is to this that we must now turn.

A system of cousin marriage, that is a marrying-in or endogemous system, tends to create a vertical or monolithic structure in which the family resources are kept within the family, and can be shared out amongst all its members according to custom. By contrast an exogamous or marrying-out system, like the European one, produces a relatively weak vertical structure and a relatively important horizontal one, in which family relationships straggle away into an extended series of affines. This has two important consequences. The goods that have been associated with marriage, whether as a dowry provided by the girl's parents to go with her or bridewealth provided by the man's family to go to her parents, will be lost to which ever family is making the provision because the two groups are not blood-kin. This means that goods can circulate in such a society in a much less regulated and more random way than is often possible. Coupled with this has been a range of heirship strategies which operated at various times and places. But in order to retain a solid core of wealth within one family line, it is necessary to create some inalienable property rights, of which the most obvious is the concentration of heirship in the eldest son, a strategy which Roman society embraced and bequeathed to later generations, and which may have operated earlier in some groups. This, however, has the result – another European, and particularly English, classic – of creating sequences of younger sons who, although educated as gentlemen, have no visible means of support and must make their own way in the world.

The effects of this have been significant. There is a very real sense in which some of the later (and perhaps some of the earlier) history of Europe is the history of poorly endowed younger sons who have always had to move on, open up new lands, look to acquire a well-dowered female, or take to commercial ventures. They have contributed considerably to the restless, aggressive, acquisitive character, which, for better or worse, is typical of Europeans. Their existence is part of the reason why European trade, industry and colonisation developed as it did. Europeans are accustomed to the idea that, because cousins are not booked to each more or less in their cradles (an approach the contemporary press describes as 'arranged marriages'), the marriage market operates much like any other market. The potential choice of marriage partner is very free and so very competitive, and this has helped inspire both our notion of romantic love (see de Rougemont 1956) with all the specially orientated forms of production which this has entailed, and a steady but ever-shifting pattern of the accumulation and dispersal of material goods. We instinctively recognise all this with our range of social stereotypes – the comfortable widow, the youthful heiress, the nagging mother-in-law, the young lovers, the man who marries the boss's daughter. In sum, one of the effects of the European kinship pattern has been to create a society in which, over a long period, material goods have been significant in a way which transcends their universal relationship to human needs, to encourage the inventions of ways in which the range and number of goods can be increased, and to create habits of object accumulation; and with all of this goes a mind-set materially attuned.

CONCLUSION: LONG-TERM THEMES IN A MATERIAL WORLD

The themes of the long term in European society which have emerged from this discussion (although not an exhaustive list) have and do shape the nature and the flavour of European life, and in particular its relationship to the material world. They represent the particular twist which European culture has given to universal human concerns, twists which, in sum, have produced a culture complex that is different in character from the great majority of human cultural systems, and which contains within it the potential for those historical developments which have indeed (for better or worse) taken place, and which we identify as materiality-based science, technology, industry, and the social developments which accompany these forces.

The broad thrust of European social life, as we have just seen, is organised around a family system which produces many restless, competitive individuals with their way to make in the world. Family property is difficult to keep together, so that there has emerged a distinct tendency to create rigorous and exclusive notions of heirship. Individuals, including female individuals, loom large in the system. This has helped to generate a characteristic relationship to the material world, in which that world's ability to generate wealth achieves a particular significance. It is worth noting that, unlike most of the world's language systems, the languages of what became the economically and politically most developed of the European countries, that is, Greek, Germanic and Latin (and their descendants) have verbs which enable a speaker as subject to describe direct possession of a thing, perceived as object. So we can say in English, 'I have a book', a characteristic construction which creates a firm individual in a direct relation of ownership, even though 'have' can be used in a variety of less clear-cut possessive ways ('I have children', 'I have a cold', etc). Many language systems, including those Indo-European ones east and west of the Latin/Greek/German area use oblique constructions of the 'There is a book at me' variety, with their stress on feeling rather than ownership. This distinction must be a part of the particular way in which classical and western European society developed (Kiernan 1976: 365).

The European approach to the social organisation of kinship is relatively unusual; unusual also is the oath/ordeal character of European society, and the two fit together to produce a communal ethos, which seems, at least on this kind of population scale, to be without real parallel across the people of the globe. The oath/ordeal paradigm creates a society whose mind-set works on the notion that one thing can be distinguished from another on the basis of 'truth' and 'falsehood', with their companion ideas of 'reality' and 'causability', and that the capacity for recognising these distinctions belongs, not within a social group, but within each (albeit usually each male) individual. There is seen to be a dichotomy between men and outward things, which generates a characteristic relationship to the material world, in which it becomes an objective reality and the suitable medium for the exercise of thought and aspiration: those aspirations which the nature of family life forces upon many individuals.

Such a society is likely to see the accumulation, exchange and deposition of specially chosen objects as a prime way of creating relationships between men and men, and men and the divine. This, in the broadest terms, is the role which the archaic hoards of bronze and gold are playing. In economic terms, the ability to create surplus which can be frozen into enduring craftwork, and to offer it to the gods, legitimises and sustains inherited authority, itself also often (certainly in its later stages) backed up by long-reckoned descent of characteristic European form. Similarly, the capacity of gift objects to create a long-term relationship between lord and man – a relationship which is the equivalent to blood-kinship and links with all the oath and fealty swearing which Europeans find so deeply familiar – help together to create the kind of material parallel to the world of blood ties which the kinship system makes necessary. It is probably no great exaggeration to suggest that in this we see one of the tap roots of what will ultimately become the superstructure of commerce and paid employment.

All this is set in characteristically emotional terms. In the archaic world, specially chosen objects are full of beauty and power, they are treasures, casting their spell over the beholder. Assembled together, they glow with psychic force, working strongly on the hearts and minds of those who behold them. They can work within the world, creating relationships of mutual obligation, or they can be laid up in the dark, by way of earth and water. They seem to bear a special relationship to the mighty dead, from whom they may have come, and to whom they may be given; in a mysterious way they can make the past a real presence in the present. Objects which are laid up, therefore, may be set apart, but they are not set aside. They continue to be among the sources of social power.

This power is sacred power. For totem/tabu societies all is equally numinous. For Europeans, as we have already noted, the sacred is characteristically divided into that which is charged with the presence of the divine (Latin *sacer*, Greek *hieros*, Gothic *hails*) and 'that which is cut off from contact with mortals' (Latin *sanctus*, Greek *hagios*, Gothic *weihs*) (Markey 1972, 1985; Benveniste 1969: 2, 179–202). This accounts for the typically European tendency to see a distinction between the numinous and the world, and between nature and the social world, and to create sacred propositions in the form of oaths and prayers which take the form of intensely private, personal experiences, and which are capable of modulating into conceptual theories and individual acts of artistic creation.

Here lies the heart of the relationship between individuals and the world of objects. Material can be worked upon in every conceivable way to yield profit, prestige, social and emotional power, and knowledge. But objects themselves are imbued with the transforming power to bring these things about. They are a bridge between undifferentiated divinely charged nature, from which they come and to which they belong, and the world of men. Much of this book is directed towards discussing the consequences of these propositions.

CHAPTER FOUR

MEDITERRANEAN THEMES

——— •◆• ———

But everything would be straightforward, my dear Gallus, if you had bought what I needed and within the price had wished to pay. Not but what I stand by these purchases you say you have made, indeed I am grateful.

Not being acquainted with my regular practice you have taken these four or five pieces at a price I should consider excessive for all the statuary in creation. You compare these Bacchantes with Metellus' Muses. Where's the likeness? To begin with, I should never had reckoned the Muses themselves worth such a sum – and all Nine would have approved my judgement! Still that would have made a suitable acquisition for a library, and one appropriate to my interests. But where am I going to put the Bacchantes?

Letter of Cicero to M. Fabius Gallus, December 46 BC
(Bailey 1978: 104)

You will then know clearly and unmistakably when your spiritual work is inferior to you, and exterior; when it is interior and, as it were, on your level; and when it is superior to you, and inferior only to God. Everything physical is external to your soul, and inferior to it in the nature order.

Your soul has within itself, as part of the natural order, these faculties: the three major ones of *Mind* (which includes *Memory*), *Reason*, and *Will*, and two minor ones, *Imagination* and *Sensuality* ... There is nothing higher than yourself in the natural order, save God alone.

The Cloud of Unknowing (Wotters 1961: 128–9)

INTRODUCTION

Historically speaking, thus far we have drawn our themes from the early northern European world, although the themes themselves have proved to have far-reaching implications. But the southern European world of the Mediterranean, although drawing on the same parameters of the Long Term, added some characteristic and immensely influential phrases to the tunes. In the peninsulas of Italy and the Balkans, where traditions may already have been very mixed, events ultimately converted a sequence of small states, many of them city based, into the complex market economy state which we know as the Roman Empire, in which a characteristic relationship to the world of things was an integral element. This complex market state eventually came to embrace the whole Mediterranean basin and Europe west of the Rhine and south of the Danube. When the empire disintegrated politically around AD 450 into a sequence of Germanic kingdoms (whose ancient northern traditions we have just discussed), these kingdoms inherited much classical practice now translated into Christian terms, and fused these with their northern inheritance to produce what we see as early medieval and feudal Europe. Here we shall look first at the ways in which material was accumulated in the states of pre-classical and classical Greece, and then in the cosmopolitan Roman world. The next section will tackle the classical notion of the 'museum' and its (highly doubtful) relationship to the gathering of material goods. Then we shall turn to medieval Christian notions about the collecting of objects and its place in the scheme of things.

TEMPLES OF ART

During the Greek later Bronze Age around 1500 BC, and drawing on sophisticated predecessors, there developed what was in many ways a palace state version of the contemporary northern chiefdoms. This society was afterwards remembered in the poetry connected with Homer's name to have cherished appropriately European attitudes towards duals, gift exchange, the burial of heroes and conduct in general; as a family Odysseus, Penelope and Telemachus are all what we would expect. In the centuries after 1000 BC, following political and social changes, a series of small-scale units developed. In terms of their social structure, with its central institutions of ruling class, priesthood, temple and legitimising ritual, and relatively small-scale economy largely redistributive but with some nascent market features, the early Greek city-states, inside and beyond the homeland, may not have been so very different to the small-scale Iron Age states to their north. Greeks, too, buried grave goods with the dead, although usually rather limited ones by the standards of the northern aristocrats. But, as Snodgrass has shown us, in Greece the European-wide custom of object accumulation and deposition at sacred sites and shrines was significantly developed. Moreover, because Greek society was already semi-literate, and because their sacred sites went on to be extremely famous, we know much more about them, and the books in which much of this knowledge was recorded have been read and reread subsequently by educated Europeans, upon whom the whole assemblage has had a powerful long-term effect.

	Eleventh and tenth century BC	*Ninth century*	*Eighth century*	
Bronze figurines at Delphi	0	1	152	(1969)
Bronze tripods at Mount Ptoön (Boiotia)	0	0	7	(1971)
Bronze dedications on Delos	0	1	19	(1973)
Terracotta figurines at Olympia	10	21	837	(1972)

	Eleventh and tenth century BC	*Ninth and early eighth*	*Later eighth and seventh*	
Bronze fibulae at Philia (Thessaly)	0	2	1783+	(1975)
Bronze pins at Philia	1	4	37	(1975)
Bronze fibulae at Perachora	7	1	50+	(1940)
Bronze pins at Perachora	0	15	81	(1940)
Bronze fibulae at the Argive Heraion	16	10	88	(1905)
Bronze pins at the Argive Heraion	3	c. 250	c. 3070	(1905)
Bronze fibulae at Lindos (Rhodes)	0	52	1540	(1931)
Bronze pins at Lindos	0	0	42	(1931)

Figure 4.1 Dedications at temple sites in Greece, eleventh to seventh centuries BC (after Snodgrass 1980: 53)

Snodgrass has analysed the deposits of bronze goods in a series of important temples in a period covering the eleventh to the seventh century (Figure 4.1). The chart shows clearly the considerable increase in bronze dedications in the eighth and seventh centuries, and, as he points out, to a certain extent this mirrors a corresponding dip in the grave goods which accompany Greek burials: the total numbers of fibulae and pins known from eighth-century graves in central and southern Greece are to be numbered in hundreds rather than thousands; tripods and pieces of armour are rarities, and bronze figures unknown (Snodgrass 1980: 54). The growth of the dedications, and hence of the sanctuaries themselves, is connected with the growth in metal supplies, and a sixth-century inscription from Athens refers to the 'collecting' of bronzes (p. 62). Snodgrass continues:

A final link which is worth emphasizing is that between the sanc-tuaries and warfare. Many Greek sanctuaries were in a real sense war museums, and on occasion they served as armouries too. Not only were the portable dedications of arms and armour usually a tithe of the spoils taken from defeated enemies, or else personal offerings of their own equipment by grateful victors; but sometimes the temples themselves were built with the proceeds of successful campaigns.

(1980: 63–4)

Like their counterparts in the northern world, the bronze goods offered to, and collected by, temples served to make legitimate the social structure of hierarchy and its public relationship to the Gods, reinforced in the case of Greece by the athletic contests, with which some of the bronze dedications are linked. Olympia seems to have served as a meeting place where the petty chieftains of the west asserted their status by making dedications in the Early Iron Age (Morgan 1991: 29). The value of the bronze metal was itself very considerable, and the temple holdings represent wealth frozen into holy immobility, to be admired but not used, in a kind of conspicuous consumption which adds material prestige to the status quo. Tripods, in particular, may have had a social value which depended upon their previous role as gifts within prestige exchange networks and interestingly, one of the tripods dedicated at Olympia, apparently in the eighth century, was an heirloom piece, a tripod from the Cypriote Late Bronze Age (Morgan 1991: 31).

A striking feature of the Greek world was its stability. Most of these temples, together with many of the assumptions which underpinned them, and probably at least some of the very early material which they acquired, were still in existence when Pausanias visited and described them in the second century AD. By then, of course, Greece, like the rest of the Mediterranean and western Europe, was a part of the Roman empire and local editions of wealth-accumulating temples were appearing throughout the Roman world, drawing partly from the traditions of the classical world, and partly on those of the northern Late Iron Age. By Pausanias' day the temple of Zeus at Olympia had a collection which included the great ivory and gold statue of the god made by Pheidias, the throne of Arimnestos, King of the Etruscans and the first non-Greek ever to dedicate to Zeus at Olympia, and the bronze horses dedicated by Kyniksa, daughter of Archidamos II, a fifth-century king of Sparta. There were also statues of Hadrian and Trajan, portraits in niches of Augustus and Nikomedes of Bithynia, three wreaths in the form of wild olive branches dedicated by Nero, twenty-five bronze shields used for the race in armour, and various stone tablets (Levi 1971; see also Elsner 1992).

The whole assemblage reads very much as we would expect that of a large late-Renaissance or nineteenth-century collection, partly because the material there would be much the same, if not so important, but also because the mixture and the context is very similar: a varied collection of works of art and historical material, laced through with piety and patriotism in which the current imperial dynasty, whether of Augustus or Victoria, looms significantly.

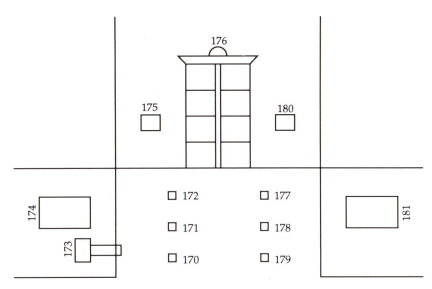

170 golden statue of Victory
171 clay figure of 'The Leisurely Boy'
172 painting of Apollo
173 panel painting of Hyacinthus
174 marble figure of Hermaphroditus
175 painting of Danaë
176 mask of a German
177 bronze of Hercules
178 clay figure of Hercules
179 silver figure of Minerva
180 painting of Europa
181 marble figure of Leander

Figure 4.2 Possible arrangement of an early imperial Roman art collection, perhaps that exhibited in the temple of Divus Augustus (after Lehmann 1945: Figure 1)

By Pausanias' day, Rome had acquired an extensive public collection of works of art, most of them Greek in origin, which were housed in temples and public buildings around the city (Strong 1973b). By the first century AD Cicero can list three buildings, the Porticus Metelli, the Porticus Catuli and the Temple of Felicitas, which contained a group of Mummius' treasures, as housing the outstanding collections of his day. Towards the end of the first century, Martial's last book of epigrams refers to eleven works of art, and Lehmann (though not without his critics) has argued that these relate to an actual collection on show in the pronaos of the temple of Divus Augustus, and, indeed, that the arrangement of the collection can be reconstructed (Figure 4.2) (Lehmann 1945). This interesting idea suggests that the marbles, clay models and pictures were displayed so that related subjects, like the Apollo statue by Praxiteles and the painting of Hyacinthus showing the youth dying having been struck by a discus thrown by Apollo, were placed together, and so were the two figures of Hercules, although they differ in medium and style.

Efforts to develop the public collections continued while the Empire lasted. Both the Forum of Augustus and the Forum of Trajan became, in Strong's phrase, a kind of National Portrait Gallery. In AD 365 Caracalla ordered his Baths to be decorated with statuary, and as late as 483 an inscription records the restoration of a statue of Minerva. An imperial administration, in the form of a curatorial board, originally established by Augustus sometime between 11 BC and AD 14, was responsible for the collections and the buildings which housed them, and there seem to have been difficulties in deciding which belonged to the State, and which to the Emperor – a wholly familiar problem. Around AD 200 we hear of an *adiutor rationis statuarum*, responsible for the three-dimensional statues and a *procurator a pinacothecis*, the curatorial official in charge of pictures; there is a curator of statues in 335–7. Rome possessed art historians and advisors and an art market.

In reading the histories of the classical public collections, one is constantly struck by a sense of *déjà vu*: the tone is so very much what the contemporary collector and curator (or perhaps the collector and curator of some three or four decades ago) understands, partly because Imperial Rome was in some respects a society not unlike later modern Europe (although in some important respects, of course, very different), and partly because late modern Europe in some respects, especially directly cultural ones, deliberately modelled itself on Imperial Rome. The temples of Olympia and Rome were the National Museums of their day – or the National Museums are the Olympias of our day.

The temple collections have their roots in archaic ideas about sacred depositions of enduring bronze and marble which mediate between men and the Otherworld. They are linked with great men and glorious deeds, as Snodgrass reminds us when he describes the early Greek temples as 'war museums', as such depositions have frequently been, creating the sense of 'the past with us' which links with the social effort necessary to meet the cost of making offerings, and the social bonds of family and obligation which this represents. As Rome developed its complex later society, established temple and collection forms were harnessed more directly to the Imperial project, as witnesses of the spiritual power and prestige of the state. Like Napoleon and Hitler nearly two thousand years later, the Roman generals of the centuries either side of AD 1 appropriated works of art, in their case principally from Greece, and redisplayed them as national trophies in the capital city. In the Roman public collections a note both cosmopolitan and sophisticated, yet in some ways curiously narrow and local, has been struck which will not be heard again until the later centuries of our own era.

A WEALTH OF COLLECTIONS

The classical world also had its private collectors, some of whom gathered material very like that found in the public temple collections. In the late Republic and early Empire we hear of art collections accumulated by well-known public men like Cicero, Mummius and Verres. For Verres, collecting in itself was a passion. As Cicero puts it 'the passion for building an art collection had reached a maniacal and violent degree in Verres. His passion (*studium*) was soon transformed into illness (*morbus*) and even insanity (*cupiditas incredibilis, amentia, furor*)' (Chevallier 1991: 113). It is, perhaps, the first time we strike a description of what will become so familiar a collecting state. Characteristically, Verres filled all the rooms of his house with art objects, but, so Cicero tells us, hid his favourite statue away in a purely private room. Cicero himself was different. His collecting was influenced by Platonic idealism as this had been developed over the preceding centuries, and so he rejected purely aesthetic criteria of artistic form and replaced these with the moral criteria of appropriateness (*decor*), virtue (*virtus*), humanity (*humanitas*), and worthiness (*dignitas*) (Chevallier 1991).

We know that some of the early emperors, Hadrian conspicuous among them, had collections of works of art. Lausus, chief chamberlain of the Byzantine court in the early fifth century AD had a substantial collection of ancient sculpture in his palace near the Hippodrome at Constantinople (Mango 1963; Mango *et al.* 1992). During this time pagan temples were being demolished or converted into churches, offering a unique opportunity for the acquisition of earlier statuary. Lausus' collection seems to have included the Pheidias Zeus, together with works by Lysippus and the Cnidian Aphrodite by Praxiteles. The collection seems to have been arranged in the long apsidal hall of the palace as is shown in Figure 4.3. The arrangement is dominated by the enormous Zeus, believed by Beckenridge to have been the inspiration behind the Byzantine image of Christ Pantocrator (1959), and the whole display apparently sets out to give an *Imago Mundi* intended to show that the Virtue and Justice, God indeed, are infinitely greater than the puny products of (pagan) Eros or Chance. We are reminded that up to the eighteenth century most arrangements of sculpture were programmatic, with underlying symbolic or allegorical meanings (Mango *et al.* 1992), until this notion was replaced by an emphasis on style and technique, rather than content.

Alongside these formal collections of *objets d'art*, the Roman world also had its personal or family collections of gold and silver plate. Some of these accumulations were very large: the Mildenhall Treasure, found in Suffolk and dating about 360 contained some thirty pieces of silver plate, many very elaborate and altogether representing the richest and most prestigious face of the common Roman family practice of accumulating

Figure 4.3 Suggested arrangement of statues inside the Palace of Lausus
(after Mango *et al.* 1992: 94)

silver tableware; the Kaiseraugst Treasure buried within the walls of the late
Roman fortress near Basle in 350–1, which contained 257 items comprising a
luxurious table service and 187 silver coins and medallions, and is the largest
late Roman hoard yet discovered; and the humbler hoard from Dorchester,
Oxfordshire, dating to before AD 400, which contained five silver spoons,
some with animal head decoration (Kent and Painter 1977: 40–3, 57).

As Kent and Painter put it,

> the importance of silver plate in the domestic, political and economic
> life of the Roman Empire cannot be over-estimated. The evidence of
> literary and legal texts gives proof of the vast quantity of silver in
> private hands, the changes of fashion, the enthusiasm of collectors,
> the ostentation of owners.

(1977: 53)

Collections were sometimes held by temples and town councils as well
as by private individuals and families, and a mass-production trade was
needed to supply the demand. A complete set of domestic plate, known as
a *ministerium*, comprised eating silver, *argentum escarium*, and drinking
silver, *argentum potorium*. A family's collection might also include ladies
toilet sets and domestic cult objects.

Family prestige depended to a considerable extent upon collections of silverware, an area where money could buy visible gentility, and this social taste resulted in the immobilisation of silver, and to a lesser extent gold, which created serious stresses to the Imperial economy, helping to bring inflation once the supplies of precious metal could no longer be replenished by conquest. Disruptions in the system during the third century AD resulted in something close to a breakdown in the skilled crafts, so that in 337 Constantine was forced to issue a law stating:

> We command that the practitioners of the arts enumerated in the appended list, whatever city they may live in, shall be exempt from all public services, on condition that they devote their time to learning their crafts. By this means they may desire all the more to become more proficient themselves and to train their sons: architects, makers of panelled ceilings, plasterers, carpenters, physicians, stonecutters, silversmiths, builders, veterinarians, stone-masons, gold-weavers, makers of pavements, painters, sculptors, makers of perforated work, joiners, mosaicists, coppersmiths, blacksmiths, marble-masons, gilders, founders, dyers in purple, markers of tessellated pavements, gold-smiths, makers of mirrors, carriage-makers, glass-makers, ivory workers, fullers, potters, plumbers, furriers.
>
> (Kent and Painter 1977: 18)

Many of these craftsmen would be contributing to the stock of prestige goods, taken from circulation into collections, in a constantly self-defeating spiral of withdrawal. Kent and Painter (1977: 18) quote figures suggesting that four or five gold *solidi* represented a year's living wage, and they compare this with the thirty *solidi* and pieces of silver plate hidden around AD 350 and found at Water Newton in 1974; clearly the market value and consequent market loss represented by Roman silverware was significant.

Here for the first time, but not the last, we strike significant material accumulations which are in one sense family collections, recognised groups of heirlooms which pass from one generation to another and are a source of pride and identity, and in another sense household goods which also carry an investment value. Collections of family plate assembled in the sixteenth and seventeenth centuries, and later, like the Armada Service (see p. 296) carry a similar character, and so, in some ways, do the collections of ornaments and decorative materials which women tend to gather (see p. 207). Equally, there is a clear link between this kind of accumulation and that characteristic of many collections of applied art in the eighteenth and nineteenth centuries: collectors like William Burrell, too, used their furniture and tapestries to create the tone of their physical surroundings, and seem sometimes to have used some of their pieces on the dining-room table.

Just as the Roman public temple collections have given us some of our institutional vocabulary, particularly the word 'curator', so the Roman private art collections have provided characteristic collecting rationales which lay stress on the moral and ennobling qualities of accumulated art. The notion of *objets de vertue* has become both an indication of personal excellence and a justification for the acquisitive habit. The Roman silver-ware gives us another insight. Collections, it becomes clear, can be set apart mentally and emotionally while still being integrated into the fabric of daily living in association with material to which this special status is not accorded. This is one of the most significant and characteristic collecting modes, but also one which is among the more elusive. The collections of silver plate in some Roman households allow us a glimpse of this process at work in the archaic world, and, as we might expect, it comes to us from just the kind of landed or high-bourgeois families who have always been well-placed to achieve such accumulations.

The late classical world, a complex market society more like our own than any other past society, shows us how, in a world where material goods of all kinds are available in quantity, social practices to do with family prestige, gift accumulation, and the fine discriminations between the qualities of one object and of another, are converted into the accumulation of material collections. The late classical world both produced its own versions of European collecting patterns in the Long Term, and bequeathed these versions to all subsequent generations.

MUSES AND MUSEUMS

The use of the Greek word *mouseion* in the classical world had a meaning, or a related series of meanings, quite distinct and separate from any notions to do with the collection of material culture. The relationship of the *mouseion* idea to the collecting process is a tangential one, which results in part from the way in which the classical world and its institutions were adopted by the world of the Renaissance a thousand years later and, partly, by the way in which a range of terms, including *museion*, were developed as the Renaissance world came to require an extended vocabulary for its ideas and their institutions. This point needs to be appreciated clearly, through direct reference to the texts, because it has given rise to a large and irritating shoal of what Hercule Poirot calls red kippers.

Mouseion meant 'the shrine or home of the muses', and as such would be used to describe an actual shrine or holy place: so, as part of the story of the wars following the death of Alexander the Great, Pausanias refers to Demetrios who

> brought a garrison into the city (of Athens) itself, and fortified what
> they call the Museum. The Museum is a small hill opposite the

Acropolis, inside the ancient ring-wall, where they say Mousaios used to sing and died of old age and was buried.

(Levi 1971: 72–3)

The word is used generally by the Athenian writers in a metaphorical sense to imply the home of music and poetry, and clearly was extended to mean a school in which letters and the arts were taught, because it is used in this sense by Arienaeus and Aristotle, although whether Museum Hill at Athens, or any similar shrine elsewhere in Greece, was the site of such a school is unknown.

It is in this sense that the word was used as the name for the most famous philosophical and literary school of the later Greek world, that of Alexandria. Strabo has left us a description of the Alexandrian Museum:

And the city contains most beautiful public precincts and also the royal palaces, which constitute one-fourth or even one-third of the whole circuit of the city; for just as each of the kings, from love of splendour, was wont to add some adornment to the public monuments, so also he would invest himself at this own expense with a residence, in addition to those already built, so that now, to quote the words of the poet 'there is building upon building.' All, however, are connected with one another and the harbour, even those that lie outside the harbour. The Museum is also a part of the royal palaces; it has a public walk, an Exedra with seats, and a large house, in which is the common mess-hall of the men of learning who share the Museum. This group of men not only hold property in common, but also have a priest in charge of the Museum, who formerly was appointed by the kings, but is now appointed by Caesar.

(Strabo 1949: 17, 1–8)

The Museum seems to have been founded by the late third century BC, and perhaps by Ptolemy I Soter, (*d.* 283) although other members of the Ptolemaic dynasty are sometimes suggested as founders.

Inscriptions from Egypt show that the Alexandrian Museum was divided into various faculties – philosophy, rhetoric, poetry, medicine and so on – and that scholars were maintained at it free of cost (Hirschfeld 1916: 207). Excavations at Antinoë, founded by Hadrian in Middle Egypt in AD 130 as a city on the Hellenistic model, yielded an inscription engraved on stone dating probably from the third century AD, now in the British Museum, which refers to such a scholar:

For good fortune. The Council of the citizens of Antinoöpolis, New Greeks, in honour of Flavius Maeeius . . . Dionysodorus one of those maintained in the Museum immune from charge, a Platonic philosopher and councillor.

(Johnson 1914)

We do not know what formal relationship, if any, the Museum had to the legendary Library of Alexandria (see Canfora 1990) nor how long it continued, although presumably it will not have survived the closing of all Pagan schools by Justinian in AD 529. What is clear is that it was a college rather than a collecting institution, and as such has no bearing on the nature and history of the accumulation of objects and specimens, a process which was taking other forms in the classical world. What the classical museum did contribute to later collecting process was a name, one endowed with all the prestige of an eminent ancient past, and offering a link with the arts associated with Platonic philosophy which would prove capable of fruitful development when the neo-Platonic world of the Classical revival started to define its own terms.

In general terms, the history of the word 'museum' is not unlike that of 'academy' which was also associated originally with an Athenian shrine, gave its name to the philosophical and teaching activity which Plato established at the site, continued as a school until AD 529, and then was consciously borrowed by the Medici to describe the community of scholars which they established in Florence. The word became, like 'museum', one of the characteristic Renaissance Greek adoptions, with a long and important institutional history before it. But while the history of 'academy' is relatively simple, that of 'museum' is more complex and only became linked with the idea of material, to us its essential meaning, at a relatively late stage in post-Renaissance usage (see Findlen 1989).

TREASURES IN HEAVEN

The later stages of the northern heroic world ran parallel with that of the late classical world, and as the Roman empire in the west was super-seded by a series of Germanic kingdoms which gradually became formally Christian, so another mode of accumulating collected material developed, one which inherits most of what had gone before in both the north and Mediterranean, and fuses the strands together through the catalyst of Christian practice. The idea that the burial places and the corporeal relics of Christian holy men and women carried significance for the living was well-established by around AD 400, the end of Imperial Rome in the west and the beginning of a Christendom whose theocratic power was exercised by a church hierarchy descending from, and modelled upon, the old imperial bureaucracy. Historically, this practice arose from the persecutions which the early Church suffered, and from the martyrs' relics which resulted. But far more was involved than the simple act of remembrance and the moral encouragement which it provided. The holy graves where relics were buried or, eventually, enshrined mediated between God and men. They were, as we shall see in a moment, the locus where Heaven and Earth touched, where this world and the Otherworld met.

Such graves were the focus of Christian communities and, especially after the formal Peace of Church negotiated by Constantine soon after AD 300, they became the spiritual and economic heart of many of the late Roman and subsequently medieval cities of the old Western Empire. Since burial grounds and execution grounds were, by Roman law, without the city wall, this often involved a physical change in which the old civic centre was replaced, or rivalled, by a fresh centre focused upon the holy graves and the churches which came to occupy the site.

Numerous examples could be cited, but let us be content with two. Outside the great late-Imperial fortress of Cologne is the cemetery site of Xanten – which is a modern corruption of its late Roman name *Ad Sanctos*, 'at the Martyrs' – where a double burial of the 360s was enclosed in a small wooden structure about 390, and had attracted a surrounding cemetery in Frankish times. The burial achieved enclosure in a stone-built chapel by about 450, and, by the eighth century, the first in a series of full churches (Radford 1968). Cologne itself went on to become the seat of a prince-archbishop with his cathedral, but Xanten retained its own prestige. In Britain, the church of St Albans stands outside the Roman city of Verulamium, and may well occupy the site of the original burial, and possibly execution, of Alban. Constantius' *Life of Germanus*, written about 480, mentions the shrine of the blessed martyr Alban, referring to events which took place in 429 (Thomas 1981: 42–4, 48–50). The abbey went on to become one of the greatest of the English medieval houses.

Churches which possessed holy relics came to accumulate earthly treasures which matched those spiritual, and those which did not took pains to acquire both: heavenly treasure and the earthly riches which surrounded it seemed to have been indissolubly mixed in the early (and later) medieval mind. Bishop Ulrich of Augsberg made two visits to Rome in 910 and 952–3 to obtain relics (Beckwith 1964: 84). Rather earlier, by 684 Benedict Biscop had founded the Northumbrian monasteries of Wearmouth and Jarrow and undertaken four journeys to Rome to secure manuscripts and books, religious ornaments and relics for his new houses, which left them an endowment unparalleled in England (Stenton 1955: 185). Alcuin of York (*c.* 730–804), the head of Charlemagne's palace school and abbot of several monasteries wrote, among others, to Abbot Angilbertus, chancellor of King Pepin of Italy, asking in the same breath for gifts of relics and other 'objects of ecclesiastical beauty' (see Geary 1986: 182).

The kinds of objects involved may be seen in the Cross of Lothair, made in Cologne about 1000, and in the possession of the cathedral church of Aachen. It is a magnificent piece with goldsmiths' filigree work and mounted precious stones, and incorporated both the rock-crystal seal of Lothair II of Lotharingia (855–69) and, in its centre, a superb cameo of the

Emperor Augustus (Beckwith 1964: 140–2, 259–60). A classical gem, an aquamarine intaglio showing the portrait of Julia, daughter of the Emperor Titus (AD 79–81), formed the top jewel of the elaborate piece known as the *Crista* or *Escrin de Charlemagne* (although probably the gift of Charles the Bald) in the possession of the Abbey of St Denis, where the relics of the saint and his companions were held (Panofsky-Soergel 1979: 190). These two examples, chosen more or less at random from the great wealth of possible illustrations, give an idea of the richness involved and the trouble taken to collect it. They remind us that material wealth from the imperial past retained a potent symbolic value; and the Cross of Lothair must stand for all the objects of high craftsmanship and art made in ecclesiastical work-shops during the period, from the west of Ireland to the eastern borders of Christendom.

Relics were the place where this world and the Otherworld met, and this explains why they were able to attract so much collected treasure to themselves and their churches, but their nature needs more explanation. Relics belong within that quite large class of material which in life were part of a living human or animal, but which in death are turned into things. Relics are objects which are both persons and things, and their corporeal reality – frequently obvious to the eye as a limb or a skull – reinforces their double condition and ties them to the experienced 'real' world of time and space. As persons they are true saints living with God; as relics they are documents for understanding the world.

The way of understanding was through an appreciation of God's inter-vention in the affairs of the world, of knowing how sometimes the divine could directly affect the mundane. The importance of life lay not in diur-nal regularities but in anomalies, strange occurrences, interruptions and miracles, and of these miracles the relics themselves were physical proof. This notion draws upon the oath/ordeal paradigm in its view of the sacred as separate from the human world and liable to disrupt it, as also in its belief that such irregularities can be documented and exhibited in visible, tangible evidence. It was to cast a long shadow before it, as we shall see, but for the present, let us express the essential nature of the relic in a simple semiotic form (Figure 4.4). It is the relics' documentation of the miraculous which stimulated the great thesaural activity which they attracted.

We can now see that the treasuries of the great early medieval churches gather together most of the threads which have characterised object accu-mulation in preceding centuries, and weave them together in a form which will greatly influence the shape of things to come. Values and land accrued because the pattern of family and inheritance permitted personal bequests, and the Church itself was at pains to preserve and enhance this notion of individual freedom as opposed to family solidarity by putting its moral weight behind the system of exogamous marriage. The treasures belong

Relic

	Signifier	Signified
Matter	corporeal survival of holy body	document of God's miraculous intervention
Content	presence of saint in Heaven	possibility of miraculous intervention on behalf of worshipper, bringing him to Heaven

Figure 4.4 Medieval relics as signifier and signified (drawing on discussion with P. Süler)

to God and to the holy ones who dwell with him. Consequently, they themselves are things set apart, both holy and dangerous, ominous in their power. They are gifts to God, and to the mighty dead whose graves and shrines occupy the imaginative place which burial mounds had held in the minds of those northern barbarians now gradually converting to Christianity.

The giving of gifts at the altar is still honourable and still a rite of passage in which the divine and the mundane are brought together and the status of the donor is changed, although, as Markey has shown, the Church found it necessary to make a clear distinction between old Pagan and new Christian practice in which the older vocabulary of *meithom* came to mean 'earthly reward' and *laun* to mean 'heavenly/true reward'. Gifts to a church, like pagan gifts to the dead or the powers to be reached by way of earth and water, are valuables withdrawn from circulation, frozen assets, to be seen primarily as creating a relationship between man and God, from which proper relationships between men will depend. Oaths once sworn upon Thor's rings will now be sworn upon the holy bones in their reliquaries of gold and gemstones.

From the old northern world the church treasuries took notions of gift exchange, the depositing of treasure with the dead and at sacred places, and the link between royal hall and royal church, usually built close together in the early medieval world. From the Mediterranean world, they took the idea of substantial stone-built structures, as the pagan temples which they superseded had been. They succeeded the temples, also, as repositories of community memory, materially expressed. The link between the old imperial world and the new devotion was sometimes made explicit in the value accorded to ancient cameos and similar pieces. The early medieval church treasuries, are, then, a meeting point of significances. In appearance, they were immensely impressive: treasure withdrawn from the working world still worked on through the vision of eye and mind. It is to the treasure displays of the later medieval and early Renaissance world that we must now turn.

CHRISTIAN COLLECTING: OBJECTS OF ENLIGHTENMENT

In 1122 Suger, son of a poor family and dedicated to St Denis as an oblate when a boy of about nine, became Abbot of St Denis. The Abbey of St Denis was founded near Paris by King Dagobert in honour of St Denis and his legendary companions, St Rusticus and St Eleutherius, believed to be the Apostles of Gaul. Together with the relics of St Denis and his friends, the Abbey housed the tombs of the French kings, and was in every sense the 'royal house' of the medieval French monarchy. Under Suger much of the Abbey was rebuilt, particularly its choir with its rib vaulting and sixteen great stained-glass windows, to create, when it was opened in 1144, the first truly Gothic structure (Crosby 1981: 19), the new style which was called *opus modernum*, modern architecture.

The splendid objects gathered to enhance the church were as important as the new architecture which enveloped it. Many details of these objects were described by Suger himself in his autobiography *Book of Suger, Abbot of St Denis* (Panofsky-Soergel 1979). A number of accounts and inventories of the treasure were compiled, notably that of 1634, and the history of the Abbey published by Dom Michel Rélibien in 1706 contains five large engravings showing the armoires (Plate 2) in which the treasury was displayed in the eighteenth century (Rélibien 1706).

Suger tells us how the tomb of the patron saints was embellished by 'the exquisite industry of the goldsmiths' art and by a wealth of gold and precious stones' , and the altar of St Denis with a gold front enriched with gems sent by bishops, by the King, who contributed emeralds, by Count Thibault, who gave hyacinths and rubies, and princes and peers who gave pearls 'of diverse colours and properties' (Panofsky-Soergel 1979: 104–7).

The liturgical objects included the newly made Great Cross, lost during the seventeenth century. Among the older pieces was a rock-crystal cabochon engraved with the Passion, probably made in one of the workshops of Charles the Bald (823–77), which Suger had mounted on the tabernacle of the saints' shrine. Suger was particularly fond of early hard stone vessels. The incense boat known as the 'Vase of Saint Eloi' comprised a green aventurine bowl of Byzantine manufacture around 600, embellished with an upper rim of silver gilt, blue glass, emeralds, garnets and pearls of probably contemporary Early Merovingian work (and of the same general sort as much of the jewellery from Sutton Hoo): the bowl had been pawned

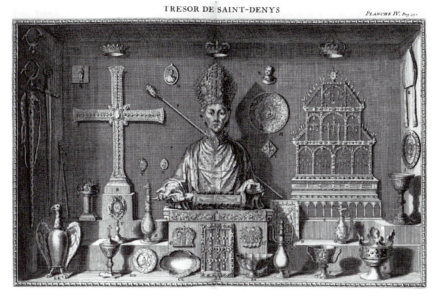

TRESOR DE SAINT-DENYS

PLANCHE IV. Pag.357.

Plate 2 One of the five armoires which contained the treasures of the Abbey of St Denis, France, as shown in an engraving in the *Histoire de l'Abbaye Royale de Saint-Denys en France* published in 1706 by Michel Félibien. Among other pieces, the engraving shows the Eagle Vase, bottom left, and the elaborate jewelled piece known as the *Crista*, back right. (photo: British Library)

by Louis VI and was redeemed by Suger. The Chalice comprised an agate fluted cup made probably in Alexandria around 150 BC, to which Suger probably added the elaborate gold and jewelled stem, foot, handles and rim. The Ewer, similarly, comprised an elaborately mounted Byzantine sardonyx vessel; and the Eagle Vase consisted of a necked porphyry vase to which goldsmiths added the neck, head and swept-down wings of an eagle.

Suger's collection – some ancient material embellished, some recent, some newly commissioned – made around 1130, is characteristic of, though not surpassed by, many collections which will be gathered together in the succeeding three centuries (and, in parallel with other kinds of collections, in the five centuries following these). Henry of Blois, Bishop of Winchester around 1140 and brother of King Stephen of England, bought antique statues in Rome, before the shocked gaze of his retinue (Beckwith 1964: 85). Matthew Paris in his *Deeds of the Abbots* (c. 1250) gives interesting accounts of the metalwork commissioned for his abbey of St Albans, and tells us of a piece Abbot Simon ordered from the pre-eminent goldsmith Master Baldwin, a great golden chalice than which we have seen none nobler in the kingdom of England. It is of the best and purest gold, encircled by precious stones, appropriate to work in such a material, made most subtle with a delicate composition of intricate little flowers.

(Alexander and Pinsky 1987: 31)

The list could be greatly extended into the fourteenth century with the collections made by men like William of Wykeham, Bishop of Winchester in England, and the Duke de Berri in France.

Cosimo de Medici (1389–1464), known as Cosimo the Elder, was born in the fourteenth century of a relatively humble family, and amassed the largest, but by no means the only, fourteenth- and fifteenth-century Italian banking fortune. By 1444 he was in a position to express his political dominance of Florence by the building of the Medici Palace. Here Cosimo was to be followed by his son Piero (1419–69) and his grandson Lorenzo the Magnificent (1448–92). There survive inventories taken of the collections and the contents of the palace in 1456, 1469 and, a very detailed inventory, in 1492 after the death of Lorenzo (Alsop 1982: 360, 395–409). These show that Cosimo had collected classical coins and medals in gold and silver, antique carved gems, and hard stone vessels, very much the kinds of objects which had attracted Suger. His son, Piero, had his own private room, his *scrittorio* decorated with coloured majolica tiles, and Antonio Filarete (*c.* 1400–69) describes how here

> Piero takes great pleasure in whiling away his time by having himself carried to his studio . . . there he would look at his books as if they were a pile of gold . . . let us not talk about his readings. One day he may simply want for his pleasure to let his eye pass along these volumes to while away the time and give recreation to the eye. The next day, then, according to what I am told, he takes out some of the effigies and images of all the Emperors and Worthies of the past, some made of gold, some of silver, some of bronze, of precious stones or of marble and other materials, which are wonderful to behold. Their worth is such that they give the greatest enjoyment and pleasure to the eye . . . The next day he would look at his jewels and precious stones, of which he has a marvellous quantity of great value, some engraved in various ways, some not. He takes great pleasure and delight in looking at those and in discussing their various powers and excellencies. The next day, maybe, he inspects his vases of gold and silver and other precious material and praises their noble worth and the skill of the masters who wrought them.

(Gombrich 1985: 51)

By Lorenzo's time, the palace included a collection of paintings by Uccello, Fra Angelico and Masaccio, among others, but these do not seem to have attracted the same esteem and value as the hard stone vases, gems, classical statues and rarities such as the unicorn horn, estimated in the 1492 inventory to be worth 6,000 florins, one of the highest valuations in the list (Hooper-Greenhill 1992: 53, 71). Just as they used the word 'academy' to describe the more or less organised group of scholars and artists gathered in Florence, so Lorenzo and his court used the word 'museum' to describe the collection, a word which therefore added to its classical prestige that of the Medicis themselves, a circumstance which ensured its future significance. For several centuries until well into the eighteenth century, it was only to be one word among the many used to describe a collection, but as Findlen (1989) has shown us, it became an apt metaphor for the encyclopedic tendencies of the sixteenth and seventeenth centuries as an epistemological structure which combined both the notion of collecting as the presentation of knowledge and the social need for impressive display, and so eventually it gained the high ground.

The liberal, humanist and classical thrust of Renaissance culture, and of the Florentine court, has frequently been described and needs no stressing, even though the 'classical' tendency in later medieval appreciation and collecting is now becoming clearer, and gives us a better notion of the soil in which Renaissance ideas and collections grew. In these respects the Medici collections did begin to point the way towards new collecting rationales, but in other, equally important, ways they are of a piece with those that preceded them, and what they project into the future carries with it the weight of a long tradition. This is true, both in terms of how the collections appear to us as making political statements about their own day, and of how they were presented spiritually and intellectually by their possessors.

Politically, the motive behind the collecting is that of display, which through its sheer impressiveness can convey legitimacy. Vestergaard (1987) makes the point that riches are described very differently in the older, Scandinavian, version of the Volsung saga, and in the more recent southern German version, the *Nibelungenlied*, completed just before 1200. In the *Nibelungenlied* a large amount of space is devoted to describing material wealth, and in this version of the story the treasure hoard is so huge that it could fill 144 large wagons. The display of wealth is the basis for prestige which underpins political power: so it was thought to be at the court of the Burgundians and so it was at the palace of the Medici.

In the eye of contemporaries, the accumulated treasures fulfilled quite another need, a spiritual one, and here we touch one of the strong threads which binds together European sensibility across the centuries and ties it to the material world of objects. Plato had held various views about the moral character of art in all its forms, and his successors tended to ignore his famous condemnation of art as imitation and to concentrate instead upon his notions of ideals and the eternal, essential existence of qualities like Justice, Truth and Beauty. In the minds of thinkers like Plotinus of Alexandria who lived *c.* AD 205–70 (and, incidentally, must have known those in his day associated with the Museum) and Proclus (*c.* AD 410–85), Plato's ideas were linked with images coming from the mystery religions of the eastern Mediterranean world to produce a metaphysic which stressed the unity of the world expressed in the luminous aliveness of all things, material and immaterial, which shared in the divinity of the One Being. This opens the way for a metaphysic of material things, in which the Divine Mind reveals itself and can therefore be approached. It was also relatively easy to fuse the Neoplatonism of Plotinus and Proclus with developing Christian doctrine, although, as the piece from *The Cloud of Unknowing* at the head of this chapter shows, Christian thought usually eschewed a simple pantheism by differentiating sharply between the physical and spiritual worlds, and making reason an aspect of the soul.

The chanciness of things dictated that this fusion should be intimately associated with the royal Abbey of St Denis. The St Denis whose relics lay in the abbey was identified with Dionysius the Areopagite mentioned in the *Acts of the Apostles* (17: 34) as a convert of St Paul's, and Dionysius, in turn, was believed to be the author of works now attributed to a nameless Syrian known as the Pseudo-Areopagite writing about AD 500. A Greek manuscript of these works had been deposited at St Denis by Louis the Pius (778–840), and had been translated into Latin by the Irishman, John the Scot, guest of Charles the Bald and one of the very few at that time capable of such a feat. Suger read these writings, believing them to be by the patron saint of his abbey and his kingdom, and found in them philosophical justification for his collecting and artistic drive.

The Pseudo-Areopagite wrote that the universe is created, animated and unified by 'the superessential Light', with God the Father designated 'the Father of Lights' and Christ as the 'first radiance' (drawing upon the fourth Gospel) which 'has revealed the Father to the World' (Panofsky-Soergel 1979: 19). There is a huge distance from the highest, purely intelligible plane of existence to the lowest, material one, but no break in the divine hierarchy of harmony through all of which flows the Divine Light, and therefore man may embrace the physical world through his sensory understanding in the hope that ultimately he may transcend it. At the beginning of his major work *De Caelesti Hierachia* (*Of the Heavenly Hierarchies*) the Pseudo-Areopagite says that our minds can rise to that which is not material only under the 'manual guidance' of that which is. He continues:

> Every creature, visible or invisible, is a light brought into being by the Father of the Lights . . . This stone or that piece of wood is a light to me . . . For I perceive that it is good and beautiful; that it exists according to its proper rules of proportion; that it differs in

kind and species from other kinds and species; that it does not transgress its order; that it seeks its place according to its specific gravity. As I perceive such and similar things in this stone they become lights to me, that is to say, they enlighten me (*me illuminant*). For I begin to think whence the stone is invested with such properties . . . and soon, under the guidance of reason, I am led through all things to that cause of all things which endows them with place and order, with number, species and kind, with goodness and beauty and essence, and with all other grants and gifts.

(Panofsky-Soergel 1979: 20)

This passage, deliberately quoted at some length, is crucial to our understanding of how the material world, and the collections made from it, are understood in the European tradition. The Pseudo-Areopagite takes ideas about the nature of distinctions and classification, expressed in the ancient world most fully by Aristotle but drawing upon a predisposition to see the world in terms of distinction and contrast, of 'this and that' which we have described as at the heart of the European tradition. He links these with mystical intuition about the creativeness of God, and writes the whole in terms of a Christian theology which ensured its continuing influence. Delight in, and study of, the material world, is a religious exercise in which aesthetic expression, contemplation of rarities – those miracles where the heavenly world touches this earthly one directly – and reasoned understanding of material organisation, come together for the greater glory of God. The Pseudo-Areopagite looks backward into the classical world from which his ideas came; his notions were the touchstone for the collecting activities of the high medieval world, and, rewritten by contemporaries, of the early Renaissance also, and, constantly reinterpreted, provided an important element in the notions of natural theology within which the scientific tradition of the later seventeenth century developed.

At St Denis itself, Suger responded blissfully to ideas which clearly ran with the grain of his own nature:

When – out of my delight in the beauty of the house of God – the loveliness of the many-coloured stones has called me away from external cares, and worthy meditation has induced me to reflect, transferring that which is material to that which is immaterial, on the diversity of the sacred virtues: then it seems to me that I see myself dwelling, as it were, in some strange region of the universe which neither exists entirely in the slime of the earth nor entirely in the purity of Heaven; and that, by the grace of God, I can be transported from this interior to that higher world

(Panofsky-Soergel 1979: 21)

CONCLUSION

The collecting habits of the period between roughly 1100 and 1450 can, then, be seen to epitomise the mind-set of the time, a mind-set which draws together the themes of the northern past – royal hoards, honourable gifts, sacred offerings in places set apart, the richly endowed dead – and those of the classical past – Platonic and Christian cosmology, notions of classification and hierarchy (as Foucault pointed out), an aesthetic of form and content – and fuses them into an intellectual and psychological unity which invites a spiritual pilgrimage. Behind both traditions lies a broader consensus about the nature of distinction, and sacredness, and of property and its rights. It is a view of the collected world which the next five centuries will develop and refine.

CHAPTER FIVE

EARLY MODERNIST COLLECTORS

————— •◆• —————

A World of Wonders in one Closett shut
  Epitaph on the tomb where the Tradescants, father and son,
    are buried, St Mary's churchyard, Lambeth, London

INTRODUCTION

Early modern Europe, roughly the period from 1500 to 1700, saw fresh attempts to understand the world which (among other things) involved an enhanced interest in collecting and the organisation of collections, which was both a manifestation of the developing cast of mind and an important element in the way in which that mind was shaped. Collecting became a passion. As the decades progressed, cities like Paris, London, Venice and Amsterdam became particularly prominent, the centres for those who were intellectually, as well as acquisitively, curious, and of dealers who could supply their needs. By 1714 Valentini in his *Museum Museorum* was able to list a total of some 658 known collections, many from their published catalogues (Hüllen 1990: 270). But many more persons were involved than this because collections were passed from hand to hand, the whole forming an intensive web of contact and descent which spans the centuries and is one of the most conspicuous and interesting aspects of the tradition, and one which needs tracing in detail.

A number of words were in use by contemporaries to describe these accumulations, each of which probably had its own shade of meaning. The German term was *Kammer*, meaning 'room' or 'chamber', to which would be added *Wunder* ('wonder'), *Kunst* ('art'), or *Schatz* ('treasure'), as appropriate. In Italy in the sixteenth century the main terms are *studio*, *studiolo*, *galleria* and *museo* (Hooper-Greenhill 1992: 88). The notion of 'cabinet' in English could mean the small room in which the whole collection was housed, or the cupboards which held it, or the collection itself. In English, too, the whole assemblage can sometimes be referred to as 'cabinet of curiosities' or 'cabinet of rarities'. The usage overall is very loose, benefiting the many-faceted and individualistic character of the whole enterprise.

Underpinning all this, but also dependent upon it, was the gradual development of the cast of mind to which we have just referred, which it is convenient to label 'modernist', that is, the cluster of mental attitudes which came to dominate European thought as the sixteenth century gathered momentum, and the seventeenth century culminated in the work of the French Pascal and Descartes, and the English Newton and the Fellows of the Royal Society. 'Modernism' as a term creates its share of heart-burning (see Jameson 1991; Hall and Gieben 1992) because it can be used either in a relatively straightforward historical sense, or as an analytical tool in its own right.

In the first sense, modernism, or modernity, means that complex bundle of characteristic modes of thought which saw its preliminary early phase between, roughly, 1500 and 1600, its full early phase between *c.* 1600 and 1700, and its later, or classic, phase between 1700 and 1950, to be succeeded by post-modernism in which the modes of thought were re-examined. In the subtler, second sense, modernity is seen as describing the condition of change, and the social and intellectual movements which create and respond to change, and which are, therefore, always self-conscious and self-regarding. In this sense, all the movements of heart and mind described for historical convenience as 'modern' and 'post-modern' are implicit in each other (as, of course, all changes must be), and represent the power to question the basis of preceding certainties. In a sense, therefore, it is true to say that European society has always been more or less 'modern', and, as we have been at pains to suggest, modernism in this sense is part of its fundamental long-term character. But in the more limited sense, the terms 'modern' and 'post-modern' are useful, and generally accepted, ways of describing particular moments in the flow, and as such they will be used here.

Modernism, then, as it matures towards the end of the seventeenth century, was concerned with the development of an interlocking cluster of meta-narratives, over-arching general theories or discourses through which objective realities and general truths could be defined and expressed. These were set within a framework of natural theology which demonstrates their descent from the preceding generations – investigators perceived themselves as approaching the mind of God, an image which sustained much enquiry through the eighteenth and nineteenth centuries and in some quarters still does – but, at bottom, rested on two crucial premises. The first of these, which has been treated many times, at great length and with great respect, was the belief in human reason, and its ability to observe, to infer and to understand the workings of the cosmos, and, we may add, to transfer this understanding from one person to another so that agreed structures and superstructures can be built on the basis of accepted fundamental facts. The second premise is the supreme significance of the material world through which alone correct deductions about the nature of the world may be achieved. The universe becomes its component material parts and the relationships between them. The rational mind achieves a true understanding of objective natural knowledge by the physical process of observing and arranging material evidence.

A number of crucial axioms appear in this. There is the notion that the human mind is capable of comprehending objective knowledge, a presumption which post-modernist thinking has gradually regarded as increasingly insecure. Equally, there is the importance accorded to the physical evidence, the material objects, upon which, in the last analysis, the modernist narratives depend. Material must be observed and arranged in order to yield up its inherent knowledge, and important material must be preserved in order to continue to demonstrate the truths that are asserted. Collected material, in other worlds, stands at the heart of modernist knowledge, both as evidence of particular truths, and as demonstrating what constitutes evidence, itself the underpinning narrative upon which the other stories depend. Collections, therefore, do not merely demonstrate knowledge; they are knowledge.

The relationship of this to characteristics which we have described as at the heart of the European cultural tradition is obvious and immediate. Measurement and classification of the material world is implicit in a culture which sees as central notions about legal evidence and demonstrated assertion, with all that this implies of importance given to eyewitness, the idea that events have causal sequence, and that 'true' and 'false' are distinct, objective qualities with practical consequences. From the same cultural bundle comes the desire to catch and explain the causal sequence, which gives a particular grip on the notion of historicity, and, linked with the evidential assessments, the notion of historical accuracy and judgement. A culture whose social and familial arrangements encourage a proprietorial attitude to the world of goods is likely, given an allied bent towards comparison and classification, to create that surge of material manufacture and the consequent immense rise in object numbers which is one of the most significant, and most neglected, aspects of what we can loosely call capitalism, itself the meta-narrative which forms the economic strand in the modernist weave.

In this chapter we shall examine first the preliminary or proto-modernist collecting rationale of the sixteenth century, and see how, gradually, emphasis shifted from the notion of the representation of the cosmos, which stressed perceived similarities between particular or remarkable things ('wonders' or 'curiosities'), which Foucault emphasised in his Renaissance episteme, to that which stressed the perpetually repeated patterns which typical material demonstrated and from which holistic classifications could be predicted. In this next chapter we shall explore the classic modernist collecting of the next phase, and its post-modernist successors.

HEAVENLY CONJUNCTIONS: SIXTEENTH-CENTURY COLLECTING

During the 1570s, Francesco I (1541–87) (descended from the younger branch of the Medici family, through Lorenzo, younger brother of Cosimo the Elder) set up in Florence what was known as the *Studiolo*, physically a small room without windows, intended to hold artefacts which represented the hierarchical order of the world as a microcosm of art and nature, in which the prince could appear symbolically as ruler. The material was kept in closed cupboards, effective through the symbols painted on the doors, and the room held paintings hung so as to represent the correspondences of the world (Rinehart 1981: 14–27; Olmi 1985). An air of secret access hung about the whole. The *Studiolo* was dismantled less than twenty years after its establishment, and its contents seem to have been redisplayed in an open, airy part of the palace which was open to the people of Florence (Hooper-Greenhill 1992: 108). But during its short life it linked what had gone before with what was to come, and epitomised the conceptual and emotional complexities of its day. The key words are 'hierarchy', 'microcosm', 'symbol' and 'prince' – and perhaps also 'secret' – words which, once linked up together into contemporary early modernist notions of knowledge and evidence, constituted an understanding of the world.

Francesco's experiment was broadly contemporary with the famous collections gathered by members of the house of Habsburg, north of the Alps, that of Duke Albrecht V of Bavaria at Munich, that of his brother Ferdinand II (1529–95) at Castle Ambras, and that of their nephew, Rudolf II (1552–1612) at Prague. The Munich collection included antiquities and sculpture. That at Ambras was arranged in four large, interconnecting buildings of which the first three held arts and armour, including trophies of the Turkish wars, and the innermost was the *Kunstkammer*, which contained pictures, covering the walls very densely, and a total of twenty cupboards. These held a large collection of worked natural materials, like coral, scientific instruments, material from the natural worlds of animal, vegetable and mineral, and things which were monstrous, misshapen, especially large or particularly small. Rudolf's collection at Prague contained similar material, and has been characterised by Kaufmann as having:

> a carefully organized content based on the system of correspondences . . . we may consider Rudolf's possession of the world in microcosm in his *Kunstkammer* an expression of his symbolic mastery of the greater world.
>
> (1978: 27)

These collections served as the models for hundreds of similar, if smaller, encyclopedic accumulations gathered by princes and men of the middling sort, across Christendom (Pomian 1990: 65–90) throughout the sixteenth and seventeenth centuries. Samuel von Quiccheberg, who was in the employ of Albrecht V of Bavaria, set out the conceptual basis of the early, sixteenth-century, phase of collecting. His book *Theatrum Amplissimum*, published in Munich in 1565, describes the ideal order of a comprehensive collection by setting down, and illustrating with examples, the desirable arrangement of material on display. The first displays are to be devoted to the person of the ruler as founder of the collection, who is seen as the centre around which the other circles of reality revolve. The remaining displays should concentrate on paintings and sacred objects, objects made of inorganic material, organic materials representing the three realms of earth, air and water, and artefacts (Schultz 1990). Translated into the terms of the twentieth century, these categories would be fine art, applied art, natural history and historical material, and the continuity of distinctions from the sixteenth century to the present day is very striking. The displays should be linked with a library, a printing shop and various workshops.

The central image of the book, from which its title is taken, is that of the *Memory Theatre*, a mnemonic system devised by Guillo Camillo (*c.* 1480–1544), which Viglius Zuichemus, writing to Erasmus, described:

> He calls this theatre of his by many names, saying now that it is a built or constructed mind and soul, and now that it is a windowed one. He pretends that all things that the human mind can conceive and which we cannot see with the corporeal eye, after being collected together by diligent meditation may be expressed by certain corporeal signs in such a way that the beholder may at once perceive with his eyes everything that is otherwise hidden in the depths of the human mind. And it is because of this corporeal looking that he calls it a theatre.
>
> (Yates 1966: 132)

The idea drew on the medieval and classical notion of the 'art of memory' a technique which enabled a speaker to arrange his material mentally in the form of a building with rooms and features which reflected the structure of his speech. Essentially, this was a device to aid the politician and lawyer in an age before jotting paper was freely available, but inevitably during the allegorically attuned Middle Ages it became endowed with a visionary force, and as the times transformed gradually into the full Neoplatonic glamour of the Renaissance, with its faith in hermetic knowledge and the magical arts, so the art of memory seemed capable of penetrating the arcane secrets of the universe (Yates 1966).

Camillo's *Memory Theatre* was intended to translate this seductive notion into physical fact. The *Theatre* actually existed: Camillo constructed it at the court of Francis I in France (Bernheimer 1956: 225). It was big enough to walk into, and rose in seven grades or steps reflecting all the associations of the mystic number. The basic allegory was extended by the inclusion of illuminating texts, boxes and coffers, and painted images. The visitor, as he walked up through the grades, understood the relationships of the cosmos and the harmony of creation by secret wisdom revealed. He possessed himself of the esoteric mastery of proportion and wholeness. A three-dimensional pyramid appeared in the centre of the theatre which represented God, and Francis I, for whom the theatre was built, was symbolised by the triangle as God-on-earth. The whole perfectly represented the theological, philosophical and political preoccupations of the age.

Quiccheberg (Hüllen 1990: 267–8) had made the jump which brought together in an organised fashion the notion of collecting, already, as we have seen, imbued with much metaphysical lore, and the notion of cosmic rationale which the memory theatre expressed. He, as it were, used a collection to fill the boxes and coffers which Camillo's *Theatre* contained and, by bringing the two together, achieved both the organisation of the collected material in classificatory terms and a fuller realisation of the nature of the universe. Quiccheberg's theatre was imaginary, although presumably he had the collections of Albrecht V in mind, and we do not know exactly how he would have related the five categorical distinctions he makes to the imaginary hierarchies of the *Memory Theatre* and its like. However, the crucial perceived conjunction between actual, selected, material from the physical world and the cosmic realities of time and space had been achieved. It was the deeper nature of this heavenly conjunction which the next century was poised to explore, as collectors gradually came to set their cosmic preoccupations within a desire for greater understanding of the material nature of the earthly world.

TRUE AND PROPER ENDS: SEVENTEENTH-CENTURY COLLECTING

Arnold (1993) has suggested that there was, among seventeenth-century collectors, an almost ubiquitous conviction that objects could say things, a belief which, as we have seen, bears a particularly characteristic relationship to the thrust of European culture and, more specifically, descends from late-medieval and Renaissance or proto-modern, notions about the nature of the physical world as an aspect of the metaphysical, and of the relationship of the parts to the whole. The engraved frontispiece of Olaus Worm's catalogue of his collection, *Musei Wormiani Historia* published in 1655, gives us a fair idea of what such collections looked like (Plate 3). Arnold distinguishes three distinct methodologies designed to make objects speak: a narrative approach in which objects bore witness to true stories; a utilitarian strategy concerned with an object's potential economic pay-off; and a classificatory enquiry which sought to established each object within its place in a systematic order. As we shall see, these three voices separated,

Plate 3 Engraved frontispiece, *Musei Wormiani Historia*, Leiden 1655. This engraving is now known to be a relatively faithful depiction of the main room in Olaus Worm's museum. (photo: British Library)

if not wholly at any rate to a considerable degree, as the corner was turned into the classic modernism of the early eighteenth century, to reunite again in the second half of the nineteenth, but during the seventeenth century they sang together in the part songs and echo choruses beloved of the age.

The argument becomes more concrete when individual elements in the modernist rationale are separated out and viewed in relationship to Arnold's three methodologies and to specific seventeenth-century collections (see also Shapin 1994; Cohen 1994). We have already referred to the notion of historicity. This is a characteristic component of the modernist view, with its belief that things, including human things, are susceptible to reasoned explanation provided this incorporates evidence sufficient in quantity and quality, and that all things can be comprehended within an objective gaze. Such ideas lie deep in the European past. In the medieval period they appear in the form of the concrete remains of the holy men, or the holy deeds which witnessed to their sanctity, and so to the conjunction of the earthly and the divine. In the early modernist view, together with the development of 'modern' narrative history, they took the form of collected objects which occupied the same emotional place as relics but attested to the existence of historical events and personages in more general terms.

This broad assertion could take a number of colours. As early as 1587, Kaltemarckt's advice to Christian I of Saxony on how a collection, especially an art collection, should be formed, contained an argument about the nature of art in relation to history:

> In addition to such libraries and book collections, illustrious potentates also established picture galleries or art collections (whatever one wants to call them) in order to encounter the events of history and those who through their deeds created them not only in books but also through drawings and paintings, as a delight to the eye and a strengthening of memory, as a living incitement to do good and avoid evil, and also as a source of study for art-loving youth.
>
> (Gutfleisch and Menzhausen 1989: 8)

This brings home to us the didactic and moral purpose of both art and history study. The Tradescant collection contained Henry VIII's stirrups, a pair of gloves presented to Elizabeth I and the armour-plated hat worn by the president at Charles I's trial (Macgregor 1983). At about the same time in Scotland, Sir James Balfour (1600–57), having already gathered an important library, began to assemble historical and antiquarian materials because 'things and events involved in obscurity are often illustrated by ancient rings, seals and other remains of a former age' (Macgregor 1985: 154). The museum of Ralph Thoresby in Leeds contained, as the catalogue published in 1713 shows, the hand and arm of the Marquis of Montrose, executed in 1650 (Brears 1989). In all of these collections we have objects used as material witnesses to the truth of historical narrative, concrete assertions of the morals which can be drawn from the stories themselves.

Modernism's economic discourse embraced a monetary exchange economy, based ultimately on large-scale, market-based production and consumption of commodities, the extensive ownership of private property, both of goods and real estate, and the accumulation of capital on a systematic and long-term basis: all of these developments, as we have seen, were likely outcomes in an eventual middle term given the long-term parameters within which European culture works. Objects are crucial elements in this economic perspective, partly as desirable things to accumulate and therefore to produce in bulk as commodities, partly as touchstones or exemplars, and partly as raw materials and tools, through means of which alone material transformations can take place. Collections relate directly to all three perspectives and material was, and still is, amassed in order to satisfy all three motives.

This aspect of modernist collecting is expressed most clearly in Francis Bacon's *New Atlantic* published in London in 1627, but written ten years earlier (Macgregor 1989). Bacon envisaged a college, otherwise known as

'Solomon's House', to be instituted. It would include gardens and lakes, where experiments in every field of nature could be carried out, and laboratories for every kind of research. Statues would be erected to inventors or discoverers, together with samples of their work:

> For our Ordinances and Rites: we have two very Long, and Fair Galleries: In one of these we place Patterns and Samples of all manner of the most Rare and Excellent Inventions: In the other we place the Statues of all Principal Inventors.
>
> (Macgregor 1989: 207)

All this was not seen as an idealistic pipe dream. By 1647 a proposal had been drawn up by John Drury for an establishment in the London suburb of Vauxhall which would fulfil Bacon's aims:

> A Memorandum for setting Faux-hall apart for Publik Uses
> 1. to house all manner of Inventions, rare Models and Engines wich may bee useful for the Comon-wealth.
> 2. to make Experiments and trials of profitable Inventions which curious Artists oft times can not offer to the knowledge of skilful men and to public Use for want of a place of Address to meet with them, and of other necessarie conveniences to show a proofe of their skill, whereof in Faux-hall is great store.
> 3. to bee a place of resort whereunto Artists and Ingeneers from abroad and at home may repaire to meet with one another to confere together and improve in many ways their abilities and hold forth profitable Inventions for the use of the Comon-wealth.
>
> (Macgregor 1989: 208)

Some material had already been collected, conspicuously a group of some thirty models which included a corn mill, a 'waterworke to raise water' and models of perpetual motion. We are told that Charles I had been interested in the project, and efforts to create Solomon's House in reality continued in England until the end of the century, and finally bequeathed its intellectual legacy to both the Victoria and Albert Museum and the Science Museum.

The third methodology was that of the classificatory enquiry. We have seen that the inclination to regard the natural world as a separate other, distinct from humankind and so viewable as such, is an integral part of the European cultural tradition, together with a tendency towards a concrete idea of what constitutes 'truth' and 'proof'. It is no exaggeration to suggest that one way to describe what is usually called 'the seventeenth-century scientific revolution' is to say that in the later seventeenth century a handful of men, whose intellectual centres were chiefly London and Paris, came to the idea of uniting the notion of carefully observed concrete natural evidence with that of Platonic cosmic structuring, still an immensely influential image especially in esoteric circles, to produce the classificatory system of the world which comes to us as classic biological taxonomy and which unites the past and present of the natural world in a systematic whole. This fitted in as part of the wider contemporary enquiry into the mathematical and physical nature of the cosmos, and the whole could be set within an acceptable natural theology, to which it also contributed. Both Adam Olearius, whose tract *Gottorff'sche Kunstkammer* appeared in 1666, and Christian Daniel Major, whose work on *Kunst- und Naturalien- kammern* came out in 1674, stress the notion that nature is a book in which we can read the greatness of God and that collections represent knowledge of nature refined by intelligence, thoughts which are going to remain entirely appropriate for the next two, or two-and-a-half, centuries (Hüllen 1990: 269).

The late-seventeenth-century English collections serve to illustrate the point. John Woodward's collection was amassed between 1688 and 1724 and eventually came to total around 9,400 specimens, all of which were deposited in what ultimately became the Sedgwick Museum, Cambridge (Price 1989). The collection was carefully documented and served as the material basis for Woodward's ideas about classification and the nature of the material world (Plate 4). For Woodward the creation of such philo- sophical structures was the only true end of collecting. As he put it:

> Censure would be his Due, who should be perpetually heaping up of Natural Collections, without Design of Building a Structure of Philosophy out of them, or advancing some Propositions that might turn to the Benefit and Advantage of the World. This is in reality the true and only proper End of Collections, of Observations, and Natural History: and they are of no manner of Use of Value with- out it.

> (Price 1989: 80)

The Royal Society was founded in 1660. It began to accumulate material from that date and by around 1663 Robert Hooke had been made its Keeper of the Repository, as the collection was called, but its most important acquisition came in 1666 when it purchased Robert Hubert's collection of 'natural rarities'. A number of writers urged that the collec- tion should be 'completed' so that it would be a systematic representation of natural history, and in 1669 the Society employed Thomas Willisel to go round the British Isles collecting 'such natural things, as may be had in England which were yet wanting in the Society's repository' (Hunter 1985: 164). It seems that the collection was intended to be the evidential version of a descriptive universal taxonomy linked to aspirations to produce classified tables of natural phenomena, the whole to be expressed in a philosophical language. Nehemiah Grew's catalogue of the collection duly appeared in 1681, and does indeed endeavour to express some of the

Plate 4 One of the surviving cabinets which held John Woodward's collection of (mostly) natural-history specimens, probably commissioned in the 1690s or early 1700s. Sedgwick Museum, Cambridge.
(photo: Sedgwick Museum)

material, particularly the shells, in the form of taxonomic tables (Figure 5.1). Moreover, as Hunter puts it:

> In his preface Grew also echoed the cry for comprehensiveness of authors like Sprat, aspiring to 'an Inventory of Nature' which would include 'not only Things strange and rare, but the most known and common amongst us'. Grew not only attacked the cult of rarity which informed many virtuoso collections; he also criticised the obscurantism of existing catalogues, advocating a fullness and precision of description which he then proceeded to exemplify through the entries in his text.'

(Hunter 1985: 164)

Scheme 3.

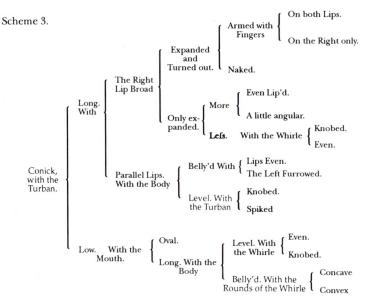

Scheme 4.

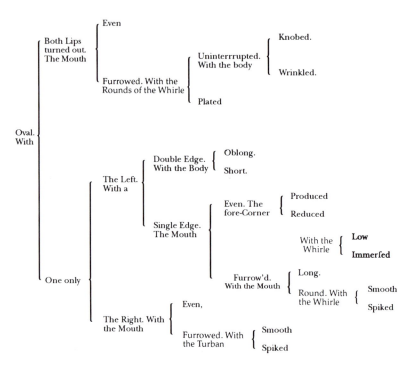

Figure 5.1 Schemes of classification for shells, drawn from diagrams in N. Grew's *Musaeum Regalis Societatis* of 1681

The collection itself, however, was too frail to bear the philosophical burden prematurely thrust upon it. As Grew noted, the 'perfect' classification was not feasible 'because as yet the collection itself is not perfect' (Hunter 1983: 166). The time for such 'perfect' collections was soon to come; as we shall see, in the next century the effort to classify the world, hand in hand with art, gained the moral and political high ground, while those curiosities and rarities, often the relics of human history, at which Grew had sneered, were, for a while, banished from the temple.

CONCLUSION

Early modern collecting saw the shift from a concentration on the rare and curious among which esoteric resemblances might be sought, to that of the normal and regular through which recurrent and reliable patterns might be perceived, Foucault's classical episteme of classification through observation and measurement. But all manifested the link between the physical reality of the world and its metaphysical reality, for transcendent being could only be approached and understood by the exercise of reason which distinguishes and divides. The mystical relationship between things and ideas could be expressed, as Suger might have suggested, by these classifications of the physical world, for they are the music of the spheres in the compass of a single room. We are in a Neoplatonist world seen through Christian stained glass, and as the eighteenth century dawns, the coloured lights will drop away and the vision of understanding clarify. It had become possible to see the world in a properly studied grain of sand.

CHAPTER SIX

CLASSIC MODERNIST COLLECTING

———— •◆• ————

Putting Jeremy's letter in her handbag, she set out for the Natural History Museum, a few hundred yards down the road; the only place she knew which provided her with fresh preoccupations, and a refuge from self.

The insect gallery was not, actually, the best thing about it. Evelyn felt that it was a mistake to see beetles arranged in rows; she felt that the bigger beasts exhibited better.

She strolled around staring at them meditatively for some hours. Then she decided to visit Harrods and have an early lunch there.

The Sweets of Pimlico (Wilson 1983: 128)

The individual who has received instructions from the Right Honourable the Earl of Waldegrave, to distribute to the world the unrivalled and wondrous Collection at Strawberry Hill, formed by his Lordship's great ancestor, Horace Walpole, Earl of Orford, and has thus had placed within his power the ability to enrich the royal and national collections of every civilised country, the galleries of the cognoscenti, and the cabinets of amateurs in every class of the highest walks of Art, has had the singular good fortune, during a long professional career, to be the favoured agent in introducing to the public, in endless variety, unique collections of all that is rare in taste and *vertu*.

Introduction to the sale catalogue of the Strawberry Hill sale by its auctioneer, George Robbins (Herrmann 1972: 116–18)

INTRODUCTION: A WORLD OF GOODS

For Britain, and north-western Europe generally (see Schama 1987; Miller 1981; Williams 1982), the mid-eighteenth century saw the explosion of material goods, which is usually described as the Industrial Revolution, and which shows no sign of abating; of all aspects of the European cultural tradition, this is the one which has had most visible influence upon the rest of the world. Recent study has suggested that, for insights into how and why this happened, we should look not at the techniques of production, but at developments in consumer behaviour (Fox and Lears 1983). As Braudel put it, 'the right string to pull to start the engine of capitalism was demand' (1973: 12). This demand, as we have seen, was not new; it was based in the idea of the individual, his social position and his view of the possibilities of the material world which had been developing over time.

By around 1750 several elements conjoined. Mukerji (1983) has argued that what she calls 'modern materialism' has its basis in the fifteenth and sixteenth century European trade with the east in calicoes and luxury goods which helped to diffuse a new orientation towards objects. McKendrick *et al.* (1982) have suggested that England, with its wealth-flushed trading class and its fluid social structure, possessed the exact conditions for a consumer revolution. Campbell, interestingly, proposes that the 'spirit of modern consumerism' arose as an ironic by-product of the Romantic movement, whose elevation of day-dreaming into legitimacy also underwrote the dynamic cycle of desire, purchase, use and disillusionment which characterises modern consumption (1987).

It is clear that the modernist collecting paradigm is a part of this consumerist tendency. It had played its part in concentrating attention upon the potential of material goods to provide explanatory narratives which could be harnessed, as we shall see, to all kinds of social goals. A materially based understanding of the world at the highest intellectual and aesthetic levels, both encouraged and help to legitimatise a materially based view of the social world as a whole.

For Quiccheberg and his contemporaries and immediate successors, collecting had come to fall naturally firstly into the broad distinction between *artificialia* and *naturalia*, and then into the finer distinctions between art, interpreted as pictures and sculpture both modern and classical, historical material, and natural specimens from the three worlds of animal, vegetable and mineral. But by 1700 the gaze was no longer trained upon resemblances between the rare and strange as a way of explaining the nature of the universe; rather it was concentrated upon measurement and distinction, and upon notions of classification as the explanatory paradigm, the elements which Foucault selects as characteristic of his classical paradigm.

This had an important impact upon what was collected and by whom, and to whom and how it was displayed. It rapidly became clear that the classificatory paradigm could be applied with considerable success to the natural world, and that, translated into an art-historical mode, it could produce an informing rationale for collections of modern European art and classical antiquities. The *artificialia* from human history, however, the personal memorials, the weapons and household goods from Europe and beyond, proved more intractable: no intellectually respectable paradigm for them appeared possible until well into the phase of classic collecting, and in some senses it never has.

The upshot of this was a complicated social dimension to collecting and display. Through very roughly the eighteenth century and into the early nineteenth, two strands became visible. One, morally respectable and intellectually acclaimed, occupied the collecting high ground; it concentrated upon art and natural history, and it manifested itself in the increasing tally of important museums, formally built and dedicated institutions to which the general public was allowed entry. The other strand, which concentrated on historical and exotic material, took a demotic turn; its exhibition was commercially organised and, especially in the bigger cities of England, it became a regular element in popular culture.

Between these two floated the major private collections of historical material, some of whose owners had a foot in both camps, and it was here that the bundle of ideas and feelings usually lumped together under the rubric of the Romantic movement had their greatest effect. As the nineteenth century progressed romantic collections seen by gaslight became the material stuff of nationalism and the exotic elements in the older (and newer) collections became nationalism's support and foil, while their new importance was intellectually justified partly by the effort to treat the material as if it were part of natural science, and partly by newer notions about context and community, which stressed the organic relationships and notion of total function characteristic of Foucault's modern episteme. Each of these four motifs needs a closer look.

COLLECTING ON THE MORAL HIGH GROUND

Linnaeus made his first collection of botanical specimens in Lapland in 1733, and published the results in his *Flora Lapponica* (1737) and *Systema Natura* (1736). He followed these with *Genera Plantarum* (1737), *Classes Plantarum* (1738) and *Species Plantarum* (1753), so establishing the taxonomic system of natural classification which has carried his name ever since (Plate 5). Linnaeus did not, of course, spring out of the void; he was in England in 1736 and took up the classificatory impulse where it had been left by the likes of Grew and Woodward. He also had his opponents. One of the most influential of these was the Frenchman, Buffon, who reluctantly accepted Linnaeus' names for plants, but only to the point of writing them on the *underside* of his own labels.

It is not true that Linnaeus retaliated by naming the toad *Bufonia* (Whitehead 1971). But he was one of those men who change the way the world is perceived. The establishment of a patterned system into which all the diversity of nature could be fitted chimed in at once with the deist theory of the Enlightenment, and the corresponding modernist belief that the physical process of material observation and measurement by a rational man could result in objective knowledge and truth. When the

Plate 5 Sheet from the herbarium of Carl Linnaeus, showing a specimen of the tulip tree and a label (centre right) written by Linnaeus. Manchester Museum. (photo: Manchester Museum)

British Museum opened to the public in 1759, one of its founding collections was that made by Sir Hans Sloane, essentially a collection of early collections, which contained natural-history material that Linnaeus seems to have worked upon, including the famous herbarium of Leonard Plukenet which Sloane acquired in 1710 and the collection of Dr Herman, Professor of Botany at Leyden, which Sloane bought in 1711 (Brooks 1954: 186). The decision to turn this into a great national institution provided its own endorsement of the classificatory project, an endorsement which matched that of the visit of the Prince and Princess of Wales to Sloane's collection when still in Chelsea some eleven years earlier.

Natural-history collecting became a passion, especially in England where as time went on innumerable societies and field clubs were founded as a context within which the collecting might be pursued. Such collecting afforded an intellectual outlet for the middle class, actual and aspiring, and gave collectors the feeling of being at the cutting edge of their time; indeed, as the taxonomic net was woven many individuals did contribute to its strands. A characteristic collection – albeit very significant and made by a woman – was that of Miss Ethelred Benett (1776–1845), whose collection of fossils, mostly from the Jurassic–Cretaceous strata of Wiltshire, is now largely in the Academy of Natural Sciences of Philadelphia. This collection was the basis for the creation of new taxonomic groups, and still contains the type specimens which constitute the primary physical evidence upon which the whole system depends (Spamer *et al.* 1989).

Outside northern Europe, collections of art retained their privileged place. Gradually, many of the great royal art collections (although not that of the English sovereigns) were turned into public museums by royalty itself. The Viennese Royal Collection was moved out of the Stallburg to the Belvedere Palace in 1776; the Royal Collection in Düsseldorf and the Dresden Gallery were opened to the public in the middle of the century; and the Uffizi was donated to the state in 1743 by the last Medici princess. The Glyptothek in Munich was built as a public museum for the Bavarian royal collection by Ludwig of Bavaria about 1820, and even the Hermitage was opened to the public in 1853, although as Bazin shows, it kept much of its character as a princely reception room:

> The [Hermitage] museum was completely integrated with the palace, being used for evening receptions and after-theatre suppers . . . The Czar permitted the public but on conditions recalling those of the *Ancien Régime*. One visited the emperor, not the museum; full dress was *de rigueur* and visitors were announced.
>
> (Bazin 1967: 198)

The new public art museums required a new philosophy and a new iconography which would draw upon the idea of classification inherited from the previous century and link this with the applied intellectual ratio-nale characteristic of the developing European middle class, who wanted to see a clear increase in knowledge and understanding for their efforts, and who preferred this knowledge to underpin their own position. The outcome was the idea of the history of art, in which pictures could be placed in chronological sequence, to show 'high' and 'lower' points. Collections of classical marbles and other similar antiquities, either already existing or as they arrived in the national collections from private hands, took their natural place in this arrangement, both as the touchstones of spiritual excellence and as the glorious past to which the splendid present was heir.

All this gave visitors something to learn, a positive possession, rather than just something to appreciate – a much less clear yield. It had the effect of creating historical depth for a generation whose habits of mind were only just accustoming themselves to the idea of the present as the product of the past, and inevitably this turned upon that simplest view of progression and change, the lives of great men and great artists. The contemporary bourgeoisie felt very comfortable with all these interlocking pedagogic, judgemental and spiritually affirmative ideas.

The arrangement of the new galleries made this quite explicit. When the Royal Viennese Collection was rehoused in the Belvedere in 1776, the pictures were divided into national schools and art-historical periods. They were put into uniform frames and clearly labelled, another change necessary for public visitors. A walk through the galleries was a walk through art history, as the accompanying *Guide* written by Christian von Mechel made clear. The new museum, he wrote, was to be 'a repository where the history of art is made visible' (quoted in Bazin 1967: 159). The Düsseldorf collection had had a similar arrangement since 1756, and the Uffizi since 1770. The Louvre adopted it in 1810, and it has been the scheme usual in art museums ever since.

THE LOWER GROUND: SCARCELY FIT TO BE LOOKED AT

In elevated collecting circles the more curious aspects of the older collections became an embarrassment as the eighteenth century wore on and their apparent lack of intellectual potential became more pointed. But in society as a whole, and in each individual in certain moods, an appetite for sensationalism had never lost its hold.

Sometimes this involved material relating directly to the famous dead, including parts of their bodies, and is the lineal descendant of the earlier relic displays, although, at any rate to our eyes, the elements of ghoulishness seem more explicit. Yorkshire had participated in all the earlier collecting movements and had had its own cabinet of curiosities in the ownership of Ralph Thoresby (*b.* 1658) whose *Musaeum Thoresbyanum* at Leeds contained, amongst a very large and varied collection, as we have seen (p. 116) the actual hand and arm of the executed Marquis of Montrose (Brears 1989). This was more in tune with the needs of visitors, of all social classes. By the 1790s no visit to York was complete without seeing the museum at the castle, then the county gaol. Here:

a small room adjoining the house of the governor [has] its walls covered with implements of crime, murder and robbery &c. Here are preserved the coining apparatus used by David Hartley; the razor with which Jonathan Martin, the incendiary, struck a light to burn the minster; the bellrope by which he let himself down from the window; a part of the skull of Daniel Clark, the victim of Eugene

Aram, dug up in Knaresborough; the strap with which one Holroyd hung his father on a cherry tree; the knife and fork with which the rebels were quartered, 1745; the fetters [24 lb] which confined Dick Turpin's legs, and the belt which went round his waist, while in prison here . . . and many other articles which would do substantial duty in a sensation novel.

(quoted in Brears and Davies 1989: 7)

The gaolers who showed people round were presumably given a consideration for their trouble, and certainly by the early decades of the nineteenth century the public had become used to paying an entrance fee to see collections which were primarily intended to be commercial operations, making a living for their proprietors. A number of such collections are known. That of John Calvert in Leeds, which opened to the public in 1795 and contained a large collection of natural-history specimens, and that known as the Liverpool Museum, which included some 4,000 curiosities of natural, historical and artistic interest, toured the north country in the early 1800s, spending a week or two at a time in towns like Wakefield (Brears and Davies 1989: 9–10). But the most famous of these collections was that originally founded by Sir Ashton Lever, a county gentleman of Lancashire who was born in 1729. He assembled a large collection, including natural-history specimens and Pacific material, and by 1774 decided to open the collection as a public museum in London, in Leicester House, charging an entrance fee partly to offset expenses, and partly to regulate the flow of undesirable visitors.

A letter from Susan Burney to her sister, Mme d'Arblay, dated 16 July 1778 gives a good idea of what the collection was like:

Saturday morning we spent extremely well at Sir Ashton Lever's Museum. I wish I was a good Natural Historian, that I might give you some idea of our entertainment in seeing birds, beasts, shells, fossils etc. but I can scarce remember a dozen names of the thousand I heard that were new to me. The birds of paradise, and the humming-birds, were I think, among the most beautiful. There are several pelicans, flamingos, peacocks (one quite white) a penguin. Among the beasts a hippopotamus (sea horse) of an immense size, an elephant, a tyger from the Tower, a Greenland bear and its cub – a wolf – two or three leopards – an Otaheite dog (a very coarse ugly-looking creature) – a camelion – a young crocodile – a roomful of monkeys – one of them presents the company with an Italian song – another is reading a book (are these alive perhaps?) – another the most horrid of all, is put in the attitude of Venus de Medicis, and is scarce fit to be looked at. Lizzards, bats, toads, frogs, scorpions and other filthy creatures in abundance. There were a great many things from Otaheite (probably from Captain Cook's voyage) – the complete dress of a Chinese Mandarine, made of blue and brown sattin – of an African Prince. A suit of armor that they say belonged to Oliver Cromwell – the Dress worn in Charles 1st's time etc.etc.

(Ripley 1970: 33–4)

By 1806 the museum had sunk in popularity and the material within it sold off by lottery. Much of it was bought by William Bullock and re-exhibited in Bullock's London Museum, Egyptian Hall, Piccadilly, another fashionable resort. Bullock's collection was itself sold off in 1819, and the pieces were widely dispersed into a large range of private hands. One of Bullock's exhibits, a case showing a tiger and a snake in battle, has been traced through a succession of owners to its present place in Rossendale Museum, Rawtenstall, Lancashire (Plate 6). This display was Lot 98 in the Bullock sale, described as:

A most superb and finely prepared specimen of the Royal or Bengal tiger, seized by the boa constrictor. The beautiful manner in which this group is preserved renders it worthy of a place in the first museum in the world. A fine picture copied from it by the Chevalier de Barde is now in the Louvre. It is enclosed in a large mahogany glass case.

(quoted in Hancock 1980: 175)

The snake is, in fact, constructed of two specimens joined together and fitted with a wooden head, although the tiger is a genuine specimen, probably preserved according to Bullock's own arsenic, burnt alum and tanner's bark recipe. The naturalistic pose and the semi-habitat setting demonstrate the new display techniques which Bullock successfully introduced into Britain. As Bullock's museum makes clear, in display terms the line between sensation and education is a fine one.

ROMANTIC COLLECTING: RESURRECTIONS OF THE BODY

It has sometimes been suggested that the new modes of thinking and feeling which appear across the range of European culture in the final third of the eighteenth century represent one of the few genuine shifts of sentiment which our history has seen, comparable, perhaps, only to that which produced the notion of courtly and romantic love in the later twelfth century. This may in part be true; but it is also clear that a European *mentalité* disposed to emphasise the separateness of each individual and to speculate about the nature of individuality in relation to the whole, is likely to bring forth that cast of mind which we call romantic, with its desire to enhance the experience of the individual. It is equally clear that, just as the economic dimension of the Romantic Age was the gathering strength of

Plate 6 'One of those dreadful combats': tableau of tiger and python shown in the Bullock Museum, now in Rossendale Museum. (photo reproduced by kind permission of Rossendale Museum)

that discourse of labour and mass production which it is convenient to call modern capitalism and which tended to disrupt nostalgically viewed 'traditional' patterns in the interests of creating a social world of goods, so Romanticism itself will take a material form. It is this material form which we see in the Romantic collections of the period.

The enhancement of individual experience took a number of forms. The desire to extend sensation took some collectors to the exotic, and is in part the genesis of contemporary accumulations of Chinoiserie and 'primitive' material where, as we have seen, there was a link with popular sensationalism. The accumulation of exotic and artistic pieces sometimes went hand in hand with a highly developed self-image and the desire to create a world within a world. William Beckford is the paradigm here: the author of *Vathek* pursued his collecting with an insatiable hunger that reached its feverish peak with the creation of his Gothic dream of Fonthill Abbey. His excesses were much admired. There survives an account of Samuel Rogers' visit to Fonthill in 1817, relayed by his friend Lady Bessborough to Lord Granville:

> He was received by a dwarf, who, like a crowd of servants thro' whom he passed, was covered with gold and embroidery. Mr Beckford received him very courteously, and led him thro' numberless apartments all fitted up most splendidly, one with Minerals, including precious Stones; another the finest pictures; another Italian bronzes, china, &c. &c., till they came to a gallery that surpass'd all the rest from the richness and variety of its ornaments. It seem'd closed by a crimson drapery held by a bronze statue, but on Mr.B's stamping and saying 'Open!' the Statue flew back and the Gallery was seen extending 350 feet long. The doors of which there are many, are violet velvet covered over with purple and Gold embroidery. They pass'd from thence to a Chapel, where on the altar were heaped Golden Candlesticks, Vases and Chalices studded over with jewels; and from there into a great musick room . . . returning the next day he was shewn thro' another suite of apartments, fill'd with fine medals, gems, enamell'd miniatures, drawings old and modern, curios, prints and manuscripts, and lastly a fine and well furnish'd library.
>
> (Chapman 1940: 283–5)

Equally characteristic is the fact that Beckford overreached himself, and the Abbey with much of the collection was sold in 1823. Horace Walpole's collection at Strawberry Hill was similarly famous, and was also dispersed under the hammer.

Perhaps even more significantly, the desire to achieve experience prompted a shift in notions about the past and how it might be seen. Objects which were already seen to be 'true relics' by reason of their 'real relationship' with past people and events were transformed by the romantic eye into a sensation of knowing the past, of resurrecting the body of the past intact so that it might be experienced in the present. Here the influence of Sir Walter Scott was crucial, and the importance he placed upon the objects he gathered around him at Abbotsford, many of them relics of Prince Charlie and the Highlanders of 1715 and 1745 in the simplest sense, prefigured the shape of things to come and altered for ever ideas about what history is.

Bann (1988) has drawn attention to a paper by Riegl (1982) in which

Riegl discusses the 'meaning of monuments in relation to three separate criteria: their 'art value', their 'historical value' and their 'age value', and the argument applies equally to both architectural fragments of the kind Riegel discusses and movable objects like Scott's weapons and mementoes. 'Art value' gives an aesthetic mark out of ten, while 'historical value' relates the object to a particular and recorded sequence of historical events. 'Age value' is different. It is a perceptible property obvious to all, and not dependent upon cultural understanding of history or art: we can all see (or think we can see) if something is old. As the later eighteenth and earlier nineteenth centuries progressed, the 'age value' of objects witnessed by the visible signs of age and decay became a part of the way in which the seeing eye attributed quality and importance to the artefacts which passed before it.

Once relics, the tangible remains of great men and great events, had been united with a particular historiography of the past seen as re-creation, it was a short step to turn such collections to the political account of constructing nineteenth-century values, particularly that of nationalism, and it is to this that we must now turn.

NATIONAL INSTITUTIONS: PRACTISING WITH THE STATE

By around 1850 the collecting river, which had diverged into several streams, albeit braided by many cross-dykes and backwaters, runs again into a single water as the relationship between material collecting and society developed new forms in the century which spans roughly 1850 to 1950. To put it less fancifully, the identifying and classificatory gaze of the previous century or so becomes a panoramic view into which eventually all aspects of human history and human relationship are fitted, together with those that tie together the natural world and the perceived place of humans within it. In all areas of human understanding hierarchy and knowledge are one, and are available for inspection, one of the great Victorian words which expresses the characteristic link between the active gaze and moral gravity. One of the principal arenas for inspection becomes the great national and civic museums, founded in strength during these decades and still, by their architectural presences, dominating the new city centres of Europe as churches had once dominated the old.

The contradictions and tensions which had split collecting into several streams in the eighteenth century – some prestigious, some demotic, and some occupying the Romantic wilderness between the two – are drawn together in the nineteenth century as notions about human history and its remains take a new turn. Equally, the economic prosperity, which, in general terms, underpinned nineteenth-century Europe, was able to support the massive development of building and professional superstructure which the appropriate institutional – another great Victorian word – housing of the accumulating collections appeared to need.

Not all actual collecting was, of course, part of this new strenuousness. One of the long-term characteristics of the collecting habit is its ability to carry on quite happily into a new generation modes of operation which belong to the previous generation, or generations. The collectors themselves seem quite untroubled by this; indeed they have frequently seemed to glory in their archaism. Collections of rarities in the sixteenth- and seventeenth-century sense were made throughout the eighteenth and nineteenth centuries, and continue to be made today. Collecting in the fine and decorative arts has, in many ways, remained in ancient modes, as very important but highly eclectic collections like the late nineteenth-century one created by Sir William Burrell show; and the collectors and curators concerned probably regard this description as a compliment. This undertow, significant in human terms and powerful in collecting terms, should never be forgotten when the visible shape of the new forms is considered.

Several factors can be singled out as contributing to the new relationship between accumulated objects and specimens and social life. Collecting in the natural sciences comes of full age as the principle of taxonomy is gradually linked with an understanding of the related principles of stratification and evolution. History and historical material assumes a new importance. The material layout of knowledge becomes the way in which it is understood; and all these motifs are brought together in the institutions of the Museum Age.

The detailed collecting and classification of natural-history material, which gathered force during the second half of the nineteenth century with the founding of innumerable county and civic philosophical societies and field clubs and even larger numbers of private collectors, gradually contributed to the perfecting of the Linnaean system so that it became all-embracing. Displays like that of the Bird Gallery at the Natural History Museum (Figure 6.1) followed this scheme until as late as the 1980s. The result was the creation of a chronological series of flat planes of knowledge which offered a description of the natural world at what were gradually realised to be a range of points in past geological time as the fossil record began to be understood. The imaginative leap which made this sequential notion possible was the idea of stratigraphy, usually attributed to R. Murchison and Adam Sedgwick whose collections and field notes are still in the Cambridge museum which bears his name (Speakman 1982).

The flat planes themselves needed to be linked into an intelligible lattice work by the addition of a vertical idea, and this idea was provided in 1859 with the publication of the *Origin of Species* which, together with Darwin's later writing, offered a chronological structure and a corresponding development of hierarchy to account for the diversity of earth

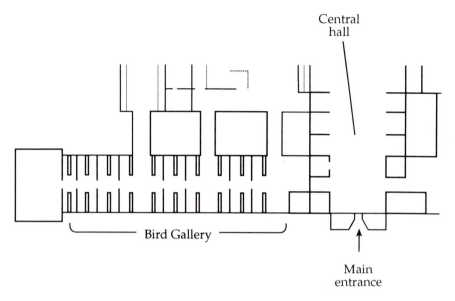

Figure 6.1 Plan of Bird Gallery, Natural History Museum, London, about 1980, showing traditional approach to the layout of cases and knowledge

life-forms. This was cast within a moral tone which endorsed the crucial link between form and context, which was seen as the forum within which successful forms and types developed, and which applauded survival as an ethical quality. Darwin was a child of his times, and his ideas, and the broad surrounding climate which had produced them made the obvious connections between natural history and human history irresistible.

The result was a new view of the historical past and of the material which had come down from it, or which could, by the application of 'scientific' principles like improved excavation technique, be retrieved from it. Such relic material, transformed by romantic sentiment into the truthful objects from an authentic past, could easily be harnessed to developing post-enlightenment notions of national history, national character and national moral virtue; and this was made all the easier in that such objects, like the cruder manifestations of nationalism with which they were sometimes linked, could draw upon an existing well of popular enthusiasm for spectacle and show.

The outcomes were manifold. They include the collecting of memorabilia of the great, produced as national shrines, often encompassing museum displays within the house where the great man (usually) lived and worked. The Dickens Collection made by Alain de Suzannet and shown in the Dickens House Museum (Slater 1975; see p. 319) (whatever Dickens himself would have made of his presentation as an establishment-validated national hero) is one such; the production of Mozart in Salzburg and Vienna is another, and one with similar ironic shadows. The lives of these men have been reified into material terms through the power seen to be inherent in objects which they actually touched and used, and these have been lifted out of actual historical process into a mythological present which helps to support ideas about 'greatness' and, in Dickens' case, 'Englishness', objectified ideas which are gazed at, not directly experienced. As Hawes has put it, drawing interestingly on the ideas of Jung:

> These myths are one key support for the identity of a culture. Just as the identity of an individual gives a *raison d'être*, so does that of a culture. The myths give people in that culture a sense of themselves, who they are, why they are here, where they are going, where they could or should go. Just as the identity of an individual has a conscious dimension in the Ego, and an unconscious dimension in the Self, the identity of a culture also has conscious and unconscious dimensions.
>
> (Hawes 1985: 136)

Unconsciously or otherwise, and in spite of their own actual life stories, the official heroes were identified in Darwinian terms as the fittest who had survived, the successful who had developed, and whose success encouraged and underpinned the success of others.

The national shrines were matched in spirit by the great temporary international exhibitions which were such a feature of the period between 1851 and 1939 (Greenhalgh 1988). These were on a scale of unparalleled opulence; for them, as Greenhalgh says (1988: 1) urban centres were replanned, national economies damaged, fortunes made and wars postponed. They usually served several purposes including the stimulation of trade and industry and the encouragement of good practice in craft and design, ideas which take us straight back to Bacon's Solomon's House, and a spectacle of cultural pageantry, all brought together under the general rubric of national glory. The Great Exhibition of 1851, mounted in South Kensington, was the first of these exhibitions to be truly international in intention, and it set the benchmark for all that was to follow, a fact regarded as fitting by the British establishment which had created it. The Crystal Palace became a prime symbol of national pride of achievement, matched by the grandiose, spectacular and often downright vulgar displays within. Half the space was devoted to Britain and her empire, and half to the rest of the world, a division which appeared wholly appropriate. Greenhalgh describes the mix of exhibits as

> extraordinary, ranging from classical sculpture to giant lumps of coal from a Nubian Court to wrought iron fire-places, from steam engines

to Indian miniatures, from rubber plants to stained-glass windows. The artefacts in this lavishly orchestrated jamboree had only one thing in common, the awesome power of the technologies that had taken them there. Everything was explicable directly or indirectly in terms of technology; the prefabricated building housing the exhibition, the steam engines, the manufactured products, the colossal objects transported to the site by machinery, the imperial produce won with commercial and military technology. The Great Exhibition, like virtually all its successors around the world, fetished the machine, choosing exclusively to see in it a glorious past and the chance of a blemishless future.

(Greenhalgh 1988: 13)

National pride, imperial glory, the mastery of history, the progress of technology and the free operation of the market are woven into a seamless whole.

At South Kensington, the Darwinian diversity of human life and its arrangement in hierarchical terms of mother country and imperial possession through which the fittest were ensured continual survival at the top of the tree, were all made unmistakably manifest. These notions, crudely expressed in the Great Exhibition, were capable of considerable refinement as the imaginative power of Darwin's ideas to generate models for understanding were applied to human history and, especially, its material culture. The Scandinavian prehistorians Thomsen and Worsaae had already by the 1830s classified ancient objects according to their material – stone, bronze or iron – and achieved the conceptual leap which turned this classification into the stratigraphic Three Age System. In the hands, preeminently, of Augustus Pitt Rivers (Chapman 1991) concepts of taxonomy became ideas of typology by means of which human artefacts could be classified and allotted their respective places in the scheme of things, while ideas of technological progress, equated with moral progress, offered a satisfactory yardstick against which human communities could be judged and ordered. Henry Balfour, the first Curator of the Pitt Rivers Museum in Oxford expressed Pitt Rivers' views well in his address to the British Association in 1904:

Through noticing the unfailing regularity of this process of gradual *evolution* in the case of firearms, he was led to believe that the same principles must probably govern the development of the other arts, appliances, and ideas of mankind.

Although as a collector he was somewhat omnivorous, since every artefact product fell strictly within his range of enquiry, his collection, nevertheless, differed from the greater number of private ethnological collections, and even public ones of that day, inasmuch as it was built up *systematically* with a definite object in view . . . Suffice it to say that, in classifying his ethnological material, he adopted a *principal* system of groups into which objects of like form or function from all over the world were associated to form series, each of which illustrated as completely as possible the varieties under which a given art, industry, or appliance occurred. Within these main groups objects belonging to the same region were usually associated together in *local* sub-groups. And wherever amongst the implements or other objects exhibited in a given series, there seemed to be suggested a *sequence of ideas*, shedding light upon the probable stages in the evolution of this particular class, these objects were specially brought into juxta-position. This special grouping to illustrate sequence was particularly applied to objects from the same region as being, from their local relationships, calculated better to illustrate an actual continuity. As far as possible the seemingly more primitive and generalized forms – those simple types which usually approach most nearly to *natural* forms, or whose use is associated with primitive ideas – were placed at the beginning of each series, and the more complex and specialized forms were arranged towards the end.

The primary object of this method of classification by series was to demonstrate, either actually or hypothetically, the origin, development and continuity of the material arts, and to illustrate the variations whereby the more complex and specialized forms belonging to the higher conditions of culture have been evolved by successive slight improvements from the simple, rudimentary, and generalized forms of a primitive culture.

(quoted in Gray 1905: 5)

Many of these strands came together at the South Kensington site in the years following 1851. The substantial profit which the Exhibition made was used to organise displays on land purchased at South Kensington. These included the exhibition of Pitt Rivers' collection, displayed at South Kensington from 1874 to 1885 in property held by the then Science and Art Department, and a catalogue résumé of the collection, written by Pitt Rivers, was published by the Department, going through two editions in 1874 and 1877. Ultimately the money from the Great Exhibition helped (1857) to fund the building and organisation of what finally (1899) became the Victoria and Albert Museum, one among the array of permanent museums in what is now Exhibition Road.

National pride was matched by civic pride. The Liverpool Museum was opened in 1853, the Nottingham Museum in 1872, the Sheffield Museum in 1875; and many more followed suit. After a tangled history of thwarted intentions and false starts, Birmingham Museum opened in 1885, and its visitors still pass an inscribed stone which includes the line 'By the gains of industry we promote Art'. Nothing could better express the sentiments of the substantial middle class who were the moving spirits behind the major public collections.

The grandeur of these public buildings, the deliberate visual link they make with the admired cultures of Greece and Rome and (to a lesser extent) Gothic Europe, and the notions of the temple and the sacred which they express, were intended to impress and instruct the underclass in the hope of weaning them equally from gin and from revolution. Viewing the Great Exhibition, Gideon Mantell could describe the working class as

> Vulgar, ignorant, country people: many dirty women with their infants were sitting on the seats giving suck with their breasts uncovered, beneath the lovely female figures of the sculptor. Oh! How I wish I had the power to petrify the living, and animate the marble: perhaps a time will come when this fantasy will be realised and the human breed be succeeded by finer forms and lovelier features, than the world now dreams of.
>
> (quoted in Greenhalgh 1988: 31)

By the time the South Kensington Museum (predecessor of the Victoria and Albert) had opened in 1857, Henry Cole could write:

> The working man comes to this museum from his one or two dimly lighted, cheerless dwelling rooms, in his fustian jacket, with his shirt collars a little trimmed up, accompanied by his threes and fours, and fives of little fustian jackets, a wife in her best bonnet, and a baby, of course, under her shawl. The looks of surprise and pleasure on the whole party when they first observe the brilliant lighting inside the museum show what a new, acceptable, and wholesome excitement this evening affords them all. Perhaps the evening opening of public museums may furnish a powerful antidote to the gin palace.
>
> (Cole 1884: 293)

The tone may be patronising, but it is infinitely kinder and more hopeful than Mantell's inability to see the profound identity of the artistic female form divine and the actual women of flesh and blood. By the end of the century Pitt Rivers could see an ideological purpose in the museum demonstration that Nature worked by slow evolution rather than by swift revolution.

At a second level, deeper but interlinked with the first, the grandeur of the ceremonial architecture and the self-evident quality of the material which the buildings displayed made visible the idea of the state through the deployment of architectural rhetoric which recalls past European glories and harnesses these to the needs of the present establishment (Duncan and Wallach 1980). The totality of the architectural form which embraces the pictures on the walls, the relics of the mighty past, and the wonderful diversity of God's world, organises an experience from which the visitor emerges as from a religious ritual, but one which is intended to reconcile him to the role of ideal citizen. Notions of quality in collected material culture are made to underpin the status quo, as the state owns and validates these things and offers to share the important experience which they embody with its citizens.

CONCLUSION

Beneath the diversity of collecting, the modernist exploration emerges with increasing clarity as the eighteenth and nineteenth centuries unwind. The big collections, and particularly the public museums as these crystallise out of the earlier accumulations, demonstrate the central fact that organised material is knowledge, and knowledge is organised material. The belief that material display creates both knowledge and proper social relationships is a fundamental aspect of the European *mentalité*, matched by the corresponding belief that material evidence embodies distinctions which can be determined by thought to reveal the pattern of things. Museum exhibition is one of the most significant modern transformations of these abiding presumptions. It is an overarching explanatory narrative of the modern world, together with printed books or scientific experiment, and, like these, the kind of knowledge it creates is deeply dyed with economic and ideological thrust of the times.

By the nineteenth century public collections, on show in their palaces of culture, are part of the European mainstream, as how could they fail to be. It is no accident that state museums and their collecting emerge at the same time as the phase of that late-eighteenth-century and nineteenth-century free-market economy which it is useful to call mature capitalism. As we have seen, notions of individual enterprise and the importance of ownership are part of the heart of what it means to think like a European, and one matched by a corresponding emphasis on the sacred quality of carefully chosen goods. The mature phase of market capitalism naturally went hand in hand with the mature phase of public collection and display, in which spiritual, intellectual and property values are united, the educated middle classes confirmed in proprietorship and the state assured.

CHAPTER SEVEN

COLLECTING IN A POST-MODERNIST WORLD

———— •◆• ————

Look! Out they come, from the bushes – the riff-raff. Children? Imps – elves – demons. Holding what? Tin cans? Bedroom candlesticks? Old jars? My dear, that's the cheval glass from the Rectory! And the mirror – that I lent her. My mother's. Cracked. What's the notion? Anything that's bright enough to reflect, presumably, ourselves? Ourselves! Ourselves!

Between the Acts (Woolf 1978: 133)

INTRODUCTION: MAKING EXHIBITIONS OF OURSELVES

The cultural logic of late capitalism, to use Jameson's (1984) phrase, has penetrated the world of objects, of those who collect objects, and of those institutions – particularly museums – whose business is objects, for just as mature capitalism, that characteristically European use of Europe's own inheritance, generated a world of objects whose use and value was carefully regulated by accepted social parameters, so post-modernist late capitalism has, from its own entrails, produced a world in which the multiplicity of objects float free in a culture landscape in which boundaries seem to have dissolved.

The main strands in the bundle can be sketched out relatively easily. In classic Marxist terms, the workers are now further than ever from the product and from participation in the whole cycle of production and consumption. The job market becomes yearly more complex and fragmented as employment stability disintegrates and more work is linked to computers and satellites which breach the once restrictive time–space barriers. With this has gone a similar instability of aesthetic. As Harvey puts it:

> The relatively stable aesthetic of Fordist modernism has given way to all the ferment, instability, and fleeting qualities of a post-modernist aesthetic that celebrates difference, ephemerality, spectacle, fashion, and the commodification of cultural forms.
>
> (Harvey 1989: 156)

As a result, we are

> so far removed from the realities of production and work in the world that we inhabit a dream world of artificial stimuli and televised experience: never in any previous civilization have the great metaphysical preoccupations, the fundamental questions of being and of the meaning of life, seemed so utterly remote and pointless.
>
> (Jameson 1989: xviii)

This pointlessness has been provided with its own philosophy in the post-structuralist writings of men like Baudrillard, Barthes, Derrida and Foucault (for a good discussion see Harland 1987). For Foucault the operation of power in the modern state is all-pervasive, running up and down society at all levels and linking the whole together. Power and knowledge are much the same thing, and they in their turn are linked to ideas like 'truth' and 'reason'. Power is exercised as an intentional strategy, but because it is everywhere, it is not linked, as Marx thought, with one particularly oppressing group. It cannot be clearly located in a distinct and manageable set of personal relationships, and consequently individuals, enmeshed in power relationships like flies in webs, have no hope of extricating themselves by normal processes, because these would simply set up more of the same.

The semiotic argument arrives at much the same conclusion. In language as in all others forms of communication, including material culture and institutions like museums, the link between signifier and signified has been severed. To put it another way, there is no reason why the meanings which have traditionally been attached to anything should continue to be attached; meaning is what anybody cares to make it. Signifiers, objects and exhibitions among others, can trigger off a large range of meanings within the minds and feelings of those who experience them, and since the inherited signification of the past – roughly the consensus of meaning resulting from history – has been demoted, there is no way of judging between the validity of these experienced meanings. As Baudrillard has put it, 'today especially the real is no more than a stuck pile of dead matter, dead bodies and dead language' (1981: 103). For Baudrillard there can be no reality, no meaning and no history, for what is history but a way of pretending that meaning exists?

In our relationship with the material world, the philosophical and social uncertainties of the post-modernist period have produced a reflexive state of mind in which the old hierarchies of value seem less secure and are perceived as social constructions rather than as explanations of natural truth, while the various kinds of popular culture and the material collections which come from it, traditionally given a low ranking in the judgemental hierarchy, are correspondingly taken to be orders of interest in their own right. The result of this across the collecting scene in terms of what we might call the institutional practice of collecting has been an interesting threefold mixture.

Collections which have come to us from the earlier periods are attracting considerable attention as historical documents in their own right, particularly as displays mounted in museums by whom the material is held. Equally, and again the principle agents are the museums themselves, there is much anxiety about how collections of twentieth-century material should be assembled as the material documents of our century to those who come after. Finally, there is the immense scope of popular collecting by individuals who keep their collections largely in their own homes. The psychological and social basis of this is of great interest and importance, and will be considered in Part Three of this study; what concerns us here is the way in which such collecting is emerging, gradually, into institutional recognition and so into acknowledged practice. Each of these three topics needs examining in turn; what binds them together is a collecting eye now turned not to the vertical structures of the hierarchy, but to the spreading landscape of human society and the human heart.

MATTER FOR REFLECTION

The desire to see collections and collecting as of significance in their own right, as constructions which ask to be unravelled and understood within their own terms of reference, has given us an extremely interesting sequence of exhibitions in which an inward-turning museum gaze attempts to demonstrate upon what premises material has been selected for accumulation over the last four centuries or so and how the museum as collection-based institution has come about. The genesis of this activity was the exhibition and accompanying conference mounted in 1983 by the Ashmolean Museum, Oxford, in order to celebrate the tercentenary of the opening of the museum in 1683. The Tradescant Collection was researched, redisplayed (Figure 7.1) and published (Macgregor 1983) and the conference volume (Impey and Macgregor 1985) discussed a European-wide range of similar collections which, as we have seen, belong within the cabinets of curiosities and related traditions and stand at the origins of many of the great European museums.

The efforts of the Ashmolean have concentrated attention upon the extent to which the study of early collections, and so of course of all collections, can throw light on our relationship to the material world, and the way in which we create our understanding of ourselves and our surroundings by selective manipulation of this relationship. The early modern collections, in particular, are now perceived as what they are: important moments in the history of thought through which the characteristic modernist gaze of material analysis which yields truth by physical comparison

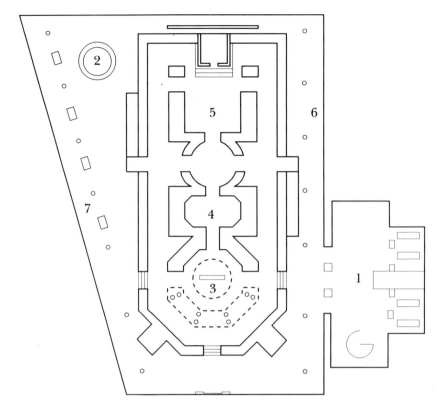

Figure 7.1 Plan of *Museum Europa* exhibition, National Museums of Denmark, 1993: 1–4 historical phases, 5–6 The Collector, 7 paintings (after exhibition literature)

and inference took much of its shape. A number of similarly self-reflexive exhibitions have followed the Ashmolean one, like that entitled *Birds' Eggs* (1992) at the Oxford Museum of the History of Science (in the old Ashmolean building) which gave us the opportunity to see what is probably the world's oldest collection of birds' eggs made by John Pointer (1667–1754) in the first half of the eighteenth century, which he used to teach a course at Oxford on natural history and *materia medica*.

The point made at Oxford has been taken by several of the major museums of northern Europe, whose collections are broadly similar. In 1992 the Historical Museum, Amsterdam, mounted the exhibition *Distant Worlds Made Tangible* which displayed the art and curiosities in the collections made between 1585 and 1735 by wealthy Dutch burghers. In 1993 the National Museums of Denmark put on an important exhibition entitled *Museum Europa: An Exhibition about the European Museum and Europe. Museum Europa* was described as an exhibition about the European Museum and about Europe herself, both as concept and reality. With this exhibition, the National Museums of Denmark wishes to illuminate the relationship between European thought as expressed through science, art and philosophy, and the museums of Europe, expressed in their methods of classification.

The way a museum exhibits its artifacts always mirrors the march of time. We see the objects of the past through the eyes of the present and only understand the past by the amount of light it sheds on our own present time. Therefore the ways of display found in the European Museum are as vibrant and alive as, for instance, the narrative styles of European literature or the painting techniques of European pictorial art.

(National Museums of Denmark 1991: 3)

Museum Europa was therefore intended to 'exhibit' the exhibition itself by displaying examples of the epoch-making changes in the methods of exhibition, beginning with the first encyclopedic collections and ending with the 'imaginary museums' of today, where objects are transferred to computer screens from databases, regardless of where they may be found in time or space (National Museums of Denmark 1991: 4). In this exhibition the objects themselves determine the arrangements in order to show how collections can reflect a cosmology and how the grouping of objects creates meaning. The whole enterprise was intended to be an examination of the museums as an idea (p. 7).

In order to achieve this the Museum drew on its rich collections, which include the surviving 2,000 or so objects in the Royal *Kunstkammer*, the first inventory of which dates from 1674, and which itself included material deriving from the collections of Olaus Worm (*d.* 1624). The physical appearance of the exhibition was that of a montage, a fragmented presentation of history open to more than a single interpretation. Accordingly, the exhibition morphology is not linear, but a labyrinth in which the visitor was allowed to make his own discoveries. To achieve this, the gallery was divided into seven areas, in which four areas showing historical phases were accompanied by the Introduction Room which showed medieval treasures in boxes and chests, The Collector which showed a bower-bird with its 'blue collection' in a wood, children collecting at a beach, and a book collector at his desk, and the Gallery of Paintings which showed paintings of collectors and collections (Figure 7.1). *Museum Europa* represents the grand gesture of self-reflection, coupled with an important statement of the significance of the collected world in the history of European consciousness.

A similar desire for self-examination and the assertion of significance is shown in the projects mounted by a number of regional museums in Britain. In 1992 Jersey Museums Service put on *From Whales to Winklepickers: A*

History of Collectors and Collecting in Jersey. This demonstrated the Jersey collections and collections in relation to themes like 'The Classics', 'Art', 'The Empire' and 'Evolution'. In May 1992 the Tolson Memorial Museum Huddersfield (Kirklees Museum Service) opened its *Waxwings, Waistcoats and Wooden Legs: Collectors and Collections in Your Museum* exhibition (Figure 7.2). This has sections on the origins of the museums' collection, what the museum has collected, and why it has done so. There are displays of specific collections of bottles, stamps and cigarette cards, and sections

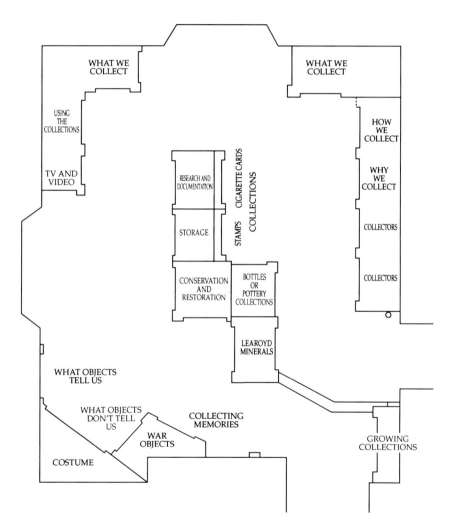

Figure 7.2 Plan of Collections Gallery, Tolson Memorial Museum, Huddersfield, 1992

on the core of collections and the uses to which they are put. Two sections consider 'What objects tells us' and 'What objects don't tell us', where attention is drawn to the selective, generally middle-class, view that surviving objects give us of our historical past. The tone here is that of a museum service explaining itself to its public, and the emphasis is therefore rather upon the way the collections are managed and used rather than upon the presentation of an intellectual framework within which the collections can be understood. The importance of exhibitions like those at Huddersfield and Jersey lies in the way in which they focus attention upon collections and the collecting process.

All this museum activity bears a close relationship to similar reflexive – some would say narcissistic – efforts much on the minds of some contemporary literary critics, pointing up the similarity between the analysis of written narrative and that of narrative constructed from material culture. Here, as in the museum, we see a textually self-conscious and critical approach to fiction in which the reader (or viewer) becomes a collaborator instead of merely a consumer, and reader and writer understand the responsibilities which the better-understood complexities of interpretation require. As Hutcheon has put it:

> The artist reappears, not as a God-like Romantic creator but as the inscribed maker of a social product that has the potential to participate in social change through its reader. Such an acknowledgement of the power of language is also an acknowledgement of the potential for ideological manipulation by the wielder of that language. The best way to demystify power, metafiction suggests, is to reveal it in all its arbitrariness.
>
> (Hutcheon 1980: xvi)

Her 'power of language' is for museums and collectors the 'power of objects' and her 'metafiction', essentially fiction which reveals the nature of fiction, is our meta-exhibition, exhibitions of collections which reveal the nature of themselves.

THE TWENTIETH CENTURY: OUR COLLECTIVE SELVES

One of the sections in the Huddersfield exhibition was called 'Growing Collections' and was concerned with recent acquisitions. One very particular, but very important, aspect of the whole late-twentieth-century collecting debate is the question of how museums should go about selecting and accumulating material from the twentieth century, and especially from the second half of the century, so that these collections can represent our time to those people of the twenty-first and later centuries who will (we must suppose) come after us. The kernel of the argument revolves around the difficulties implicit in selection and representation which, however self-conscious and open the process may be, will inevitably involve lop-sidedness and bias.

One approach attempted to find a path through the difficulties by concentrating upon issues which are visibly and clearly important in the neighbourhood in which the collecting museum works. As King puts it very clearly in relation to the People's Palace Museum, Glasgow:

> You have to decide what the issues are for your own locality. The Falklands War was not an issue for Glasgow, in the same way as it was for Southampton or London. Glasgow's war in Argentina took place in 1978, when Ally's Tartan Army was routed in the World Cup Finals. In the aftermath, we were able to acquire quite a variety of souvenirs at bargain prices for the museum collection. This may seem to some to be a facetious outlook, but in a country which is politically effete, football often assumes a disproportionate cultural importance. In comparison with the heated fervour generated by the '78 World Cup, the '82 Falklands War had the aura of a distant B-movie media event.
>
> (King 1985–6: 4–5)

King goes on to detail some of the popular culture which can and should be collected in contemporary Glasgow: new shops and their immediate predecessors ('the Patisserie Françoise, née City Bakery'), city Christmas decorations, the material culture of the Peace Movement and the 1984/5 Miners' Strike, comedian Billy Connolly's stage costumes and material relating to pop and folk music. As Mayo puts it, drawing on her experience in the Division of Political History at the Smithsonian, collecting contemporary historical artefacts requires a great 'leap of faith' (1984: 8) because political problems can never be solved to everybody's satisfaction and yet material must be selected if museum collectors are to do their job.

Another way is to steer through the theoretical problems by admitting cheerfully to bias on the grounds that how a late-twentieth-century museum curator sees contemporary collecting is itself part of the history of our time, and consequently endowed with its own interest and significance. When in 1990 the Victoria and Albert Museum mounted the exhibition *Collecting for the Future: A Decade of Contemporary Acquisitions*, it became clear that the museum sees itself as collecting on the basis of aesthetic, technical and historical criteria arrived at, essentially, on the strength of curatorial interests and taste. By 1992 the Museum had opened both the Twentieth Century Gallery and the European Ornament Gallery. The Twentieth Century Gallery features Doc Marten boots, Lycra leggings, the Bic ball-point pen: ephemera treated as art because of its design qualities and its ability to define the essentially political tastes of an era.

In 1992 the European Ornament Gallery featured a display of 'outrageous, charismatic and kitsch ties' by inviting all and sundry to send in ties for display. The London *Evening Standard* for 19 March 1992 told us:

> London's temple of style, the Victoria and Albert Museum, is playing host to the worst that the British male and his dubious sense of fashion can throw at it. Men – and women – from all over the country have responded enthusiastically to the V & A's appeal for outrageous, charismatic and kitsch ties. Every day, parcels containing more examples of bad taste arrive at the museum's new European Ornament Gallery.
>
> (*Evening Standard*, 19 March 1992)

Claudia Bigg, a member of the museum staff, was quoted as saying 'One man said he had 2,000 but was forced to stop buying because he was spending too much money' (*Evening Standard*, 19 March 1992). Here we have the national 'Temple of Style' as the *Evening Standard* put it, exploring contemporary popular taste through the medium of a standard late-twentieth-century piece of male clothing, and doing so by inviting popular collectors to send in their own accumulations for display. The demotic spirit of the age comes into its own here, as collected objects, politics and institutions come together.

ONLY COLLECT

Like the ties exhibition, the Victoria and Albert Museum's *Collecting for the Future* exhibition, with its *Objects for the Collector* section showing objects like David Shilling hats, craft pottery and Aldo Rossi coffee sets, which, although sold for use or decoration, are manufactured above all to be collected, made an explicit link with contemporary collecting being carried on outside the museum walls. The same link was at the heart of the People's Show Project launched by Peter Jenkinson at Walsall Museum.

In 1990 Jenkinson conceived the idea of a People's Show, which would put on display in the museum collections formed by private individuals in their own homes. The first People's Show gathered together some 16,000 objects by sixty-three collectors from diverse backgrounds. The display packed out the museum's walls, floors and ceilings and included collections of neckties, eggcups, international hotel soaps and gambling machines. Further People's Shows have taken place since 1990 throughout museums in the Midlands. The Walsall show attracted much attention in regional and national media, where it linked up with the enormous superstructure of collectors' fairs, magazines and clubs, all of which support the popular collecting which is one of the most interesting and significant aspects of contemporary culture.

The notion of what is collectable ranges from recognised antiques (that is, those pieces which are more than a century old), to discarded contemporary bric-à-brac, or even contemporary material bought in a normal market outlet. The collectors hunt in antique shops, car-boot sales and mail-order magazines, but also in ordinary shops carrying contemporary commercial stock. Their interests are served by enterprises like the BBC's Antiques Roadshow and its various spin-offs, Miller's magazines, trade papers like *Antiques Trade Gazette*, which are often read by collectors, and a large range of magazines.

A characteristic magazine is that issued by Marshall Cavendish entitled *What's it Worth: The Complete Guide to Everyday Collectables*. The first issue appeared in the winter of 1993. It features articles on blue and white china, men's pocket watches, teddy bears, first aid for wood, comics and rocking chairs. Each article is lavishly illustrated and is backed up by inserts on 'Dealers' tips', 'Close-up on trade marks' and 'Tomorrow's treasures'. Each individual piece shown has a price-guide tag attached to it: prices range from under £5.00 to over £5,000. The emphasis is on becoming knowledgeable enough to find one's way about the collecting world and to avoid being made a fool of in a world presumed to be full of pitfalls.

CONCLUSION

At first sight, post-modern collecting, like the post-modern world, might appear to have abandoned the old cultural parameters of the long term in favour of eclectic freedom, both personal and material. Notions of classification and relationship, including those where value judgements are implicit, seem to have been subverted in favour of idiosyncratic assemblage which has no point of reference beyond individual quirks of partiality. The breakdown of traditional material structuring can be linked with the dissolution of other traditional social parameters – the family, authority, law and order, and so on. This is accompanied by the now-inevitable agony on the part of the professionals involved, here museum curators, who embark on honest endeavours to come to terms with the new world.

But what abides is the clear propensity of European individuals to define themselves and their cultural relationships in material terms. Viewed from this angle, popular collecting reinforces long-term habits and attitudes; now more people collect than ever as post-modernist capitalism and its cultural freedoms opens up more and more material to the collecting gaze. Perhaps (perhaps!) many European individuals are in some important ways more 'free' than they were, but they are using this freedom in traditional ways in the aggressive accumulation of goods, in the cherishing of material relationships and in individual assertions of sense and meaning.

CHAPTER EIGHT

COLLECTING CULTURE

—— •◆• ——

For the three or four last years of her life She checked her purchases (it is like trying to control a vice!); but some few months before her Death She was tempted by the celebrated Barberini Vase, imported by the noted Virtuoso (savant collector) Sr. William Hamilton. The Duchess gave 2000 pounds to Sr. William for it, a fine cameo of Augustus, and a fragment of an Intaglio of a Hercules.

Account by Horace Walpole of the Collection made by the Duchess of Portland (Ripley 1970: 31)

COLLECTING CULTURE

The thrust of this Part of the book has been to perceive a range of inter-related themes which constitute important threads in the weave of European culture in the Long Term, and which can take on different colours and tones as they both draw on and contribute to that European identity as it can be seen to develop through successive generations. Characteristically European notions about the way in which a family unit should be achieved, and, in part at least, about how property should be selectively distributed within this family, suggest that implicit in European culture has always been a tendency which we now recognise as typical, that is, a peculiarly intimate relationship to the world of goods. This has contributed to the European cultural pattern a willingness to speak with things in a way unusual across the world's cultures, and to do this both by way of community hoarding and depositing and through individual accumulative efforts which draw on notions about fame, honourable gifts, exchange and social prestige. We have traced the progress of these social ideas from prehistory to the present day.

Hand in hand with such cultural traits goes the corresponding way of seeing the world in terms of distinction and classification, in line with a fundamental oath/ordeal paradigm. The two together produce a disposition to understand the universe by analysing its material substance, to unite mystical ideas of the divine with a method of understanding which depends upon physical evidence and its scrutiny. This gives us the epistemes, the ideas of knowledge, characteristic of the European mind-set which can be seen in ancient times, appear in the classical world, and are easily traced in the world of the early modern period to the present. This urge towards classification has its temporal or historiographical side. Individuals are important and must be remembered: their barrows, relics and surviving possessions must be honoured with all the emotional force which surrounds the remains of the mighty dead and which, in due course, will produce historical writings and chronological distinctions once it is transmuted into the new understanding of the modernist rationale.

Objects which carry the freight of all these significances and combine them with the characteristics of treasure – valuable materials, superior craftsmanship and the capacity to enchant the eye – are endowed with sacred knowledge and power. Such objects, it has always been felt, must be set aside to be held in veneration and to act as (in the words of the older anthropology) the external souls of the group. For this, sacred places are needed, institutions cut off from the world. There is a clear and unmistakable line of descent which runs from the hoards and graves of the Bronze Age, through the shrines and temples of the Iron Age and classical world, and the royal halls and churches of the medieval world, to the royal collections of early modern times, and so to the museums of the past three centuries. All are sacred depositories of material selected by virtue of its inherent significance, its ability to show us to ourselves. All guard their material as jealously as any Fafnir, and all, as contemporary circumstances permitted, take compelling iconographic and architectural forms, whether of classical or of that neo-Romanesque we call Gothic. All are embedded, generation by generation, in the contemporary European version of political solutions to long-term social enigmas.

Some collected objects, by reason of the value attributed both to their intrinsic artistic and craft qualities and to their accumulated history, seem to encapsulate the relationship of the European tradition to the production of material meaning and so to collecting in practice. One such piece is the cameo glass vessel now known as the Portland Vase (Plate 7), described by the staff of the institution which now holds it, the British Museum, as

> The Portland Vase, named after the Dukes of Portland who owned it from 1785 to 1945, is the finest piece of Roman cameo glass in existence. It owes its reputation to the skill of its manufacture, the art and content of its decoration, and the historical importance of the people with whom it had been associated. Its fate has been one of breakage, damage and repair, both in antiquity and over the last two hundred years, and much of its fame, ironically, is a direct result of the misfortunes that have dogged its history.
>
> (Williams 1989: 22)

The vase was probably made in the decade 30–20 BC. It consists of two

Plate 7 Portland Vase undergoing conservation treatment in the British Museum laboratory in 1989. (photo: British Museum)

layers of glass, the inner dark blue, the outer white, and the white layer has been cut back to create superbly detailed decoration in cameo style. The decoration consists of a frieze of figures divided into two scenes, which Denys Haynes has interpreted as scenes from the events leading up to the birth of Achilles (a hero whom imperishable fame has certainly attended), although other interpretations are possible. Why it was made and for whom has been the subject of much debate, but most suggestions revolve around the idea that it was initially intended for Julius Caesar and his adopted successor Augustus (or Octavius as he was before he came to absolute power in 29 BC), or possibly originally for Cleopatra and her lover Mark Antony and so acquired by Augustus after he had defeated the pair at Actium in 31 BC. In any case, it was seen to represent the divinity of the Imperial family and their mastership of the Roman world.

The Vase was discovered in 1582 by Fabrizio Lazzaro, when he tunnelled into an Imperial burial mound three miles south of ancient Rome; the mound contained a sarcophagus which seems to have held the remains of Alexander Severus, emperor from AD 222 and his mother, Julia Mamaea, both of whom died in Germany in AD 235. The whereabouts of the Vase between roughly 20 BC and AD 235 is unknown, but presumably it formed part of the Imperial holdings of art and treasure which, as we have seen, had accumulated in Rome. Once excavated, the Vase passed first to Cardinal del Monte, and then, in 1627, to the possession of Cardinal Antonio Barberini, one of the greatest collectors of the age. By the end of the seventeenth century the Vase had become an acknowledged treasure which had to be seen by every young man on the Grand Tour. The fortunes of the Barberini family declined and by about 1780 the last of the line, the Princess of Palestrina, had sold it to a Scottish antique dealer living in Rome, James Byres, who around 1783 sold the Vase on to Sir William Hamilton. Hamilton, in turn, sold it to the Dowager Duchess of Portland (a widow possessed of her own means) and by 1784 it was installed in her private museum of natural and artificial curiosities in Privy Gardens, Whitehall. A year later she died, and her collection was broken up, probably to pay her debts. The Portland Vase, lot 1455 in the sale of 7 June 1786, was sold through an agent to the Duchess's son, the Third Duke of Portland. His son, the Fourth Duke, who inherited through the normal hereditary process, placed the Vase for safe keeping on loan in the British Museum in 1810, where it was put on display in a glass case in the ante-room to the Hamilton Gallery. Here, on 7 February 1845 a young man, apparently suffering from a severe hangover, picked up a weapon later described as 'a curiosity in sculpture' and smashed both case and Vase to pieces.

The Vase had been broken into some two hundred fragments. It was to be restored three times. John Doubleday, the first restorer, succeeded in getting the reassembled and glued Vase back on show in September 1845. It was a famous exhibit through the rest of the century, but by 1929 its prestige as a masterwork had dropped to the point where, when its owners, the Portland family, attempted to sell it at auction, it did not fetch its reserve price. It was returned to the British Museum, and in 1945 sold to the Trustees. Soon after, it was taken to pieces again to be put together with more modern adhesive. By the mid-1980s this had deteriorated in its turn, necessitating a third reconstruction, carried out in 1988–9 by Nigel Williams and Sandra Smith of the British Museum. This reconstruction was the subject of a BBC TV *Chronicle* programme.

The Portland Vase has its place within, and contributes to, most of the paradigms which structure European thought, feeling and social action. The striking appearance of the blue and white glass, the obvious quality of the craftsmanship, and the theme of classical gods and heroes portrayed in naturalistic style which conveys imperial glamour even to those who do not know its story, add up to a piece which, through all its two thousand years of European life, would always be highly desirable. Pieces like the Vase were treasured in the classical world, they feature among the grave goods of the barbarian world – pieces of broadly similar glass as we have seen seem to have been associated with the barrow at Hoen (p. 67) – and they, or carved classical gems very like them, figured in the medieval collections, and those of the Renaissance and later, up to our own day. These are the pieces which for the anonymous seventh-century author of *The Ruin* offered the joy of gazing upon treasure (p. 71), for Suger the transportation in seeing the loveliness of the many coloured stones (p. 107), and for Piero de Medici the greatest enjoyment and pleasure to the eye (p. 104). Viewed as experience, the intensity surrounding such a piece burns away the grosser motives of materialism to leave the religious exaltation which has always clung to our most precious objects. Viewed in terms of analysis, the Vase and its fellows have become the vehicle for social norms, the embodiment of the normative tradition which allows the notion of hierarchy and high culture, and so of a distinctively European notion of contrast and difference.

In notions of contrast and difference, of evident truth and fiction, rest also the historicity of the Vase. It is important because it possesses the moral force of the real thing, which alone has the ability to be genuinely of the past and to transfer this past into the present. We believe, as a result of the labour of various historians, that the Vase truly comes to us from the court of Augustus, and had the subsequent history described here. One of the reasons why its prestige suffered in the early part of this century was because in 1909 the then Director of the British School at Rome claimed to have disproved the story of its discovery. Characteristic rational and positivist notions are apparent here, in which the tracing of provenance and history, and the ability to carry out satisfactory scientific conservation work which will somehow convert the shattered fragments into a new but authentic whole, endorse 'reality'. Process through time easily acquires the moral twist which makes it progress through time, and the Vase personifies the value of history for a society for whom such values have always had an implicit importance, broadened and sharpened by the romantic eye. The Vase points up the nature of historicity by virtue of the individual history which it embodies in relation to the timeless qualities which it enshrines.

The Vase makes clear the intimate link between artistic or aesthetic quality and politics of prestige and display. It seems to have been produced originally as a political piece, and to have been used so by the Emperor Augustus. Once it had been rediscovered in 1582, it immediately again occupied the same central cultural position: as an important fragment of the classical inheritance, it itself produces prestige for its owners and, in a different but still important way, for its viewers and admirers. Hence the great influence which the Vase itself has had upon taste and design. Only a week or so after it had been bought by the Third Duke, he lent it to Josiah Wedgwood, who copied it in the firm's famous Jasperware and used it as the inspiration for many of the blue Jasperware designs, all of which reproduced the cameo effect. Throughout the nineteenth century, as it stood in the British Museum, it was constantly copied by artists and industrial designers. Even though at moments its power has waned, as during the

1920s and 1930s, its images are so integral a part of our mental stock that they constantly reassert themselves. When, in the early 1990s, the London underground station at Holborn, near the British Museum, was refurbished, images of fragments of the Vase were incorporated into its design.

The treatment of the Vase as a possessable object, which must always exist in time and space and therefore in a social relationship, is very revealing. It seems to have existed firstly as a piece of Imperial or state property about which a divinity clung, since it portrays divine beings which were intended to support the claim of the Imperial family to divine origins. It was then, some two centuries later, formally dedicated to the Otherworld as an appropriate object to accompany the Imperial dead. When it reappeared it went immediately into one of the most renowned collections of the age, that of Barberini, and thence through several collections scarcely less famous, particularly those of Hamilton and Portland. In 1810 it was transferred to what is arguably the world's greatest collection in arguably the most magnificent of museum buildings, and this at a moment when Britain – fresh from the victory at Trafalgar in 1805 gained by Nelson who knew the Hamiltons well and must have been familiar with the story of the Vase – was poised to exercise the Imperial power which the public collections helped to underpin. Through all its life, the sacred character of the Vase is clear. It belongs among the objects set beyond the world of commodities by virtue of its capacity to mediate the sacred meanings of value and history.

The Portland Vase remains in the British Museum. It will continue its sacred task of representing ourselves to ourselves as far forward as we can see. But it has one further dimension, not yet touched upon. It is an infinitely desirable object with, like some of the famous weapons or jewels, an 'unlucky' history, a character and a personality of its own. These are magical qualities, which lie beyond the immediate production of social practice and its deconstruction, although they may help to support them. Things seen in moon shadow appear otherwise than in the bright of day, but both are real; and it is to the shadow land of the human heart that we must now turn.

PART III

THE POETICS OF COLLECTING

CHAPTER NINE

COLLECTING OURSELVES

——— •◆• ———

Our subject being Poetry, I propose to speak not only of the art in general but also of its species and their respective capacities; of the structure of plot required for a good poem; of the number and nature of the constituent parts of a poem; and likewise of any other matters in the same line of inquiry.

Aristotle, *The Poetics* (Bywater 1920: 1)

Welcome to a secret world – a secret world that is usually hidden behind people's front doors and glimpsed only by friends and family, a secret world of extreme interest, humour, passion and even obsession.

(People's Show 1992)

INTRODUCTION

The crucial question which this Part tries to answer is, why do people collect? It is helpful to set this question within a framework, and remind ourselves of the working definition of a collection arrived at earlier (p. 23): that a collection is a group of objects, brought together with intention and sharing a common identity of some kind, which is regarded by its owner as, in some sense, special or set apart. The importance of collecting in the contemporary Western world, as in its past, is manifest: it has been calculated that one in three Americans collects something, and the figure is unlikely to be less for much of Europe (Belk 1988). We are clearly dealing with a social phenomenon of considerable significance, which it is important for us to understand. Individuals do not live in isolation; they are a part of society, and that society comes from its past, the past we have discussed in detail in the previous Part. But individuals also have particular ways of relating to their society and its past, in order to construct their own personalities and create Braudel's dimension of the short term. European individuals will have European hearts and minds, shaped by social and family practice and the mechanisms of inheritance, and will construct themselves and their relationships in European ways. Collecting objects is one of these ways, and a very important one. Understanding how this operates is the task of this Part of the book.

To approach it we have first to form a view of the relationship between the individual and the material world. This will lead us to a notion of how the role of individuals can be appreciated, and what kind of nature objects have. We then need to understand the poetics of the mutual relationship and how this leads to collecting. But not everybody collects, so we must ask ourselves why in a substantial minority of cases the universal pattern of relationship between individuals and things is diverted into deliberate accumulation. Finally, we will establish a framework for a discussion which will be pursued in the following chapters.

THE INDIVIDUAL AND THE MATERIAL WORLD: MIND IN MATTER

At the beginning of the first Part, we suggested that a useful model for understanding the collecting process was that which expressed the simplest Saussurian principles of semiotics to show us how the material culture available at any one time could be turned into collections through a double structuring process which drew on both the accumulated history of social practice and the make-up of the individual (Figure 1.7, p. 24). The nature of the social practice of collecting was considered in some detail in Part Two, and it is now time to turn to the second of the structuring axes. In order to come to grips with this we must form a view of the nature of the relationship between an individual human and the surrounding world, some of it immaterial in the obvious sense, some of it material in the physical sense, but all of it in European thought traditionally considered as objective in relation to the human subject. It is this notion of personal objectivity which needs a long, hard look.

Embedded in the European consciousness is the idea of duality, of 'this and that', of 'now and then', which, as we have seen, draws a large part of its strength from the oath/ordeal nature of European social practice and has had profound implications for our rational, classificatory and 'scientific' approach to life. Its implications for our view of ourselves have been equally profound, and both can be traced down a philosophical tradition which runs back through the Enlightenment to Descartes and Locke and, bypassing much theological elaboration, to Aristotle and to the part-philosophical, part-religious traditions on which he drew. Swinburne, describing a modified Aristotelian understanding of the criteria for the identity of substances, notes that this wider Aristotelian framework was taken for granted by Descartes, when he expressed a classic dualist position in passages like:

> Just because I know certainly that I exist, and that meanwhile I do not remark that any other thing necessarily pertains to my nature or essence, excepting that I am a thinking thing, I rightly conclude that

my essence consists solely in the fact that I am a thinking thing. And although possibly . . . I possess a body with which I am very intimately conjoined, yet because, on the one side, I have a clear and distinct idea of myself inasmuch as I am only a thinking and unextended thing, and as, on the other, I possess a distinct idea of body, inasmuch as it is only an extended and unthinking thing, it is certain that this I [that is to say, my soul by which I am what I am], is entirely and absolutely distinct from my body, and can exist without it.

(Swinburne 1984: 129, quoting Descartes, *Meditations*. Swinburne notes that the clause in square brackets occurs only in the French translation approved by Descartes)

The fundamental oppositions which structure this binary view of the individual and the surrounding world are set out in Figure 9.1. We can see

nature	: culture
proper	: improper
moral	: immoral
self	: other
soul	: body
mind	: matter
pure	: applied
subject	: object
creator	: created
sensible	: insensible/senseless
divine	: profane
player	: game
substance	: accident
active	: passive
immaterial	: material
thinker	: thing
worker	: field
eternal	: passing
time	: times
knowing	: known
unchanging	: changing
person	: non-person
divider	: divided
right	: left
male	: female

Figure 9.1 Oppositions which structure the European view of the individual and the world

that under the broad rubric of an antithesis between Nature and Culture, they fall into a number of groups each of which gives an account of the relationship between the self and a particular aspect of experience. The immaterial core of the individual, irreducible in both conceptual and material terms since it is beyond sight or touch, is the soul, and closely linked with this is the thinking mind; both are in opposition to grossly material body and matter. Mind is capable of knowing, matter of being known; mind is capable of creative thoughts and created things are the result; mind and soul are active while the world is passive. Mind is sensible, in both senses, while matter is insensible. Mind, in godlike utterance, creates reality by naming names and making boundaries. The soul shares in divinity and is therefore eternal and unchanging, in contrast to the fickleness of the profane world. This, the immensely flattering metaphysic of the business, is matched by a corresponding ethical appreciation. The soul is capable of good while the world is very evil, and from all this it follows that only minds and souls are proper persons in both the social and the legal sense, for in law material things, including animals and dead bodies, do not exist as principals and cannot be active in affairs.

The active self works within his field, organising and allotting, whether of real or of intellectual space; he, the divider, carves up the divided world into socially meaningful slices; he lives within Eternal Time, but creates allocated times within the world. He belongs with the right, the correct, the dextrous, the adroit, the legal and the legitimate, and, we may add, the conservative forces of stability and established values. The left is in opposition, sinister, gauche, cack-handed and clumsy: it is as unthinkable for God to be on the left as it is for him to be left-handed. The final pair in Figure 9.1 needs no comment: the gendering of the sexual and social metaphors which run up and down the columns speak for themselves, for women, like matter, are known.

We see that metaphysical, ethical, social, intellectual, and temporal and spatial, activity are set within an overarching image of active and passive within which the self describes, orders and uses a world of passive objects. This pervasive image is, of course, why in intellectual enquiry material culture was not deemed worthy of investigation in its own right until recent decades. Much the same could be said of collecting as an activity, and of the museum world of assembled material evidence. The same feeling crops up again in the academic and social convention which says that fine art or pure mathematics is somehow superior to applied commercial art or applied mathematics and technology. In the classic world, the self is the player; and, provided he plays within the established social rules which give substance to structure, the world is his game.

This ancient and sustaining vision has come to seem increasingly flawed as our century has progressed. It is obvious that an active–passive duality is a wholly inadequate way of describing our relationships with other people, for these relationships are governed by those reasons of the heart which reason knows not of, but which both the tradition of European fiction, especially in novels, and of psychoanalysis, have steadily revealed to us. In the same way, our relationship with society in the broader sense is a complex mixture of sensible immediate self-interest, self-denial in the interests of a more distant but still rational goal, and obscure self-promptings which have no intelligible motives in terms of classic duality.

The same is also true in the material world of production and acquisition. Classic economics, and related disciplines like marketing and consumer research, which have focused primarily on the acquisition of goods rather than upon their consumption and possession, work on the general assumption is that we seek to manipulate the world of goods in a rational fashion in order to satisfy human wants by using and extracting utilities from what we own. In the rationalist view, we purchase things in anticipation of the benefits they will provide and then use them in ways which bring the desired results (Belk 1991b: 18). So much is this the case that we might have added 'consumer' and 'consumed' to our list of opposed pairs. The rationality of possession is central to the belief that our way of living is logical and sensible. But, in fact, our relationship with our possessions is far from reasonable, and, broadly speaking, the more we cherish them, the more unreasonable it becomes. We consistently buy things which we do not want, purchase things which we cannot afford, use things in ways for which they were not intended, and hang on to things which other people think would be better thrown away. Sometimes, even frequently, the material which we chose to collect is worthless in the eyes of the world. It is, indeed, the disassociation between reason and acquisition which helps to account for the feelings of guilt and unhappiness which material goods often arouse in us, and in general for the emotions which flow between things and people, and which are not satisfactorily accounted for in terms of acceptable social practice.

To put the matter in a rather different way, a notion of duality leaves out of account the many filaments which must, in any way of thinking, link the two sides together. In terms of the kind of structural analysis developed by Lévi-Strauss and Edmund Leach, it is in the middle ground of ambiguity where emotions form, decisions are taken, and social attitudes are crystallised, the attitudes which then emerge as social practice on each side of the equation. The link between thinker and thing lies in the middle ground where the possibilities of things are understood, something which belongs as much with thingy-ness as with humanity, and potential shapes emerge. The link between male and female rests within the local tradition of appropriate sexuality; the link between divine and profane lies in the sacrifices which turn the one into the other; and so on down the list. What is needed is an integrating rather than a divisive framework of understanding, a theory of action which can comprehend, in both senses, both sides of the ancient duality in a way which matches our actual experience rather better. Such a framework is offered by George Herbert Meade and Sidney Shoemaker, and their ideas of social psychology and symbolic interactionism, but, as is usual among philosophers, these writers are still so in thrall to the world-view which they look to leave behind that they privilege language as the defining communication medium, at the expense of material culture, our other (in its broadest sense) great means of communication. Consequently, I shall describe their views through a material rather than a linguistic lens.

Shoemaker, among others, has developed a materialist view of personal identity, that identity which, as he says, can be viewed as an aspect of the mind: body pattern (Shoemaker and Swinburne 1984: 69). The core of his complex arguments can be expressed like this:

> an account of personal identity ought to make intelligible the knowledge we have of personal identity, including the special access each of us has, in memory, to his own identity, and it ought to make intelligible the special sort of importance personal identity has for us. It ought also to cohere with the rest of what we know about the world. In my view, this last requirement means that an account of personal identity ought to be compatible with a naturalistic, or materialistic, account of mind. To a large extent, the mind–body problem, including the problem of personal identity, arises because of considerations that create the appearance that no naturalistic account could be true; and I think that solving the problem has got to consist in large part in dispelling that appearance (while acknowledging and explaining the facts that give rise to it).
>
> (Shoemaker and Swinburne 1984: 71)

This is to say that, since we cannot show that mind and body are distinct, as the dualists would have it, and since there is no reason to suppose that they are not the same, then to think that they are the same is the best working hypothesis. At the level of empirical existence, admittedly a problematic guide in these matters, this notion of the identity of mental and bodily states fits how things seem to us: we are less sharp when we are tired, less good when we are hungry, and it seems likely that what is true at these humble levels is also true in broader ways. We are, therefore, faced with a working personality, with its notions of its own identity, its memory, and its thoughts and feelings which are inseparable from its bodily self, but which is also capable of 'seeing itself' do things, that is, of carrying on an internal dialogue between 'I' and 'me' which embraces intentions and judgements about success and failure. This complex self, in structuralist terms, might be said to exist only in the obscurity of the middle ground and to be, not in the steady state represented by either binary opposite, but always in the process of becoming.

What is true of the mind : body dimension, is apparently equally true of the others expressed in the duality range. It is the task of social psychology, so Hewitt tells us, to create a theory of action which is capable of examining the details of action and interaction in order to show how people are influenced by society and culture, but also to show how their everyday actions sustain and change these larger realities (Hewitt 1988: 7). For Hewitt this theory of action is best developed within the perspective identified as symbolic interactionism, which draws on the pragmatic approach developed by figures like Charles Peirce, William Jones, John Dewey and George Herbert Meade. Hewitt expresses the core of this approach as

> for pragmatists, life has a probing, testing quality. Truth is not an absolute, but exists relative to the needs and interests of the organism. An idea – for example, the idea that the sun rises in the east – is true if it leads to correct empirical predictions that make possible human actions that adjust people to the requirements and circumstances of their world. Questions of how members of a species know and interact with their environment are, for pragmatists, matters of great moment, not merely peripheral concerns. Knowing and acting, in the pragmatist view, are intimately linked: we act on the basis of our ideas about the world. The reality of the world is not merely something that is 'out there' waiting to be discovered by us, but is actively created as we act in and toward the world.
>
> Meade's theory attempts to account for the origins and development of human mind – or intelligence – by locating it within the process of evolution, by seeing mind and conduct as inescapably linked together, and by showing that the origins of human mind lie in human society. Meade felt that one had to explain the nature of the human organism by seeing it in the context of evolutionary development. Moreover, the mind had to be seen, he was convinced, not as a separate, disembodied entity, but as an integral aspect of the *behavior* of the species. In this, Mead sought to avoid the *dualism* of mind and body that had plagued philosophy, a dualism that led people to separate the physical organism from intelligence, and to imagine the latter as existing within some ethereal real of ideas. For him, mind, body, and conduct were inseparable aspects of a process of evolution that had produced a uniquely human life form.
>
> (Hewitt 1988: 7, 8)

Meade saw people as neither godlike souls nor as antlike behaviourist automata, but as individuals in whom valid inner experiences and real individual acts are part of more complex social activities involving other people, and so he achieved a style of explanation which could deal with both inner or personal experience and the social nature of human life.

The link between the two is what Meade called 'significant symbols', and by this he meant primary language which can describe inner experience and bring it into the social arena by making that description intelligible to others. In fact, of course, as subsequent investigation into the nature of symbols has shown (e.g. Hawkes 1977) not merely language, but all social communication systems like the disposition of time and space, and the human relationships of kinship, have symbolic value in broadly the same way. All of these aspects of life may be described as objects in the sense that they have an existence which is independent of that of any individual human and in this sense are external or objective in relation to him. Here we wish to concentrate upon material things, and so for linguistic culture we will substitute material culture. Material symbols, then, can bring private experience into the social world, and social experiences into the private world.

Material objects, like all other kinds of objects, are constantly created and recreated by human beings through their symbolic designation of them and their actions towards them. Human beings turn a world of blank matter and simple physical stimuli into a world of objects, because they act with purpose towards this world. Objects are therefore both created by human activity and are the goals of activity; it is the purposeful attention directed by the human actor which transforms inert matter, or indeed, other people's things, into objects in this sense, objects which have meaning for the individual concerned. Like language, therefore, objects are creative of reality and not merely reproductive. Just as we can agree to form new words or create new phrases with new shades of meaning, so we can create new objects or new sets of objects which convey novel meanings. This is how technology and the language of technology moves forward. It is also how new slang helps to shape new social perceptions, and new combinations of material things help to bring about new attitudes.

Once objects, material and otherwise, are seen as both constituted by acts and as goals of action, it becomes important to look at terms like 'motive' and 'purpose'. At both a social and individual level, actions typically look forward to an outcome which fulfils some need, even if the individual is only dimly aware of the nature of the need. Objects, therefore, represent a plan of action. Objects do not exist in a pre-established form; on the contrary, the perception of an object has within it the idea of a series of experiences which an individual might have, or might hope to have, if he carried out the plan of action the object represents. Objects, then, are not inert. They represent and remind us of the variety of experiences which we have or might have, and the motives and goals which seem to be open to us. Objects embody human purposes and experiences, and they invite us to act towards them in ways which may give us what we desire.

Society, we can say (Figure 9.2), consists in its history, in the trajectory through time which has produced the notion of a given community to

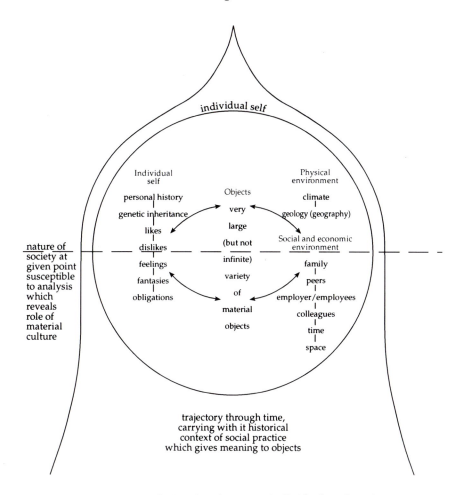

Figure 9.2 Relationship between individual and society

which individuals belong, and within which all its content, including its material culture, has symbolic meaning and value. It is this historical trajectory which gives us our notions of 'English' or 'black', and which gives to a video machine one kind of meaning and to a garden spade quite another. This society and its relationship to its things is analysable at any given point in time from a number of perspectives, which boil down to a functionalist view which sees all things as working because they contribute to social survival, and a semiotic view which explores the effective symbolic and mythological power with which social attributes are endowed (Pearce 1992: 166–91; see also Jackson 1991). These two analytical views are the two sides of the same penny, and together they shed much light on how societies and their material culture operate.

So far so good; but the important point is that what is true across the social scene at large is more or less true across the mind of each of its individuals. Each individual's mind is a microcosm of the wider whole; each self *understands* his social surroundings in much the same way as does his society as a whole (although some individual appreciations are subtler than others), although, of course, each person may *feel* all kinds of discordant things. Within the individual self is everything which we think adds up to individual identity, that is, a genetic inheritance, a personal history which lives in the memory, an economic and social situation, and a range of feelings, fantasies and obligations. Surrounding him is an environment, both physical and social, about which something perhaps can be done. The social environment consists of his family, his peer group, his colleagues and employers, and also of his personal time, that is, the span of his life, and his achievable personal space. An important part of this environment is the material culture which it holds, and which is privileged in Figure 9.2 because the relationship between the individual and the accumulation of things is the topic of this part of this book. As we have seen, the relationship between the individual and his material environment is a matter of complex intention and interaction, the outcome of which follows certain inherent tendencies but is, in the last analysis, unpredictable. We have, then, to ask how the role of individuals can be appreciated.

THE ROLE OF INDIVIDUALS

To come anywhere near a satisfactory view of the nature of human identity in relation to society is a tall order, but we shall be helped by a need to restrict what we say to those aspects which relate most nearly to the accumulation of things, and by drawing on notions which have already appeared among some of the fundamental attributes experienced in the dual scheme. The key image, the image which gives us the necessary range and flavour is that of the self as 'player', an appropriately ambivalent word in English which describes both an actor in a play and a participant in a game. At root, both are much the same. They set out a scheme in which each protagonist works through a developing situation in relation to a number of other players, within a recognised spatial arena and a specific lapse of time. The action takes place within agreed conventions – the rules of the game – which are intended to provide a sense of closure and hence of outcomes, to give a psychological framework for individual struggles, and to offer a group plan which, although in one sense limiting, also enables an action with significant form and content to take place. The action allows abundant scope for personal quirkiness and odd results, and for the interpretative appreciation of the audience, but the given structure means that this takes place within an understood framework. It also permits all levels of grandeur and commitment: cricket is recognisably cricket whether it is played at Old Trafford or in a street with a wicket chalked on the wall. At a different level, a play is still a play however introverted, reflexive or deliberately absurd its style may be.

The metaphor bears a little pursuit. Plays, of all kinds, are, across the world, a normal way for humans to construct themselves, but the play does seem to be at the heart of European culture in a specific sense. The Greek development of both theatre and athletic competition needs no labouring, but it is worth making the point that physical trials seem to have been an integral part of both the Celtic and the Germanic traditions (see Kinsella 1969), and that the notion of dialogue, of tension between competing characters, is at the heart of ancient Indo-European poetics (see Polomé 1982). Since then, it has been at the core of some of the most characteristic forms of European consciousness: Roman notables ran round the racetrack (*cursus*) of honours, and medieval academics disputed points of theology as a way of arriving at orthodoxy. Debate is at the heart of all democratic process, and the notion of the champion is closely allied to that of the actor and the representative. For English speakers, particularly, much of institutional life is cast in the form of a play or game, whether in the law courts, in Parliament, or in public debate, and our habitual use of language, from 'Parliamentary whips' to 'running for office', brings out its sporting and adversarial character. It is, indeed, arguable that the structure of Indo-European languages, with their verb and pronoun forms and the relationships which can be created between them, are integral to the culture of play as action, as is the European-wide tendency to exalt the statement and counter-statement of extended rhetoric as a cultural form. Finally, plays, whether of field or theatre, are very close to religious ritual. Historically, ritual is accepted as their point of origin, and as continuing to contribute the peculiar flavour of significance which hangs about them.

'Game' is itself an extended metaphor which operates across the dimensions of life. The rules of the game may provide the ground rules within which the drama is played out, but within them each of us will have his game plan and his notions of gamesmanship, and his own views about cheating. Adroit handling of the developing situation enables us to make a play for what is seen as fair game, and those who fail are likely to be made game of. Game is both the process of the play and the name we give to animals hunted down according to the rules; and if game animals are too well-hung, they become gamey, a liking for which we count as a perverted taste. Collectors habitually speak of themselves both as 'hunting for finds' and as 'playing with their things' (see also p. 183 and p. 178). We see that play is a transforming process whose power touches every aspect of ourselves, and in which the player, the chosen ground, and the materials of play are equally significant. Play ramifies across and through all the important aspects of our lives, and constructs them as we go forward. It is to the playing out of the game that the following pages will be devoted, but first we must look at the objects themselves.

THE NATURE OF OBJECTS

We have seen how people, far from existing in splendid isolation on the left-hand side of Figure 9.1, are actually drawn across into the right-hand side through the processes of interaction and intention. We might say that, in some ways, people turn out to be rather like objects; and now we must turn to the objects and see how they can behave more like people. This is complex, because, of course, the characters of physical objects can only come by endowment from human beings. But this is not how any given individual at a specific time and place experiences the world of material things. For him, things, or some of them, have a power of their own to which he responds. We need, therefore, to come to a view of the nature of objects, particularly as this affects them as collectable pieces.

The fundamental point about objects is that they, like ourselves, but unlike most other aspects of our social lives, have a physical, tangible reality. They take up space, which means that they can be physically organised within space; they can be seen and handled; they are highly possessable in an extremely direct fashion and this means that they are capable of simple accumulation and simple transfer as gifts, sales and bequests, although naturally the social and legal arrangements may be complex. An ownerless object is something of a contradiction in terms, and objects which happen to stray often find masters, even objects which have sunk pretty far down into the rubbish category.

Finally, because objects are physical, they live their lives, as do we, within a specific time span, although their span may be much longer than ours: there is a moment when they are new, a period, potentially a very long period indeed, when they are alive, and then, like us, a phase of deterioration, fast or slow, followed by dissolution. All of these aspects of materiality mean that objects exist in a mode quite different to that of much social process. They are with us and of us in a particularly intimate fashion which is approached otherwise only by close members of the family or particularly favoured pets. They are woven into the fabric of our lives, a common simile which, let it be noted, makes its point precisely by linking our lives with our material goods.

One particular aspect of object nature needs more elaboration because of its great significance, and this is the relationship of objects to time, and to past events. The material nature of objects means that they, and they alone, have the capacity to carry the past physically into the present. An object which was once part of a Roman kitchen or a Polynesian settlement or a 1930s cinema retains the reality of that historical involvement, even though it may also be the subject of many fresh interpretations and rein-terpretations. The object is, in colloquial speech, the 'real thing', it has sincerity, validity and authenticity. Of course the argument is, in a certain sense, circular. The perceived historical reality of any piece derives from intellectual notions of evidence and demonstration which are part and parcel of our conceptual mind-set, and therefore of our ideological frame-work, and as such are part of material politics; but for the present let us take perceived historical reality at its face value.

This historical reality is best explained by making use of a variant of the arguments already used to describe the nature of collections and expressed in Figure 1.7. In Figure 9.3, using the same fundamental semiotic notions of *langue* and *parole*, we can see how an original still from the film *Gone with the Wind*, displayed outside a local cinema when the film first went on general release, still retains its real relationship with that event, just as the style and content of the photograph retain their cultural relationship to the event. The still emerged into *parole* from material categories within the *langue* of its society, and was used appropriately. It then survived, materially, for fifty years or so to become part of the available material culture in the *langue* of the 1990s, when with contemporary *parole* it

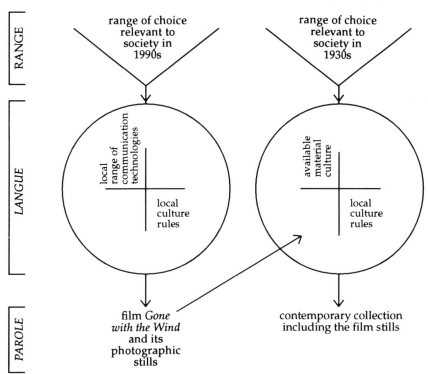

Figure 9.3 Objects as the 'real thing' and their relationship to history

was culturally reconstituted as a part of somebody's collection. The social values now placed upon it are different, or perhaps they have increased, but however the piece is viewed, it retains the historical reality with which it was born. This chameleon-like quality of objects – their ability to take on different cultural colours while retaining the same body – is an important part of that aspect of their character which defies explanation in ordinary 'rational' terms and for which we have to turn to words like 'magic', talisman' and 'spell'.

MUTUAL MAGIC: FALLING IN LOVE AGAIN

Objects can have about them a glow of significance, sending sparks of their own into the imagination of the beholder which kindles a desire for possession. Here we touch the notions of bewitchment, at the heart of which seems to lie the idea that, like all magic, objects can bring about a transformation. It is as if the frog images, which so many people collect, have the power to turn not themselves but their owners into princes through the inherent powers released by the transforming kiss. In part objects take their glow of desirability from exactly that inherent historical content which we have just discussed, for it is this accumulated meaning which gives an object much of its social value. Social value is a significant part of material politics, but for the moment let us accept that one of the things which may attract us to an object is the social value which it embodies.

But only one of the things: individual values are also extremely significant. We find ourselves attracted to objects for antisocial reasons, where the fascination lies in their worthlessness for other people, which matches the special qualities that only the owner can perceive in them. We are attracted to objects because they come with special, personal emotional attachments: a birthday present bought by a child for its mother may be hideous and valueless in itself, but this is neither here nor there. Frequently, we simply see something and want it, and we ourselves cannot explain how this happens, just as we are inexplicably attracted to other people.

These experiences, as so often, are simpler than their analysis, which is tortuous but of considerable interest, and here again basic semiotic ideas are helpful. We can see a social situation in which both people and objects exist (Figure 9.4). For each individual a particular range, or ranges, of things has the capacity to attract. As Fraser said long ago but with perennial insight (Fraser 1957), magic works by similarity, a mode which translates into modern semiotic terms as metaphor, and by contact, rendered (more or less) in modern semiotics as metonymy, that is, by a parallel but separate imaginary relationship and by an intrinsic or 'true' relationship. Effective magic is the conversion of the first into the second, and this objects

individual sees
hollow boxes

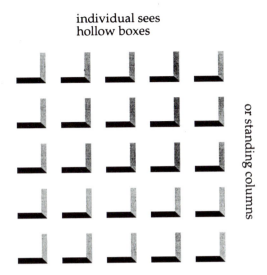

or standing columns

Figure 9.4 Individual relationship to the magic of objects as metaphor and metonymy

seem to be able to do. A metaphorical relationship exists between the desirer and the desired, where the desired object seems to embody emotional values which can be transferred to the desirer if the magic can be made to work, if metaphor can be converted into metonymy, and similarly into contact.

This happens when a meeting is made within the mysterious middle ground, and what we might call the kiss of possession takes place; when the desirer becomes owner, and the object with all its accompanying meanings belongs to him and becomes an intrinsic part of him. This is possible because, as we have seen, objects are pre-eminently ownable. It is effective because the emotional transference really has happened, and the owning individual has been transformed: we genuinely feel different if we have found something important to add to our collection. It is magic because it is essentially illusory: our capacity to experience changing emotional states which seem to us to be real, are only 'real' in the sense in which all our individual and social practices are 'real', that is, they exist as part of the social raft which, no matter how excellently or elegantly crafted, still floats rudderless on a sea of unknowing. The moment of magical transformation is at the emotional heart of the collecting process. It is the object of intention and the moment of triumph in the game. But, like a kiss, it is brief, and since we cannot prolong it, we look continually to repeat it; hence the limited satisfaction which one object can bring and the desire on the part of collectors to keep on adding to their collections.

COLLECTIVE LIVES

We all have objects around us, with which we interreact in the ways just described, but only, it seems, about a third of us interreact with these objects in ways which result in what we may agree to call a collection. Why is this? Why is it that many people choose this way of defining themselves and constructing their identities, but the majority do not? Are collectors born or do they have collections thrust upon them? Are there such things as active and passive collectors?

Occasionally (Baekeland 1988), it seems that people undergoing psychological analysis have been advised to take up collecting in the same way as they might be encouraged to develop any interest 'which takes one out of oneself' (as if anything could). The collecting literature, however, is conspicuous for the number of stories told by people who believe that their collecting was the result of an accident, usually seen as serendipity. Olmsted asked the owner of a used marine-supply store if he was a collector:

> If you had asked that two months ago, I would have answered no, I am a dealer. When I buy for the shop I often buy knives. When I get a real nice one I throw it in a drawer in my bedroom dresser. One night my wife asked me when I would bring those knives to the store. I said there was only a few, I probably wouldn't bother. She said 'I counted them last night. There are 75 pocket knives in that drawer.' They still aren't in the shop, so I guess I am a collector now.
>
> (Olmsted 1988: 3)

Typically, a woman suddenly realises that the old clothes at the back of the wardrobe constitute an important group of Mary Quant dresses, or a man is given one 'adult toy' racing car as a birthday present and goes on from there. This, however, leave us only on the edge of the question. The *content* of the collection may well be the result of such happy accidents, but since such events happen to us all and do not make all of us into collectors, we are left wondering if a predisposition to collect is an essential feature of the collector.

A number of researchers have suggested that the motivation to be in control underlies possessive behaviour. Furby (1978) found this to be true in a large survey of American and Israeli citizens, and Csikszentmihalyi and Rochberg-Halton (1981) in their survey of Chicago residents concluded that people feel one major function of possessions is to manipulate the environment. These broad findings have been borne out by the recent study carried out by Beggan at the University of Louisville, Kentucky (1991). It may follow, then, that collectors are possessed of a particular form of that motivation, or that motivation in a particular degree, which leads them to construct a special private world which they can control directly in a wide range of ways. And it is true, even granted all the idiosyncrasies of compulsive behaviour, that we can control the disposition of our collections in ways in which we can control little else.

Attention to a collection is matched, as we ought to expect, by suffering caused by its loss. Such possessions are part of self, and therefore, their loss is felt as a loss or lessening of self. Belk interviewed flood victims in the summer of 1986 and quotes from his field notes:

> The losses that concerned (the flood victim) most were those of his record collection . . . a first edition book collection . . . the tools that his father – the cabinet maker – had used . . . the ceiling and paneling of the basements that he had installed with the help and advice of his father, and (upstairs), the hutch, lowboy and stereo cabinet that his father had made.
>
> (Belk 1988: 142)

The same feelings, but with additional anger and agony, often described as violation, are reportedly experienced by those who have lost collections as a result of theft (Van den Bogaard and Wiegman 1991). As James put it in 1890:

> although it is true that a part of our depression at the loss of possessions is due to our feeling that we must now go without certain goods that we expected the possessions to bring in their train, yet in every case there remains, over and above this, a sense of the shrinkage of our personality, a partial conversion of ourselves to nothingness, which is a psychological phenomenon by itself.
>
> (James 1890: 293)

And from a different perspective this is echoed by Simmel: 'material property is, so to speak of the ego, and any interference with our property is, for this reason, felt to be a violation of the person' (Simmel 1950: 322).

This brings us as close as we are likely to get to an understanding of what makes a collector. A combination of circumstance, accident and particular traits of personality means that for some people the qualities and possibilities which objects carry are particularly significant. Collecting people have the capacity to bring their emotions and imaginations to bear on the world of objects, and are able to nourish these qualities by objects. Consoling and compensatory collections may be, but they achieve their effect through the active imagination working with and through the material world.

CONCLUSION: POETIC LICENCES

It becomes clear that for collectors collections are, in Belk's memorable phrase, 'the extended self' (1988). We feel about our collections as if they were part of our physical selves, and we identify with them: loss of

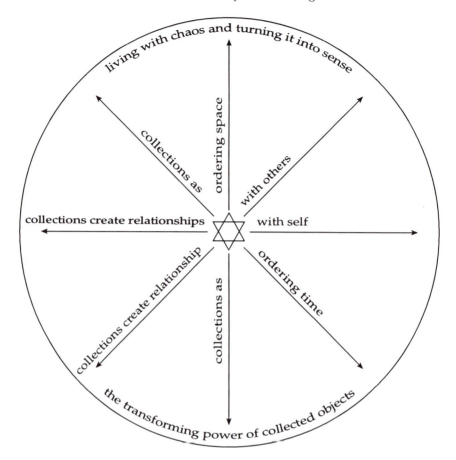

Figure 9.5 The private world of collections as the extended self

collections brings the same grief and the same sense of deprivation which accompanies other bereavements. Collections can be used to construct a world which is closer to things as we would like them to be, and the colloquial use of 'things' in a phrase such as this is revealing. We can use them as a material dialogue between 'I' and 'me', and so create a way of working out an intentional inscription on the world.

We have tried to delineate the middle ground between people and objects, an area within which the processes of interaction and intentionality are acted out. This interaction has a cluster of facets all of which revolve around the kinds of opportunities which objects can carry. The plot can be set out as in Figure 9.5, in which the central star represents the individual and the circle both his own enclosed and private world, and the social ground with which he interacts. Collected objects are possessed of a kind of freedom, a poetic licence, which gives them transforming power across this world. They can help to construct the relationships between 'I' and 'me' which create individual identity, between the individual and others, and between the individual and the finite world of time and space. Each of these facets needs separate consideration.

CHAPTER TEN

CONTROLLING COLLECTING

——— •◆• ———

The collector is by definition a man of possessive instincts; but the possessive instinct in his case is inseparable from a love of risk, or battle: he has to conquer the object he wants to own; hostility, rivalry and sharp practice only whet his appetite and rouse his fighting instincts. He stops short of no means, no ruse, trick or manoeuvre to get what he wants, and he no sooner has it than he forgets all the trials it has cost him as he sets out in pursuit of his next prize.

The Great Collectors (Cabonne 1963: viii)

INTRODUCTION: GETTING THINGS TOGETHER

We can control our collections as we can few other matters in this world, subject although this control is to the obsessive impulses discussed in the previous section, and the ground of this control rests in our ability to select or discard items for inclusion in our collections, and then to manipulate those which we choose as we wish. This throws up a range of arenas within which collecting offers the exercise of power, and we shall look at the most important of these in turn. All, however, depend upon a tradition of indi vidual self-assertion which views its surrounding social and material scene with a calculating eye.

THE GAME OF THE NAME

The Robert Opie Collection began in 1963 when Robert was 16 years old and had just purchased a pack of Macintosh's Munchies: 'It suddenly dawned on me, while consuming the Munchies, that when I threw the Munchies pack away, I would be throwing away a small fragment of history' (Opie 1988: 6). From that point he began to collect the packaging and advertising material which relates to the last century or so of con- sumerism, particularly of food consumption. In 1976 an exhibition of a small part of his collection at the Victoria and Albert Museum entitled *The Pack Age* aroused a great deal of interest, and eventually a museum to house all 250,000 items was opened in a Victorian warehouse at Gloucester Docks (Figure 10.1).

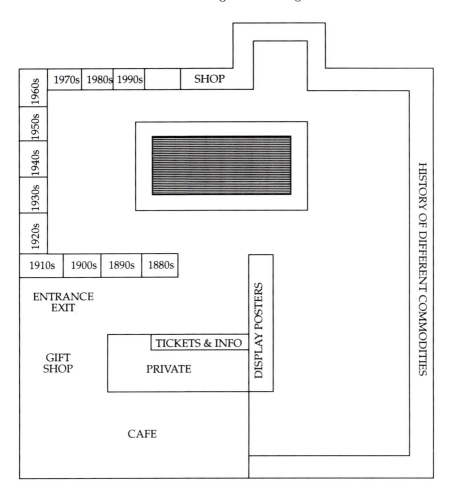

Figure 10.1 Plan of the exhibition of the Robert Opie Collection, Gloucester Docks

The Opie Collection, huge although it is, is clearly a selection from all the consumer-oriented printed material which has existed since roughly the 1880s. In this sense, the original mass represents the metonymic whole from which Opie selected his collection, and to which, therefore his collection bears a metaphoric relationship. But this is a little simplistic. The packaging and advertising material itself bears a metaphorical (in most cases, very metaphorical) relationship to the actual products which it was created to promote. More fundamentally, the sense that the original products, and so their advertising material, belong together in any organic or intrinsic way is itself pure imagination of a corporate or social kind, resting upon nothing more secure than shared personal habits which we dignify and

179

METAPHORICAL RELATIONSHIPS

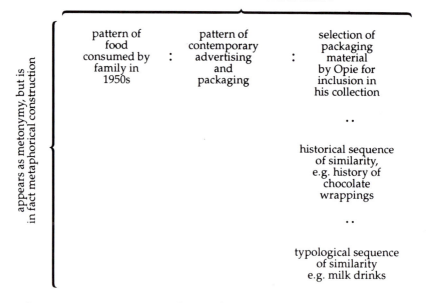

Figure 10.2 Metonymic and metaphorical relations displayed in the Opie Collection

solidify by describing as accumulated and inherited social practice (Figure 10.2).

Let us consider, for example, the food and its related advertising material consumed by an ordinary lower-middle-class southern English family in the 1950s. Much of the food came to retail shops made up in quantities suitable for small families of roughly two adults and two children, and this is reflected in both the packages and the advertising. The main daily meal consisted of a meat or meat-and-pastry dish, together with potatoes and a second vegetable, the classic 'meat and two veg', followed by a sweet usually made with a combination of fatty or dairy products, sugar, cereal, and fruit or jam, for this is the time when rice belonged safely under the skin of a milk pudding. The daily pattern would be broken on Saturdays when a less formal meal – kippers or black puddings – might be taken while the football results came out over the radio, and on Sunday, when the roast joint was ritually consumed, and its pathetic remains saved to be served cold on Monday and as shepherd's pie on Tuesday. The underlying pattern of work and leisure, gender roles, family life, and broadly Victorian values of respectability, stability and frugality need no labouring. Contemporary advertising on hoarding and packets reinforce these images as advertising always does, and, as the Opie Collection amply demonstrates to us, acting not as a passive but as an active social component.

To a child of the period (in both senses) these things seem as set as the stars in their courses, but in truth they are a result of where and when you happen to be standing. The pattern of foodstuffs and other commodities is only a metonymy in the eye of the beholders; in reality, they are as metaphorically free-floating as anything else and come together in an apparently intrinsic relationship because this is how we wish to see them. They are an inscription on the world, making patterns which exist only in our corporate imaginations, and the collections which we make from them through the act of selection are equally inscriptions in their own right, creating their own realities, their own metonymies, in their turn. This is why collecting is a more powerful activity than might at first appear. It is not merely a reflection of the material world, translated through the imagination of the collector; it is an active intervention into a social reality which is merely one construct among potential others. Consequently, collecting is a dynamic process in which the collector struggles to impose himself and to control outcomes. Collections make a difference. The Opie Collection is of great interest in a number of respects, but not least in this – that it has sharpened the vision and altered the view we take of our own childhoods.

In order to achieve imaginative constructions of material which stand some chance of keeping us within the pale of the 'normal' we require some generally understood overarching metaphors to act as mental and emotional scaffolding. This is much less simple than might seem at first sight because the whole process through which metaphors are generated is culturally determined. Crucial to an understanding of the process is some purchase on the way in which meaning is generated through the giving of names, since the naming of material in the world generally, and the renaming of it as it joins a collection, is fundamental to our construction of relative meanings and values. In Opie's collection there is much material relating to 'hot non-alcoholic bedtime drinks', an obvious social construction of the mealtime kind we have just been considering. But within this group, Opie, and everybody else, make a distinction between cocoa tins and malted-milk tins, which is a distinction of a quite different kind. In another kind of collection, we might talk about mammals which move about at night, and then draw a different sort of distinction between 'fox' and 'badger', a difference which is just as social as that between night and day, but arises from a different kind of mental activity.

Collecting (among many other activities) depends upon the ascription of names and categories to the collected material. At a very simple level, people do not take into their collections things to which they cannot give a name; if they have such a thing and it intrigues them, they keep it separate (at least mentally) from the rest until more information is forthcoming. The giving of a 'proper' (in both senses) name to an object is an important element in selection, possession and the dominance and control which underlies these activities. The issue of name semantics has had a very troubled history up to and including the impact made by Chomsky in the postwar period. To this Frege (see Searle 1983: 244) contributed the notion, important to this argument, that names are non-descriptive referents that have sense (or senses) only contingently, as a result of culturally prescribed conditioning and of contextualisation which conveys a particularised intentionality, and as a result act as a means of assigning positions within a system.

This is fairly straightforward when it is put concretely: 'fox' is the name of the particular animal because we agree that it is, and as such it will occupy its assigned place in a natural-history collection of British mammals. But how do we understand 'flying fox' which reuses the word to describe, in part, a very different kind of Australian animal, or the mechanical device for moving gravel which puts oddly shaped buckets, known as flying foxes, on to a high wire? How do we understand how humans can be called 'foxy'? And yet we can imagine a collection created on the basis of 'foxiness'. Similarly, but by a process with historical depth, we originally bought tins of malted milk manufactured by Mr Horlick; then we bought tins first of Horlick's, then of Horlicks (note the gradual dropping of the possessive apostrophe) still made by the original firm; now we speak of buying tins of horlicks at Waitrose or Asda, although we know very well that this will not be the brand name on the tin: the proceeds of all this shopping can be observed at work in collections like Robert Opie's. Clearly for each name we have a potentially ramifying but interrelated range of associations, which makes what Markey calls 'the identification of the modabilities of contingency' (1985: 179).

At the heart of this is the notion that 'likeness' – whether of form through some correspondence of appearance (the 'foxy' man has a sharp, ginger face 'like' a fox's and therefore shares in its cunning), or of content (Horlicks malt drink and Asda's malt drink are virtually indistinguishable) – can be used to generate long metaphorical strings of similarity and comparison. It is this capacity which enables us to exercise the particular form of imaginative control which allows us to act with intention, in the Serlean or Meade sense, and so to see amorphous undifferentiated material though a contrasting-and-comparing eye which shows us how things do or do not come together in self-evidently 'sensible' groups and categories. 'Sensible' is, of course, a loaded word, since a view of what is sensible is a cultural response. What we are describing here is what Europeans, with their oath/ordeal mind-set, assume to be sense. Naming and categorising works quite differently within a holistic world-view, particularly that which takes what we call a totem-oriented view in which 'like' does not exist because everything truly is 'the same' as everything else and metaphorical speculation is inhibited.

The dividing lines which make differentiation, or to put it another way, the overarching metaphors which we commonly employ to make distinctions, are then those which seem to arise from the natural world itself, but which in fact are implicit in the metaphorical cast of mind. They include the notion that genuine 'likeness' can run sequentially backwards, giving us the chronological or historical metaphor and hence the collected history of milk-drink packaging; and the notion that there is a special relationship or identity between owner and owned (or collector and collected) which can (and very often does) take the form of anthropomorphising material culture to the point where it is really treated as if it were human, like the brown mugs with human smiles on their faces which were for a time given away with Ovaltine. Overarching metaphors include the idea that things of comparable colour, size, shape or design go together, like all the foxes, and the idea of the perceiving eye which sees an internal logic of the taxonomic or typological kind as a basis for separating foxes and badgers. Figure 10.2 sets out the metaphorical relationships which our minds make available to us in a world where all assemblages are necessarily essentially metaphoric.

The collector plays with metaphors, and makes his choice among them when he comes to structure his collection. Opie has chosen a broadly sequential metaphor based on the assumption that packaging is one obvious and integrated group in our social structure, with a history which bears its own relationship to the broader history of our times. The largest section in the display of the collection takes the metaphorical choices further by chronicling the history of each commodity and its packaging, so that all the cocoa things are together, all the tea packets, cereal boxes and so on. Objects are here organised according to their type of product, one way among several in which their arrangement might be approached. Opie, like every other collector, has made an intentional inscription on the world by choosing and rejecting amongst the overarching metaphors which structure social and individual life in our culture, and has added his own creative gamesmanship to our understanding.

HUNTING FOR MATERIAL – PRIZE POSSESSIONS

'Hunting for material to add to the collection' is a characteristic expression which collectors use about themselves and others use about them. 'Hunting for material' legitimises a great deal of brooding and wandering activity, sealed by the capture of finds to add to those already secured. Hunting must be one of humankind's oldest (although perhaps not among our very oldest) activities, and the prestige which to this day clings about blood sports, for food or pleasure, washes over into collecting practices when collecting is described in these terms. Hunting is, to collectors, a helpful analogy, promoting ideas of cunning, stealth, patience, prowess, competition and ultimate success with the acquisition carried home in triumph, all of which support the collector's self-image and his social standing. Hunting is very close to quest, an image which, with its stress on individual prowess and the overcoming of ordeals, runs particularly deep in the European psyche, and for many collectors a successful acquisition is indeed the Grail Achieved.

Notions like 'hunt' and 'quest', and ideas of collections as prey or trophy, bring before us the play of dominance and control which collecting involves, painted in the brightest colours. Collectors like Joseph Whitaker (1912), whose collection is now in Mansfield Museum, straddle the two real worlds of hunting and collecting and point up the image particularly clearly. Whitaker was born in 1850, the son of a large Northamptonshire landowner, and lived at Rainworth Lodge, where he kept his collection and established a bird sanctuary. Whitaker seems to have felt no tension between his conservationist efforts and his shooting. In 1906 he was a member of a party which shot 1,500 partridges, and in 1909 his party shot some 1,200 rabbits in one day. Most of his collection specimens were acquired by shooting and then prepared by a local taxidermist.

Whitaker's collecting style, and the very obvious trophy character of his material, can be analysed by employing the broad style which Edmund Leach used to describe hunting psychology and its role in creating correct relationships between man and the outside world. We must remember that this kind of trophy-hunting is pure ritual, functioning not as part of the food quest but only as an assertion of respective roles (Figure 10.3). We see that the action can be boiled down to a set of opposed pairs, from which can be inferred the underlying reality and purpose of the action. We understand that, for Whitaker and all who collected like him or viewed his collection, it is the 'naturally' inferior quality of the natural world which the stuffed blackbird in its case makes manifest. It is obvious how the same analysis of a British regimental collection makes clear the relationship between the regiment and the rest (see p. 321), or how sporting cups and medals demonstrate dominance over competitors and rivals. But what is obviously true for such collections is, in fact, true for all collections, all of which manifest the same effort directed towards achieving the satisfaction of control. Figure 10.4 shows how this works by analysing in the same style an apparently harmless collection of Roman coins. Collecting is not only an inscription on the world; it is also an imposition on the world.

COLLECTIONS AS OPENING AND CLOSURE

The twin ideas of selection by imaginative metaphor and dominance through active choice, both of which encapsulate notions of achievement through struggle, come together concretely in the way we encourage our

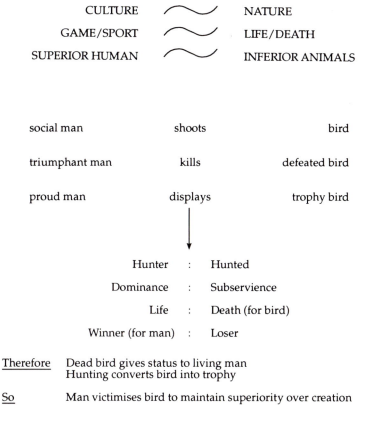

CULTURE 〰 NATURE
GAME/SPORT 〰 LIFE/DEATH
SUPERIOR HUMAN 〰 INFERIOR ANIMALS

social man   shoots   bird

triumphant man   kills   defeated bird

proud man   displays   trophy bird

↓

Hunter   :   Hunted

Dominance   :   Subservience

Life   :   Death (for bird)

Winner (for man)   :   Loser

Therefore   Dead bird gives status to living man
            Hunting converts bird into trophy

So   Man victimises bird to maintain superiority over creation

Figure 10.3 Analysis of the significance of animal trophies (drawing on Leach 1977)

collections to be open and closed, and in the chosen strategies which make this possible. With this are bound up ideas about what constitutes the 'end' or the 'completion' of a collection, and what constitutes 'perfection' or 'perfect' examples within the chosen range. There is an inherent tension in this, which many collectors have remarked upon. There may be a desire to complete a collection, whatever this may mean to the individual collector, but there is also a fear of doing so, because once this has happened the collector's occupation has gone. Hence come frequently heard remarks like, 'My collecting will go on and on – I can't ever see it finishing' and 'I don't know what I'd do without collecting, so I expect I'll just carry on'. Hence, also, comes the meandering nature of many collections as they appear to the outsider, and the clear tendency, once a collector has to admit that a particular line has come to its natural term, to start immediately upon another.

CULTURE ⌇ PAST

GAME/SPORT ⌇ VICTORY/DEFEAT

present collector	seeks	Roman coins as past
successful collector	acquires	past as Roman coins
dominant collector	tames	past as named Roman coins
proud collector	displays	past as exhibited Roman coins

↓

Collector	:	Collected
Dominance	:	Subservience
Present	:	Past
Exhibited now	:	'Then' displayed

Therefore   Collected past gives status to living collector
Collecting turns past into tamed present

So   Exhibitionist displays collection to maintain dominance over past

Figure 10.4   Collection of Roman coins analysed as victory trophy

As a result of their study of Israeli collectors, Danet and Katriel (1989) have tabulated five strategies which allow the collector to pursue completion, and backed these up with five examples to demonstrate what they mean (Figure 10.5). As we have just seen, the notion of discrimination, of 'this and that' through which a series or a set can be defined and then subcategories with the set distinguished, is central to collecting both intellectually and emotionally. When this is intentionally directed towards particular groups of actual material, then a collection is formed within the applied parameters. The collector has the fun of deciding which broad area, defined through these processes, he will collect within, and then of how he will define the subsections. This comes across as an intention to 'specialise', a very significant aspect of the collecting mentality. The liberty to take these decisions is experienced as very important. The Brick Collector expressed it succinctly:

> Oh and I've got some tiles, a lot of brick companies made tiles too so it seems natural, but I don't collect decorative ones, they're

Strategies to Pursue Closure/Completion/Perfection

	Strategy	Example
1.	Completing a series or set Acquiring all of something Assembling exemplars of sub-categories Putting together items that 'go together'	Completing a series of stamps Acquiring all editions ever published of a book Collecting examples of pipes made by different manufacturers Furnishing a room with country furniture
2.	Filling a space	Filling a wall with a displayed collection of plates
3.	Creating a visually pleasing, harmonious display	Attending to the composition created by a display of plates
4.	Manipulating the scale of objects Collecting very small objects Collecting very large objects	 Collecting miniatures, e.g. doll's house furniture Collecting vintage cars
5.	Aspiring to perfect objects Acquiring items in mint condition Restoring items to mint condition Acquiring aesthetically perfect objects Improving the physical quality of items Improving the aesthetic quality of items	 Acquiring a mint condition vintage car Restoring a vintage car Acquiring an exquisite painting Replacing a rusted stamp with one in better physical condition Trading a painting for one of superior aesthetic quality

Figure 10.5 Strategies to pursue closure, completion and perfection in collecting (after Danet and Katriel 1989: Table 1)

too dear and there's already a heavy collecting scene there. And I've got a granite set. That's totally cheating but I fancied it because you could see how it'd been worked and it is my collection.

(Austin 1993)

It is the collector who decides upon the rules of the game, and allows himself whatever licence he feels like.

Filling a space in an agreeable fashion which is visually harmonious and emotionally pleasing is an important piece of material self-construction. So is aspiring to perfection, usually perceived as inherent in a 'good' example, one which displays clearly all the principal characteristics singled out as important to the creation of description and difference, and in a piece which is clear and undamaged. Aesthetic perfection, and the self-realisation through which aesthetic notions are formed in the first place, is important here. This can operate in obvious ways, like the development of taste in water-colour paintings. Less obviously, it can be viewed subjectively by a collector who sees his collection as complementing his developing notions of quality and 'correctness'.

A characteristic expression of the urge to manipulate the world through collecting is the decision to concentrate either upon miniature things or upon huge things. In the nature of the case giganticism in collecting looms less large as a result of the practical difficulties it entails, but probably material like the various collections of locomotives which exist around the world come into this category. The collecting of miniatures, in the sense of things represented by much smaller copies of themselves, is very much more common. A typical collection is that formed by Angela Kellie of Strathpeffer in northern Scotland, whose assemblage of dolls forms the basis of the Museum of the Social History of Childhood which opened in Ross and Cromarty in 1992. By the time the material was donated to the new museum, it included over 300 dolls, baby clothes, books and toys, but the original dolls came to Angela from her mother and grandmother. Angela seems to have treated the dolls like real children, giving them names and talking to them, itself an interestingly anthropomorphic side-light on collecting, and something we might have anticipated where dolls are concerned. The collection is clearly a manipulation of scale, the attempt to create a world in miniature in which the collector has ultimate control.

COLLECTION PROPER AND IMPROPER

The relationship of each of us with the rest of our world is not a simple matter, because each of us is possessed of a complex personality, and is able to promote, resist or change the colour of relationships in more ways than the obvious and overt ones of prestige and power. To put it another way, collecting is an activity eminently capable of giving flow of expression to these aspects of ourselves which we have already listed under 'left': the aspects of subversion, illegitimacy, deliberate gaucheness, deviance and sinister wisdom. 'Proper' and 'improper' are, of course linked with notions of possession and its lack, so we may expect that improper collections have less of the world's regard attached to them in the financial sense, and this is, generally speaking, true. What they do frequently engage is that most subversive of all human activities, humour, in all its mocking, ironic or sick moods, and with these are linked fine shades of evasion, disillusion and disenchantment. In games, we must not forget, it is possible to bend the rules, and this kind of creative tension has its own importance.

In a sense all of this kind of collecting is an act of subversion, in that the theme which runs through it is the intention to overturn the world of accepted material values, not just of monetary values although this element is not absent, but also the values of quality, fidelity to evidence, purity and normality in which the social world is grounded. The accepted order is subverted when very ordinary, everyday things, things which are worthless by 'accepted' moral or aesthetic standards, are collected with the same obsessive care which others would lavish upon 'acceptable' material. A huge amount of contemporary popular collecting is directed towards material which hovers on the edge of this broad category. Here belong the glass animals, the tobacco tins, the oilcans, and the old spectacle frames, and, indeed, discussions with many of these collectors do show the tongue in the cheek, the lurking sense of deliberate and prideful difference which is clearly one important part of the collector's self-image. Usually, though, this is linked with a sincere obsession, and a hope that the world will be converted to the collector's view of the value of his material.

An insight into the mind-set of such a collector is given by the Brick Collector (Austin 1993). The Brick Collector collects ordinary building bricks, and has them stacked around her house. She explained:

> I'd done some architecture at college; studies of church buildings and peasant housing. It just made me look at how things were put together and think about the time and work it takes to build a house. It's not just the actual construction, it's finding clay, mining it, refining it, grinding it and then making it into bricks. I grew up in a farmhouse that'd been knocked about for years. I could spot changes in the bricks: colour, shape, size, texture and that sort of thing. It was easier to try and work out the house's history by looking at it than by ploughing through papers and legal stuff. Then I did some voluntary work which meant I had to learn about bricks and making them. I hated it to start with, I couldn't get my head round how different chemicals and firing temperatures made bricks look a certain colour. But once I could tell one brick from another I felt like I was getting somewhere. I hated industrial history but now I could see it wasn't about nuts and bolts, it was about people. Bricks began to have lives of their own if you like.
>
> (Austin 1993)

This provides a 'respectable' rationale for the collection by relating it to normal historical pursuits. But the Brick Collector is well aware of the social values bricks carry. When it was suggested to her that bricks don't impart knowledge or prestige, the following conversation ensued:

BRICK COLLECTOR: Yeah, but they do. People think here's a person who's into something really boring. What are you doing here? You've come because you think collecting bricks is weird; so I must be weird or there must be something unusual about me. It's not like train spotting, you don't see loads of people out looking for bricks. It's like bricks look really boring, they all look the same if you don't look really hard. They don't move or make noises, they don't even catch your eye. I can look at a brick and give it a sort of life.

AUSTIN: If you don't mind me saying, that sounds a little sad. You make it sound like you think of bricks as friends.

BRICK COLLECTOR: I suppose so. It's not that I don't have friends or anything. I'm not lonely but sometimes I want something that's special to me. I'm too scared to talk to people who know about bricks in case they make me feel stupid or small; like I don't know enough and shouldn't be allowed to collect bricks. I talk to my boyfriend about them, he's getting quite good at spotting bricks I'd like and now he goes out on brick raids for me if I'm busy. But at the end of the day the bricks are mine and he knows that. I do get emotional about them, I know. If people want to get at me they threaten to get an angle grinder out. It's just not funny, if people can cry about smashing their car up, why can't I worry about bricks?

AUSTIN: So you think bricks are as beautiful as say, a Porsche?

BRICK COLLECTOR: Not beautiful, but they are attractive in that they're solid and strong. They endure a lot, they glow. I don't think Porsches are beautiful anyway. It's no more stupid to find bricks attractive than to find lumps of painted metal sexy.

(Austin 1993)

The emotional sincerity of the collecting came out loud and clear when the Brick Collector talked about her feelings for her collection:

At family parties people always talk about jobs and how your family is. I don't really have either yet but at least now they remember me as the one who collects bricks. I have an identity, a character, I'm not floating in some sort of social limbo. Yes, I'm insecure, isn't everyone in some ways? Finding a brick can turn my mood around: if I'm angry or stressed out it distracts me; if I'm sad it cheers me up; if I'm feeling small it makes me feel better about myself. With my collection I'm strong, interesting, motivated and most of all safe. My bricks are inside me, they are something no one can ever take away from me. I can walk down a street of Victorian terraces and feel so excited I think I'm going to burst. No one can take that enjoyment away from me. It's free, it's harmless, it's mine.

(Austin 1993)

The genuine potential importance of the material emerged in a further reply:

Without [bricks] there'd be no great nineteenth century cities and a lot of people'd be without homes. It's a bit like eggs, most people know they come from birds but they don't know how. If eggs stopped people'd wonder what they'd eat with their soldiers. If bricks stopped, people'd be stuck for new houses. Brick makers have tremendous power.

(Austin 1993)

These kinds of experiences have been recorded by many collectors, and seem to be characteristic of a part-jokey, part-serious way of thinking and acting. The joke acts partly as a defence of the collector's obsession in the face of a dubious world, and partly as a way of undermining what is seen as stuffiness of that world.

Collectors themselves sometimes perpetrate deliberate jokes on those who might come to appreciate their collections. Charles Waterton, born in 1782 to a substantial Yorkshire Catholic family, became a collector of natural species in British Guyana, where his family had sugar interests. He established his collection at his home, Walton Hall, where it followed well-established forms: preserved animal specimens and material culture of the Guyana Indians, together with purchased specimens of European oil-paintings. Waterton opposed the practice of slavery and allowed free access to the Walton Hall collection to the general public: so far, so good. But there was another side. Using his considerable skill as a taxidermist, Waterton created strange and grotesque creatures as a form of satire. One, called 'John Bull and the National Debt' was created from a porcupine with a tortoise shell weighed down by the national debt represented by six reptiles got up as devils. Another, more notoriously, was 'The Nondescript' in the form of a bearded man but made from the hindquarters of a howler monkey. Waterton may have meant this as a joke, but he used it as an illustration in one of his books, and allowed stories to circulate about its capture (Blackburn 1989). This freakishness can be interpreted as the reply of a Catholic gentleman to a society which rejected him, but the gesture was made as much at his own expense as anybody else's, because it damaged his reputation as a serious scientist.

The same kind of feelings come into play where fakes and forgeries are involved, although here the malice aforethought is much clearer, and is usually directed against the collectors, who are seen as dupes and victims, tricked by their own complaisant arrogance and, when the plot is revealed, made to look very foolish. You can be badly bitten by deliberate fakers, we say, treating them as mad dogs spreading disease into the healthy population. 'Proper' collections may become contaminated in unknown and ramifying ways which upset markets and damage reputations. The outside world usually watches this with unholy glee, and this is why important forgers rank with murderers and mystery men in the popular press, and are always good for a reworking if sensational copy is running low. Readers are delighted to see experts and collectors revealed to be as fallible as the rest of us and to see the values represented by the experts rendered as flawed as most readers had always hoped them to be. We might say that if the 'unacceptable' collectors make honest, if sometimes mocking, efforts to subvert, fakers and forgers are the dishonest side of subversion, at one with the smiling faces of poisoners with whom they often share column space.

The 1990 *Fake? The Art of Deception* exhibition at the British Museum brought together a revealing world of forgeries. A husband-and-wife team working in Devon were responsible for porcelain pieces such as that which imitates a rare figure of the 'Girl in a Swing' group, made at an unknown factory in London in the mid-eighteenth century, whose pieces are much sought after by collectors. The makers of these recent fakes were never prosecuted, following the normal reluctance to take to court all varieties of blackmailer. In 1980 two inmates of Fetherstone Prison, Wolverhampton, successfully knocked up 'Bernard Leach' pottery during prison classes. Their pieces carried Leach's impressed seal mark and monogram, and were sold as genuine by Sotheby's Belgravia and Christies, among others. Eventually, the forgeries were recognised and the men successfully prosecuted: the pieces remain in the Metropolitan Police Museum (Jones 1990: 243). We are offered the perennially popular picture of the humble country couple or the likeable rogues cocking a snook at important people, and even the most committed of us cannot resist a sly smile.

If various kinds of illegitimacy show up in the 'unacceptable' collections and the forgeries, another appears in what may be called the collections of intentional gaucheries. Here, it is our notions of what is pure which are transgressed, for these are the collections of old false teeth, historic lavatory paper, lavatory seats and the like. The People's Show Project 1990 brought to light a Walsall collector who specialised in aircraft sick bags, and subsequent national media coverage revealed at least half a dozen more people who also collect them. It seems likely that this kind of collection is a distinct subset in the collecting range. The peculiar resonance of these accumulations hinges on the fact that they deliberately bring out, and bring together, material expressions of those aspects of life which we regard as acceptable in ourselves but disgusting in everybody else, other than lovers or children who may be regarded as extensions of ourselves. These aspects group into a cluster, all the members of which have in common the notion of what goes into and out of the human body (Douglas 1966), particularly what comes out of it. Bodily excreta can be summarised as in Figure 10.6.

We rationalise our disgust at this sort of material by treating it in medical terms, so that ancient desires to avoid contamination and impurity become a matter of personal hygiene and the avoidance of infection, so that, for once, the ritual process and modern science do indeed seem to hang together. But, as Douglas notes (1966: 160) an important criterion for disgust at others' intimate possessions is the possession's ability to convey the identity of their original owner. Rubbish, she suggests, is not disgusting unless it is disturbed to reveal the wrappings, bits of food and

Tangible products

nail/hair clippings

spittle, snot

blood, including menstrual blood

remnants of childbirth, e.g. cauls

semen/vaginal secretion

urine

faeces

perspiration

vomit

partly chewed food/food left on plate

<u>and</u> the stains of all these

Sensory products

smells from flatus, bad breath, body odour

body heat, e.g. on lavatory seats

Figure 10.6 Bodily excreta

hair combings that it contains. Personal identity adds greatly to the emotional force of such material, and this is why the collectors of lavatory paper, for example, are always anxious to know which important building the sample comes from, and who might have had access to the roll.

The anthropological literature abounds in examples of approaches to these tangible and sensory products as the focus of ritual importance, from the black drinks which caused deliberate vomiting among the north American Indians, to the purges beloved of traditional European medicine. Association with excreta can be used to make a political point. A number of collections of contemporary Irish material include relics of the 'dirty protests' made by prisoners who smeared their cells with faeces. Original punk gear included bin-liner trousers, and more:

The style alluded to sado-masochism, porn, sleaze and tawdry glamour and inscribed itself by means of shaven or partially shaven heads and a sort of anti-make-up (reddened eyes, black lips, make-up painted in streaks across the face or in a pattern) on the surface of the body. Punks created an alienated space between self and appearance by means of these attacks on their own bodies; this was truly fit wear for the urban dispossessed, constructed out of the refuse of the material world; rusty razor blades, tin cans, safety pins, dustbin bags and even used tampons.

(Wilson and Taylor 1989: 196)

One wonders how often these ritual vestments were worn in their full glory.

The degree of disgust and shame which this material arouses shows how significant it is to us, and what powerful feelings collections made within the area can tap into. Such collections, and the area of activity they relate to, exist in the middle ground where blood and sweat mingle with intense human activity to produce new outcomes. They are a part, sometimes a humble, sometimes a very important, part of the transformation of one human state to another. Like all such material, they carry risks, chiefly the risk of symbolic contamination, and these we dissolve in gusts of deliberate merriment. When a collector of lavatory seats, flushed with success, adds a new model to his collection, we and he know that its public reception will follow a well-trodden social and ritual path.

COLLECTIONS DEVIANT AND SINISTER

As we have already seen (p. 4), there is a powerful tradition, both literary and psychological and now of some antiquity, which considered that the process of collecting is abnormal, and that all collectors are necessarily deviants, with flawed personalities whose neuroses power their collecting urge, so that they turn from people to things, an immoral act in the classical view of our proper relationship with the material world (see Figure 9.1). Unquestionably, this notion has coloured both earlier research into collecting, and earlier ways in which collectors have, therefore, viewed themselves. Modern approaches to the study of collecting, as we have seen, reject this as too limited and partial a view of what should be seen in the broader frame of our relationship with the material world as a whole. Once this has been said, however, we are left with those areas of collecting around which cling uncomfortable feelings, areas we are likely to use words like 'perverted' or 'deviant' to describe.

One such area surrounds the collecting of material from the German Third Reich. Harris, whose researches into the forged Hitler diaries took him into this world, says

It has been estimated that there are 50,000 collectors of Nazi memorabilia throughout the world, of whom most are Americans, involved in a business which is said to have an annual turnover of $50 million.

In the United States a monthly newsletter, *Der Gauleiter*, published from Mount Ida in Arkansas, keeps 5,000 serious connoisseurs and dealers informed of the latest trade shows and auctions. Prices increase by 20 per cent a year. 'In the States,' according to Charles Hamilton, 'the collectors of Hitler memorabilia are 40 per cent Jewish, 50 per cent old soldiers like me and 10 per cent of them are young, fascinated by people like Rudel.' In Los Angeles, a collector enjoys himself in private by donning Ribbentrop's overcoat. In Kansas City, a local government official serves drinks from Hitler's punch bowl. In Chicago, a family doctor has installed a reinforced concrete vault beneath his house where he keeps a collection of Nazi weapons, including Hermann Goering's ceremonial, jewel-encrusted hunting dagger. In Arizona, a used-car salesman drives his family around in the 1938 Mercedes which Hitler presented to Eva Braun; it cost him $150,000 to buy and he expects to sell it for $350,000.

(Harris 1986: 183–4)

Clearly, the Nazi era was of great importance in the history of Europe and therefore the accumulation and study of its material culture is as important as that of any other era. When we reflect that much the same actual material – the jackets, the insignia, the proclamations – might be part of the collection in one of the Jewish museums, we can see that intentionality, in Meade's sense becomes the crucial issue, however clouded by individual obscurities intentions may be in any actual collector's case. A Jewish collection is likely to hold such material as historical evidence of events which happened in the 1940s, in order to assert a moral conviction about the fundamentals of good and evil, and their implications for the future. A Nazi memorabilia collector is unlikely to concern himself with moral issues at all, in any other than a lip-serving way. For him, the issue appears as one not of ethics but of personal identity; his relationship to his material is that of worshipper to relic, who hopes that his possession will bring about the magical transformation of himself into something closer to his hero. Hence the peculiar reverence such collections arouse; hence, also, the desire to drive in the cars and, above all, to wear the uniforms. We have to conclude that most of those who collect Nazi material now would have actually been Nazis then. Ethics and identity come together, because the collector (blind to the significantly appalling bad taste of Nazi material culture) sees glamour in evil and wishes to identify with it through its relics.

CONCLUSION

The argument here suggests that collecting is an important way in which we can assert our impulses towards dominance and control. Practical restraints aside, the choice of collecting area, and of selection within that area belongs with the collector alone, who is king of what he surveys. The idea of naming and classifying is itself an exercise of power, and so are notions of what constitutes beginnings and ends.

The power inherent in collecting practice can be turned to mocking and subversive ends. 'Unacceptable' collectors, among other things, are making important assertions about the 'ordinary' material world and our relationship to it, which we ignore to our detriment. Collectors of lavatory paper and the like similarly remind us of our vile bodies, and do so within a very broadly based human tradition, which treats this disgusting material with a deep and sacramental seriousness and so shows how profoundly it can resonate in our emotional lives.

At the further end in the scale of attempted dominance are the Nazi fantasies which the collectors of this kind of material act out. What this tells us about collecting is that it shares its nature with every other human activity. It is not uniquely deviant in itself, but will call to deviant impulses where these exist. The reality of the material has, as we have seen, its own power, which derives from its ability to comprehend similar deviant impulses in the past and carry them into the present, there to reinforce similar feelings among that proportion of people who always seem to harbour them. Much the same is true of collections of erotic art, especially that which is sado-masochistic in character, and the even sadder little accumulations which surface in the technical literature from time to time. This brings us to the engendering capacity of European collecting, which is the subject of the next chapter.

CHAPTER ELEVEN

ENGENDERING COLLECTIONS

—— •◆• ——

'What', Utz's mother asked the family physician, 'is this mania of
Kasper's for porcelain?'
'A perversion,' he answered. 'Same as any other.'

Utz (Chatwin 1988: 20)

But once, at least, Giulio had done an oil painting in the same
manner. It was known as 'Nanna and Pippa', and had been very
celebrated in its time. Several detailed descriptions of it were extant.
Long ago, however, it had disappeared, and historians were inclined
to suppose that, after agreeably adorning for many years one of
the more private apartments of an art-loving cardinal, it had
been destroyed by a succeeding cardinal during a fit of religious
morbidity.

A Family Affair (Innes 1972: 36)

INTRODUCTION: CATALOGUE SONGS

Given that the act of collecting enables individuals to create themselves, it
follows that the whole of this creative process, in which both individuals
and objects are both active and passive, will be shot through with
emotions about sexuality and gender, since these are most significant,
perhaps the most significant, defining attributes. We know that this is an
all-embracing topic, and, whether because we ourselves live in a time
of change, or (as seems more likely) because human sexuality is always of
absorbing interest to humans, no aspect of any subject pricks up our interest more. In terms of the gendering of collected material the kinds of
questions to which we would like answers are: who collects most, men or
women? What and how do men and women collect? And how does this
relate to social practice, or to put it more simply, how does it affect how
people see each other and themselves? We may soon begin to wonder if
the received answer to these questions, that collecting life is structured
around a simple male : female polarisation, is itself based on superficial
notions of gender. We must endeavour to go below these simplicities.

FOOD FOR THOUGHT

It is generally accepted, at any rate in anthropological circles, that sex has to do with human reproduction and is a biological process common to all members of the human species, while gender has to do with human practice and is therefore a social construct, in which we would expect to find wide differences across time and space. Allowing for a good many glosses, and accepting that psychology has revealed to us swathes of feeling and action which occupy the middle ground where biological reproductive activity is affected by social practice and vice versa, this seems to be broadly true. Since notions of gender and the relationship of this to collecting practice will feed off each other, and since, as is argued in this book, self-definition by collected material is a characteristic European practice, and European custom will also include its own notions of what constitutes gender, it follows that we must first gain some purchase on what these European notions are. They are best appreciated by thinking about one paradigmatic social situation, one cluster of interactions as dense and rich as a plum pudding (as Henry James is reported to have said), which, although open to the objection that it is limited in time and place, and social class, nevertheless crystallises social action and so resonates far beyond itself, offering a chance to catch the elusive breath of human relationships. The late-Victorian dinner party offers such a chance.

Here we have a quintessentially European ritual, transacted by the middle and upper ruling classes of the continent which, at the time, ruled much of the world. The men and women sit down to eat together, a fairly unusual thing in human culture generally, alternating one by one around the table, with husbands and wives carefully separated. The table is oblong, and at either end, facing each other, sit the master and mistress of the house, the host and hostess. No children are present, and one's first appearance at a formal evening dinner marked an important moment of passage. The men all wear their black and white uniforms, and show the very minimum of exposed flesh. The women, especially the young ones, are décolleté, exposing shoulders, neck and bosom; a nice calculation for the glimpse of a nipple would be a major solecism. The young, unmarried women are likely to wear paler colours and softer silks or gauzes while older women, whether married or not, will have stronger colours and heavier brocades.

The same food and wine is available to all, but while the men will eat and drink everything, and heavily, and the older women will, like men, drink red wine and partake of strongly flavoured dishes like game, the younger women will put on a pretty flutter of preferring white meat and lighter drink. Women who are not 'respectable', that is, whose extramarital sexual habits have caused them to be disowned by families and husbands, will be excluded from the gathering. So will unrespectable men, but for them this relates to acts of cowardice or cheating. The women will have been taken down to dinner, each with a cavalier who will pull back her chair when she sits and who, with her other neighbour, will continue to be attentive throughout the meal. When the final eating course is over, the lady of the house will gather the women with her eye and a man will hold the door open for them as they walk out together, to sit in the drawing room, perhaps relieved, perhaps dull and bored, until the men come in from their port and cigars and from what is presumed to be conversation of a serious and substantial nature. Meanwhile, everybody has had a chance to go to the lavatory, without manifesting this need to the opposite sex.

Images of gender emerge from this social web, many of them peculiarly European in tone, which suggests that gendering is an infinitely more complex affair than most discussion about collecting suggests. Apart from one brief interlude, the men and women are together all the time, talking and eating. The clothes which the younger women wear appeal to the male preference (whether biological or cultural is unclear) for visual sexual stimulation, but the women themselves are unavailable, the unmarried ones without honourable matrimony, the married ones without, at the very least, considerable time and trouble, throwing the men back on the excluded women and the huge prostitute population of Victorian Europe. In terms of human cultural dynamics in general, it is strange that women, particularly young women, should be both closely visible and unattainable, especially in sexually charged situations which allow them to wear silk, fur, perfume and jewels in the late evening.

We touch here a significant aspect of characteristic European kinship, marriage and property arrangements which, once they had united around 1150 to create the notion of romantic love that linked the unattainable woman to an erotic satisfaction in possession endlessly deferred, naturally produces the split images of woman as whore and virgin with which we are so familiar. The virgin may, in fact, be a married woman with her own child in her arms, as one of the central icons of Christendom suggests, and in this condition, together with her unmarried sisters, she will be treated with the erotic deference which the formal good manners of the dinner party reflect. But the serious conversation through which the business of life is arranged happens when she is not there. Mentally, she is reduced to a little girl from whom full adulthood will be withheld. Throughout, the general idea of look but not touch is central to the situation, and generates a great deal of emotional tension, in which, as we shall see, collections play their part.

Living in parallel with this multiple image of young (or youngish) femininity as virgin-mother, whore and girl, we have the hostess at her end of the table, and her equivalents elsewhere in the room. The substantial woman, married or widowed, perhaps with property of her own, running her own household, although excluded from the public institutions of the world, is, and perhaps always has been, a typical character in the culture.

She is associated with nurturing and loving qualities, being a woman of experience as well as substance, and the combination of these things gives her a quality of adult womanhood to which society accords respect, symbolised by darker colours and stronger food.

The overt male image which matches all this is much simpler, although the inner reality, of course, is equally complex. The men, broadly speaking, treat each other all alike except for a certain social leadership accorded to the host. Just as social custom works to provide a many-faceted gender image for women, so it works in exactly the opposite way to produce a single image for men, for male solidarity is one of the linchpins of social life, and it is reflected in the food and the conversation in which all the men present partake, and in the identical evening dress which covers them all.

Our dinner party then, granted its temporal and social limitations, gives us a cast of gender characters which run back into the distant past and forward into the future (Figure 11.1). Social life comes from the interplay between them, and in their capacity to change from one to another, modifying, perhaps, each other's character as they go. Brokering and negotiation is implicit in the situation. Human gender relationships are in a constant state of fluctuation as they are played out, and there is a sense, too, in which human relationships in this sense are a European invention, just as the fiction which explores them is a characteristically European art form. As much of this fiction shows, gender patterning can be destructive because individual temperaments do not fit into prescribed forms. We may expect that collecting will be a passive and an active strand in the pattern,

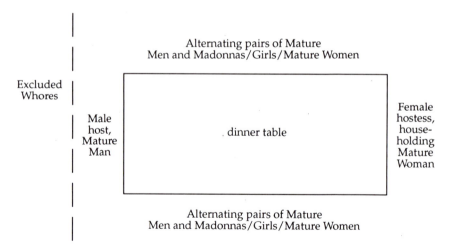

Figure 11.1 Cast of gender characters represented by a traditional European dinner party

and that this will operate in terms both of the content and the style through which the collection is formed.

We will consider first women and then men. Women, as we have seen, are faced with self-images which present them as whores, madonnas, little girls or house-holding adults. The accumulated evidence suggests that women gather collected material in ways which support these roles, with the exception of the second. Women do not seem to collect to sustain the image of themselves as unattainable madonnas, presumably because such an image has little appeal. Sometimes, though, the same woman's vision of herself may embrace more roles than one, just as the entertainer Madonna deliberately chooses to confuse several sexual identities.

COLLECTING ON THE GAME

The whore image can be subtly and satisfactorily smoothed to that of vamp or temptress, and this seems to be the animating story which informs many women's collections, like those of 1930s clothes, cosmetics and Hollywood material. Two of the women collectors presented in the Walsall People's Show 1992, interestingly two of the youngest, collect Marilyn Monroe material. Leanne Edwards commented 'I like Marilyn Monroe because her acting was brill. Every weekend I look around the shops for anything I haven't got.' 'My Mom's friends think that it is unusual for such a young girl to be interested in a star of the forties/fifties' (Edwards 1992). Rachel Baker said 'It's very important as it has taken some time to collect and she is an inspiration to me to want to act in films . . . My friends do not really see why I like her though – they think it's a bit weird to like such an old movie star.' (Baker 1992). There is a clear element of self-identification with the admired star, and with the kind of universal seduction symbol which she was.

Collectors of 1930s clothes frequently seem to dress up in their material, and to create a satisfactory *mise-en-scène*, with cosmetics, music and dim lighting, usually in the privacy of their own bedrooms. The strain of wishful thinking is obvious, but the interesting point is the theme it takes, identification through material goods with a decade dominated by female entertainment stars like Josephine Baker or Marlene Dietrich, whose dresses cut on the bias emphasised what they concealed, but about whose allure hung the scent of ambivalence, as powerful as the great perfumes of the period, *Je Reviens* and *Chanel Numero Cinq*. The most compelling personal image of the decade, adult emotions in the warm darkness of the cinema, can be translated by collecting into the contemporary woman, playing with dialogues, interesting to men and women, self-loving, self-absorbed.

Often, among women, this kind of collecting takes the form of a passion for jewellery, where it may be linked with less introspective ideas about the history of design and use. Anne Hull Grundy is characteristic of many. She was born in Nuremberg, but her family moved to England in the early 1930s. All her family collected and her father's company produced Corgi Toys, themselves material which figure in a good many collecting histories. By her mid-teens Anne declared herself 'fanatical' about jewellery (Griggs 1981). She concentrated upon eighteenth-, nineteenth- and early- twentieth-century jewellery, which was often inexpensive when she started to collect in the 1940s and 1950s but which leapt in value as Victorian material became fashionable.

By the 1970s Anne had succumbed to a limb-wasting disease, and from her bed despatched parcels of jewellery as donations to museums, including the British Museum, Kenwood, Northampton and Abbot Hall, Kendal. As the graph in Figure 11.2 shows, parcels of material arrived regularly, sometimes from Anne, sometimes from other museums to whom material

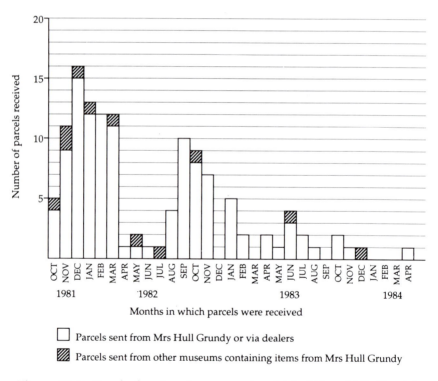

Figure 11.2 Graph showing the pattern in which Abbot Hall, Kendal, received donations of jewellery from Anne Hull Grundy (after information from Janet Dugdale and the Lake District Art Gallery and Museum Trust)

had also been sent, and sometimes direct from the dealers with whom Anne dealt (Tait and Sere 1978). In her collecting life Anne managed to achieve a very characteristically feminine unity of interest in the female body, and its enhancement and adornment through ornaments, an interest which gained poignancy as her own health failed. She linked this with an equally characteristic need for generosity through a dispersal of her material which, through the particular way in which it was done, achieved a close and continuing relationship with the receiving curators.

Close cousin to much of this female collecting interest in bodily adornment comes collecting which, certainly within the older analysis of collecting, would be called 'fetishistic' in the sense that this term is (or was) used by sexologists to describe a state of mind in which the use of a non-genital object is a necessary part of the sex act or as the exclusive sexual goal (Freud 1927; Sargent 1988). It has been suggested that fetishism, in this sense, is more of a continuum ranging from a slight preference for the fetish object (which we all probably share), to a strong preference, to needing the object for sexual activity, to complete substitution of the fetish object for a living sex partner (Gebhard 1969). Characteristic materials in fetish collections are objects of leather and items of female clothing. Received wisdom says that women (as opposed to men) seldom have this kind of relationship to objects, since they are the objectified rather than the objectifying (Ellen 1988; Belk 1991a, 1991b), and in terms of direct sexual action this may be true, although a good deal hangs on how 'fetish objects' are defined: nobody is likely to attach the phrase to, say, a particular set of duvet cover and pillowcases, although this kind of thing seems to be sexually important to many women. We strike here the softer-edged feeling women seem to have about much of their relationship to the material world, an ability to invest objects with feeling without separating them in name and thought from the flow of things, a mental attitude which is indeed the antithesis of the sexologists' fetish-making, and which we shall come upon again.

This interesting line of thought notwithstanding, it is clear that women do sometimes make collections of clothing which are lingerie rather than 'underwear', and which are not simply intended for ordinary use: these seem to be the contemporary material equivalents of the 1930s vamp material and reflect similar preoccupations. Sometimes collections come to light which, if collected by men, would instantly attract the fetish label. Karen Hendry of Glasgow joins film star Sharon Stone and *femme du monde* Imelda Marcos in her passion for buying shoes. Karen Hendry is aged thirty, did a degree in psychology, and has more than a hundred pairs of shoes:

Karen has shoes crammed into every corner of her tiny west London flat. She opens cupboard doors and pulls yet another pair from its depths. All her shoes are very precious to her, no matter how old or battered. Ms Hendry is particularly proud of her Forties brown suede Ferragamo shoes, bought for £17. Being a size 3, she finds lots of old shoes that fit her perfectly. Her most recent acquisitions include not one, but two pairs of Gucci clogs, and a pair of original Seventies mules from a market.

(Blanchard 1993)

And Blanchard adds, 'Even with her huge collection laid before her, she mutters something about really needing to buy some more.'

Karen is not alone. Janine Ulfane, an actress who lives in Los Angeles, has at least one hundred pairs of shoes made by Johnny Moke. According to Blanchard:

> Ms Ulfane does not like to be described as either a fetishist (too seedy) or a collector (too grand), but as an accumulator: 'I never throw anything away,' she says. 'I have shoes I bought years ago, which are now scruffy and holey, but I can't part with them. They become old friends.' One of the problems of owning more than 50 pairs of shoes is finding enough room to store them. Janine Ulfane has the perfect solution – two homes. She keeps her shoes stacked in their original boxes and has inherited a cupboard in LA with built-in shoe racks so they can be on display.

Blanchard tells us that Karen Silverstein, a public-relations officer and owner of at least sixty pairs of shoes, does not object to being called a fetishist, saying simply, 'I'm obsessed with shoes.'

Shoes have always had strong metaphorical powers separate from, or complementary to, their sexual significance: hence their appearance in folklore like the Old Woman who Lived in the Shoe, Puss in Boots, Seven League Boots and their modern equivalents like *The Wizard of Oz* and *The Red Shoes*. Hence also their appearance in phrases like 'stepping into somebody's shoes' where the shoes themselves clearly hold the essence of the new position and authority, and hence also the many traditional practices in which shoes are concealed in buildings, the European version of a widespread need to make material depositions of this kind, which has been carefully documented by Swann for the shoe collection in Northampton Museum (Swann 1969). Women, it seems, are relatively comfortable with the notion of themselves as obsessives, and probably the important point which separates women collectors of this kind from men is that women collect *women's* shoes, or underwear, or other clothing, not men's; even the further reaches of psychological literature do not seem to throw up cases of women who collect men's shoes obsessively, even though they may wear men's clothes.

OF MICE AND MEN

From female collecting which has a specifically sexual construction, let us turn to a type of feminine accumulation for which the point is that overt sexuality is absent from it: this is the kind of collecting which supports the role of woman as little girl, and is linked with qualities like innocence, trust and a certain kind of charm. Belk quotes the telling example of the Mouse Collector, whose collection has been established as a museum known as Mouse Cottage by the collector's wealthy husband. The brochure for Mouse Cottage invites the visitor to

> Enter the Mouse Cottage and you'll squeak with delight! Once upon a time, in the early 1920s, there was a little girl so clever and charming in character and petite in stature that her mother quite naturally called her 'mouse'. The childhood name inspired the little girl's imagination with a life long passion for collecting mice of every description.

> (Belk and Wallendorf 1992: 5)

The collection consists of mice replicas displayed amongst pseudo-antique golden oak household furniture in a home-like setting. There is a mouse doll's house with a miniature Christmas tree, and another Christmas tree with mice ornaments and presents wrapped in paper printed with mice. The display is cluttered, almost chaotic, and casual. Both the display tone and the emphasis on Christmas, pre-eminently a family festival for which women make elaborate preparations of food, home decoration and gifts all of which are largely consumed by men and children, can be seen to stress feminine subservience and mindless triviality.

A vast range of feminine collections belong within this general mode. Here come the collectors of pottery animals, like the Walsall Frog Collector, dolls (treated in some moods) and 'typical feminine' objects like miniature thimbles. A good deal of female bonding is part of this kind of collecting, because it often involves commercially available gift ware, which can easily be bought for presents; but, of course, the clear female tendency to gather such material is why the gifts are available in the first place. There is also a tendency to treat the material as if it were human. This is clear in Mouse Cottage, and it is made explicit in statements like that by Eileen Webb, who is a china cat collector: 'My collection is very important – I would miss them sitting in their various poses, some happy, some sad' (People's Show 1992). The Box Collector in the same show said 'I use parts of my collection daily so I will miss it even when its away at the [Walsall] Art Gallery.' She added also, 'My collection grew from being given a special box as a child. I do not add to the collection any more as it is rather large, but people still give me boxes and I do rescue others', which makes a clear link between childlike collecting and childhood itself.

FEMININE ENDINGS

A great deal of feminine collecting unites around the warm maternal images that cluster about the persona of mature wife and mother. We can approach this best by looking at an interior, like that painted by Edouard Vuillard in 1910 (Plate 8), coincidentally in roughly the same period as our dinner party (see p. 198) although Vuillard's scene would stand today with only superficial changes, supposing that one was lucky enough to inherit the mantelpiece and fireplace. It is, immediately, a woman's room. In such rooms the women come and go, reading, sewing, talking by the fire. In such rooms are made the friendships of winter afternoons, confidential, intimate, sustaining but not signalled by public formality. On the mantelpiece and along the tops of the bookcases are a mixture of pictures and ornaments, apparently carelessly disposed. Without them the room would be quite different and, most of us would feel, much the poorer, but does the assemblage count as a collection or is it merely a random accumulation of assorted objects?

Plate 8 Oil on canvas, interior showing lady with dog, painted by Edouard Vuillard in 1910. The painting shows Marguerite Chapin in the sitting room at 44, Avenue à Jena, Paris. (photo: Fitzwilliam Museum, Cambridge)

This question is at the root of why there are seen to have been relatively few 'major' women collectors with 'important' material, why women collectors have been seen to be very many fewer than men whatever the character of the collection, and why their collections do not emerge into the same sharp-edged sunlight of public recognition and esteem. Traditional wisdom takes a predictable view by assuming that women who do collect in the grand manner do so because they are more 'masculine':

> grand scale collecting almost always calls for aggressive and material ambition to a degree uncharacteristic of women, aside from women's historic economic position. Those who came within hailing distance of collecting giants were women who seemed to exhibit the masculine strain of a highly developed competitiveness, although this in no way detracts from the position of women as amateurs.
>
> (Rigby and Rigby 1944: 326–7)

This kind of argument simply begs many questions without offering answers. The first point to establish is that, during the last century and a half or so, the number of women collectors has probably not been lower than men. Surveys of contemporary collecting make it clear that today at least as many women collect as men, possibly slightly more. Research at the Victoria and Albert Museum is revealing nineteenth- and early-twentieth-century collecting circles, particularly of china and similar material, in which women played a prominent part, both numerically and in terms of influence. The same story seems to emerge wherever it is looked for. The number of nineteenth-century women known to have collected natural-history material grows as records are searched.

What is true is that women collectors are relatively absent from formal collecting records, especially museum acquisitions and the corresponding museum registers. Part of the aesthetic movement of the 1870s and 1880s was a craze for blue and white china, often, as we might anticipate, expected to be largely a woman's passion. Important cities had shops which catered for this taste: in Liverpool, Bunneys, on the corner of Church Street and Whitechapel, had an Oriental Emporium which sold such wares, and several pieces in the National Museums on Merseyside collections still carry its labels (Liverpool Museums 1971). But most of the collections themselves seem to have disappeared, and all that they would have told us about contemporary collecting habits in relation to social life has disappeared with them.

What we have had, and still have, is a largely domestic history of women's collecting, in which collected material mixes, as in the Vuillard painting, with other kinds of goods, and the whole forms a unity to which no dividing or specifying self-consciousness is attached. A mass of contemporary accumulated material belongs here. Eggcups kept in the kitchen, flower paintings hanging in the hall, lace bobbins displayed on framed squares of velvet, cups and saucers on the window-sill, willow-pattern plates on the dresser: the women themselves could not tell you whether or not these are collections. The Leicester Collecting Project (1993–4) produced a number of replies from women who said that the questionnaire itself had prompted them to think of their objects as a 'collection' for the first time.

Clearly, these women's domestic collections support notions of personal identity and are as much extensions of the self as are the collections made by men. What they are not is closely defined, separated off from normal living, and embodying a vision or a philosophy which is itself distinct. The women who accumulate them are, therefore, seen as mere consumers of objects, acquiring pieces through the sheer joy of shopping, and intending them either for themselves or for women very like themselves. Men, on the other hand, are serious and creative, acquiring in relation to an anticipated rationale. What this is saying is that we tend to define our idea of what a collection is in terms of men's collecting practices, a tendency, of course, not confined to this aspect of our social life. But such definitions are not merely limited, but also fatally flawed: a proper account of collecting in the European tradition must be capable of self-reflexive understanding of why we think as we do.

Recent studies on gender and work on moral development (Beckett 1986; Gilligan 1982) stress that women's descriptions of themselves are embedded in their connections to others and are presented in a 'relational mode of discourse,' and this is borne out in how they seem to view their collecting. Dittmar's study (1991) of the meanings men and women in Britain attach to their possessions underlines the thrust of this argument. She was interested in discovering how on the one hand men and women, and on the other hand those from different economic and social situations, regard the significance of material goods. The eighty-six participants all from Brighton, England, were invited to list their five most treasured possessions. This information was then coded against the table of systematised reasons why possessions are important (Figure 11.3) and the results cast in the form of a bar chart (Figure 11.4).

Business women proved to place the highest value of objects which linked to their personal history, while business men and unemployed women felt much the same about objects from their own past. Both kinds of women were markedly less interested than men in use-relationships, and both felt much the same about intrinsic value. Business women were least interested in instrumental value, a view presumably reflecting their relatively different circumstances, but both expressed positive value for relational and emotional qualities, and also for self-expressive qualities, although considerably less emphatically. On the whole, Dittmar's work broadly bears out the view that women have a similar relationship to material regardless of social position, so that ideas about gender are more influential than economic circumstances, and that this relationship stresses

A. Qualities 'Intrinsic' to Object
    (1) durability, reliability, quality
    (2) economy
    (3) monetary value
    (4) uniqueness, rarity
    (5) aesthetics

B. Instrumentality
    (1) general utility of object
    (2) enables specific activity associated with object

C. (Other) Use-Related Features
    (1) enables social contact
    (2) provides enjoyment
    (3) provides entertainment or relaxation
    (4) enhances independence, autonomy, freedom
    (5) provides financial security
    (6) provides information or knowledge
    (7) provides privacy or solitude

D. Effort Expended in Acquiring/Maintaining Possession
(dropped from analysis as few responses referred to it)

E. Emotion-Related Features of Possession
    (1) emotional attachment
    (2) mood enhancer or regulator
    (3) escapism
    (4) emotional outlet/therapy
    (5) provides comfort or emotional security
    (6) enhances self-confidence

F. Self-Expression
    (1) self-expression *per se*
    (2) self-expression for others to see
    (3) individuality/differentiation from others
    (4) symbol for personal future goals
    (5) symbol for personal skills/capabilities

G. Personal History
    (1) link to events or places
    (2) link to past or childhood
    (3) general symbol of self-continuity
    (4) long-term association

H. Symbolic Interrelatedness
    (1) symbol for relationship with specific person(s)
    (2) symbolic company
    (3) symbol of interrelatedness with particular group(s)

Figure 11.3 Coding system for reasons why possessions are important
(after Dittmar 1991: 175)

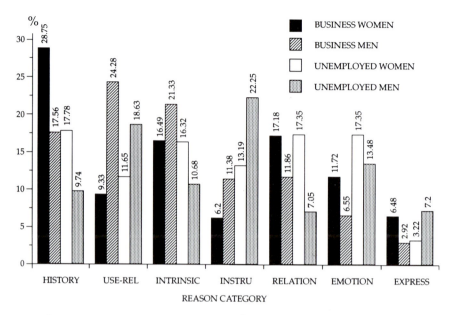

Figure 11.4 Average percentages of reasons why possessions are important to employed and business women and men (after Dittmar 1991: 177)

the ways in which objects create emotional interplay within an individual personality and between individuals.

Dittmar suggests that the gender-identity-related meanings of possessions range from a 'male' self-orientated, activity-related functional extreme to a 'female' relational, symbolic pole (1991: 180). The analysis here suggests that although this is true, it is a partial truth. When women are seeing themselves in the role of nurturing adults, they do indeed collect relationally and in an unemphatic style which so merges with their broader lives that its emergence as a true collection tends to be written out of the story. But when they are seeing themselves as vamps or child brides, the style of their collections is in a male mode, intense, specific, separate and serious (although of course the content of the collection is usually of 'feminine' material), and its emotional resonance is self-loving, narcissistic and absorbed.

INTO THE DOLL'S HOUSE

Unsurprisingly, perhaps, the collecting of dolls offers the clearest pattern of how the gendering of women works in our society. The collection at Mouse Cottage included a number of dolls in human as well as mouse form, which supported the collector's role as 'little girl'. This is balanced by the collecting habits of Flo, who has been collecting Barbie dolls for some eleven years (Belk and Wallendorf 1992). A few years ago Flo underwent radical mastectomy, which required extensive corrective and reconstructive surgery. Flo now has a complete collection of the outfits manufactured by Mattel for Barbie, and it is difficult not to relate her satisfaction at this completeness, associated as it is with the very full feminine form of the dolls, with her own difficulties following the removal of her breasts. Flo's Barbies are the acceptable face of vamping, desirable but well within the accepted constraints of Middle America.

It is interesting to realise that woman as loving mother does not figure in the collection. Flo says that Barbie is 'not a baby person', noting that Mattel had never produced maternity clothing or a baby for Barbie. Her euphemism was 'Barbie is more a woman of leisure' (Belk and Wallendorf 1992: 10). But Flo herself uses her collection to enact feminine qualities like generosity, sympathy and bonding by selling spare items at reasonable prices to other collectors and by giving away pieces at Barbie convention dinners. She says she views her collecting as a mothering activity, since mothers are supposed to keep things for their daughters, and her daughter and granddaughters will inherit her collection.

Brent collects the same material but uses it to produce a very different range of gender constructions. Brent is gay, with a history as an exotic dancer and male prostitute. His relationship with his own mother was very poor and, perhaps as a consequence, figures of a loving mother are absent from his collection, although, as we have seen, this image is in any case not a standard part of the Barbie repertoire. For Brent, this role is filled by his Gay Bob doll wearing a pink fairy costume acting as male fairy godmother, a deliberate material pun on his own homosexuality. In the house which Brent built for Barbie, the little girl dolls are relegated to the top of the wardrobe: Brent recognises that the image of woman as good little girl exists, but it holds no interest for him, except perhaps as a commentary on other kinds of image. Brent does have one Madonna figure, a blonde doll dressed in blue whom he calls Carol, and to whom he refers as 'the wholesome one'.

What Brent's dolls primarily express is his simultaneous anger and fascination with feminine images of evil and impure sexuality. He describes an oversize Barbie doll, to which he has given heavy eye make-up, as a whore, and places her next to a Miss Piggy doll to make the direct connection between whores and swine. He dressed one Barbie in a silver lamé evening dress put on backwards to show more cleavage, and then disparaged this doll's supposed desire to show off her breasts. Most vivid of all of his images is that of the Ice Queen, the most valuable doll in his collection, who is, Brent says, beautiful, cold, rejecting of men, and hated and feared by all the other dolls in the collection.

Flo and Brent are good – though admittedly rather extreme – examples of collectors whose creation of gender images through their material is particularly sharp and revealing. Together with the Mouse Cottage collector, they construct all the characteristic images of women including that of woman as loving mother, for Flo uses her collection to develop this aspect of her own persona. Meanwhile, Brent's collection also includes Ken dolls which display male images, and it is to the construction of masculine images through collecting that we must now turn.

COLLECTING MEN

Earlier, the point was made that the masculine gender image is not fractured into several figures, but remains single and, culturally speaking, true for all men, a fact symbolised at the dinner party by their equal participation in food, drink, talk and dress. Man as a cultural figure is a single whole, for although each man is composite, each is also perceived as capable of including some or all of the range of roles at any given time. A female cannot in the public gaze be a young girl, an impure vamp or a mature mother simultaneously because society regards their figures as mutually exclusive and life is adjusted accordingly. But men can see themselves and, just as importantly, are generally seen, as embracing a range of characteristic images in unison. Most of these images are the subject of collections which men make in order to encourage a correctly masculine view of themselves which they and others may be induced to hold, and they are, therefore, men collecting themselves in the direct sense. But some are to do with men collecting in relation to the gender images of women; that is, they are concerned to encourage images of women which they find support their masculinity, and which, probably for this reason, conform to the deep-rooted notions about femininity which we have already discussed.

MASCULINE PIECES

The admired male qualities are easily listed as strong, brave, potent, clever, protective, and so forth. These can easily be divided into a coherent range of attributes all of which reflect the central theme. Each is backed by a range of mythical characters which sum up the motif, and each is supported by a characteristically male approach to collecting, for examples of which the collecting literature overflows. Militaria and weapons are very common collecting material for men. The Walsall People's Show 1992 produced two militaria collectors. Timothy Hudson identified himself directly with the Second World War in which he was too young to fight. 'When I started at the age of seven I just wanted to own a bit of the war, I had heard it talked about so often and read about it in comics and books . . . I spend a lot of my free time acquiring new items or looking after those I already own, many are irreplaceable' (People's Show 1992). He says he spends most of his free time acquiring new items and caring for those he has. G. Clarke could genuinely be described as obsessive: 'It takes up all of my life, when I can I phone up my friends to talk about it. There are also club meetings during the week. My wife and I got married in full kit, we ran off to Gretna Green and also had the witnesses in kit' (People's Show 1992). His life seemed to begin when he started his collection.

Equally common, as every reader of the specialist magazines knows, are those who collect machine parts of various kinds, including complete machines. These are the oily handed collectors, who spend most of their free time working on their material in sheds and garages. Linked with these, but probably separable from them, are those for whom the apparent power and potency of their material is important. The size and speed of trains and cars, collected in harsh reality in a range of less inspiring ways – train numbers, train memorabilia, pictures and cards – seem to offer this kind of power. Gun collecting is extremely common, and whether or not guns are really phallic symbols scarcely matters because everybody knows that they are supposed to be. The language of guns and of firing is so laden with sexual innuendo, and has been since at least the seventeenth century (typically in phrases like 'Present your piece', 'Cock your locks', 'Discharge'), that *double entendres* in gun labels are well-nigh impossible to avoid, as anybody who, as I have, has tried to write them well knows.

Some male collections express a desire to assume the qualities possessed by the rescuing and saving professions. A good example is the Fire Museum, which houses material collected by the husband of the Mouse Cottage collector, who was himself a business man. The Fire Museum brochure invites the visitor to 'See the world's largest exhibit of fire-fighting equipment. Over 100 fully restored pieces dating from circa 1725 to 1950 . . . Learn about the history of the American fire-fighter – America's most dangerous profession – from Ben Franklin's Philadelphia volunteers to the modern era.' As Belk and Wallendorf put it:

> The exhibit is considerably more spacious than the Mouse Cottage. The fire trucks and other pieces of fire equipment are restored to perfection, and are individually presented in spacious roped-off areas that impart importance and honor to these objects. Carefully displayed exhibits of fire hats and other fire-fighting regalia line the museum walls. Historic photos, along with dates and plaques, help to give the impression that this is an historical museum. Whereas Mouse Cottage charges no admission and has no guidebook, both are found at the Fire Museum. The Mouse Cottage brochure positions

that museum as a tribute to childhood, while the Fire Museum is organized as a place for an adult educational experience.

(Belk and Wallendorf 1992: 10)

The Fire Museum collector is presented as a serious adult, akin with those whose bravery and devotion have always been at the service of the community.

Saviours sometimes rub shoulders with common men, and there is a large range of collectors whose material expresses mateyness, the masculine values of the barracks and the rugby club: here lie the collections of beer-mats, football souvenirs and ashtrays stolen from pubs. Similarly, some men take pride in a deliberate lowness, tricksters who knowingly display the seamy underside of things: here lie the subversive collections already described, the false teeth, the pepper and salt pots in the form of lavatory pans. Curiously close to this mental attitude, but its respectable other self, are the aesthetic collections of material like very modern art, modern glass or advanced studio pottery. Here connoisseurship is at the same work of undermining accepted values and drawing unacceptable analogies between objects and meaning, from which new insights and standards will emerge.

At the opposite pole to the virtues of mateyness lie those of the scholar, seen romantically as dedicated and secluded, engrossed in the search for arcane wisdom, although they may be perceived by their womenfolk with an affectionately ironic eye. Here lie the collectors of antiquities, coins and medals, and stamps. Close kin to these collectors are the scientists, a large detachment in previous decades and considerable now, who collect natural-history material, either actual specimens as before or photographs as is now considered proper. Among other things, these collections serve a role image of cleverness, of intellectual dominance of the world through the capacity to make correct identifications and proper organisation.

These collections also show particularly well the characteristic male style of collecting, which in fact seems generally true across the world of male collectors. Male collecting is seen as a distinct, and important, even self-important, activity. It frequently happens in a specific place, usually one set aside. It involves set times, and settled practices. The paraphernalia which surrounds the collection – cabinets, records, books and catalogues – may well be as striking as the collection itself. The whole assemblage is obtrusive in every sense, and clearly, for the collector, this is a significant element in its meaning.

MEN ON WOMEN

Men do not only make collections in their own images, they also collect to encourage images of femininity. They do not do this across the board:

we do not find male collections which are in the mature feminine household mode. But large fields of male collecting have to do with the image of women as whore, including a subset which emphasises little girl qualities in an erotic fashion. Equally, a similarly large collecting field links up, at least in part, with the image of woman as untouchable virgin and mother.

The subversive nature of the trickster collections has just been noted. One aspect of this kind of subversive collection are the accumulations of Nazi material and similar material relating to famous murders, like that held in Scotland Yard's Black Museum which has kitchen utensils from serial killer Christie's house at 12 Rillington Place, London. The pornographic vein in most of this is obvious, and it links up with the collections of erotic or pornographic images of women. Probably, too, a good deal of the Oriental and other exotic material within collections was accumulated in this state of mind, which wishes to develop the whore-like image of women.

The collection of Egon Schiele pictures exhibited at the Royal Academy in 1990 under the title *Egon Schiele and his Contemporaries* shows the problems inherent in this kind of pictorial material. Schiele's pictures hover in the twilight zone between erotic art and pornography. Presumably we know that they are art because they are on show in the Royal Academy rather than resting on the top shelf at the newsagents, but the difficulty of making any distinction was brought home in the most practical way by the problems the Royal Academy experienced when it tried to find commercial sponsorship for the exhibition (Graham-Dixon 1990). The instinctive response of the big banks is matched by the appropriately curious poses adopted by the art critics in their finally fruitless efforts to convince us that there is a categorical difference between art and pornography. The implications are of fundamental importance. As Graham-Dixon put it:

> Erotic art troubles the liberal mind because while taking to an extreme its ideas about the radical, exploratory nature of great art, it also punctures one of its fonder delusions. This is the received idea that the contemplation of great art is necessarily good for people. Major works of erotic art demonstrate, in a blatant and troubling way, that this is simply not true. They have what might be termed cultural significance – but they are hardly edifying or improving.
>
> (Graham-Dixon 1990)

The same might be said for many images of war, or for that matter in respect of that vein of sadism which runs back through much religious art, just as it does through some religious practice.

All of this is shot through with uncomfortable eroticism, but it is also, in its way, a legitimate vision of the human condition, or perhaps of the European capitalist condition, since images of this especially pornographic and semi-underground kind seem to be more common with us than with most cultures, and, like our approach to prostitution, reflect our characteristic ambivalence to women. Schiele perceived this condition as essentially one of loneliness and vulnerability, which all humans, men and women, share. Collections of erotic material unquestionably help to establish the motif of woman and whore and man and whoremaster.

Similar impulses are at work in that erotic subset which involves grown men being unduly interested in little girls. This seldom takes the form of collecting 'little girl' material – pottery mice and the like – but does, of course, fall into line with a well-established literary and pictographic aspect of the erotic. Lurie (1991: 68–84) has described the relationship between the artist Kate Greenaway and John Ruskin, when Ruskin was in his sixties. Greenaway specialised in drawing children, particularly sweet, pretty girls wearing loose, light-coloured clothes in an idealised country landscape. For Ruskin, her pictures were rarefied and decorous pornography of which he could not get enough, however many she drew and sent to him. But, as Lurie puts it, even the most delightful of her figures seemed to him to have one fault: they were overdressed. He wrote to her persistently on this topic:

> Will you – (it's all for your own good – !) make her stand up and then draw her for me without a cap – and, without her shoes – (because of the heels) and without her mittens, and without her – frock and frills? And let me see exactly how tall she is – and – how – round. It will be so good of and for you – And to and for me.
>
> (Lurie 1991: 76)

Kate never did undress her girls, and Ruskin had to be satisfied with what he got; Kate was in love with him, but he had nothing of the kind to offer her, and the relationship ended in her disillusionment.

As we have already seen, both sexes may have stakes of their own in these engendering images, but the emphases are different, underlined by the fact that only very seldom do women seem to collect erotica in all its various moods.

If pornographic art is seldom collected by women, the same is equally true of 'high' or 'fine' art, and this, it seems, for reasons which run beyond mere access to funds. Where women have been involved in this kind of collecting, investigation suggests that it is usually in conjunction with a husband or family prestige, or linked to a non-intrinsic meaning like that shown by Peggy Guggenheim, who seems to have collected most of her pictures as souvenirs of her various artist lovers (Guggenheim 1979). The metaphor should not be pushed too far, but there is an obvious correspondence between the sublimated sex on offer in much high art and in the image of woman as madonna, a metaphor which, of course, derives its visual aspect from exactly those same pictures in their earlier historical

aesthete	:	trickster
knight	:	whoremaster
mate	:	scholar
saviour	:	scientist
warrior	:	magician

Figure 11.5 Masculine images and male collecting habits

manifestations: both pictures and gender image spring from the same cultural context. Similarly, a reverential and moral quality surrounds high art and its characteristic collecting practice; a quality that corresponds directly with notions of the pure and the set-apart which surround the woman on her pedestal, an image not intended to allow us to see her legs better, but one appropriately chaste and chilly for both the human figure and the museums which hold much of this kind of collected art.

All these male collecting habits and the masculine images with which they are bound up can be arranged, without too much special pleading, in a set of opposed pairs (Figure 11.5). The 'high' aesthetic matches the subversive trickster, since both are concerned to draw attention to neglected values and relationships. Knights who serve ladies in paint and flesh match whoremasters. Saviours balance scientists because both intervene on our behalf, the one with warm action, the other with cold calculation. Gregarious mates match solitary scholars and warriors balance magicians who make their engines work with a puff of blue smoke, and show that spells are mightier than swords. The mythology of the male collector, in other words, is deeply rooted in the mythology of our society, and in social practice this matters as much as the fact that one side of the set represents 'good' qualities and the other side 'dark' or evil ones.

COLLECTIONS AS GENDER: ASPECTS OF LOVE

Collections, it seems, do engender masculine and feminine images, and they do this in ways which both fit and help to encourage images of men and women which are part and parcel of the European cultural inheritance. Figure 11.6 sets out a plot of the argument advanced here, with the many-faced image of woman set against the single one of man, single because a simple image is the social norm to which split female images relate, although as we have just seen, this simple image embraces its own complexities. 'Mother' and 'man' are at opposite poles just as their collecting styles are opposites, women low-key and unemphatic, men sharp and demanding.

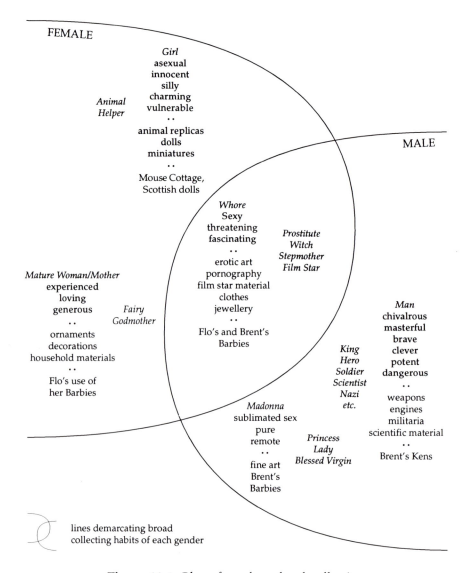

FEMALE

Girl
asexual
innocent
silly
charming
vulnerable
..
animal replicas
dolls
miniatures
..
Mouse Cottage,
Scottish dolls

*Animal
Helper*

MALE

Whore
Sexy
threatening
fascinating
..
erotic art
pornography
film star material
clothes
jewellery
..
Flo's and Brent's
Barbies

*Prostitute
Witch
Stepmother
Film Star*

Mature Woman/Mother
experienced
loving
generous
..
ornaments
decorations
household materials
..
Flo's use of
her Barbies

*Fairy
Godmother*

Man
chivalrous
masterful
brave
clever
potent
dangerous
..
weapons
engines
militaria
scientific material
..
Brent's Kens

*King
Hero
Soldier
Scientist
Nazi
etc.*

Madonna
sublimated sex
pure
remote
..
fine art
Brent's
Barbies

*Princess
Lady
Blessed Virgin*

lines demarcating broad
collecting habits of each gender

Figure 11.6 Plot of gender-related collecting

'Girl' and 'Madonna' represent linked but contrasting images on the other axis, and 'whore' occupies the centre for reasons which we will explore in a moment. The correspondence between these images and the seating arrangements at the dinner table need no labouring.

Each character is listed with its ascribed qualities, and under each list is a résumé of the typical collections made to support and confirm the role.

I have added to each the doll collections as they relate to the characters, because dolls as human representations capable of manipulation offer the clearest statement of characteristics which are implicit in less obviously hominoid collections. Beside each column I have added a second which gives the mythic or archetypal image which each figure reflects and enhances. All of these are clear enough, although I have added 'Animal Helper', that typical figure of European folklore and fairy story, to the young girl and her animal replica collections because there is indeed a sense in which such animal collections help a girl through adolescence and into adulthood, just as Dick Whittington's cat, or a host of other animal helpers, assist their friends to self-realisation.

This takes us into the next important point. On the English stage, let us not forget, Dick, however masculine his name, is played by a long-legged lady called a principal boy, and various confusions or complications of gender have been a characteristic feature of the European stage from its visible beginnings, now 2,500 years ago. One way and another, these give us pretty well every combination of cross-gender image and serve, of course, as an acceptable form of representation and release, both socially and psychologically. This warns us that the gendering of collecting, like the gendering of every human activity, may not be quite what it appears. People may, always or sometimes, understand their collections self-consciously and view them with an ironic eye which appraises their statements and evasions: Brent's material puns have something of this flavour.

Equally, there are, as we would expect, clear contradictions within a collecting habit. Flo's actual Barbies are available but wholesome young women – tasty but class with it – but the use she makes of them, though shadowed by the loss of her own figure, is to create for herself a maternal image among other collectors. What can be said is that what emerges most clearly in collecting studies generally is a sincere, indeed often painful, emotional honesty. People may collect privately, and find this, a socially accepted part of collecting, very helpful. But when the investigator penetrates to the collection, he almost always finds that there is a correspondence between the collector, the collection and the established patterns of gender, as these can be played out. Seldom, it seems, do people collect outside the gender roles on offer to them.

How these gender roles are played out, and their implications, form a fascinating area. The accumulated literature of collecting, although no doubt it could produce some contradictions, suggests that the overwhelmingly large number of collections follow the distinctions set out in Figure 11.6. In their collecting habits, women construct themselves as women, little girls or whores: but not much as madonnas. Women seldom construct men in their collections, either as wish-fulfilment for themselves or as a means of projecting a male relationship which they find exciting. Women collectors of guns or fire-engines or zoological specimens certainly exist, but they are relatively rare. Men commonly construct themselves in their collecting habits but, through their erotic or pornographic collections and their fine-art collections, they also construct women as whores (including the 'little girl' version) and madonnas. They seldom, apparently, collect material presenting women as mothers or as normal girls. They may help and encourage their womenfolk to collect in these modes but they would reject suggestions that the resulting collection is theirs, just as the Fire Collector wanted his museum and Mouse Cottage geographically separate.

It appears that only one gender-orientated collecting habit is common to both genders, and that is the representation of woman as whore through all its softer or more strident modulations. The image of the whore occupies the centre of the system, or rather, like the whole of the theatre with which it has ramifying links, it occupies the middle ground between real life for men and real life for women (or at any rate, for the huge majority of us most of the time). It is a fantasy land, exciting to men and women both, provocative to men, self-absorbing to women, inward-turning yet able to achieve material expression in many forms. If, for both sexes, 'Man' is the positive social norm, sustained by 'Mother' at the negative pole, then the whore is everybody's image of availability and change.

A PASSION FOR POSSESSION

Underneath the specific gendering with which collections are involved, however, lies a further question: is collecting itself, in itself, a variety of sexual experience? The older generations of psychologists, as we have seen, gave an emphatic 'yes' to this question, linking the accumulative habit with a range of sexual practices, and it would, doubtless, be perverse, in our turn, to deny some sort of linkage here. In his study of art collecting, for example, Baekeland suggests:

> The collectors are remarkably uniform in their descriptions of how they feel when they choose an art object. To a man, they report that they usually know immediately whether or not a piece really appeals to them and whether they want to possess it. They often compare their feeling of longing for it to sexual desire. This suggests that art objects are confused in the unconscious with ordinary sexual objects, an idea that gets some confirmation from the fact that many collectors like to fondle or stroke the objects they own or to look at them over and over from every angle, both up close and at a distance, activities that are impossible in a museum. The only other context in which looking, fondling and caressing loom so large is sexual foreplay.
>
> (Baekeland 1988: 51)

Certainly in the popular mind, feeding perhaps on this older technical literature, collectors are generally considered to have uncertain private habits, and this is, of course, one of the reasons why collectors are often secretive about their accumulative lives.

There are many relevant things which we do not know. Do collectors tend to be single people, for example, either those who have never been in a long-term relationship or those who have become single when such a relationship ended? Do collectors tend to be childless? Such information as we have does not suggest that such correlations exist, although, as we have suggested, it may not be true, either, to argue that collecting is an activity which may happen to anybody. What seems likely is that collecting, in general terms, does not relate to any specific sexual orientations, or particular kinds of life-history, although, naturally, individual collections may, and probably will, reflect individual tastes and experiences. Rather, collecting is so part and parcel of human personality, as this is seen in the European tradition, including those gendered aspects of it, that it is more pertinent to think of the broader erotics of collecting, of a passion for possession.

'Passion' ties up in one word a complex knot of feelings which embrace the notion of passivity, of having things done to one, of strong and powerful feeling, and of suffering (de Rougemont 1956). Our multiple use of the word reflects, among other things, the apparently deeply held conviction of our species that sex is a variety of religious experience or, perhaps, indeed, that religion is a variety of sexual experience. In the same way, but more simply, 'possession' also carries two linked connotations, one material and the other sexual. All this complexity stands behind the simplest assertion that 'Mary has a passion for antique clocks' or 'John likes possessing railway-train name-plates'. In the same way, and carrying much the same burden of meanings, we tend to use the language of war, of hunting and of sexual conquest interchangeably as metaphors for each other, and to apply all of them to the collecting habit. Collections are hunted down, opposition is beaten off and collectors are carried away by the excitement of the moment, with frequently unfortunate consequences.

But being carried away is an experience which we all ardently desire. Many collectors report on the state of excitement which finding, or hoping to find, an important piece arouses in them. The pleasure of this sensation, the sense of being lifted out of oneself into a sharper, brighter, more interesting world of feeling, is the central experience for many collectors, and a large part of the reason why they collect at all. Handling the existing collection then becomes a train of memories of past enjoyment, and a promise of more such memories in the future. The decision 'I'll buy it' is accompanied by a rush of heightened feeling, release, pleasure and self-realisation, which is a kind of love. These are transforming experiences, or at any rate we live in hope that they will be, and hence the image of collection as the transforming kiss which lifts us from one state to another. But the flow of feelings aroused by a newly acquired object does not last, although they may take their place in the solid structure of our lives. Passionate possession, in every sense, lies as much in anticipation and recollection as it does in the ever-passing present. Hence our continuing emotional appetite, and hence the need to go on adding to what has already been collected.

CONCLUSION

Probably most collections have an element of gendering, although it must be stressed that some are much more emphatically gendered than others. European images of gender are intrinsically complex, and, as we would expect, collecting habits support and encourage them. Style of collecting is, in terms of gender, as significant as the content of collection. Over the last two centuries or so, women seem to have actually collected things as much as men, but frequently in ways which emerge much less often into specific and recorded social practice. Interestingly, this seems to have worked across the class system. Working-class and middle-class women have and do collect in much the same way; equally, working-class men and middle-class men have and do collect in the same masculine style.

Perhaps, rather oddly, there is not much evidence that people collect in order to subvert the gender roles available to them, possibly because, as analysis shows, in some ways these are diverse enough in themselves to keep most of us happy. Collecting, perhaps because it must be both visual and tactile in the most direct ways, obstinately remains embedded in traditional erotic experience, and when it encourages change, it does so by enabling us to develop our understanding of our own erotic natures.

CHAPTER TWELVE

COLLECTING RELATIONSHIPS

—— •◆• ——

Oh, they *did* enjoy themselves!
They were the sort that went trampling all over your pet stamp
collection, or whatever it was, and then spent the rest of their lives
atoning for it. But you would rather have had your stamp collection.
                    Cold Comfort Farm (Gibbons 1956: 60–1)

My family think I'm a nutter and should grow up.
                                        (People's Show 1992)

INTRODUCTION

As we have recurrent cause to remark, humans do not and cannot live
alone. Our paradox is that we can only be ourselves in so far as we do so
in relation to other people, and this is true even for natural hermits who
nevertheless define themselves in relation to the absence of others.

We touch here two major, and parallel, aspects of collecting. On the one
hand, there is the mythology of the subject, the way in which collectors *en
masse* are traditionally viewed by a society which sees them as separate from,
and different to, itself. On the other hand, there are the actual lives which
collectors lead, and which, as we shall argue, for the most part, take place within
the normal social contexts of the primary group (the wife or husband, parents
and children), the peer group (friends and colleagues in general and fellow-
collectors in particular) and the reference group (those people whom the
collector desires to despise or join). It is worth remembering that both the
structure (and disintegration) of the family itself and the nature of the further
referential groups are the current late or post-modernist version of the continuing European tradition. The 'actual lives' of collectors are concerned with
multiple levels of the self, and will, therefore, require correspondingly extended
treatment, but first we will turn to the popular mythology of collecting.

POPULAR MYTHS

Collectors are always good for a laugh. So runs the conventional wisdom,
and its works appear in an enormous range of cartoons and comic writing

which have been with us since at least the mid-eighteenth century. As the collecting of curiosities ceased to be at the avant-garde as the Enlightenment gathered momentum, it became the butt of much heavily humorous verse. Sir Charles Hanbury, when asked by Sir Hans Sloane (whose medical treatment had saved his life) to look out for material, replied:

> I've ravaged air, earth, seas and caverns,
> Mountains and hills, and towns and taverns,
> And greater rarities can shew
> Than Gresham's children ever knew.
> From Carthage bought the sword I'll send,
> Which brought Queen Dido to her end,
> The stone whereby Goliath died,
> Which cures the headache, well applied.
> A whetstone, worn exceeding small,
> Time used to whet his scythe withal.
> The pigeon stuff'd, which Noah sent
> To tell him when the water went.
> A ring I've got of Samson's hair,
> The same which Delilah did wear,
> St Dunstan's tongs, which story shows
> Did pinch the devil by the nose.
> The very shaft, as you may see,
> Which Cupid shot at Anthony.

And so on, ending with:

> This my wish, it is my glory,
> To furnish your nicknackatory.

Lord Hervey, in one of the pieces he wrote to amuse Queen Caroline, compliments her:

> Who every Sunday suffers stupid Sloane
> To preach on a dried fly or Hampstead stone,
> To show such wonders as were never seen,
> And give accounts of what have never been.

> > (Brooks 1954: 193)

Heavy-handed though this stuff is, it does not lack a touch of the genuinely malicious, typical of the vicious satire of the day. This acid gradually modulates into the fun on offer in periodicals like *Punch*, where the ponderous levity has a more kindly tone. One *Punch* cartoon published on 21 September 1878, the year after Canon William Greenwell had published *British Barrows*, shows a barrow opening scene on the Yorkshire Moors with, in the foreground, a labourer putting what looks like a food vessel into his coat. The caption reads:

North Country Labourer (who has been engaged to dig). '"They that eat alone may howk alane!" These archi'logical chaps never so much as asked if ah'd tak' anything, and while they're havin' their Denners ah've found the "burying" – (Pockets Urn and several flint arrowheads) – and they may whustle for't!'

(Bray 1981).

The tone changes very little with the passing decades. A *Punch* cartoon of 7 December 1938, shows two venerable old buffers either side of an ancient Egyptian coffin. One is saying to the other, 'Many happy returns Cathcart. I didn't know what to get you.' On 18 November 1959 we see a museum scene, with a visiting family of two adults and 2.4 children in classical clothes. They are gazing at a large mounted skeleton of a creature with a horse body and a human upper torso. The museum label – in Greek – says CENTAURS. Gary Larsen brings the theme up to date a little (but not much). In a cartoon published in 1987 we see a desert scene with an overweight, knobbly-kneed investigator, holding a skull with a near-human gaze in one hand, and a bosomy blonde, bigger than himself, in the other. The caption reads, 'The anthropologist's dream: a beautiful woman in one hand, the fossilised skull of a *Homo Habilis* in the other.'

This is Collectorland, not collecting, an instantly recognisable fantasyland like those which popular culture creates for cavemen or Mickey Mouse. Here collectors are mildly dotty but entirely harmless and their obsessions are a small eccentricity but not a threat. The world of traditional social class is well in place, but is without sting: the Yorkshire labourer slyly outwits his betters because they do not offer him any dinner. The two beside the Egyptian coffin are funny but unmistakably middle class, and 'Cathcart' used by an equal without any prefix bespeaks the public school; indeed, the choice of this surname itself makes mild fun of the school system. In a similar way, Larsen's cartoon laughs at the peculiarities and contradictions of academic life. Essentially, we are being offered a reassuringly familiar cast of cardboard cut-out characters, and are then prompted to find the incongruity between their appetite for essentially useless things and the rational man's view of the real world amusing. So, semi-official humour brings collecting well into the social frame, a tolerated eccentricity, which can be absorbed, regulated and digested without impairing the natural balance of things.

Up to a point, collectors seem comfortable with this image of themselves. It is not simply that they are generally ready to laugh at themselves, but that they do so in very much the same kind of terms. Collectors usually glory in their difference, accepting the ways in which they are described, although, naturally, rearranging the language to flatter rather than disparage. Typical comments from collectors are: 'At work they think I'm absolutely loopy – that I'd want to spend all of my time and money on 50 year old tat', 'Most people think I'm a bit eccentric – the one who collects the daft things', 'They think I'm mad.' Collectors like to be thought of as mad; they enjoy seeing themselves as possessed by a state which holds interesting psychological complications, and, once the ice is broken, they are often (although not always) happy to talk at length about themselves and their material, so that the cloven hoof of exhibitionism soon starts showing through the skirts of decent reticence. The varieties of prestige which collecting can give are many, but one of them seems to be conferred simply by being a collector at all.

But the investigator sometimes senses the effort behind the smiles: the collector is comfortable not because such humour is truly along the grain of his nature, but because it provides an acceptable social self which diffuses criticism. At heart, collectors are seldom ironic about either their material or themselves in relation to their material: collections are a way of taking oneself very seriously indeed. We are reminded of the Walsall collector who said, with a straight face, that his collection of American World War Two militaria arose entirely by accident; all he had wanted originally was one contemporary uniform to wear while he drove around in his 1940s jeep.

The collector's unease is compounded when the popular image modulates into one which is not just funny in a way which can be seen as self-enhancing, but which, drawing at least in part on the older psychological literature, sees the collector as a pathetic fellow who hangs around railway stations in a plastic mac and a woolly hat collecting engine numbers, overweight and probably impotent; or as a precious aesthete whose sexuality is open to speculations of a different kind. These are interesting notions, particularly in their characteristically gendered colouring, but they are probably the kind of descriptions any large minority attracts.

Both the kind and the unkind faces of popular mythology make assumptions about the social and family life of collectors, which hinge on the notion that their social habits are, in various ways, abnormal, and that this is linked with abnormal traits of personality. This assumption is contradicted by current investigations now under way in both north America (Belk 1991a, 1991b) and Britain (Pearce forthcoming 1996). In particular the data being assessed from the British study suggests that the family relationships enjoyed by collectors broadly match those in the wider community. Contrary to some popular belief, collectors are no more likely to be living solitary lives than anybody else. Their patterns of partnership and of parenthood broadly mirror the national norms, and, in simplistic terms, it is clear that the great majority of collectors lead lives which fall well within contemporary social norms, and would be generally regarded as 'quite natural'.

This is obviously very important. It suggests that ideas about collectors as a specific type, compounded from a mixture of unusual (or deviant) psychological and social characteristics, should be abandoned. Collectors may have a temperament which relates to material culture particularly easily, but this does not work in a way which turns them into a particular kind of social being, in a comprehensive sense. Collecting colours the collector's social life, as do many other kinds of activity, but that life is usually more or less 'normal' as this is generally understood. Like everybody else, collectors live their lives on a number of levels.

COLLECTING AS A FAMILY AFFAIR

I said at the beginning of this chapter that we are concerned here with multiple levels of the self. Another way of expressing this is to say that the principle which structures this aspect of each of us in relation to the rest of us is that of private : public. Important elements in our collecting relationship with others concern things like who can see the collection, who can touch it or parts of it, who knows exactly how extensive it is, who knows about the mistakes as well as the triumphs, and who knows how much the individual pieces have cost. A good deal of *amour propre* is invested in collections and with this goes a desire to exhibit the best part of them, including the successful stories of the chase, and to suppress those which show the collector up as dupe or victim, either of other's malice or his own folly. Collectors, like other shoppers, sometimes find that when they get the piece home, it was not quite what they thought it was, and the dress which the *vendeuse* persuaded them would make them look like the sultan's favourite turns out to do nothing of the kind. The persons to whom we confess these things are intimate indeed, but confess we do, driven presumably by an urge to clean the slate and start again.

Our families usually live in the same domestic space as our collections and ourselves. Children collectors, young or adolescent but still living at home, have a wholly unsurprising tendency to be secretive about their collections, since this, particularly for adolescents, is a normal way to behave in general. Collections seem likely to be kept in locked spaces, sometimes bedrooms or spare rooms, but more probably secure cupboards within a bedroom. Senior adults can behave in very much the same way. If the older generation of grandparents are living with the family, then they too have a tendency to keep collections private, and this, sadly, is often linked with a miscalculation, financial or emotional or both, about the intrinsic value the material has for others. Curators doing museum enquiries and identifications frequently find themselves in the position of having to give unwelcome news either to the elderly persons themselves or to their children after the grandparents have died, and on such occasions one often hears a tale of the grandfather's secrecy and possessiveness, presumably in an attempt to maintain a dwindling store of personal significance.

The most important relationship within what we still call the standard family is that between husband and wife (or long-term partners). Baekeland makes the interesting point that 'if the marriage is a poor one, the husband's collecting may be but one of a number of disputed areas', but 'in a harmonious marriage the collector's wife usually enthusiastically approves of his collecting' (1981: 51). In other words, collecting stands as one of the many activities and outlooks which make up a marriage and does not operate out on a limb by itself. Baekeland cites one example known to him, in which the marriage was already in trouble:

> one collector was reproached by his wife, who said, quite accurately, 'You are more interested in art than in me.' His collecting became such a source of conflict that finally he never brought his art friends home. He often left objects with the dealers from whom he had bought them for many months in order to forestall the resentment and arguments that disclosure of their purchase would inevitably engender when he took them home.
>
> (Baekeland 1988: 51)

In good marriages the wife may be the guiding hand behind the collection, contributing her 'superior' taste and understanding, although the business-man husband will pay, and will take the credit. As Baekeland again points out

> Since they are unflattering to the man, such marriages are rarely documented by art historians. A well-known example is that of the sugar millionaire H. O. Havemeyer. With his wife Louisine, he amassed an important collection of European old master and Impressionist paintings, most of which were ultimately left to the Metropolitan Museum of Art. In 1879, before he met Louisine, his collection, like that of most rich American collectors, consisted of currently fashionable French and German salon painters with a sprinkling of Barbizon school artists. By 1889, six years after the marriage, under her tutelage his tastes had veered to Courbet and 17th-century Dutch paintings.
>
> (Baekeland 1988: 51)

These examples, however, reflect one particular kind of marriage, that in which it is assumed that the husband will be the dominant partner, with the power to decide and spend and the willingness to take the responsibility for good or ill, while the wife's influence, whether supportive or its opposite, is decidedly backstairs. Many contemporary marriages are much more like equal partnerships, and of this, too, joint collecting can be an important element.

The Studio Pottery (Hillier 1993) collectors work very much as a pair. They have some thirty pieces by potters like Quentin Bell and Bernard

Leach, and also some twenty acrylic paintings, many of them by contemporary painters based in St Ives, Cornwall. Interestingly, neither the
husband nor the wife choose to think of themselves as collectors, because
the material is primarily used to furnish their home, and because the
pottery is used for serving and eating food, as it was originally designed
to be. Both agree that they started collecting immediately after their
marriage in 1959. Both were asked if there was a sense of any particular
object belonging more to one than the other, and if so, if one only had
decided to buy it, if it was a gift from one to the other, or if one simply
grew to like it in the course of time. In answer to this the husband said,
'We always seem to agree on what to buy so the objects belong to both
of us' and the wife said, 'I don't think of anything being particularly mine,
but I do think that two pieces are more the other's, because the other
likes them more.' When asked how they would compare the collection of
objects to other ways of spending time and money, the husband stressed
the importance of the material to the home through its capacity to create
the mood and style of rooms. The wife replied, 'This is more satisfying,
very evocative and, for a married couple, gives a sense of permanence and,
yes, bonding.' The role of the actual collecting in the marriage and in
creating the home which is an intrinsic part of the marriage comes across
very clearly.

These three images – hurtful, supportive and bonding – we may call the
three faces of marriage, but what of the collecting habits of single parents,
who either have never been married or whose marriages have come to
an end? Sadly, very little information exists about the collections which
people – mostly women – in this social group do or do not form, because
they have never been studied as a distinct group. It would be easy to assume
from general indications that neither their incomes nor a certain instability in the lifestyle make it probable that collecting will be part of their personal cultures; but such judgements are impossibly crude and better avoided
until better information becomes available.

One further point should be made. The significance of gift exchange in
European culture has already concerned us, and we have considered the
role of the gift in the deep structures of our social and psychological lives.
We shall touch again on the transforming power of the gift when we
consider the political nature of commodity material. What is important here
is that in modern society the normal area for gift-giving is the family,
enhanced by close friends who almost count as family members, signalled
by the honorific 'uncle' and 'aunt' titles given to them by the family's
children. The link between gift-giving and the collecting process is
extremely close. It is normal practice for human collectors to receive
additions to their collections, and the collector himself is frequently invited
to take part in the choice. In this way, the interrelated elements of close
personal relationship, the presentation of gifts as an important expression

of those relationships, and the physical presence of the steadily growing collection, form a strong bonding web.

PEER COLLECTING

A collector's peer group embraces all those he comes in regular contact with outside his immediate close circle of family and friends, and therefore includes acquaintances and colleagues at work, and these, of course, are the people most likely to respond to him in the ways we have discussed as popular responses. But for the collector there is another ramifying network of peers which is constituted by the specialist groups in which collectors gather. There is across north America and northern Europe particularly, an immense and intricate network of collecting clubs and societies which encompass a very broad range of collecting activities indeed.

Organisations of this kind have considerable historical depth, running back to the eighteenth century with the great names like the Society of Antiquaries of London (founded 1717), the Dilettante Society, also in London (founded 1733) and the many city and county philosophical, archaeological and natural-historical societies of the nineteenth century. Those whose histories are well-known and frequently published (see Piggott 1976) tended to cover broadly archaeological and natural-history material, but research is beginning to uncover similar collecting circles in London and elsewhere through the nineteenth century devoted to collecting in the applied arts. As the twentieth century has progressed the numbers and range of such clubs has increased hugely, and with them are linked the proliferating collectors' magazines, radio and television programmes produced locally and nationally, collectors' sale days at antique markets, car-boot sales, white-elephant stalls, and all the apparatus associated with collectors in the mass.

The Russell Society is a good example of the more organised of such clubs. In its literature, it describes itself as:

> the country's leading society specialising in topographical mineralogy. It is named after the eminent amateur mineralogist Sir Arthur Russell (1878–1964) and attracts a wide spectrum of amateur and professional people ranging from beginners to professors. The membership of 500 is spread throughout the United Kingdom as well as overseas and is organised into six branches.
>
> The principal aims of the Society are the study, recording and conservation of minerals and mineralogical sites. The Society works closely with museums and other like-minded organisations in the pursuit of these aims. It encourages only responsible collecting and exploration.

Each branch of the Russell Society organises programmes of winter meetings inviting guest speakers and holding social events. There are excursions to sites of mineralogical and geological interest. Over forty winter meetings and fifty field trips take place each year. Any member can attend any meeting.

The Russell Society publishes a Journal and a Newsletter which are both free to members. The Journal records new and important mineral occurrences and studies and has an international standing. The Newsletter reports the activities and affairs of the Society and occasionally includes articles on minerals or mineralogical sites. There is a library which is free to all members.

Both formal symposia and informal discussion groups are held as well as laboratory sessions. There is always a free exchange of ideas and knowledge between members and hands-on experience with mineral specimens is common.

(Russell Society literature 1992)

Similar societies exist in comparable collecting areas, and the level of organisation shades down from this to much smaller and more local enterprises.

This is a phenomenon of undoubted social significance, but one which is only just beginning to attract attention as the subject of sustained research. Some significant shapes are beginning to emerge, but any hard conclusions would be improper, given the current state of knowledge. It is clear that, active and extensive though the club network is, the majority of collectors, probably the very substantive majority, do not identify themselves as club members. They do not subscribe to any regular magazine, or pay a subscription, or attend meetings. The reasons for this seem to be complex, and normal human lethargy plays a surprisingly small part because the collectors concerned are no less passionate than their club-orientated fellows. The heart of the matter seems to be a strong sense of singularity and of the unique importance of themselves as individuals and of their collections as a part of themselves: this holy ground would be profaned if others came too close to it or turned out to collect the same things in the same ways.

Collecting-club members have an ambivalent relationship with each other. They too, wish to protect the joint identity of themselves and their material, but they also wish to impress others with what they have achieved, and to put themselves in the way of fresh acquisitions. The result, as experienced by a club visitor, is a curious mixture of mistrust and complicity, characterised by cryptic conversations and elliptical pronouncements, all embraced within a good deal of jockeying for position. What sustains the group is partly the good opportunities which it offers for acquisition, and partly, of course, the feeling of solidarity. Collecting, as we have seen, is regarded with some ambivalence by society at large, but within the group a collecting norm can be established, which is supportive and nourishing. Clubs have their own kind of legitimacy.

COLLECTING AS REFERENCE: PAY AND DISPLAY

Collections, as we have seen in our discussion of improper accumulations, are sometimes gathered in order to cock a snook at society, and to exhibit its underbelly to the light of day. But, and much more frequently, collections are undertaken in order to impress contemporaries, to arouse admiration and amazement, and to secure an immortal place for the collector through the building of the collection as his monument. Prestige has unquestionably been one of the principal collecting motives over the last five centuries, to go back no further. It is likely, indeed, that all collectors, whatever the nature of their material and however trivial or laughable it may seem to others, derive *some* prestige from being known as a collector, even if this may have a strong element of deliberate perversity in it. But prestige in the normal sense of accruing social honour has usually belonged with those collectors whose material is deemed to be intrinsically important, and therefore valuable, and this means, *par excellence*, pictures from the European schools of acknowledged masters.

It is clear that many such collectors down the generations have deliberately chosen fine art as their target for the prestige which it conveys. It is also clear that pictures have the art of turning base metal into fine gold, of transforming money acquired in trade into nobility in every sense of the word. Business men have always been able to acquire genteel polish by demonstrating their taste in the purchasing of works of art, and their public munificence in the bequests of art which they make to their fellow citizens. This was true of the Medici, whose collections helped to transform doctors turned bankers into princes; it was true of the great nineteenth-century collectors like Rockefeller, Guggenheim and Burrell; and it remains true of the Sainsburys and the Saatchis today.

The point needs no labouring, but one or two details may serve to bring out the flavour of the thing. When George Villiers, Duke of Buckingham, was assassinated in 1628, his art collection consisted of over 330 pictures, which included Titian's *Ecce Homo* and a number of works by Rubens purchased from the artist. Buckingham may well have actually liked the works, but it is clear that they were, equally, an important counter in his rivalry, political and personal, with the Earl of Arundel, also an avid collector. The collection, on display at York House, was intended to impress visitors to the state functions held there, and to present himself as what Arundel was, but he was not, an aristocrat of birth and lineage.

Buckingham's collection was gathered for him by agents who searched Europe on his behalf, particularly Balthazar Gebier (who became Keeper of the Collection at York House), Sir Dudley Carleton and Sir Henry Wotton. The essense of Buckingham's collecting is preserved for us in a revealing work of Gerbier's:

> Sometimes when I am contemplating the treasure of rarities which Your Excellency has in so short a time amassed, I cannot but feel astonishment in the midst of my joy; for out of all the amateurs and princes and kings there is not one who has collected in forty years as much pictures as Your Excellency has collected in five.
> (Gebier to Buckingham, 1625, quoted in Lockyer 1981: 409)

The same note is struck at a slightly humbler social level at the other end of the century. In the Castle Museum, Norwich, there survives a painting dating to about 1679, perhaps by Pieter van Roestraten, which is probably a *pronkslilliven*, or 'boast still-life'. This was commissioned by Robert Paston of Oxnead Hall, Norfolk, who became Earl of Yarmouth in the same year. The pictures show sixteen carefully chosen pieces from the Paston collection of treasures and curiosities, of which we have relatively complete accounts, including two inventories drawn up in 1663 and 1673. A visit to Oxnead in 1639–40 mentions cabinets, and the word *musaeum* was used to describe the collection in 1658.

Robert was the late-seventeenth-century representative of the well-known letter-writing Pastons, who had started as fourteenth-century husbandmen, entered the ranks of the Norfolk gentry through successful legal concerns, and managed a baronetcy in 1641. Robert achieved the final translation to the aristocracy, and the collection can be seen as helping to legitimise the family's dazzling rise. It also sustained it in the most literal sense: the pieces had to be sold in 1679 to help pay for the new dignity, and the picture may have been intended as a record as well as a boast of the family material.

The sixteen pieces in the painting include several mounted seashells, some in the form of cups, several flagons, a pair of coconut cups with silver gilt mounts and various elaborate flasks. One of the most important pieces was a nautilus shell cup with silver gilt mounts, sold in 1679 for £68 to the Walpole family of Houghton Hall. It crops up again when Horace Walpole's collection at his Strawberry Hill villa was sold in 1842. The Walpole sale catalogue mentions 'A Nautilus shell richly mounted in silver gilt, representing Neptune Riding on a Dolphin, the arms of Paston supported by satyrs on a turtle pedestal with sea monsters, of very rare workmanship.' The present whereabouts of this daunting piece are now unknown (Wenley 1991; Ketton-Cremer 1957).

I have deliberately chosen two collections from the seventeenth century, because they show so clearly how personalities, prestige, politics and collections were intimately intertwined and so act as a benchmark for so much that was to come in the centuries leading up to the present day. But collections of the seventeenth century, like their immediate predecessors, relate to prestige in a more fundamental way. This was the period above all when the image of the great man at the centre of his splendid treasure came to full power, an image which fused mortal and material magnificence in a moment of apotheosis, rendering both godlike together. It has been a potent image for all latter-day prince-collectors, lifting the prestige of accumulation from the mundane to the sublime.

CONCLUSION

Collections, then, are one of our principal ways of structuring our relationships with the human world outside our own skins. This world is itself hierarchically structured in relationship to each collector in terms of a private : public opposition, and this works, on a sliding scale, from intimate partner to the larger public world of power and politics. Accumulating evidence is suggesting that collectors are normal members of the contemporary social and family world, structuring their basic human relationships in ways which are not intrinsically different to those of non-collectors. But within this structure collections are a part of the dynamic: they help the collector to alter his perceptions of other people, and other people's perceptions of him.

CHAPTER THIRTEEN

COLLECTING IN TIME

—— •◆• ——

It is a permanent record of my life.

(People's Show 1992)

INTRODUCTION: NOW AND THEN

Collecting is an essentially spasmodic activity. Acquisition takes place over an extended period, and we feel that this is an intrinsic part of its honesty and sincerity. 'Instant' collections, our instincts tell us, are not true collections at all; in order to be honourable and genuine, collections must have been acquired gradually over the years, and piece or group at a time. There are, of course, some legitimate exceptions to this. One may inherit a complete collection, and it will have a sincere place in one's own life. But unless it is added to, it remains essentially the collection of the dead person, which in the nature of things has passed into other hands. One may purchase complete collections, or substantial parts of complete collections, and add these to the total of one's own accumulation. The history of collecting in the grand manner is replete with such major purchases: to take only one, the collection of Sir Hans Sloane was, by the time he passed it to the nascent British Museum, essentially a collection of collections for Sloane had acquired not only much material of his own, but also the entire holdings of several well-known collectors of the previous generation, especially those of William Courten and James Pettiver (Brooks 1954: 176–81). But this kind of acquisition does not really transgress our notions of what is proper. Sloane, and most of those contemporaries and successors who have collected like he did, were unmistakably genuine collectors who happened to be able to structure their collecting lives through the occasional major addition to what they already had. Our instinctive objection relates to those who buy collections by the yard, in the attempt to establish a spurious material pedigree and past.

From this some fundamental characteristics of collecting emerge. Pieces enter a collection now and then as the collector is prompted to acquire them, and the collection gradually gathers size, scope and momentum as time goes by. Collections are therefore both the product of a personal life (or whatever of his time the collector has spent building up a collection), and a means of structuring that life span, of giving tangible form and content to

235

the experience of time passing. They are an outward and visible sign of what otherwise leaves no trace upon the empty air, and it is this capacity of material to carry experience which makes it so dear to us. But they are not merely the memorials of time past. They have an active role in that they themselves provide the structuring principle for important aspects of our lives. They can serve as rites of passage which help us through periods in our lives, and create distinctions between one period and the next.

The capacity of collecting to give meaning to the passage of time is, however, itself a cultural trait, a construction not an aspect of innate nature. The notion of 'now and then' works both in the sense of 'occasionally', and in that of making clear-cut distinctions between what is 'now', that is, the ever-passing present actually conceived as time spans of varying width, and 'then', that is, the time before 'now', capable of being chopped up into various 'thens', variously understood. These notions, in turn, depend upon the sense that time is an arrow, a dimension in which things happen only once and bear a sequential and a determining relationship to each other. This is, as we have seen, a characteristically European way of looking at the world, and it is, among other things, part and parcel of the particular European relationship to material goods.

From this springs our ability to perceive that collected objects have a unique place in relationship to passing time. As we have already seen (p. 170) objects have the capacity to be perpetually reinterpreted, re-formed within a desired contemporary context. But they also, always, carry with them the characters they acquired in their original and subsequent contexts. As we saw earlier, the rabbet plane made about 1910 (Plate 1, p. 26) remains for ever a rabbet plane and always, providing it is in repair, retains the capacity to shape wooden mouldings. But it also accumulates additional meaning in its century of life, as junk, as collector's piece, as part of museum exhibition. Objects are therefore both content and interpretation, both past and present; in semiotic language they are, always, both signifier and signified. It is this quality of reality, of 'really' bringing the past, as per-ceived in the European tradition, 'into' the present, of possessing a unique capacity to re-present the past, which makes collected objects so eloquent and so desirable.

This is where Braudel's structuring notion of history as long-term mentalités, medium-term mentalités and immediate mentalités touches the emotional life of the individual collector in a particular way. Collectors use their collections to create their own particular view of the long, medium and immediate terms, and they do this through the perspective of their own lives. What happens before and after their own lifetime becomes the long term, what happens within the lifetime becomes the medium term, and the moment of each significant acquisition creates the immediate act. I shall structure this discussion accordingly. We will consider how collected material can structure our relationship with the pre-lifetime past, a relationship which divides into two styles, that of the impersonal past represented by historical relics, and that of the family past represented by family heirlooms. We will look at the role of souvenir material, that is, material which bears an intrinsic relationship to the lifetime of the collector; and we will look at the hope of immortality which collections represent. But first we must consider the notion of acquisition as rite of passage, as one immediate or short-term act follows another through life.

COLLECTING AS A RITE OF PASSAGE

It is clear that, for many collectors, their collections themselves act as a structuring principle in their lives. Many collectors have a weekly routine in which a certain span of time in the evenings or at weekends is spent working on their material in various ways, and this serves as the principal way of structuring leisure time, and as marking the distinction between work and leisure. Others have regular monthly forays to collectors' meetings, car-boot sales and similar events. In these ways, the collecting habit provides the framework for day-to-day living.

Additions for the collection are frequently given, especially by other members of the family, as Christmas and birthday presents. In the same way, many people buy collection objects while they are away on their regular summer holiday, or have material brought back for them by other people, usually close friends or family. These recurrent moments of transition in every life therefore become identified with the growth of the collection, and with particular items within it: the collection accumulates experiences in the same way that we do ourselves. The collection may itself provide the significant moment. The finding of a particularly sought-after piece is an important moment in the life of every collector, and can become a mental point of reference in its own right, so that other events, both collecting events and more general ones, are thought of as before or after the special acquisition. In all of this, as in many other ways, collections act in a curious way as if they were people, providing, as it were, a parallel sequence of encounters.

In a similar, but rather broader, sense collections help to 'get us through' periods in our lives, and these periods are frequently themselves times of transition. Several studies have shown that children are avid collectors, and use their collections as a means of creating external relationships with each other through competitive acquisition linked with intensive swap sessions (Burk 1900; Whitley 1929; Witty 1931; Durost 1932). The flurry of this work in the 1930s was, indeed, a part of the considerable work done at that time on the psychology of childhood, for collecting is one of the most visible aspects of childish behaviour. Durost reported that boys' collecting activity peeked at age 10, and girls' at age 11. A recent study in Israel found that between first and seventh grade at least 84 per cent of both boys and girls collect something, although in eighth grade these figures drop to below 50 per cent (Danet and Katriel 1989).

It is clear that collecting is more common among children than it is among adults. Some child collectors become adult collectors, some children abandon collecting for good as they leave childhood behind, and some adults collect who never did so as children: this seems to be clear from the collecting literature and probably rules out the otherwise seductive conclusion that collecting adults are experiencing a prolonged childhood – or that collecting children are experiencing a form of neoteny, giving us materially, rather than sexually, mature infants.

Bereavement is another period in life when collecting sometimes seems to be important, particularly if the collection bears some relationship to the dead person, and can be seen as a way of continuing to respond to that person. Recovery from an illness can have the same result. We have already seen that the Barbie Doll Collector linked her material with her cancer surgery, and in the People's Show 1992 the Frog Collector reported of her collection: 'it has helped me recover from my illness' (People's Show 1992).

Adolescence, similarly, can sometimes be eased through the process of collecting. The Toy Collector (Wallace 1993) started collecting when he was 16 when, though British, he lived in northern Italy. In October 1985 he moved to Edinburgh and recalls

> When I first came to Edinburgh I had a huge big old cardboard suit-case which was filled with metal toys and the weight of the suitcase was incredible . . . and the journey was by bus and I had to put the suitcase in the bus . . . it was really funny cause this huge suitcase was just full of toys and clothes – I just had a bag of clothes and that was it! . . . But I felt it was important to have them with me so I took them over.
>
> (Wallace 1993)

The Toy Collector himself distinguishes two fundamental principles in his collecting which set the notion of the collection itself in perspective: a love of craftsmanship, and a fascination with the creative and imaginative qualities of toys:

> what I appreciated in collecting toys was something to do with crafts-manship – toys are made of metal, colours, simplicity, and there is something to do with the imagination and creativity as well. The idea of collecting wasn't so important for me, what I liked and what it taught me, I think, was appreciation for objects and shapes and things . . . that was what I liked most, not so much the idea of collecting or showing off a collection.
>
> (Wallace 1993)

This is doubtless true, but it is also significant that the collector made sure that his collection accompanied him intact from Italy to Scotland. As Wallace (1993) points out

> The notion of collections representing the extended self is also relevant in this case. It is evident both in the importance, for the Collector, of bringing his collection with him to Britain, and in the enthusiastic shows he gave to people interested in the collection. His collecting activity spans the years of adolescence. It is perhaps significant then, that the toy car, the most prominent object in the collection, symbolically straddles the world of childhood and that of adulthood. On the one hand, as a symbol of fantasy and play, on the other as a powerful symbol of the male gender, speed, and status.
>
> (Wallace 1993)

The Toy Collector, now grown up, speaks of his adolescent self in critical terms:

> When I first started collecting I used to buy items which were not in such good condition and I used to try to improve them, repaint things over them and make them look better, while later I lost that. In fact, in the collecting activity something that had been re-painted or restored was looked upon as something that had lost value and originality.
>
> (Wallace 1993)

He now feels very differently about collecting; expressing himself with the strength of revulsion:

> Now I dislike the idea of collecting, it is something that I dislike in people, for example I hate people who collect stamps . . . It's something that I've quite rejected this collecting business, I think that there is something 'perverted' in collecting.
>
> (Wallace 1993)

Collecting, it appears, is not just a time one can pass through, it is also, in itself, a pass which time can open out.

HEIRLOOMS: AT THE MATERIAL TIMES

In 1985 the National Trust took over the house and home park of Calke Abbey in Derbyshire, the family seat of the Harpur-Crewe family. This was in many ways a new departure for the Trust, and its special claims to attention are made clear in the Trust's information literature:

> Calke Abbey is one of the most unusual country houses you will ever visit. Why unusual? Because, although certainly large, Calke is

not the classic stately home full of priceless treasures which you might be expecting but a family home which has remained largely unchanged for most of this century – in some rooms since the 1880s! It contains a rare mixture of fine showrooms, dilapidated corridors and rooms where innumerable items from oil lamps to children's toys were stored away in heaps.

(National Trust Information leaflet 1992)

Calke was built in the early years of the eighteenth century, and occupied continuously by some twelve generations of the Harpur-Crewe family. As Colvin puts it, 'Calke Abbey is a house, where for the last 150 years, scarcely anything has been thrown away . . . Calke today is therefore a treasury of Victorian life and Victorian taste with a substratum of Georgian furniture, pictures, silver and glass' (Colvin 1985: 111). The State Rooms, in particular, remain almost precisely as they were in 1886, the year of Sir John Harpur-Crewe's death.

So far, so interesting, but, more remarkably still, upstairs in the bed-rooms are the accumulated personal possessions of four or five generations of the family (Figure 13.1),

for at Calke successive owners, instead of clearing out the predeces-sors' belongings, have tended simply to close the door and move to another room. Indeed, it is remarkable that scarcely a single owner of Calke has chosen to occupy the same bedroom as his immediate predecessor.

(Colvin 1985: 115)

Here survive tissue-lined cartons containing collections of Victorian dolls, toy soldiers from Germany in mint condition, a case of presentation silver, clothes and uniforms.

Elsewhere in the house are collections of mounted heads and antlers, of caricatures by Gildray and Cruickshank gathered by Sir Henry Harpur (*d.* 1819), and of Egyptian material collected by Sir Gardner Wilkinson (1797–1875), cousin of Georgiana, Lady Harpur-Crewe. Over all loom the enormous natural-history collections of lepidoptera, birds' eggs, and stuffed birds accumulated by Sir Vauncey Harpur-Crewe, baronet from 1886 to his death in 1924. As early as 1793 household accounts record payments for preserving, or 'naturalising' birds, and by 1840 there were already 200 cases of stuffed animals at Calke, many collected by Sir Vauncey's father, Sir John, who also gathered the collections of fossils and minerals still to be seen in the saloon. But by the time of Vauncey's death the number of specimens ran to several thousand, and their glass cases invaded every floor of the house.

This is an extreme example of what happens on a smaller and more manageable scale in many families, particularly those of the stable home-

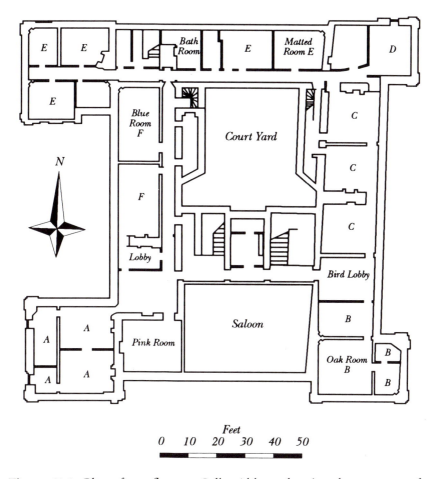

Figure 13.1 Plan of top floor at Calke Abbey, showing the sequence of occupancy of principal bedrooms A - Sir John and Lady Harpur-Crewe, 1845–86; B - Sir Henry and Lady Caroline, 1741–8; D - Sir Vauncey as a bachelor; F - Sir Vauncey and his wife, 1886–1924
(after Colvin 1985: 115)

owning classes, where the same family will inhabit the same house for several generations. The wealth of material goods gathers densely about such families, sometimes beginning as collections gathered deliberately by a member of the family, sometimes originally acquired simply as desirable pieces which then take on a collection quality in the minds and actions of successors as time passes.

Heirloom material of this kind stands between relic collections gathered from the impersonal past and souvenir material which relates to the life of its owner. It takes its value from its ability to make material the blood-line connections which link one generation to the next, and so provide each living generation with a satisfying place in the flow of things. It is a kind of ancestor worship, where part of the point is to participate in the power which can flow from the mighty dead of one's own kin and partly, in a more limited and snobbish sense, to enjoy the prestige which accrues from having ancestors at all. So the individual takes on an extended personality which reaches backwards through ancestors and forwards through putative descendants.

REMEMBRANCE OF THINGS PAST

In the film *Throw Momma from the Train*, written by Stu Silver in 1987, Owen tries to persuade Larry to murder his dreadful harridan mother. The film parallels Hitchcock's *Strangers on a Train*, and eventually Larry visits Owen's house where he meets his mother and where Owen shows Larry his prize coin collection. There follows one of the most touching scenes in modern cinema, which is worth quoting in full:

OWEN: You want to see my coin collection?

LARRY: No!

O: I collect coins. I got a dandy collection.

L: I don't want to see it Owen.

O: But it's my *collection*.

L: I don't care. Look, Owen: I'm just not in the mood. OK?

O: [Removing a box from under the floor boards, lying on his belly like a small child at play, and beginning to extract the coins from their envelopes] I never showed it to anyone before.

L: [impatiently] All right. I'll look at it.

O: No, it's OK.

L: Show me your collection.

O: No, you don't mean it.

L: [With exasperation] Show me the damned coins!

O: [Happily] All right. This is a nickel. And this one, also is a nickel. And here's a quarter. And *another* quarter. And a *penny*. See? Nickel, nickel, quarter, quarter, penny . . . And here is another nickel.

L: [Bewildered] Why do you have them?

O: What do you mean?

L: Well, the purpose of a coin collection is that the coins are *worth* something, Owen.

O: Oh, but they are. This one here, I got in change when my Dad took me to see Peter, Paul and Mary. And this one I got in change when I bought a hot dog at the Circus. My Daddy let me keep the change. Uh, this one is my *favourite*. This is Martin and Lewis at the Hollywood Palladium. Look at that. See the way it shines, that little eagle? I loved my Dad a lot.

L: [Realizing . . .] So this whole collection is, uh . . .?

O: Change my Daddy let me keep.

L: [tenderly] What was his name?

O: Ned. He used to call me his 'Little Ned.' That's why Momma named me 'Owen.' I really miss him.

L: That's a real nice collection, Owen.

O: Thank you, Larry.

(Belk *et al.* 1990: 199–200)

Here we have, in small compass, a paradigm of all the collected material kept in remembrance of things past, as souvenirs of what once was. Owen's coins are of no 'intrinsic' value, that is, they are not involved in the system of intellectual or financial values which support large tracts of human life. Their worth lies in the feelings of which they are an intimate part. The burden of the scene rests in the relationship between Larry's early remark, 'the purpose of a coin collection is that the coins are *worth* something,' and his final statement, 'That's a real nice collection, Owen.' Larry has passed through a moment of redeeming feeling as he comes to understand the importance of the coins, just as we the audience experience a brief catharsis through the dialogue as, momentarily helpless with tenderness, we recognise ourselves.

Collected material which comes from the personal past is capable of expressing and embodying profound meaning and deep feelings. After an emotional catastrophe, it is always the sight of the scarf which the absent lover used to wear which enables us to enter more profoundly into our sense of loss, showing ourselves to ourselves in ways which nothing else can do. Its characteristics are the painful pleasure and pleasurable pain of all aspects of love, and here of the self-love which contemplates a personal history and draws other people and places into it. Souvenirs are past life, past loves, past happiness or sorrow; they are, for all of us, the past which makes the present. How this can happen we must now tease out.

Souvenirs possess the quality held by all objects to be at once a genuine part of the past where they played a part, and a genuine part of the present where they can be the focus of a variety of feelings; they both attach themselves metonymically to their original context and present metaphorical potential in the present. The sights, the sounds, the taste and touch of the battle or the wedding, or the home or the holiday, are written on water which closes over without any trace save that on the memory; only the tin helmet or the silver cake ornaments, or the curtains, or the postcards, come authentically from an otherwise vanished past. They, alone, can offer tangible contact with a time that is gone, and at the social as well as the philosophical level this is of great significance to modern people for whom a feeling of rootlessness becomes increasingly oppressive, and for whom also the easy portability of objects which can move from place to place with their owners is important. A past can be represented quite adequately in the contents of a small suitcase.

Unquestionably, then, objects have the capacity to serve as the unique trace of genuine experience. But they are experience worked upon by feeling. They become the vehicles for a nostalgic myth of contact and presence in which a selected view of the personal past is vaunted over the grey and difficult present. This is the more persuasive in that souvenirs often belong to youth and are reviewed in middle age. Never again will the ageing man be a young soldier, and no matter how dreadful war was, he and his comrades seem now to have been strong, confident and either happy or affectingly tragic. Never will the mature woman be a girl again, wearing miniskirts and fancy tights, but she can remember herself and her friends as young, attractive, touchingly immature. Souvenirs toll out 'never again' and as they do so they move the authentic into the domain of the significant, where the past is endowed with satisfactory meaning. Turning-points emerge from the flow of time, and are seen as dramatic, whether happy or sad; periods of the past become stretches of pastoral content or vacant misery contributing to the flow of a life, and so personal narratives are made, supported in their 'truth' by the 'real' objects to which they refer, and a personal past is created. Origin stories are told of a past which is not repeatable but is reportable, in narratives which spiral backwards and inwards into the interior of a life. Gradually, the souvenir itself becomes the point of the story, and where once it was a product of life, now life is used to explain it.

Part of the souvenir's capacity to create narratives of the past lies in its ability to help us make sense of situations and experiences which are essentially beyond our control. The little heap of cigarette case, piece of shrapnel and cap badge which makes up somebody's memories of the War in the Western Desert serves, also, to reduce an intrinsically unmanageable and confusing experience to something about which 'sensible' memories and stories can be constructed. The same is true of souvenirs of Niagara or of the Alps, where the naturally awe-inspiring and indifferent is reduced to a memorable human dimension. Mementoes of the pyramids or the Taj Mahal or the Tower of London work in the same way: here the weight of fame and human history is brought within the scope of a simple appreciation. The same kind of reduction happens when, after a serious operation, the hospital staff offer the patient the metal clips used to hold the wound together as a souvenir of the event: a terrifying experience is turned into low humour, complete with story and supporting objects. The souvenirs of a lifetime serve to make time itself personal, familiar and tamed.

As Owen's coins show, souvenirs gathered over time come to be a kind of collection in their own right. But it is also true that many collections, ostensibly of other kinds of material, are in fact valued in large part for their personally commemorative characters. The collector may view his collection as miniature trains or examples of Victorian lace, but he knows, and the investigator soon discovers, that each piece also acts as a memory which carries a particular narrative of time and place, which of course in no way impairs its other intrinsic qualities but rather adds to its richness of association. Collections, like human lives, are seldom entirely all they seem, and much of their significance is on the inside.

The contrast between external value and the inward construction of significance explains why other people's souvenirs are, generally, supremely uninteresting, and why souvenir collections, unless they are either of 'intrinsically interesting' material or illumined by a scene like that in *Throw Momma from the Train*, are irredeemably banal. The emotional urge is well expressed by Cynthia Hughes (People's Show 1992) who, because she happens to come from Blackpool, collects commercial Blackpool souvenirs as the memorials of her own life, a telling double reflection of how souvenirs can work. She says:

> Wherever we went in the country we could usually find a Blackpool souvenir . . . It's a very good talking point . . . It's a bit of nostalgia – wherever we went in the country it was nice to have a focal point and a purpose . . . I just have so many fond memories of Blackpool as a child. You can never really escape from the place you were born, it figures strongly in your life . . . The collector in me will always be there now.
>
> (People's Show 1992)

To the outside world, the accumulated material is one of many similar collections, and of interest only in so far as it strikes a similar chord in its viewers. But to Cynthia, the collection means a good deal, so much, indeed, that she now defines herself through it, seeing herself as a collector and her collections as the fond enjoyment of a past redeemed.

COLLECTING THE DISTANT PAST: SIGNS OF THE TIMES

We define 'distant' against ourselves, and so, to each of us, the distant past is that which begins as far back as we can see, and runs up to the limits of personal and family memory: the distant past begins where heirlooms end. The ways in which as feeling individuals we desire material which comes to us from a distance plays a large part in structuring our relationship to these distances and to the material which comes from them. This is doubly piquant when the particular past also represents a cultural distinction, when it is exotically as well as chronologically far from the collector, for this will add to the complexities of his feeling.

The material which comes from the Indian communities of the southwest United States is a case in point. This material has been avidly collected down the generations since Europeans first set foot in the area. As early as 1540 Francisco Vasquez de Coronado sent – from near what is now Zuni, New Mexico – to the Spanish viceroy in Mexico City:

> '. . . a cattle [i.e., bison] skin, some turquoises, and two earrings of the same, and fifteen Indian combs, and some boards decorated with these turquoises, and two baskets made of wicker, of which the Indians have a large supply.' He also sent 'two rolls, such as the Indian women wear on their heads when they bring water from the spring, the same way they do in Spain,' as well as 'a shield, a mallet, and a bow and some arrows, among which there are two with bone points.' Finally, he included two painted blankets, all destined to be carried on foot and horseback more than 1,700 miles even by the shortest possible route.
>
> (Fontana 1978: 75–6)

Assemblages of Zuni, Hopi, Navajo and Hohokam material abound in collections, both private and in public museums, and it seems that a principal reason for the popularity of this material is the way in which the smaller pieces, especially the turquoises and the ceramics, have an appeal to Western eyes.

The material culture from the region has had a complex history of its own, beginning from about 1540 when Francisco made his shipment. At this time the artefacts were made 'prehistorically' and, by definition, subject to no influences from non-Indians. Secondly, and apparent through the eighteenth century in material like the whole elaborate range of horse furnishings, there are artefacts made by Indians for Indian use but clearly expressing white influence on the material culture. Thirdly, there are artefacts made by Indians solely in response to white culture: here belong the turquoise bracelets and tie clasps much favoured by some contemporary American males. Finally, we reach the artefacts made by non-Indians but now widely used by Indian people, like the tools used to smith silver, a non-local craft, into designs genuinely characteristic of the traditions of the area (Fontana 1978).

Here we have a particularly complex relationship to the collectable material from the past, which is worked out in some detail. Material from all stages of this historical progression has been the subject of collection after collection, and all of it accumulated in the belief that, as well as offering the acquisition of historically beautiful and interesting pieces, it offers some kind of personal contact with the past. This desire – like so many – becomes self-defeating. As the available quantity of genuinely prehistoric and genuinely Indian-made-for-Indian-use material dries up, by being swallowed into collections, the desire can only be assuaged by the deliberate production of 'collectables' which somehow carry the association of the past without actually being from any past which our notions of 'traditional' would consider acceptable. As Fontana puts it, (p. 107), 'We collect the horse gear, or even decent replicas of it, quite happy in its ability to sustain the myth of contact which is what we want'.

What sustains this myth of contact above all is the tangibility of objects, their capacity to be handled and felt. We see in collectors, and we recognise in ourselves, the special excitement which arises from the genuinely ancient object in the hand, the ability to feel the beads which were once in an Egyptian tomb, to put one's own fingers beside the fingerprints left inside a bowl by the Neolithic potter. We feel that the mute stones can speak, and tell us in eloquent language of their own time, and of how it was both different and the same as ours. We feel that if only we could stare at collected pieces from the past long enough and hard enough, we could compel them to yield up their secrets; but the effort of concentration always breaks, the hypnotic link is broken and the collector awakes to the cold hillside of his own limited here and now.

The erotic parallel for this experience of the past through its remains is irresistible (Shanks and Tilley 1987: 79–80). The desire and pleasure which the collected objects from the past can give us is played out through the tensions of presence (of the actual objects, and of the metaphor or myth of the past associated with it) and absence (the past which the pieces come from and reality which this once was), and of gratification, the grasping of the artefact, and distress, which follows the failure to attain the desired experience. The themes of the past are uncovered, but the collection is finally frustrating because it withholds the living encounter, a frustration not unknown to other kinds of lovers.

With all this goes a field of feeling which colours all our erotic relationships, whether with people and things in our own personal pasts, or the personal pasts of people who lived and died before our time. Here are our capacities for yearning, for reaching out into the hopelessness of lost encounters, for longing for what we know is forever beyond our grasp. Given the complexities of the human heart we experience this as both painful and pleasurable; we are able to enjoy our loss. Hence the refinements of satisfaction which our incomplete meetings with the past through its objects are able to give us. Here, too, we may remind ourselves, rests that long tradition in European sentiment in which self-denial is completion, and the absence through death of the beloved is an emotionally satisfactory erotic alternative.

There is a further thread to the skein of our erotic relationship with the past. A number of writers (e.g. Sontag 1979: 23–4) have pointed out that our approach to the objects of the past is voyeuristic. This is at its most obviously true when the memorials of named individuals are concerned, the desire to collect the effects of dead statesmen or writers, but there is an unquestioned element of the peep-show in all our strained relationship with the objects of the past, and the way in which we feel that these things can open doors to hidden places is one measure of our fascination with them. The opening of a sealed tomb is the classic locus for this sentiment, but it comes into play whenever material is collected from ancient homes and workplaces: the collector hurries down the dark street of the past trying to conceal his hasty glances through the windows into other people's lives. Enjoyment is a kind of appropriation, and appropriation is violation: what is seen is possessed, and to view is to rape. We are left with a kind of pornography of the past. The collected objects themselves are innocent, but they are used to provide a doubtful excitement for their possessors.

A KIND OF IMMORTALITY

If collections can create the sense of a life-history, stretching back, perhaps before the collector's own birth, they can also create the sense of immortality, of life extended beyond the individual's death. As Rigby and Rigby put it in 1944, 'because the collector has identified his creation so closely with himself (a very strengthening bond for some men), he sometimes feels that, like a strong boat, it will bear him through the centuries after his body has gone to the earth again' (Rigby and Rigby 1944: 27). The collection becomes the reified self, the tangible and enlivening aspect of an individuality which is otherwise fragile, vulnerable to the decaying processes of time.

It follows from this that the collector usually gives considerable thought to the destination of the collection, particularly as he himself starts to grow older. This process can be fraught with much sadness. As Lord Kenyon, contemplating the fact that he must leave his autograph collection behind him, said:

> No one will ever be as fond of my pets as I have been . . . I look upon them almost as one might upon the children whom he must leave behind . . . None the less dear to me are these relics of the leaders of life and of literature. Someone will preserve them, and perhaps fondle them as I have done. I trust that they may come under the protecting care of a true collector, a real antiquary – no mere bargain-hunter, no 'snapper up of unconsidered trifles,' but one endowed with the capacity to appreciate whatsoever things are worthy of the affection of the lover of letters and of history.
>
> (Joline 1902: 306–7)

The 'capacity to appreciate' seems to be an important strand in this leave-taking. Sometimes collectors skip over their own children, who would otherwise be the natural heirs, in order to train up a still-pliable grandchild in the appreciation of what has been accumulated. Belk (Belk *et al.* 1988: 551) quotes the case of the elephant-replica collector who hopes that his granddaughter, now two years old, will take over his collection, and is preparing her by reading elephant stories to her, and giving her elephant gifts. A baseball-card collector had already willed his collection to his two-year old grandson. Probably collectors of this kind realise the intrinsic limitations of their collections, and in their heart of hearts understand that their best hope of some afterlife rests in the mark which they can make upon their descendant's early childhood.

Collectors who are more ambitious for themselves and their material tend to think of their collections' futures in terms of permanent disposition in a museum, and there we touch two important motifs: the particular character of the museum and the view collectors take of the final act of self-surrender. Museums, as we have seen, are the natural heirs, or, to put it in slightly different terms, the modern representatives, of deep-rooted preoccupations in the European psyche which revolve around the capacity of material to create relationships between gods and men, the sacred significance of relics, and the need for a building in which sacred wealth can be set aside on behalf of the community. A collection once accepted by an accredited museum shares in this divine nature, and so does its collector, who is added, quite literally, to the pattern of names inscribed in stone or in accession registers, as once abbeys added the names of benefactors to their Golden Books.

Museums are immortal – to be so is one of the objects of their existence – and so collections received within them share this immortality. Collections so received have also been judged worthy by the curators, priests of the mystery, and thereafter are transformed into a new state in which mortal years have become eternity. All this is greatly eased if the collection itself is composed of material intrinsically desirable, that is, of objects to which a high cultural value is attached. This can accrue from a collector's perseverance and accuracy, as was the case with most collections of British flora and fauna. It can come from his eye for the future, allied perhaps to good fortune in the turns taken by public taste: Opie's packaging material is a collection of this kind. Most reliably, it comes in the fine and decorative art fields, especially when the collector was wealthy enough to buy in a demanding market. Behrman notes of Duveen's sales to wealthy collectors that 'he was selling immortality, and since most of his protégés were ageing men, the task of making them yearn for immortality was not hard' (1952: 102). Their immortality was, of course, assured by the purchase of pieces which museums would be very anxious to accept.

However desirable collectors may find museums, the reverse is not always true. The sense of the identity of one's whole self with one's whole collection frequently creates that most characteristic urge among collectors: to keep the entire collection together and to prevent the sale or dispersal of it or any part of it after the death of its owner. In the tensions which this generates, desire can be marred and confused by bickering about the exact terms of a donation or bequest. The museum may not judge the whole ensemble to be worthy of reception; the collector may wish to impose special terms, like perpetual display or special exhibition areas and special markings. Nevertheless, the huge majority of the collections now in museums arrived as donated collections: the collector's urge for this material eternity is so sharp, and the curator's acquisitive drive so keen, that, surprisingly often, mutually satisfactory deals are struck.

Where this does not happen, the collector, if he can afford it, may take the middle course and set up a museum of his own, specifically to act as a home for his collection and a memorial to himself. This has the advantage of giving the collector a free hand; he can arrange the material exactly as he wishes, as did the husband of the Mouse Collector with her collection and with that of his own fire-fighting equipment. Its disadvantage is the struggle to achieve recognition. To write one's own epitaph certainly counts as a derangement, an attempt to subvert the natural course of things, which only the gradual passage of time can endorse. Many great museums began as such pieces of private enterprise and have transmuted successfully into genuine institutions. But many others are more like vanity publishing, with no life of their own.

What shines through all of these acts of deposition is the comfort and relief which collectors often find in the planning and arranging. To consider the future fate of one's collection is part of coming to terms with one's own approaching death. Separating oneself from beloved possessions is as painful as any other parting, but it carries, also, a sad hopefulness. The negotiations and agreements, the conversations and the busyness, soothe the spirit and give some satisfaction in leave-taking. These last rites, too, are rites of passage.

CONCLUSION: RE-COLLECTING

The wealth of evidence from collectors and from what is recorded about the purpose and significance of surviving collections makes it clear that the capacity of collected material to create a sense of the past within the present is emotionally immensely significant to us, so much so that it is the mainspring of much collecting activity. The peculiar quality of objects make it possible for us to create an active relationship with the distant or relatively distant past, which has otherwise no intrinsic relationship to us, and in so doing to achieve a sense of continuity and psychic well-being.

Heirlooms play the same role in a more decidedly personal way. They are part of our desire to discover family history and keep photographs of family graves. Heirlooms attach us to the flow of past, present and future. Souvenirs help to create for us our own life-histories, attaching us in material form to an unreachable past, making experience concrete and so constructible into a personal narrative which makes transparent what is obscure. The transfer of collected material helps us to come to terms with our own mortality and, or so we frequently hope, may confer a little immortality upon us. Through all of this the gradually accumulating collections are not beside us, but in us, helping themselves to create the changing relationships or the changing view which we take of relationships, giving support and easing our passage.

Collections can do these things in different ways at different times. The Angela Kellie doll collection shows how the dolls and their owner inter-reacted variously over a period of some sixty years (Figure 13.2; Kellie 1983; Mackenzie 1993). Angela was born in 1930, and during her earliest years she was given dolls which had belonged to her mother and her aunt when they were children, two late-nineteenth-century wax dolls by a friend of the family, and, when she was about eight, two French dolls which had belonged to her paternal grandmother. By about 1940, then, the collection spanned three generations of the family, in fact of both sides of Angela's family: the dolls which were the souvenir of childhood for the adults had come together to create an heirloom collection for the little girl, a fact of which the adults were well aware.

'Heirloom' is not a misnomer in any sense. The oldest of the French dolls, known as Fifi, was made in Paris in 1868, in porcelain and ceramic and bought as a fashion doll from a couturier. The other French doll, known as Jane, was also made in Paris, of clay and ceramic, about 1865: both of these dolls, and the wax examples, count as 'significant' pieces, with a sales valuation. It is worth noting, too, that the objects concerned are passing along the female lines. We would expect this, perhaps, with dolls in any case, and the male role in creating heirlooms must not be underrated, but it is probable, particularly in families not of the landed class, that the cherishing of objects across the generations rests largely with the women.

As Angela became too old to play with the dolls, they were put into family storage, but during the Second World War the Kellie women would sometimes exhibit them to raise money for the Red Cross. Their role as toys of passage in Angela's childhood was over, but by the time she was an adult in the 1950s, she began to add to the collection deliberately by searching antique shops. Between 1950 and 1978, the years of her marriage and her young family, the dolls became a collecting interest occupying the role in her day-to-day life, which collecting does by structuring leisure time and shopping trips and, in Angela's case, by creating a personal position and relationships through showing the dolls and giving talks to local women's clubs.

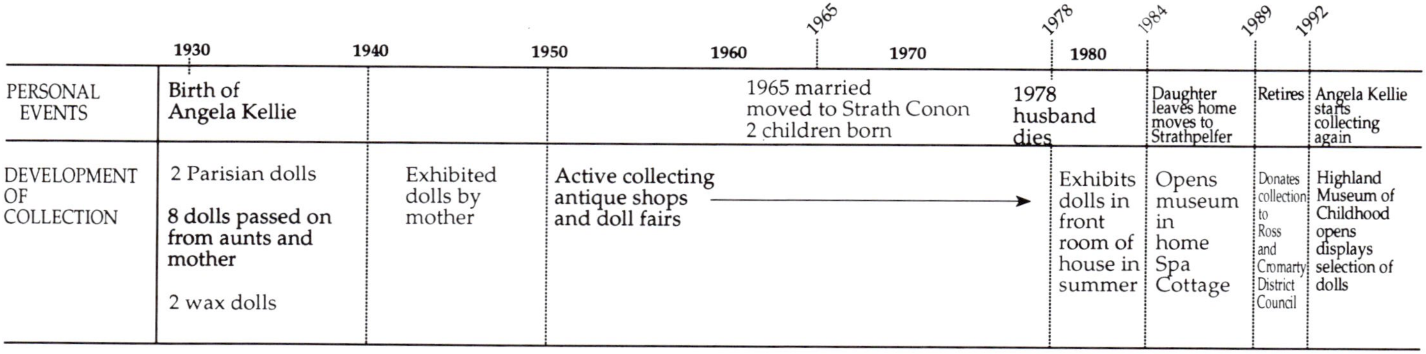

	1930	1940	1950	1960	1965	1970	1978	1980	1984	1989	1992	
PERSONAL EVENTS	Birth of Angela Kellie				1965 married moved to Strath Conon 2 children born		1978 husband dies		Daughter leaves home moves to Strathpeffer		Retires	Angela Kellie starts collecting again
DEVELOPMENT OF COLLECTION	2 Parisian dolls 8 dolls passed on from aunts and mother 2 wax dolls	Exhibited dolls by mother	Active collecting antique shops and doll fairs					Exhibits dolls in front room of house in summer	Opens museum in home Spa Cottage	Donates collection to Ross and Cromarty District Council		Highland Museum of Childhood opens displays selection of dolls

Figure 13.2 Development of the Kellie Collection in relation to the events of Angela Kellie's life (after information from Lorna Mackenzie)

Angela's husband died in 1978, and the collection helped to structure her response to this event. She set up an exhibition in the front room of her house in Strath Conon, Western Ross, establishing what was in effect a small, private museum. The collection then numbered twenty-five items, but donations soon raised it to over a hundred. In 1984 Angela's last daughter left home. This prompted her to move to Spa Cottage, Strathpeffer, and there establish the museum on a more formal footing with the assistance of several grants. In 1989 came a third life-change, when Angela decided to retire. She did not wish her collection to be split up (that so-familiar phrase to every collector) and so donated the whole to Ross and Cromarty District Council, where it forms the basis of the new Museum of the Social History of Childhood which opened in 1992. Changes in the status and the style of the collection clearly have an intimate relationship to changes and new departures within Angela's own life cycle. The dolls offer both opportunity and consolation at these times. By linking her acceptance of her own old age with the establishment of a permanent memorial museum, Angela has managed the prospect of her own death more faithfully than most of us do.

By 1989 the collection had grown from the original group of about twenty-five pieces in 1978, to over 300 dolls and doll-related material. Interestingly, as the collection grew gradually more public so its 'intrinsic' quality declined. The original French and wax dolls were joined before 1978 by some material like an oak clothes-peg doll, hand-carved around 1880, but the collection was already becoming more mixed, and from 1978 onwards, the accepted donations included reproduction Victorian dolls, a doll in Swedish national dress, a beefeater doll, Sindy dolls and Action Man figures. It looks as if the fact of the collection as such, with its own qualities and capacities, was more important than the nature of the newer material within it, a suggestion borne out by the very mixed nature of the displays. Objects like the peg doll, however, show how the collection was able to absorb 'genuine' relics from a non-personal past, and incorporate these into one woman's life-story.

We see how the doll collection and Angela's life are intertwined, providing for each a kind of symbiotic relationship, which structures time passing. The collection has given Angela a way of working out her life, and in doing so, it has provided her with an identity. In Strathpeffer, a tourism-orientated village, it has given her a niche among the shops and hotels; here she is known simply as 'the woman with the dolls'. The collection has come to define the life of the collector.

Angela's collection is a particularly striking and well-documented example of how one of the most important capacities of the collection-forming process works, but at a profounder level this capacity depends upon a number of culturally characteristic assumptions which we have already touched upon. The first is the notion of time as a progression, as a flaming arrow fired across the dark, in which past moments never recur but shine for a little in the light cast backwards from the ever-passing present. Europeans predicate all their mental processes upon this image, even though it is a notion not shared by much of the rest of the world, or indeed, perhaps by Europe's own physicists and mathematicians.

The second is the belief that individuals exist, that there is such a thing as an essential personality, capable of being the same, unique individual from birth to death, and of remaining so in the memory of others. This key European idea is sometimes called 'the humanist fallacy', humanist because it is at the heart of metaphysics and morals of the traditional kind, and fallacious because we are created as much by social and personal circumstance as we are by any inner, spiritual flame. We prefer to believe in our true individualities, but we acknowledge the role played by the outside world in shaping us, and we see memory, with all its admitted evasions and constructions, as the thread which binds a remembering individual to the past which constitutes his unique selfhood.

This helps to explain both the importance and the paradoxical nature of collected objects. They are themselves a part of the external world by which individuals are shaped, but our ability to manipulate them, in both the literal and the metaphysical sense, and their relationship to the thread of memory which they help to constitute, sustains our sense of ourselves as meaningful people passing through time. Our collections, with all their potential for selection and dismissal, offer us the romantic chance to complete ourselves, to create significance and meaning out of nothing by the power of need and imagination, and so to sustain a sense of dignity and purpose. They are both autobiography and monument. But the vertical axis of time is only one within which we must live and invent ourselves. Equally significant is the horizontal axis of space, and to this we must now turn.

CHAPTER FOURTEEN

COLLECTING IN SPACE

—— ·◆· ——

Its important that I own a bit of the universe.
I will not stop as long as there is room in the house for them.

(People's Show 1992)

INTRODUCTION: HERE AND THERE

Just as collecting structures the vertical dimension of time through its ability to help create the notions of 'now' and 'then', so it also has the capacity to structure the companion lateral axis of space by defining notions of 'here' and 'there'. Indeed, as we shall shortly see, the two together can marry up to give us the three-dimensional lattice-work through which we make sense of ourselves and the world in which we find ourselves.

The most important point to make initially is that the many ways in which material can be laid out spatially depend upon two interrelated things. Firstly, each arrangement is, in its way, an act of imagination, and the truth of this is not diminished by the fact that some arrangements seem to be entirely subjective, while others seem to relate to, or reflect, the objective realities of the world. As we shall see when we come to discuss the politics of knowledge, the problem of the objective nature of under-standing is an acute one; here we are concerned not with the ultimate reality or unreality which any arrangement of collected material may constitute, but with the ways in which our minds seem to approach the creation of meaningful spatial patterns.

Secondly, here, as in all their aspects, collections are the fruit of a select-ing process in which both the collector and the objects themselves enter into a symbiotic relationship. Notions of how one piece will 'fit' with another, from a large range of reasons about what 'fit' means, is frequently implicit in the collecting process; the desirable spatial pattern exists in the mind of the collector, perpetually modified and revised as new pieces are taken into the collection and some, perhaps, discarded. It is a common experience in all kinds of collecting that suddenly, when seen in juxta-position to other pieces, an object shines out with a hitherto unrecognised significance, which may entail a fresh evaluation of many other pieces and relationships.

This very ordinary, but immensely heartening, experience, begins to bring us closer to the heart of the matter. Many collected objects are shorn of most of their significance if they are separated from their fellows. This is, to a certain extent, true even of objects like pictures or perfect specimens of fossil fish, which embody an intrinsic aesthetic satisfaction, for here the pieces mean more if the viewer can, in his mind, supply the images amongst which they belong. It is entirely true of that great mass of collected material for which an understanding of significance primarily lies not in the pieces themselves but in the relationships between them.

We arrive at three key ideas. The use of lateral space is one of the ways in which collections achieve significance; and, because they are material and must, literally, always be somewhere, this happens in the most crudely physical way when a collector's hand puts one object here and others there. Secondly, spatial relationships put one thing beside another so that our eyes can take in both, or several, together, and come to a view about their appropriate neighbourliness. Thirdly, significance lies in the perceived relationship between collected objects. This perception is complex. It rests partly in the objects themselves and what they, with their intrinsic shapes, and histories suggest, and partly on how and what the collector can see in them (a revealing phrase). At the end of the day, the purposefulness and appropriateness of this depends upon an act of imagination, which will itself be endorsed, to a greater or lesser extent, by the surrounding social imaginative consensus, and by the extent to which the spatial relationships which result from the collector's efforts find favour in the eyes of his friends and peers.

It follows from this that the layout of collected material in its selected space is a complicated acknowledgement of a single statement in its intellectual, emotional, and physical domains. Since we and collections live together in the 'real world' of physical entities, the selected space will be 'real' space, parts of a house, special shelves, purpose-built containers and so on. Because we are the creatures we are, the kinds of sense and meaning which we conspire with our collections to create around us will cover a wide spectrum, with aesthetic, emotional and intellectual satisfactions emerging as broad, but overlapping, bands of colour. We shall concentrate on each of these, and discover that each is made up of several distinguishable shades.

Two final points. We tend to take much about the spatial nature of collections for granted, and this is one excellent reason for looking at it here. Also, we tend to grant more importance to those collections whose spatial arrangements generate 'knowledge' than we do those which generate other kinds of satisfaction. There are reasons for this, which we explore in Part Four of this book, but here we start from the assumption that all collectors and their arrangements are of equal interest.

THINGS DO FURNISH A ROOM

A great deal of collected material is gathered in broadly domestic situations, and is expected to help create the particular furnished, and therefore social, character of the room in which it is placed. Indeed, even allowing for reservations in the exact correspondence between 'room furnishings' and 'collections' in any pure mode, a purity which is in many ways unhelpful, there is a sense in which, in many actual situations, collected material and room contents are so much the same that they have to be discussed as a unity.

The relationship between a deliberately accumulated group of related objects and the furnishing of domestic rooms goes back as far as we can see in the history of both, and this history can be traced through the classical, or (to a lesser extent) through the medieval world, and so into modern times. It is an important aspect of the way in which the northern-European middle class developed from about 1400, and it is the century following this time that domestic inventories start showing us groups of material like plate and pewterware, which were certainly carefully gathered, and displayed, and which are the direct ancestors of later and contemporary collections of ceramics and glass.

We can trace the history of the accumulation of this kind of material quite easily once the china trade got underway in the sixteenth century and well-off families began to acquire porcelain, some of it custom-decorated, mostly for use but some of it purely for display (National Museum of History 1990). A high watermark in the taste for chinoiserie on (superior) domestic display was created with the Prince Regent's Brighton Pavilion, where the Octagon Hall, for example, had a pair of elbow chairs in the Chinese style, and the figure of a Chinese court official in plaster composition made in China about 1820 for the English market (Royal Pavilion 1991). The then existing Marine Pavilion was decorated in the Chinese taste from 1802, and the present Pavilion was transformed into its present Indian-inspired style by 1822.

What is true of the broad ceramic class is also true of the other great class of room-defining collections – framed pictures. These begin very grandly in the Renaissance, deliberately collected right from the beginning as the abundant detail surrounding the collections of princes and cardinals makes clear. The pictures tend to occupy those special long rooms which we still call galleries, and are being placed in increasing density on the walls as the sixteenth and early seventeenth centuries progress. Thereafter, we might say, pictures have never looked back, although naturally the tastes of the time have always dictated the subject-matter of the picture, the design and elaboration of the frame and the mounting, the number of pictures displayed together and details of the hang like the use of picture rails, the visibility of string or wire and distance from the floor. In a domestic setting especially, these matters are scarcely less important than the character and quality of the work itself in contributing to the overall effect, as any professional picture framer will testify. All this accumulation of material taste has long since brought us to the point where we expect some of the rooms in a well-found household to be filled with furniture, itself an area of collecting but a relatively uncommon one, displayed ornaments chiefly of glass, metal and ceramic, and framed artwork. We will form a view of the inhabitants of the rooms largely on the strength of how we react to the collected taste on display.

For one must, as Wilde put it, live up to one's blue china. Collections of this kind, essentially, do three interrelated things. They compose accumulations of material which somebody simply likes, for all the complex social and individual reasons which make up personal taste. They are intended to be displayed, something which is by no means true of all collections. Their place is to be seen, by family, friends and visitors, and so they have a role which is, as it were, public in a private setting. They are consciously intended to put the impress of the owner upon domestic space, to create a room of one's own in which one is at home. And, as part of doing this, they help to define the functions of rooms, and separate one from another.

All of these things are made clear by the Willow Pattern Collector (personal communication). The Willow Pattern design is interesting in itself because, more or less alone of designs, it has managed to retain its hold over our affections over a period of some three centuries. This is remarkable given the history of social change over the period, and seems to bear partly on the perennial grip which Oriental design in general has over the Western imagination, especially when, like much Chinese food, it has been carefully adapted to Western palates. Partly, it has to do with the character of the design which is almost always rendered in the traditional style with relatively little alteration down the decades, and in the conventional blue on white. The result is something which fits in with many styles of décor, for those who enjoy, rather than despise, a touch of wholesome convention. Partly, of course, it arises from the charming nature of the depicted scene, with its lovers and secret garden. All these matters the Willow Pattern Collector bears in mind.

The collection, however, is not exclusively of Willow Pattern. There are altogether some forty-five pieces, and of these about a third show different scenes, including pieces of Spode Italian design and several Chinese pieces showing traditional dragon and flowering-branch motifs. This does not disturb the collector, who thinks that they all go together well, and is more interested in this than she is in gathering examples of particular manufacturers and styles, or completing sets. The pieces are disposed about the sitting room, some on a mixture of shelves, and some hanging on the walls. They are confined to this one room, and they do a good deal to confirm its special character, and its distinction from the other rooms in the house.

OBJECTS IN SETS

The emotional satisfaction taken in the spatial arrangement of collections comes in many different guises: aesthetic and intellectual satisfactions have their emotional side, and so does creating the kind of object fantasy which we shall look at in a moment. But one of the commonest kinds of collecting has always been the urge to fill up blank spaces with the right piece, with the object that takes its proper place and completes the set. Here belong what we may call the album-based collectors who devote themselves to accumulating stamps, cigarette cards, autographs, matchbox tops, and more recherché but essentially similar material like the labels from Heinz baked-bean tins through the decades. With these collectors belong those whose objects are too large or awkward to fit into an album, but whose mental processes seem similar. Here come those who collect record sleeves, the programmes of theatre shows or sporting fixtures which they did not attend, and a huge range of printed ephemera. Here too, in many ways, come the collectors of coins and medals, and here also are some of the book collectors, especially those who are interested in first, or partic-ular, editions (and who are to be carefully separated from those who buy books to read, and who put them on visible shelving because they like to feel them close).

This kind of collecting was so widespread in the earlier part of this century as to constitute what many people would then, and perhaps still do, regard as the collecting paradigm. Everything which we know about contemporary collecting suggests that it is still very popular, although it looks now as if people try to avoid the most obvious kinds of things, like stamps, and try to choose something a little different, which they can regard in a favourable light as a tribute to their individuality. For it is, above all, this kind of collecting which has given collecting in general its dowdy, fusty image, to plumb the psychological depths no further. There are clear reasons for this. The collected material is usually devoid of much aesthetic resource. Similarly, although it may well possess considerable historical and social significance, this is not the aspect of it which usually animates the collector. It does not display well in a larger domestic context (or any other: museums always have difficulty exhibiting stamps), and cannot be said to have many home-making qualities. Against our classic yardsticks of quality therefore – artistic, intellectual and imaginative – this kind of col-lected material falls well short. It may occasionally have a financial value worthy of respect, but since this value relates solely to its collected value, and what collectors are prepared to pay, the argument is a circular one.

And yet such collections do have their satisfactions. These seem to rest in the thrill of chase, particularly when rare objects are being sought, and, above all, in the satisfaction of filling in all the blank spaces and being able to contemplate the completed set. The collector may know supporting information about the individual objects, but the sense of their collection rests in its truly collective nature, and in the investment of time and effort which have gone to make it so. The point of such collections is the finite conclusion which they offer, for the sets are genuinely delimited and completion is a possibility, where generally it is not. These collections, *par excellence*, demonstrate the joys of possession and control, and of opening and closure in a closely defined context of spatial layout.

SPACE FANTASIES

Greenblatt has drawn attention to what he describes as 'two distinct models for the exhibition of works of art':

> one centred on what I shall call resonance and the other on wonder. By *resonance* I mean the power of the displayed object to reach out beyond its formal boundaries to a larger world, to evoke in the viewer the complex, dynamic cultural forces from which it has emerged and for which it may be taken by a viewer to stand. By *wonder* I mean the power of the displayed object to stop the viewer in his or her tracks, to convey an arresting sense of uniqueness, to evoke an exalted attention.
>
> (Greenblatt 1991: 42)

But these qualities are not necessarily separate, for there are a range of collections where the collector has brought together his sense of both resonance and wonder to create a private universe of fantasy and deliberate illusion. Such universes are ordered by an individual sense of form, colour and symbolic meaning through which the personal vision is turned into physical reality through the manipulation of objects in space. The intention is that of the theatre, to create a stage set, a spectacle, in which states of mind and feeling can be invoked and the dramatist's intentions played out.

These characteristics are very fully developed in the extraordinary collection of Charles Paget Wade at Snowshill Manor in Gloucestershire, which has, as an entity, been in the hands of the National Trust since 1951 (Wade 1945). The Manor is a typical domestic farmhouse of the sixteenth century, renovated with all the reverence associated with the Arts and Crafts Movement which had influenced Wade considerably. Here, but in a very special way, Wade organised his enormous but eclectic collection of weapons and armour, household fittings and utensils, tools of trade, furniture, costume, scientific instruments, pictures and sculpture. Eventually, by 1940, he had over 5,000 objects. He has told us how he viewed his collecting:

> Collecting gives such a wonderful opportunity for a wider view of humanity, both the present and the past. How varied are the traits of those met with when searching for 'finds', from most of them something is to be learned . . . How much more interesting any object becomes with sufficient knowledge to suggest how it was made, where and when, what its purpose was . . . To all kinds of queer places by narrow alleys, up obscure yards, to old inns, coach houses, stables long disused, scrap iron yards, ship's chandlers, sheds by the waterside, old maltings, mills and barns . . . To ancient attics, chilly cellars, gaunt garrets, cobwebby crypts, mouldering vaults. To homes rich and homes humble. To workshops of the saddler, cobbler, wheelwright, blacksmith, baker, druggist, confectioner, carpenter and to the village watchmaker's little den behind his shop where many hoards of his father and grandfather still remained.
>
> (Wade 1945)

Wade seems to have been inspired to collect from a child, when he was allowed to play with the curiosities in his grandmother's Chinese cabinet. In 1911 he inherited a private income derived from family estates in the West Indies (that dark thread of plantation-owning which runs beneath so much English collecting), and abandoned a rather uncertain career as an architect, preferring to develop his skills in woodworking and craftsmanship.

When war broke out in 1914, he joined the Royal Engineers, and it was while he was in France that he saw the advertisement for Snowshill Manor. In 1919 he was able to buy it, together with two cottages and fourteen acres of land. He embarked immediately on a large-scale restoration which took three years to complete. It is unlikely that Wade had ever intended to live in the Manor, and he settled in one of the cottages known as the Priest's House. The Manor was to be the setting for his collection and for his imagination.

Wade himself, the manor house, and the collection have to be understood together. The house was (and is) on three storeys, and each floor contains about seven rooms, mostly fairly small and with interlocking access (Figure 14.1). Wade tells us that

> I set out to find furnishings that would make an attractive series of rooms pictorially, not to form a museum. I have not bought things just because they were rare or valuable, there are many things of every day use in the past, of small value, but of interest as records of various vanished handicrafts. My guiding essentials have been

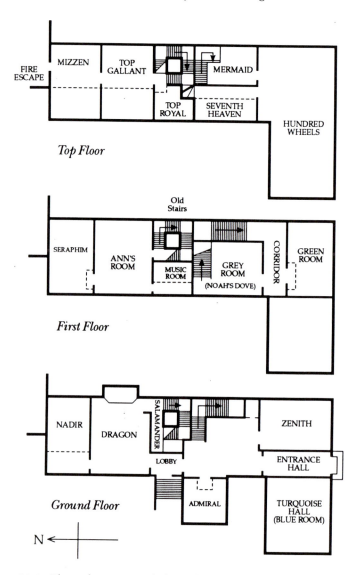

Figure 14.1 Plan of rooms and their designations at Snowshill Manor, Gloucestershire (after De la Mare and Jessup 1992)

DESIGN, COLOUR and WORKMANSHIP. I am often tempted to let colour come first, though it cannot retrieve bad design. Many of the pieces were bought for the place they now occupy. At first I intended to keep to English things but soon found that there was little indeed with colour . . . So I turned to the golds, vermilions and blues of Spain and Italy, then to Persia and eventually to the Far East.

There the three essentials of shape, colour and craftsmanship are attained to the fullest with the additional attraction of another world, a civilisation ages old where symbolism enters so much into decorative designs. What joy these old things are to live with, each piece made by the hand of a craftsman, each has a feeling and individuality that no machine could ever attain.

(Wade 1945)

Each room has a name, chosen by Wade to reflect its contents and character, and its position in the house. The Admiral holds nautical artefacts like naval swords and model ships, and these are repeated in Top Gallant, Top Royal and Mizzen, where they are accompanied by clocks and tools. The rooms reflect Wade's interest in the sea which dated back to his childhood spent on the quay sides of Great Yarmouth. Mermaid and Seventh Heaven hold the memorials of childhood, including Wade's toys from his own childhood. As he tells us, 'All the greatest experiences, the things we remember, the things our imaginations seize upon, happen in our childhood when we couldn't care less, when, in fact, we were thinking of other things.' He wrote, with some bitterness, 'Seventh Heaven is only to be attained in childhood before schools and schoolmasters have been able to destroy the greatest treasure, imagination' (De la Mare and Jessup 1992: 30).

Turquoise Hall concentrates on Oriental art, and Meridian and Zenith on early European furniture. Hundred Wheels houses transport material, including the twelve boneshaker bicycles, which Wade collected at a time when nobody else was interested in them. The instruments in the Music Room were arranged like a small orchestra with brass and percussion on the right, woodwind in the centre and strings on the left. Most strikingly of all, the Green Room holds Wade's twenty-six suits of Japanese *samurai* armour (one of the best collections outside Japan), all arranged to give the impression of warriors meeting at dusk around a charcoal brazier.

Wade has told us how and why he bought his house and his collection together:

If chosen with thought these [things] can form one harmonious background and a perfect sense of restfulness can be obtained. Furniture should . . . merge into the background, golds and glints on polished metal are far more effective in subdued light. In such surroundings a hundred and one trains of thought are enlivened, thoughts of other lands, other customs, other people, other times.

(Wade 1945)

The house acted as a frame, separating the contents from the outside world, and shaping them to the imagination of collector and viewer. The house offered Wade a secret world, a Chinese cabinet made large enough to enter, wherein mysterious discoveries could be made and objects experienced in all their provocative beauty and interest. The house is a maze without symmetry and without centre, where discoveries are made at every turn. 'Mystery', Wade tells us, 'is most valuable in design; never show all there is at once.' (Wade 1945). The notion of 'composition' haunted much of what Wade did, like the tableaux of Japanese warriors or the theatrical 'dressing-up' parties, using the collected material, in which guests, like Virginia Woolf, J. B. Priestley and John Betjeman, were expected to take part.

Wade understood the staginess of the whole conception, and its vulnerability to shafts of outside light and air:

> Flowers used as a decoration can only be used successfully against a perfectly plain background, and no such exists here . . . In this house they are just as incongruous as items from the house would be if placed in the flower beds. Each room being designed as a complete picture as it stands, the introduction of flowers may well destroy the whole effect.
>
> (Wade 1945)

Within the illusion the illusion is all, and the objects in their settings work upon us as the master intended; but flowers pressed between the pages of books have meanings different to those of living flowers, and the contrast can be painful. Wade's own life illustrates the difference between the solitary, private preoccupations of the collector making fantasies in space, and the world of living flesh and blood. In 1946 he married, and left Gloucestershire to spend most of the rest of his life in the West Indies. Appropriately, however, he is buried at Snowshill.

SERIAL KILLERS

Collections can lay out life after another fashion which also reflects a view of the truth of the world, for here belong the collections created by the serial killers, the zoologists and botanists, and their equivalents among the dead, the palaeontologists and the palaeobotanists. Historically, such collectors descend directly from the sixteenth-century gatherers of natural curiosities, whose thoughts changed direction around the last quarter of the seventeenth century, away from the 'rarities', now seen as the sports and peculiarities of nature, and towards Nature herself, envisaged as an intricate but sensible pattern of corresponding and differing forms whose relationships study, along the lines drawn out by Carl Linnaeus, could and would reveal. As Rudwick has put it, the overriding aim of naturalists was

> the systematic ordering of the whole range of diverse natural entities . . . Classification was not a means to an end, a clue to evolutionary

relationships, for example. It was itself an end, the end of knowing the true order of Nature.

(Rudwick 1972: 208)

The key elements in this approach to the understanding of nature are the elaboration of classificatory hierarchies which reflect the natural systems of the world, the creation of a systematic taxonomy.

Collections of this kind account for the majority of pieces now in public collections, and the numbers are enormous: the British Museum (Natural History) in South Kensington, one of the world's greatest accumulations of natural-history collections has something in the order of 60,000,000 specimens. Some of the collections were created by men famous in the history of science, like Adam Sedgwick, whose material is in the Cambridge University Museum which carries his name; others, like William Reed's collection of fossils in the Yorkshire Museum (Pyrah 1988), or the Earl of Enniskillen's collection of fossil fish in the South Kensington Museum, have served to add important pieces to the overall pattern. This collecting practice spans all types and classes of men (mostly), and also occurs in all periods of life from childhood to old age. Partly for these reasons, and partly because the principles on which such collecting is founded stand at the heart of modernist thought, this kind of collecting, too, is seen as a paradigmatic activity, a 'natural' and useful way of spending leisure time.

The principles of spatial classification which informed natural-history collecting operated also in other areas. As early modernist ideas of chronological and spatial order developed, picture collections began to be arranged in order to show the development of style and technique from one generation to another, and the relationships between artists of the same generation. This historicist approach required the reorganisation of art galleries into 'period rooms' within which artists would be arranged in 'national schools' to point up correspondence and influence, as well as the glories of 'national art'. Art had achieved this kind of reorganisation by the beginning of the nineteenth century, and through the century understanding in the applied arts followed suit so that the notion of an ability to define 'periods' and 'schools' developed – with intense effect, not just upon what was becoming the history of art, but upon all aspects of taste and design, and indeed, the idea of human history itself – as a visible, definable progression which could be made manifest through the arrangement of its remains.

From this it was a relatively small step to combine ideas of spatial natural classification and chronological human history, and to create the idea of typological sequence as the key to understanding those cultures – prehistoric in Europe and more or less contemporary to a man of the nineteenth century everywhere else – whose surviving evidence was primarily material culture. The remarkable thing is that this did not happen until the

1880s, by which time Darwin had given his further dimension to the natural world and its collected material, and when the link was made, in the person of General Pitt Rivers, typology in archaeology and ethnography embodied both a spatial and a chronological dimension (Chapman 1991).

The archaeological collections formed in this image are also very numerous indeed. One example will serve: the collection achieved by Dr Hugh Fawcett (Thomas 1982). This collection, which stayed in Fawcett's own hands through most of his long life (1891–1982) and was eventually purchased by Bristol City Museum, comprises over seven thousand archaeological pieces, all in their original cabinets. Fawcett deliberately collected in the style established by Pitt Rivers, and the collection therefore contains a range of tools, weapons, domestic articles and personal ornaments, drawn from many parts of the world. The objects were collected in order to illustrate the principle of 'typology – the development and evaluation of the commoner and "every-day" artefacts of early and primitive man, by bringing together and grouping, as widely as possible, a series of such objects from all over the world' (Fawcett 1960: 3). Fawcett believed that the study of large bodies of artefacts can 'not only reveal much of the evolutionary progress through the ages, but have an unbroken continuity in similarity of intention and form from the earliest types to the present day' (p. 5). The arrangement of the documentation and of the storage cabinets reflected these ideas.

We must stress that the principle of classification under discussion here – taxonomic for the natural world, typological for the human world – is essentially the ordering of lateral space through the disposition of material by means of which correspondences and differences, and so relationships, are demonstrated. It should be said, also, that although this thinking is typical of the period roughly between 1700 and 1950, it is still indispensable. There is no way of beginning to get to grips with the natural world other than through the classic basic identification of specimens, and there is no way of starting to understand the human prehistoric past other than by handling ceramics, stone and metalwork and appreciating their similarities and dissimilarities, no matter how elaborate the superstructure of understanding may have become. This, viewed starkly, is a daunting thought.

We may consider a characteristic collection assemblage, endeavouring to strip its confusing familiarity from our gaze. Plate 9 shows a view of the Sedgwick Museum, Cambridge. We see a stylised and formal layout of collection cases, placed in rows which run in both directions across the room. Each case is labelled and numbered. Each comprises a display area at the top, through which objects can be seen through glass, and each has below a series of uniform drawers. The whole is a nest of boxes – the cabinets in their spaces, the drawers in the cabinets, the compartments in the drawers, and the specimen in each compartment, together with its

Plate 9 View of upper gallery, Sedgwick Museum, Cambridge, showing the cases of geological specimens laid out in patterns which correspond to the creating of knowledge. (photo: author)

double-barrelled Linnaeum name and its museum number. We have to ask ourselves what is the nature of the specimens, what is their relationship to the web within which they have been placed, and what the implications of this are.

As with all material objects, the perceived understanding which natural-history specimens embody cannot be detached from the object itself, but only discussed with reference to it in concrete terms. Similarly, the relationship of the scientist to the natural world is not a simple one. Specimens are selected for collections on the strength of their supposed 'typicality' or their 'departure from the norm' so that they may act as referents, a process which is clearly circular and self-supporting. It is justified scientifically on the grounds that, put crudely, it seems to work – that human notions of typicality and norm do square with 'objective' or 'natural' reality in the sense that decisions made on this basis do not normally backfire.

Once collected, natural-history specimens have become artefacts in the sense that the act of selection turns them into man-made products, for once they have entered our world, they become part of the relationships which we construct for them. A simple semiotic analysis makes this artefactual

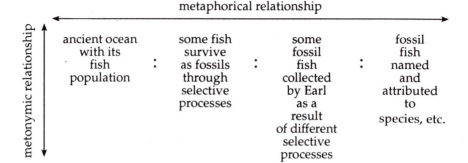

Figure 14.2 Semiotic relationships within the Earl of Enniskillen's collection of fossil fish. It should be noted that although two left columns may be intrinsically 'naturally' related as genuine metonymics, the two right-hand columns are only perceived as metonymics by humans and are, in fact, a form of metaphor

nature clear. If we take the fossil-fish collection accumulated by the Earl of Enniskillen, we can see that the fossils gathered by the Earl have a metaphorical relationship to the natural fish swimming unknown and unnamed in the ancient sea, and that a further metaphorical act transpires when the collected fish are given their systematic names (Figure 14.2).

The 'unnaturalness' of this kind of procedure is made glaringly plain when we see cases of Felidae, like that among the famous Milwaukee Museum early animal cases, showing together spotted and striped cats who may in human terms belong to the same group, but who have no connection with each other in the world where they live out their unregarded lives. These are constructions, human and social, and like all of their kind, we are more inclined to admire them than to criticise. This becomes painfully obvious when a new start of knowledge – perhaps like that which is reviewing Darwin's notions of the 'survival of the fittest', in favour of 'once a runt occupying a special niche always a runt', – disrupts the careful web of relationships and reveals then for the *ad hoc* bits of building which they are.

We can see that systematic collecting depends upon principles of organisation, which are perceived to have an external reality beyond the specific material under consideration, and are held to derive from general principles deduced from the broad mass of kindred material through the operation of observation and reason; these general principles form part of our ideas about the nature of the physical world and the nature of ourselves. Systematic collecting, therefore, works not by the accumulation of samples, as much more obviously emotionally based collecting does, but by the selection of examples intended to stand for all the others of their kind and to complete a set, to 'fill in a gap in the collections' as the phrase so often upon curators' lips has it. The emphasis is upon classification, in which specimens (a revealing word) are extracted from their context and put into relationships created by seriality. This is achieved by defining set limits which apparently arise from the material. This kind of collecting is a positive intellectual act designed to demonstrate a point. The physical arrangement of the finds sets out in detail the creation of serial relationships, and the manipulation implicit in all this is intended to convince or to impose, to create a second and revealing context, and to encourage a cast of mind.

What operates so powerfully upon this cast of mind is the congruity between the value allotted to each separate piece, and its visible place in the scheme of things, which is spread out before the viewer's eye through the layout of cabinets and compartments already described. There is something quite magical in the visual and tactile experience of this systematic classification of hierarchy – itself a word for priestcraft – which bewitches the intellectual imagination, leaving us as impressed as children with the way in which it all fits together. The visible layout presents the irreducible material evidence of the proposition of classification and relationship which for us constitutes understanding, and it does this by producing knowledge apparently made actual in physical assemblages which physically present the facts by placing one thing beside another in their correct and intelligible sequences. More than this – it is doubtful if the stratigraphic relationship between fossil-bearing beds, the typological relationship between varieties of hand axe, the historical relationship between the products of ateliers or the taxonomic relationships between starfish, could be intelligible – could really be said to exist at all in a meaningful way – without the serried ranks of cabinets and drawers which carry relationships to the enquiring eye and convince the intelligent mind. Seeing is believing, and we cannot see the pattern of the carpet until it is unrolled on the floor before us.

CONCLUSION: HOBBIES ON THEIR STAMPING GROUNDS

The point has already been made that many of the collections brought within the orbit of this discussion – the postal stamps, the fossils and the preserved flowers – are 'classic' collections, paradigms of the kind of accumulation which an older dictionary would class as hobbies, with all the air of diminishment which this word frequently carries. All of them, too, and by inference the many collection subjects for which those chosen here stand, make their points by acting as inscriptions on space, by allotting ground and arranging classificatory sets within it.

SITTING ROOM		BEDROOM		SPARE ROOM
easy chairs		bed		chairs
carpet		carpet		packing cases
books	:	clothes	:	collected material of all kinds
ornaments		personal ornaments		
pictures		books		

Figure 14.3 Room contents as sets shaping notions about privacy and access

Regardless of the content of the collection, this works in a number of interrelated ways. Collected material helps us to define our domestic space, together with other kinds of furnishings and all the other social arrangements which characterise modern European domestic life. When we consider the contents of typical rooms, set out as a series of opposed sets (Figure 14.3) we can see that collections are helping to shape our notions about privacy and broader access, about appropriate décor and activity. Natural-history material defines the non-human world in similar ways. Viewed from this perspective, collections are grounded, in every sense, in their capacity to place objects into significant spatial relationships.

I have deliberately chosen to discuss those collections generally described as 'systematic', that is, those which reflect the true relationships of things, within this chapter in order to bring out their psychological kinship with the collections of sets and fantasy; their intellectual content will concern us again when we consider the politics of knowledge. The analysis of a range of collections brings out the central point. Whether we describe the process as taxonomy, typology, set-selecting or fantasising, it becomes clear that the essence of the process is the same, the predilection which our minds have for producing distinction and order – that is, meaning – by creating sets of Chinese boxes which comprehend each other, and for doing this literally, in the physical delimiting of space.

It is worth pointing out a specially European relationship between the predilection for serial classifications in space and time, and an element in long-term mentalité. The characteristic pictorial or figured version of the systematic relationships which spatially ordered material embrace, is exactly that of the characteristic European kinship system set out as a family tree, with a clear senior line and ancillary branches, all of which operate horizontally and vertically in classificatory space. So deeply embedded in our mind-sets are our own social systems that we forget their singularities and fail to realise the extent to which they underlie and shape our

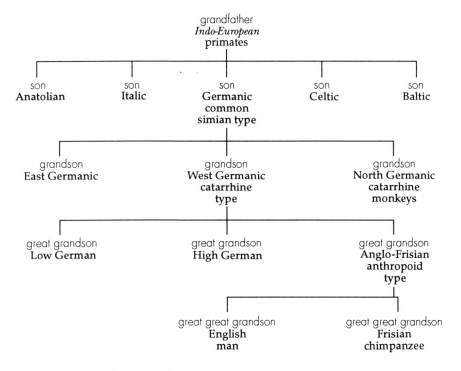

Figure 14.4 Characteristic vertical and horizontal classificatory systems for languages (Indo-European languages) and animals (from C. Darwin's *The Descent of Man*, published in 1871), with European system of kinship and descent showing underlying principle

thinking in other areas. A glance at the classificatory and kinship systems set out in Figure 14.4 will show how the last has informed all the others.

Each of the collections discussed here, like all collections, is a self-contained, internal world in its own right, and so its collector experiences it. Each is also a reflection of the rest, a microcosm of the extending series of microcosms, which eventually become the macrocosm of classified space which humans aspire to divide and rule. Hobby horses, however humble they may be, each stamp out their own ground in the scheme of things.

CHAPTER FIFTEEN

MATERIAL IDENTITIES

— •◆• —

Brekekekex ko-ax ko-ax,
Brekekekex ko-ax ko-ax,
children of freshwater ponds and springs,
gather we all together now
and swell our lofty well-becroaken chorus,
ko-ax ko-ax

Chorus of frogs, Aristophanes *The Frogs*
(Lattimore 1970: 34)

I've thought about putting it in a museum.

(People's Show 1992)

Part Three has explored how individuals interreact with the material world
to produce collections through which they can create their identity, an
identity which is essentially a play upon the world, a game which is at once
played out and pursued. The play engages all the dimensions of an individual's life: his inner relationship with himself and with the social demands
of the world; his relationship with others; his ordering of personal space;
and his view of his own place in the passage of time. Collections are
material autobiography, written as we go along and left behind us as our
monument. All this can happen in a number of ways, and we shall draw
together the threads by considering two contrasting collections. The first,
which has been mentioned before, is the Frog Collection of Edna of Walsall
which featured in the first People's Show (1990). But, lest it be thought
that between the paradigmatic glass amphibians and the avant-garde French
philosophers it all comes down to frogs in the end, Edna's collection will
be matched by that of Robert and Lisa Sainsbury and the Sainsbury Centre
for Visual Arts, University of East Anglia.

Edna is an elderly lady living in Walsall whose life is dominated by her
collection of frog images, in pottery, glass, metalwork and printed textiles
(Plate 10). The obsessive quality of Edna's interest is as clear to her as it is
to everybody else: Edna says, 'I bet there's not a week goes by when I don't
buy a frog . . . I talk to them everyday when I come down on my lift.
In the morning I say good morning and hear them croaking to one another
. . . People are always asking if I've got any new frogs.' She is known
throughout her community as the Frog Lady, and at the time of the 1990
People's Show received considered media coverage which confirmed

Plate 10 Edna and her husband, with Edna's collection of frog images, Walsall. (photo: Mo Wilson)

her identity. Her behavioural interaction with her frog images has formed a perpetual cycle, or spiral, through much of the later part of her life, which has created her identity, and this has been supported by the personal relationships solidified into the collection through the giving of gifts and birthday presents.

Edna started the collection, however, at a moment of transforming crisis in her own life, when she was faced with serious illness. The first frogs and all they stood for comforted and supported her through this time of trouble, and now enshrine the memories of that ordeal. The frogs dominate Edna's living room; they establish the physical framework within which she lives, just as they establish her social and temporal framework. Edna is married, but her husband distances himself a little from his wife's obsession, tolerating the frogs among which he lives for her sake.

In his heart, Edna's husband probably thinks as perhaps most men would, that frog collecting is the sort of thing that women do, mildly odd as all of the sex, but harmless. The accumulation of frog images is an extremely common form of collecting, so that special shops (Figure 15.1) and special collectors' fairs exist to cater for the taste. Unquestionably, frog and related collecting – pigs and cats are also very popular – is a gendered activity. These small animals have an obvious affinity to small humans, and act, like dolls, as baby images and substitutes. Edna deliberately creates

Figure 15.1 Logo of 'Frog Hollow', a shop which specialises in frog images for collectors, 15 Victoria Grove, Kensington, London

an anthropomorphic character for her frogs, wishing them 'Good morning' and 'Good evening' every day, and she is far from alone. Animal collections are thought to foster a loving, caring and essential maternal character, which, by tradition, can easily absorb a foolish and besotted strain.

But there is rather more to it than this. Frog images are frequently shown got up in human sporting and everyday clothes, and in so doing they are well within a tradition of considerable antiquity. The English folksong 'A Frog, he would a-wooing go' is one of the most regularly recorded among traditional singers on both sides of the Atlantic, and has many variants. Frog Princes are part of the standard European repertoire, and frog familiars for witches (Murray 1962: 218) or others can give advice and help, or act as a general comment upon the action, as does Aristophanes' chorus. The cultural disgust felt towards frog-eating Frenchmen – as opposed to honest beef-eating Britons – has helped to sum up the antagonism felt for 'different' neighbours only forty kilometres away at their closest point. Frogs are possessed of transforming powers, just as collections of them are, and much of this power is addressed to woman as lover and intimate. Frogs are, in other words, one of those natural phenomena which have been brought metaphorically into the human world in order to help create social relationships among people and between people and nature.

This kind of metaphorical relationship should be put beside the type of

CREATURE	:	FROG
(frog) as SIGN		(creature) as SYMBOL

CREATURE   :   FROG
(frog) as SIGN   (creature) as SYMBOL

- creature
  living unregarded
  life in wild
  according to
  natural cycles

- scientific construction
- frog as example of
  family Ranidae
- collection specimen named,
  accessioned, taxidermed,
  displayed, creating relationship
  between humans and nature

(creature) as SYMBOL

- traditional construction
- anthropomorphised frog
  creating relationship between
  humans and nature,
  Frog Prince, etc.
- collections of frog images
  played with and talked to

Figure 15.2 Analysis of modes of frog collecting

collecting which Edna does not do, that is, of frogs as natural-history specimens assembled to demonstrate the range of frogs in the world and their relationship to other life-forms and to their environment. As we have seen, this intellectual ordering of spatial relationship is as much an act of imagination as any other construction, and equally, in its way, a piece of writing on the darkness. The relationships between the various frog modes can be set out as in Figure 15.2, where the semiotic notions of sign and symbol are employed. Frogs in their natural habitat, unregarded and unnamed by humans, are living as a sign, metonymically at one with their intrinsic surroundings. But when they are brought into a relationship with humans by the giving of names and qualities, they act as symbols for this qualifying structure, which then itself forms a metonymy of its own. In fact, frogs are formed into two quite distinct human constructions, 'scientific' and traditional, which bear a metaphorical relationship to each other as well as to the natural creatures; both are constructs, and both are 'true' in their different fashions. The collection of frog images represents the anthropomorphic and representational tradition in its realised, physical or material, aspect, and is so placed on the figure.

Similar analyses could be worked out for the analogous cats and pigs, the collecting of all of which, like the frogs, would turn out to be the latter-day manifestation of a traditional inclination. Many of these animals, too, have a gender content in their metaphorical constructions, which together with their smallness, make them an appropriate way of sustaining a female and maternal image. Edna, and those like her, stand within a long line of sisters.

Plate 11 Reliquary fang head from Gabon, Africa, made of wood with brass discs, late nineteenth or early twentieth century. Height 33.5 cm. Sainsbury Centre for the Visual Arts, University of East Anglia. (photo reproduced by kind permission of the SCVA, University of East Anglia)

The Robert and Lisa Sainsbury Collection at East Anglia is offered to us in a very different way, and is an obvious topic for discussion because Robert Sainsbury has written about it. In 1973 Sir Robert and Lady Sainsbury presented their collection to the University of East Anglia. The collection consists of non-Western three-dimensional pieces, considered in this context as art objects with formal, aesthetic qualities, and nineteenth- and twentieth-century Western art pieces by accredited masters, such as Modigliani, Picasso and Moore, many of whom were interested in, and influenced by non-European art (Plate 11).

Sir Robert has told us how he views the collection and what it means to him. He writes:

I never decided to become a collector. In fact, I have never regarded myself as a collector in the most usually accepted sense of the word – that is to say, I have always refused to acquire something merely because it filled a gap, or added to the representation of a particular art form. Rarity, as such, has had no attraction for me. If asked what am I looking for, I always say 'I am not looking for anything.' On the contrary, I have spent my life resisting temptation. For although denying that I am a collector, I have to admit that, first as a bachelor and then jointly with my wife, I have, for over forty years, been a 'passionate acquirer' – a passionate acquirer of works of art that have appealed to me, irrespective of period or style, subject only to limitation of size, in relation to the space available, and, naturally, cash.

(Sainsbury 1978: 1)

He says, 'In my acquisitions I have been essentially eclectic', and that 'possibly the only valid art experience was my capacity to be tremendously stimulated by particular plastic qualities of certain works of art'. He 'discovered the additional appeal of texture or patination, and of being able to hold or touch an object', and tells us that 'my personal reaction to any work of art is mainly sensual, intuition largely taking the place of intellect . . . our aesthetic sensations . . . have their origins, deep down, in our memories of physical satisfaction' (Sainsbury 1978: 13–14). Clearly, the sensual appeal of the objects is extremely strong and belongs with a range of similar physical sensations, reminding us of Baekeland's (1988) analysis of the immediately sexual nature of collections. The notion of collection as passion comes across vividly in what Sainsbury says.

The collection has been described as 'the product of a marriage', and seems to relate both to Sir Robert's acquisitive urges and Lisa Sainsbury's Parisian connections (Benthal 1989: 2). The identity created by the Centre is a joint one, and its university, quasi-public, nature is important. The Sainsburys considered the University of Cambridge for their donation, but rejected it on the grounds that they 'would not be able to stop the University from eventually splitting' up the collection, should it so choose (Benthal 1989: 3). Eventually East Anglia was chosen, and the resulting Centre was conceived not as a traditional museum but as a new kind of institution:

People have asked me 'Why a University?' 'Why a new University?' 'Why UEA?' 'And why, in any case, "A Centre for Visual Arts" incorporating a School of Fine Arts – why not a straightforward museum or gallery?' It is because we want to give some men and women – and who better than undergraduates in a School of Fine Arts – because we want to give them the opportunity for looking at works of art in the natural context of their work and daily life, not just because they have been prompted to visit a Museum or Art

Gallery – to give them the opportunity, when young, of learning the pleasures of visual experience – of looking at works of art from a sensual, not only an intellectual point of view – above all, of realising that certain artefacts are works of art as well as evidence of history. A new University clearly lends itself to our project in a way not possible at the older Universities.

(Bethal 1989: 3)

There were early tensions between the Sainsburys, the University and the city of Norwich, which are highlighted in the story told by Benthal (1989) that when a party of distinguished foreign architects was sent by the British Council to inspect Forster's innovative building, they found themselves at the town's supermarket after asking directions to the Centre.

But the dimension which mattered most to the Sainsburys in the creation of the Centre was that of lateral space in its character and organisation (Plate 12). The Centre was to be 'an opportunity for looking at works of art in the natural context of [the students'] work and daily life'. Its underlying intention is to create a display as much like a private collection as possible, and hence the use of the unusual term 'Living Area' for the main display space (Figure 15.3). The objects are intermingled, without contextual information,

Plate 12 View of the 'Living Area' showing some of the permanent collection, Sainsbury Centre for the Visual Arts, University of East Anglia. (photo reproduced by kind permission of the SCVA, University of East Anglia)

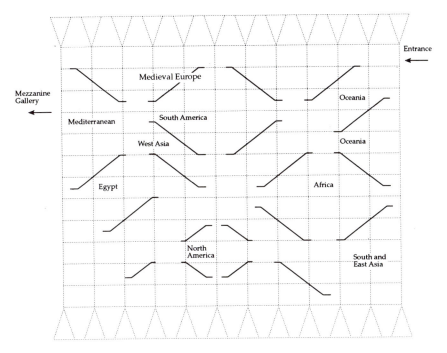

Figure 15.3 Floor plan of the 'Living Area', Sainsbury Centre for the
Visual Arts, University of East Anglia (after Sainsbury Centre
information leaflet)

and the viewer, on his daily occasions, is invited to make his own
aesthetic discoveries, an approach which underlines the Centre's paradoxical
public/private nature.

Collections are psychic ordering, of individuality, of public and private
relationships, and of time and space. They live in the minds and hearts of
their collectors, for whom they act as material autobiographies, chronicling
the cycle of a life, from the first moment an object strikes a particular
personal chord, to specialised accumulation, to constructing the dimensions
of life, to a final measure of immortality. For these personal inscriptions
on the blue void, the *content* of the collection in many ways matters much
less than its *formal* role in weaving the pattern. But collections are also
made of real objects to which intrinsic meaning is accredited, and operate
in the political arena where private pastoral can become public indecency.
In this world of exterior values, the Sainsbury Collection is seen as an
exciting mixture of European and non-European art, a juxtaposition which
is saying something important; while Edna's frogs are dismissed as unwor-
thy of attention. The implications of these judgements, the politics of value,
will be among the pressing ideas to preoccupy us in Part Four.

PART IV

THE POLITICS OF COLLECTING

CHAPTER SIXTEEN

POLITICAL PARAMETERS

——— •✦• ———

Of everything which we possess there are two uses: both belong to the thing as such, but not in the same manner, for one is the proper, and the other the improper or secondary use of it. For example, a shoe is used for wear, and is used for exchange; both are uses of the shoe. The same may be said of all possessions, for the art of exchange extends to all of them.

Aristotle The Politics (Davis 1959: 41)

Jorge feared the second book of Aristotle because it perhaps really did teach how to distort the fact of every truth, so that we would not become slaves of our ghosts.

The Name of the Rose (Eco 1983: 491)

INTRODUCTION

Let us, at the outset, remind ourselves of the shape and thrust of this study. We are concerned with the nature and implications of one significant aspect of human culture: how participants in the European tradition have shaped, and have been shaped by, their relationship to the material world of objects, particularly by the practice of accumulating special material which, in the broadest sense, we have called collecting. Collections help to create social action, and so 'old' collecting, accumulated in the past, continues to affect us through the continuing successions of presents.

We have argued that the European involvement with the notion of accumulation and collection is a particular one, both in its selective and sacred character and in the centrality of its significance. This seems to be linked with a range of shared characteristics, which are part and parcel of a shared social and historical experience. One of the most significant of these is membership of a common language family which presents a shared idea of social structure, one which particularly stresses the notion of the individual, and a shared mind-set which works by making distinctions of the this : that, now : then, and here : there kind. This is accompanied by a shared classical and Christian tradition, which has meant that for some two millennia all educated Europeans have read more or less the same books, and a shared history, particularly for Western Europeans, of internal and external expansion inextricably involved with the growth of what it is easiest to call capitalist economics. We see a system in which, for all these accumulated reasons, individuals and societies share a disposition to construct themselves in terms of distinctions which can be concretely expressed through manipulation of the brute physicality of the material world.

MATERIAL VALUES

The framework for grappling with this interrelated cluster of attributes was set out in Figure 1.8, a figure repeated here (Figure 16.1) with additions which sum up the argument so far. In Braudel's terms, the arrow represents

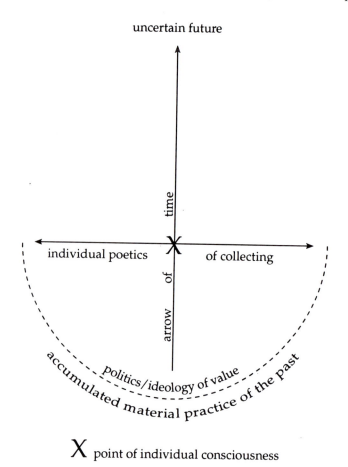

Figure 16.1 Plot which brings together the practice, poetics and politics of collection in a time frame

mentalités of the Long and Medium Term. The analysis of Long- and Medium-Term collecting practice has been our concern in the second Part of this study. The intersection of past and present, where each individual is located, is where collecting takes place and is itself a Braudelian act in the immediate or Short Term. We have seen that a collection arises partly out of the predisposition of the individual, itself a part of the flow of cultured time, and the discussion of how and why individuals relate to collected material concerned us in Part Three of this study.

In this Part, we are concerned to bring together the flow of long-term collecting practice and the motives of the individual in order to understand better how collection choices are made, what kinds of collections result, and how these are viewed. To put the matter another way, to the collection dimensions of inherited social practice and poetic individuality, we must now add that of ideology or politics. By the end of this discussion we shall hope to have shed some light on the questions posed at the end of the last chapter. Edna's frogs mean as much to her as the collection in the Sainsbury Centre means to the Sainsburys, but to the rest of us they are likely to be of very unequal value; from an ideological point of view the frogs are quite valueless, while the Sainsbury material is important, and, because it incorporates a range of Western and non-Western material, valuable and interesting in a variety of ways. We must try to understand how and why this is so.

The first and most fundamental point is that all value is symbolic value: even values which appear to relate to the maintenance of the daily fabric of life are, in fact, outcomes of the symbolic structures which constitute social life because, however oppressive the utilitarian world may appear to be, it would always have been possible to do things differently. Collections, no more or less than uncollected material but much more obviously, belong in this world of symbolic value. It is equally true, however, that societies need principles of valuation and a range of values in order to be able to function.

We are faced, therefore, with a series of interlocking questions: How are material values created? What political considerations underlie the selection of materials for collection? How and why are collections treated differently? How does this relate to the broader political patterns of dominance and exploitation? How does it affect outcomes? These are enormous questions, and since our primary business is with collected material, we must try to focus as closely as possible upon the directly material aspects of the problems; but the effort to understand their material nature will be necessarily wide-ranging.

Since political practice is of its nature self-referential and self-supporting, it follows that arguments about it tend themselves to be interrelated and circular. The best way to cut into the cake is to suggest – following what we have identified as a deep-seated European practice of distinction now

us	:	them
present	:	past
authentic	:	non-authentic/spurious
normal	:	odd
identifiable	:	unidentifiable
art	:	not-art
real	:	fake
knowable	:	unintelligible
scientifically recorded	:	no context
special/important	:	standard
interesting/provocative	:	boring
cultured	:	uncultured
traditional	:	rootless
masterpiece	:	artefact

Figure 16.2 Oppositions of thought and feeling which structure traditional value judgements

in its latter-day structuralist phase – a group of interlinked standard oppositions of thought and feeling around which, in terms of our instinctive reactions, mental and emotional values and judgements are traditionally determined (Figure 16.2). The word 'traditional' is crucial, because it reminds us that the values with which we are dealing have come to us from the history of past practice, but for the moment let us take it as underwriting the validity (however limited) of what is said here.

On the left-hand side are those aspects of material goods which modern European society traditionally prizes, and on the right their opposites. We feel that knowledge is real and can be known, that individuals truly exist, and that the accumulated weight of historical practice rightly informs the present. We privilege the authentic, and the genuine or real, over its opposites. We feel more comfortable with the normal, the knowable and the identifiable (particularly if we are museum curators), and the scientifically situated in time and place. We prefer things which are interesting and provoke us to thought, even if this sometimes conflicts with our taste for the clear-cut and the easily positioned. We think we know what art is, and believe that this has to do both with the notion of importance, as this word is used habitually by Sotheby's and Christie's, and with the ideal of the masterpiece. We understand 'culture' in its older meaning of a cultivated and informed taste, rather than in its newer one of social practice unencumbered by value judgement, and we prefer things to be intelligible and valuable against our idea of traditional cultivation. And we always think that we know best, and make use of outsiders in order to create and confirm our own yardsticks. Finally, we assume that 'proper' values are public, which is to say, shared by all right-thinking people. Their opposites are nobody else's business, the private poetry of each of our lives.

We can, if we choose, be reminded of Joyce's image of the Holy of Holies, that fine and private but ambivalent place which is sometimes a museum and sometimes a lavatory, and so add a further sequence to our set of pairs (Figure 16.3). This is to structure the worthy and the normal in terms of our own most obvious selves, and to link it with material nature, a notion which has considerable resonance.

A simple scheme like this can be read in a number of ways. It offers, however naïvely, the sketch of a politics of aesthetics, implicit in words like 'art', 'masterpiece', and 'cultured'. It offers, similarly, an idea of a politics of knowledge, implicit in words like 'authentic', 'real' and 'known'. These together add up to a politics of value as this is presented in the realm of objects and collections. At the same time, it can be read as an image of 'us' and 'them' where 'we' are normal, authentic, important and so forth, and 'they' are odd, lacking proper roots, uncultured and so on. It is, that is to say, a mechanism for endorsing distance and difference.

The politics of aesthetics, of knowledge, and of difference are so cunningly interwoven by a society bent on keeping up its strength, that they are difficult to separate out as discussion requires. Nevertheless, we can produce a serviceable scheme with a little further analysis (see Clifford 1988: 222–9; Greimas and Rastier 1968; Jameson 1981). If the notions of authentic : non-authentic/spurious, and masterpiece : artefact, meaning a special high-value work and an ordinary object, are taken as the structuring axes, then we arrive at the frame given in Figure 16.4, and on to this can be fitted the other pairs already discussed. Four quadrants emerge, authentic masterpiece, authentic artefact, non-authentic (spurious)

pure : impure

canonical : colloquial

mind : body

included : extruded

food : excrement

Figure 16.3 Further value-structuring oppositions

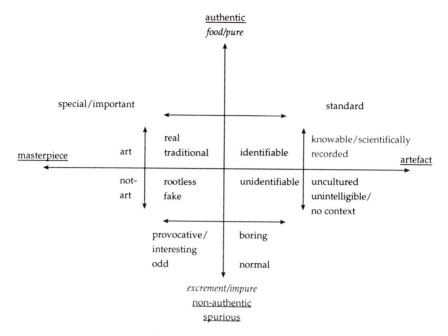

Figure 16.4 Axes of masterpiece : artefact and authentic : spurious which structure notions of value (drawing on Clifford 1988: 224; Griemas and Rastier 1968)

masterpiece and non-authentic artefact, which, as we shall shortly see, serve to qualify the material which is characteristically the subject of collection in the European world.

Within these four quadrants are structured our notions about quality and rubbish, art and non-art, and knowledge and non-knowledge. But implicit within them are also notions about the appropriate way to structure 'presence' which is identified as the values which the structure presents, and 'distance' or 'difference' to which it is opposed. An important aspect of the ways in which we select in order to construct value are the ways in which we see our relationship to difference, because such construction is our standard way of bringing our relationship to such distances into the magic circle of our understanding. Perception of value is also, always, an appropriation.

All distance is cultural distance, but it works within the two dimensions of time and space, of degrees of temporal and physical proximity. This construction of self and other, or home and exotic, begins for both time and space with 'me', and gradually moves out to a final 'them' and a distant 'past'. To anticipate the argument, both notions of distance encompass a fault line, above which the European 'I' acknowledges a certain kinship or familiarity (in both senses) and below which much becomes truly different. In terms of global culture, this line comes where 'white' gives way to 'brown/black'. In terms of history, it seems to fall amid the classical period, beyond which people stop being 'obviously like us'.

There are two further dimensions to the system. The use of words like 'art', 'masterpiece' and 'authentic' in the top half of the plot suggests immediately that this, in the politics of value, is where museums will be situated, and these hints are well taken: although, as we shall see, the matter is not without its complexities, museums do operate within the holy part of the system. Conversely 'not-art' and 'uncultured', in the genteel sense of culture, belong outside museums, in the 'ordinary' world of daily commerce and commodity. To all of this collecting bears a complicated relationship. The final dimension is part and parcel of the whole system: it is in perpetual motion at every level of detail. Individual objects and collections can and do move from one quadrant to another; how far and in what ways this represents 'change' is a point to which we will return.

CONCLUSION

This, then, will structure our discussion. We shall look first at the contents of the quadrants and at the politics of value, in its social, aesthetic and epistemological guises, which they represent and underpin. We shall then discuss how collecting has structured the distance in time and place. We shall investigate the idea of material culture value change, and how this can come about, and then relate this to the interface between commercial exchange and embedded exchange and develop the relationship of this to the range of market operations.

CHAPTER SEVENTEEN

THE POLITICS OF VALUE

—— •◆• ——

You're casting your eye round the shop, Mr Wegg. Tools, Bones, warious. Skulls, warious. Preserved Indian baby. African ditto. Bottled preparations, warious. Everything within reach of your hand, in good preservation. The mouldy ones a-top. What's in those hampers over them again, I don't quite remember. Say, human warious. Cats. Articulated English baby. Dogs. Ducks. Glass eyes, warious. Mummied bird. Dried cuticle, warious. Oh, dear me! That's the general panoramic view.

Our Mutual Friend (Charles Dickens 1865: Chapter 7)

'At least,' said the Prince, 'allow me the pleasure of arming you after the Highland fashion.' With these words, he unbuckled the broadsword which he wore, the belt of which was plated with silver, and the steel basket hilt richly and curiously inlaid . . . There was one addition to this fine old apartment, however, which drew tears into the Baron's eyes. It was a large and spirited painting, representing Fergus Mac-Ivor and Waverley in their Highland dress; Beside this painting hung the arms which Waverley had borne in the unfortunate civil war. The whole piece was beheld with admiration, and deeper feelings.

Waverley (Sir Walter Scott 1805: Chapters 40, 71)

INTRODUCTION

Europeans are what Europeans have been and so in looking at ways in which the different kinds of value are allotted we are looking into the material face of a civilisation immensely complicated in its likes and dislikes, and its automatic assumptions and rejections. We are dealing not only with the twin peaks which make, say, a Rembrandt painting or the blackboard in Oxford which bears Einstein's equations chalked by Einstein's own hand, both immensely significant cultural and collectable artefacts in their different ways; we are dealing also with small sentimentalities and snobberies, with small calculations which together add up to a view of value. We shall use the plot already set out to structure and enlarge our appreciation of how valuation works (Figure 17.1).

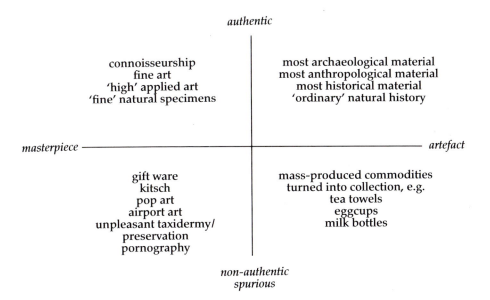

authentic

connoisseurship
fine art
'high' applied art
'fine' natural specimens

most archaeological material
most anthropological material
most historical material
'ordinary' natural history

masterpiece ———————————————————— *artefact*

gift ware
kitsch
pop art
airport art
unpleasant taxidermy/
preservation
pornography

mass-produced commodities
turned into collection, e.g.
tea towels
eggcups
milk bottles

non-authentic
spurious

Figure 17.1 Collection valuations plotted against the axes of masterpiece : artefact and authentic : spurious

The word 'authentic', over which much ink has been spilt in the recent past, carries with it not only the notion of 'real' in the forensic sense, but also the feeling of 'genuine' in the emotional sense, of sincerity, honesty and truthfulness after its own kind. It absorbs ideas like true-bred and consistent: with authentic things what you see is what you get without double-dealing or unpleasant surprises. Authenticity in material goods is the moral equivalent of lifelong friendship between people, the essence of honourable dealing. Non-authentic or spurious is the opposite of these things. Its morals are those of the bazaar, where the buyer bewares. Its glamour is sickly and its appeal curious, in the newer rather than the older sense of the word. 'Masterpiece' speaks directly to us of the older, pre-modern European system of production, before modernist industry and mass production. It carries the burden of excellence, and also of having successfully passed a social and cultural test. 'Artefacts' are simply that: the world of objects which do not make it into the masterpiece class.

The four quadrants which these two axes create structure most of our ideas of material value. In terms of food, genuine French cuisine is acknowledged to be the authentic European masterpiece; for a traditional Englishman roast beef and vegetables is a standard artefact, authentic if it is home-cooked, spurious if it is warmed-over in a poor café; for every-body non-authentic masterpieces are cakes made with egg-substitute and cream from a tube. Fabrics work in a similar way. Silk is the acknowledged authentic masterpiece, a position which comes partly from its intrinsic qualities of lightness, softness and warmth, partly from the way its shifting lights and soft colours delight our eyes, and, partly because we know that it is the 'natural' product of a particular kind of animal. Authentic artefact fabrics are 'genuine' cottons, wools and linens, while non-authentic artefacts are commercially mixed fibres, often sold under a brand name, for which one has to know in advance about matters like colour-fastness, shrinkage and behaviour under an iron. Spurious masterpieces are fabrics got up to kill but nasty to wear, the harshly dyed nylons and polyesters, and what used to be called 'art silk', artificial silk, commercially redeemed by a play on words which makes use of the fact that 'artificial', like 'artefact', and 'artful', a characteristic of the spurious, does indeed contain the word 'art' in the sense of 'raw materials transformed by cunning', a fact which reminds us of the interweaving complexities of the matter in hand.

How we feel about things, and how we give these value, it becomes clear, is a mixture of physical attraction and revulsion, itself, of course, culturally created, which has to do with notions about 'naturalness', craftsmanship, fidelity to traditional standards, and a kind of durable goodness which means that the thing will not suddenly reveal itself as hurtful and disappointing. These criteria can support an allotment of the broad range of collected material into the four quarters, bearing always in mind that here we are looking at generally accepted values in the long term, rather than relatively recent changes in valuation.

The authentic masterpiece quarter is occupied, as if by right, by everything which connoisseurship would recognise as art, that is, by those paintings and drawings in all media, those sculptures, and those prints executed by a range of techniques, which by their intrinsic qualities are entitled to the description 'fine' or 'high'. Also here come high applied art, material from the atelier and the studio rather than the workshop and the factory. Allowed entry is fine metalsmiths' work, usually in the valuable metals, the work of jewellers and enamellers, and of studio potters and glass workers.

The bulk of this eminently collectable material was made in Europe and within the last four hundred years, but a substantial proportion of it derives from beyond these boundaries. Much Greek and Roman material will be included within this quarter, and the criterion here seems to be, not any argument about intrinsic quality because this is taken for granted, but, much more simply, a measurable level of survival. A classical marble, be it never so battered, has its place without question; so has many a relatively humble bowl or plate, providing enough of it survives to give a reasonable idea of its appearance. As we move chronologically backwards beyond Greece, the matter becomes more problematic. The small pieces of pot and metal are on the whole definitely less aesthetically interesting, and the monuments to Middle Eastern political savagery have always hovered uneasily between art and a kind of archaeology. Tiny cultural details have enormous significance: hair in Assyrian crimps gives a message quite different to that of classical locks, because one is European and the other is not. Language makes these fine distinctions clear. 'Crimp' is a contemptuous word at every level, whether describing an outsider or a hair-do that has gone badly wrong, while 'lock' expresses so mainstream a perceived good quality that its meaning has become rubbed away into banality.

There is also another, and quite different, category of authentic masterpiece material, and these pieces are what might be (and often are) described as Nature's masterworks. Here are the fine crystals and plumages, the impressively complete fossils like some of the Jurassic reptiles, and the sheets of marble cut to reveal colour and pattern. These are usually displayed with the same pomp and circumstance as an important picture, and we are encouraged to view them with much the same mixture of admiration and awe. We may note that all of the material described here commands a high financial price, some of it very high indeed.

Very different is the material included in the authentic artefact quarter. Here the financial value of each individual piece in a collection is usually negligible. The occasional specimen, a particular coin or fossil, may command a certain price because it is rare and so needed by many to complete a particular set, but in general, it is the set itself, the whole collection, which is valued as a unity for the sake of the information which it holds. In the authentic artefact quarter comes all the collected material which is not in the masterpiece class but which is nevertheless, sincere, genuine and culturally true. Authentic artefacts are trusted friends not hired hands.

Here come the collections of social-history material, the tools, toys, clothes and household goods of our relatively immediate predecessors. Here come the collections of much the same character from the more distant European past, medieval, Roman and prehistoric, which we are accustomed to call archaeological. Here, too, come their equivalents from the rest of the non-European world, material that we are accustomed to call anthropological or ethnographic. Here, equally, comes the great bulk of the collected natural-history material in the world, the accumulation of which has been the life work of many thousands of people over the past three centuries, most of them Europeans, and which has resulted in the collection of many hundreds of millions of specimens. The value that accrues to these collections is not that of individual excellence, except in some rather specialised senses; rather it is the value of knowledge.

Things change as we drop below the line, into the area dominated by the non-authentic, spurious end of the axis. Within the spurious artefact class come those pieces which are perfectly authentic in themselves, but which are rendered inauthentic through a collecting process which, in terms of political value, endeavours to turn them into something which they are not. Here comes material like pepper and salt containers, eggcups, ordinary tea towels, common corkscrews and the like, which, when bought in a shop and used for their proper purpose are entirely legitimate, but which can strike us as strained or foolish when assembled into a collection, particularly when we are thinking in terms of ideological value rather than psychological resonance. On the outer edges of this collecting practice are the hoards of milk bottles and old newspapers, for which we generally feel we need a good deal of special pleading to induce us to accept them as other than both ideologically and psychologically perverse. The essence of the spurious artefact, politically speaking, is the once-decent artefact perverted into something it is not as a result of collecting activity.

Spurious masterpieces, in their unlovely way, share some of the characteristics of fine art and some of the contemporary ordinary artefacts just discussed. Their kinship with fine art rests in the fact that they too have no overt (though, for both, plenty of subvert) simple functional or practical purpose – they cannot be used or consumed in the earthy sense of these words. They have been produced to enact a wholly symbolic role, as makers of statements and creators of relationships. But, like the other contemporary commodities, they have been mass-produced through normal ways to become material lumped together as 'gift ware' and sold in gift shops. Here are all the commemorative pieces which we buy on holiday to keep or to give each other when we get back. Here are miniature baskets, often made out of inappropriate materials, or tiny coal scuttles which we buy when we 'go round' factories or heritage centres, and all the adult toys which we might label kitsch. Here is the airport or tourist art, the masks and wall-hangings and necklaces, which we bring back, in commercial reminiscence, from trips abroad. Here, too, are the garden gnomes with their wheelbarrows and fishing rods; here are delicately hued and painfully refined boys and maidens of the better class of garden centre, all shadowing authentic garden statuary in bronze and stone. Here, of course, are Edna's frogs and all their kind.

Equally spurious, but in a rather different way, are those collections of preserved human and animal remains, particularly if they are treated in ways which make us morally queasy, like seeing little girls in high-heeled shoes and make-up. Here belong the displays of small mammals – foxes, mice, cats – formed by taxidermy into 'human' poses and placed appropriately in cat cottages, clad in 'human' trousers and shirts. Here too, certainly from the standpoint of today, are the trophy-mounted heads and paws, each inscribed below with date and place, together, often, with the name of the hunter and the details of the kill. Here is the morbid taste for bones, whether as South American shrunken heads or as St John Southworth in Westminster Cathedral. Here also are the relics of famous murders, Christie's spade from Rillington Place, London, and the like preserved in the Scotland Yard Black Museum (Waddle 1993). The spurious essence of this kind of material rests in its intention to produce itself as 'important' when against traditional tests it is not, just as gift ware offers itself as 'art'. Each aspect of the spurious mocks one of the upper categories.

A little thought will suggest how all the collected material discussed in the second and third parts of this book would fall into one or other of the quarters (although for some the resting-places will be surprising), and show how tastes change with time, a point to which we will return. Meanwhile, some clear shapes emerge. Material of quality and importance is located in the top half of the plot, while the dubious and the insignificant is placed below the line. To put it another way, excellence and knowledge both belong on top (a truly political statement) and we can recognise both by comparing them with the underclasses. It is to these political matters that we must now turn.

OBJECTS OF VIRTUE: THE POLITICS OF EXCELLENCE

The collections gathered in the authentic masterpiece quarter are those which command the highest admiration and the highest prices, and we have to ask ourselves why this is so, why these collections are considered the seat of excellence and virtue. We may take three characteristic objects, not quite at random as will appear, but taken from an enormous range of comparable material: the row of saints sculpted in stone on the west portal of Chartres cathedral, Raphael's Sistine Madonna, especially the much-reproduced detail showing the upper part of the Virgin holding the Christchild, and any Stubbs painting showing a horse in a landscape. All of these are familiar images of the kind which crop up regularly on greeting cards, and each may be taken, after its own fashion, as a cultural paradigm.

All three images are capable of moving us profoundly or, to put it equally truly, we are capable of being moved by them when we are in the right mood. The moment of intense feeling passes, leaving us able to reflect upon it, and we see that we have felt love, pleasure and relief accompanied by a physical loosening of nerves and sinews. The whole experience is comparable to, if not exactly like, suddenly seeing a dearly loved person or sighting home after a difficult absence. Exactly how the images work upon us differs in detail one from another. The Chartres sculptor, working in the broadly naturalist tradition of the High Middle Ages, gives us a row of saintly figures, rather tall and narrow, partly as a result of their positions on the church wall but partly deliberately heightened. The figures, male and female, are wearing draped garments organised so as to give a series of long, slow upward-slanting diagonals set in clear but not oppressive parallels, and these are echoed by the long hand of one of the males raised in blessing and the waist-length braids of the women. The design and the meanings – the powerful reality of the Christian ideals of holiness and godliness – are finely congruent; the masses of line and form work to show us that what they are telling us is true, and, while we look at it, we are susceptible to its message.

Raphael's Sistine *Madonna and Child* belongs within that large class of art and literature about which, to traditional-minded Europeans, there is scarcely any need to say anything, apart from a modest quantity of biographical and historical detail. The picture is transparent in its simplicity, either as the central image of the Christian faith (since God-made-flesh must precede God-crucified), or as the central image of humanity for whom the picture of the young woman with her baby in her arms represents the sum of human tenderness and hope. And, of course, as with the Chartres figures, form and content, of image, line and colour, are inseparable within our emotional response as a whole.

The responses on offer from the Stubbs are less powerful and, we may instinctively feel, rather coarser-grained, one reason perhaps why Stubbs does not stand so high in the artistic hierarchy. A characteristic painting might show us a splendid piece of horseflesh being held in a grassy field by a groom. Behind the figures rolls the incomparable (at least to those brought up amongst it) English landscape of patchwork fields and trees embracing agreeably disposed gentlemen's seats and villages with spires. Behind is a summer sky and the whole is nicely framed in leafy foliage. Very soon, we know, the young master will appear and ride off into the rosy, beckoning landscape at the back of the picture, delighting in the good horse and the fresh country air, and in his own health and high spirits. It is worth noting, incidentally, that as the young mother with her baby is the essential feminine image across not only Europe but much of Africa and other parts of the world also, so the corresponding male image is that of the young chieftain on horseback, a powerful figure in much of Africa, Asia and America, as well as Europe, although, of course, treated in a wide variety of styles. The Stubbs, well within this broad tradition, shows us human pleasures within a human landscape.

Related values appear, although with a different emphasis, and one which makes their ideological nature just as clear, when the collections of high craftsmanship are analysed. In July 1992 the British Museum acquired the Armada Service, valued at £900,000. The British Museum press release told us:

> 'The Armada Service' comprises twenty-six silver dishes, each having a gilded rim engraved with the arms of Christopher Harris of Radford, Devon (*c.* 1553–1625). The dishes are the work of four different goldsmiths and bear hallmarks for London 1581, 1599, 1600 and 1601. The set has long been known as 'The Armada Service' because, according

to a Harris family tradition, it was made from New World silver captured from Spanish treasure ships after the Armada and presented to Sir Christopher Harris for services rendered. A document signed by Sir Walter Raleigh and Sir Francis Drake, now in the collections of the British Library, could be the basis for the tradition. It records that when Raleigh captured the Spanish carrack *Madre de Dios* in 1592, Harris was appointed commissioner to safeguard the booty. Sir Christopher may well have been repaid in kind for his part in safeguarding the treasure. 'The Armada Service' is the earliest known surviving set of English dining silver.

We are unlikely to be as deeply stirred by these dishes as we are by the pictures, but we note that what is evidently important about the service is the quality of the craftsmanship required to create it, and the long tradition of craft which this entails, together with the historical context in which it can be placed, and its rarity, given the vicissitudes of the English seventeenth century.

We begin to see that cultural value is assigned to objects which are seen to embody the highest levels of technical skill in areas of craftsmanship which require inherent skills of hand and eye, linked with long personal dedication pursued within a social structure which gives this appropriate space and time. The closer this skill is married to the expression of cultural norms both deep and central – the notion of sanctity, the vision of motherhood, physical joy and pride – to the ideal, that is to say, of ourselves at our truest and best – the more profoundly we are likely to be touched, and the more we value the experience and the object which can give it to us. This, of course, is why high art is also virtuous: it embodies moral goodness, and the more this seems to be of its essence and the less it is like a tiresome tract, the greater the work is judged to be. Art, like love, is held to be ennobling. To this authenticity we can add that of historical genuineness, of true provenance to artist, studio and succession of owner, where it is, in part, the business of the art historian to provide reassurance. One or another, or more than one, of these qualities the objects in the lower quarters lack. The cultural statements which they make are equally true and complex, but they are not what we perceive as the points of reference from which cultural value itself derives.

Of course, not everything which a collector might feel himself entitled to describe as fine art is as transparent as the three examples chosen here. Many pictures are culturally complex and require detailed exegesis before the intentions of the painter can be understood; Holbein's *Ambassadors* is a case in point, now known to be giving a complicated allegory of contemporary views about life, death and the politics of religion (Berger 1972). Similarly, a vein of desperation can be traced back through much early twentieth-century art to earlier modern times and so to Bosch and the Vision of Hell. But, put very crudely, these pictures either comment upon the simplicities in the more transparent works, in that they gloss them and thicken out the cultural detail of the message, or they act as companion pieces by describing the loneliness and desolation of the human condition, which, the implication is, can only be assuaged by accepting the consolation which the broad tradition offers. We are likely, the message runs, to find what content is possible to us if we are true to what our culture tells us we are: this is what admired art tells us roughly up to the First World War, and it is still what most people viewing pictures in an exhibition expect to feel.

The wall of the cultural city looks very different from the inside and the outside. Inside, instead of the smooth ashlar face and cunningly fitted blocks, we can see the supporting metal bands, the bits of old buildings used as hard core and the holes to hold the scaffolding. The construction, in other words, is not altogether what it seems. The authentic masterpieces which embody our most cultured selves may move us to love, but we must unhappily admit that it is self-love, for if art mirrors nature (as it may do in very many ways) then what we see reflected is ourselves, and what we give is a warm, emotional endorsement of the values and assumptions which these works are underpinning. If art is treated as anthropology, it can, by the normal processes of social-anthropological analysis, be shown to be operating as a social element which provides functionalist and symbolic expression and reinforcement of social practice viewed, of course, by its practitioners as morally good: and the better it does this the more highly it is regarded.

The Chartres figures show us ideals in ideal representation, echoing religious themes which run back to Plato, but a look about the world does not convince us of their existence. Feminist critique detests an imagery which encourages women to suppose that motherhood is their truth and their destiny. Young chieftains may enjoy good horses and broad acres, but they do so only at the expense of the rest of us. Here we are looking at art as a part of the mechanism of dominance and subservience which a Marxist critique can reveal for what it is, and which is seen to operate in the interests of the great European bourgeoisie who have always paid for the artists, bought the pictures, and managed the code of values and morals in their own interests.

The artistic eye penetrates more deeply than these true, but socially superficial, criticisms. As Berger has shown us (1972), the time of traditional oil-painting, culturally the most visible aspect of the European masterpiece tradition, can be set roughly at between 1500 and 1900, and it helped to create our most characteristically modern European ways of seeing, most of which are quite different from those of the rest of the world. It affected how we see landscapes and nature, important people, history and mythology, women – yes, Rubens shows a rape scene, but its very artistic – and food. Oils are especially good at rendering the high-grade and expensive materials which are part and parcel of our ideas about quality: the furs, silk brocades and marbles. All these goods are rendered in their solid material worth which is, itself, a part of the way in which we create value. Great things, in every sense of the word, the masterpieces tell us, are only achieved by acquiescence, by a kind of cultural quietism which finds its happiness in ignoring underlying themes.

OBJECTS OF UNDERSTANDING: THE POLITICS OF KNOWLEDGE

As in the politics of excellence we strike fundamental social values about 'good' and 'bad' and 'high' and 'low', so in the politics of knowledge we strike the related pair which reads as 'true' and 'false', the 'truth' or 'falseness' of which is seen as measurable by real standards. Material which is assigned to the authentic artefact quarter, God's artefacts and ours, finds its place there largely because it is collectively believed to hold knowledge about the world, revealed by the application of correct intellectual techniques and procedures.

The words used 'naturally' in this paragraph show us how to begin to unwind the skein of what constitutes this kind of knowledge. The material base rests in the collections of natural-history material through which we have come to understand the interrelationships and development of earth's flora and fauna through time, bringing to bear upon many thousands of specimens the techniques of comparison and contrast which make up the Linnaean system of taxonomy upon which identification and classification depends. Examples are legion, and one must suffice. The Abbot Herbarium, which survives in Bedfordshire (on loan to Luton Museum Service), contains about five hundred sheets holding local flora specimens collected between about 1790 and 1810 (information from Paul Hyman). This collection, a classic of its kind, takes its essential place in the interlocking network of collection, identification and developing understanding.

The equivalent material base has been created for the human past, and, as a matter of the history of knowledge, it came about when archaeologists like Pitt Rivers (Chapman 1991) thought to adapt the Linnaean/Darwin system to the world of human artefacts to produce the corresponding system of typology through which objects could be similarly allotted and classified. Human material has proved to be less tractable to this method than *naturalia*, but nevertheless typological studies still form the basis for our understanding of material from the prehistoric, and to a large extent the historic, past, including the relatively recent past from which we automatically characterise spoons as 'rat-tailed' or 'bifid', and furniture as 'straight' or 'breakfronted'.

What is true for ordinary objects is, of course, equally true for the masterpieces. Here too the brush strokes and the pigments, the style and the design, and the fact-findings of the historians, have united to create a history of art which works to give us the same sort of scheme which can be produced for other kinds of material. So, for example, by using these principles, Alfred H. Barr was able to produce in 1936 his Darwinian table of the sequential relationships of artists and art styles from 1890 to 1935 (Figure 17.2). We should add that the weight of collected material which has produced this network of interlinked knowledge is truly massive: many hundreds of millions of specimens and objects are involved, and the great

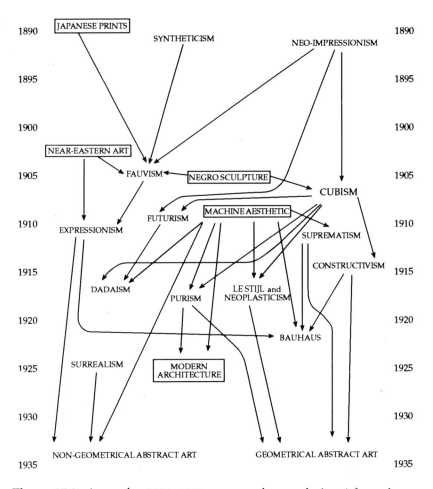

Figure 17.2 Art styles 1890–1935, expressed as evolution (after scheme developed by Alfred H. Barr, 1936), for exhibition in the Museum of Modern Art Library, New York

majority of these are now, as the result of concentrated work over the last three centuries, docketed with their correct place in the scheme of things.

The first important point is that the basis of this knowledge is believed to be, and in one sense is, material: tangible, concrete and capable of being measured, tested and assessed according to categorising principles which are considered to yield information. Conversely, such scientifically categorising principles require a material base to work upon, and without such a base they could not work, indeed could not exist at all. At the heart, therefore, of modern European notions of what constitutes knowledge is the material world, and the two together make up a privileged system of understanding through distinction and similarity. This might be described as the inevitable epistemological outcome of a social system with a deeply rooted tendency to view objects as a particularly important way of creating social position, and a mind-set which works by creating discriminations of the this/that, now/then variety, but which shares the apparently universal human desire to create cosmological systems into which all experience phenomena can be fitted. We arrive at a special kind of cosmology, which is seen to be rooted in physical realities which are capable of objective proof.

Much of this proof depends, as we have said, upon comparison, and upon the amassing of comparisons. This is another way of saying that information cannot come from single specimens, only from groups: the knowledge involved is essentially collective, and the collected existence of the many millions of pieces just referred to are essential to the existence of the system. Perceived relationships are of the essence; reality lies not in an individual item but in the relationship it bears to others which are like and unlike it. Consequently, knowledge takes the form of a three-dimensional lattice which spans space and time, and provides a space for everything, with everything in its place. As we saw when we considered how individual collectors use their material to create spatial organisation, this kind of control clearly appeals to impulses deep in our individual psyches.

It is clear that we are dealing with a closed system in which references are circular and conclusions eventually reinforcing. The system depends upon the knowing individual who is capable of understanding, and upon the faith that in the material world likeness and difference are objective and stable qualities capable of being understood in a way which allows back reference and future prediction. The objectivity of the object world is taken as given. This interlinks with efforts made over the long term (2,500 years in recorded literature, probably longer in oral tradition) in Western culture to make knowledge seem as *immaterial* and as asocial as possible. Knowledge is treated as an abstraction, divorced from any personal or intentional frame of reference. It is seen as a 'thing in itself' wholly free of the social nexus of hope and fear, or power and dominance, which otherwise informs everything which we do. As Plato first propounded in the *Theatetus*, and Descartes developed, knowledge is 'justified true belief', both a definition and a yardstick against which 'knowledge candidates' can be judged, and accepted into or rejected from, the referential circle (Fuller 1991; Chisholm 1966). Individuals are thought to 'possess' knowledge as a result of particular experiences but in ways which are entirely separate from other experiences which they may have or from what they may feel their world to be like.

Fuller expresses this classic approach to the nature of knowledge very pertinently in the light of this whole, broad discussion:

> The classical tendency to cast epistemic judgments in terms of the bare 'having' of knowledge puts knowledge in the same category as antiques and other collectible items that accrue value to their owners simply in virtue of their continued possession. Specifically, like collectibles, knowledge is pursued for its own sake, and hence, value is accrued through continual reflection on the object of knowledge, which in turns serves to personalize its significance of the object for the knower.
>
> (Fuller 1991: 109)

We have the image of individuals brooding over their knowledge cabinets, the sum of which make up all the knowledge in the world. But as Fuller points out, the power of knowledge lies not in its mere possession, but in the range of possible uses and users for it, even if these are seen primarily as the generation of more knowledge. Similarly, classical epistemology operates on the assumption that only individuals possess knowledge, and then only if they are able to proffer the right kind of reasons, based on objective study already described, to validate the knowledge they have. Knowledge, that is to say, is perceived as an individual's intellectual property, in much the same way as the collected material which he studies can be regarded as 'his'. But, in fact, if knowledge is a kind of property, it must be collectively owned, since only previously collectively endorsed earlier knowledge can give rise to new, and this new, in its turn, can only achieve 'knowledge status' as a result of collective acceptance.

Classical epistemology sees knowledge as the 'mirror of nature', in which the knower uncovers pre-existing truth, and does not himself interfere in the order which connects one part of the truth with another (Rorty 1979). But in fact, knowledge costs time, effort and money to produce and the irregular disposition of these distorts the end results. The accumulation and use of knowledge is a complex form of power in which choices are constantly made about what is worth looking into and what is not. As Fuller has put it:

> But more important in this context are the various social exigencies that bias inquiry in specific directions, ultimately forcing resolution on

even the most abstract of matters. Philosophers of science typically inquire into *which* theory is chosen. A more materialist inquiry would ask *when* theory choices are made, especially, if as Serge Mosovici's research on small group persuasion suggests, he who controls the moment of decision also controls the decision that is made. Much external history of science supports this social psychological tendency. A vivid case in point is the so-called Forman Thesis, which argues that German physicists in the late 1920s linked up behind an indeterminist interpretation of quantum mechanics because of the financial and political pressure exerted by the dominant irrationalist elements of Weimar culture, even though the conceptual and empirical argument pro and con indeterminism had not changed substantially.

(Fuller 1991: 114)

The history of science supports the notion that knowledge comes about through the operation of tendencies in social and group psychology, as Kuhn (1970) has shown when he talked about the way in which discipline and research areas emerge, and become the property of specific groups, with interlocking intellectual, social and professional lives, among whom sudden starts and jumps produce new investigative directions. Knowledge is a product of our social and psychological selves, and hence, among other things, of all the efforts to construct individual identity through the accumulation of collections which we have discussed in Part Three of this book. Knowledge is continually generated from the real world of people and their relationship to things; with all that this implies. In a fundamental way, however, it may seem to 'work' at a crude level, knowledge is what we want it to be.

And there is a further point. Just as the accumulated masterpieces of the world have an inbuilt tendency to exalt the excellence of cultural norms, in spite of the counterbalance which more recent artists try to offer, so knowledge also supports the status quo, not (or not only) in superficial and obvious ways but also by reinforcing deep cultural distinctions about what constitutes understanding and how it is achieved. Just as art collections convey moral prestige upon their owners, collected objects of understanding convey intellectual prestige upon theirs.

OBJECTS OF THE UNDERCLASS

The image of the city and its wall – that quintessentially European institution in which, as a matter of history most art and most knowledge (and, by definition, politics) has been produced, together with most material goods – may still assist us. It becomes clear that value in objects is created by a circular system, meaningful and sensible within its own terms, within which, by abiding by the cultural norms and thinking in the right ways, a person can find a measure of satisfaction. Bound up in this are moral and intellectual attitudes, and also social attitudes, which discriminate between persons, the whole operating as a self-perpetuating system of power, in which, in material terms, the authentic pieces are elevated and inauthentic pieces depressed. Those objects and collections gathered in the top half of the plot are in the significant class, while those at the bottom are commonplace, either as ordinary artefacts or as spurious (or non-authentic) ones.

A range of models has been used to describe this complex circular structure. For Chomsky the system comprises generative rules which act as an intricate structure by which patterns are formed, modified and elaborated (1964: 58). Baudrillard speaks of the 'code', a typical word in this kind of discourse, and says that, in the exchange of products, 'it is not only economic values, but the code, this fundamental code, that circulates and is reproduced' (1975: 54). For Foucault it is 'a group of rules that characterise discursive practice but these rules are not imposed from the outside on the elements they relate together; they are caught up in the very things that they connect (1972: 127). Bourdieu uses the word 'habitus', which he calls 'principles of the generation and structuring of practices and representations' (1977: 72).

Writers like Bourdieu, drawing on earlier Marxist ideas, argue that since the 'code' or 'habitus' is grounded in nebulous and unprovable assumptions, we should treat what these assumptions tell us about aesthetic and epistemological value as ideology, and look to uncover the social mechanisms which they are intended to mask. Values are not 'natural' and 'revealed'; they are constructed in the interests of specific social groups in order to enhance their dominance but these groups also attempt to conceal this naked aggression by fig-leaves of supposed tenderness, intellectual excitement and so forth. Moreover, since the knowledge and art on offer is bound to be particularistic and exclusive, it will always cut out other interests in the same social structure – whether of religion, class, gender, sexuality or whatever – so these the value system will diminish, suppress or forget.

And once the value system is revealed for the power-broking which it is, it follows that there is no reason why it should command the allegiances of those – most of us – who do not see what is to be gained from it. This reluctance is provided with its own philosophical rationale in post-structuralist thought as this has been developed by writers like Baudrillard, Barthes and Foucault. Adults have become like children, perpetually asking why; and to these questions, as all adults know, there is no real answer.

In terms of the closed system of values, the critique of spurious artefacts writes itself. Collections made from commercially available artefacts are boring and tasteless. They fail to engage our deepest sympathies and lack the capacity to move us, unless – a significant point to which we shall return – they have acquired human meaning. The humblest T-shirts and sweet wrappers can bring thoughts that lie too deep for tears if we find them while sorting out the belongings of the newly dead, that grimmest of tasks. Commercial material lacks what seems to be a 'true' context of time and space, which is carried by collections that belong in the knowledge-bearing class.

This is, of course, not true. All objects, by definition, have a true, original context, and this is partly why this century's rubbish becomes the next century's meaningful artefact, a process of value-creating particularly characteristic of our own century. What we mean when we talk of commercial material lacking context seems to be a comment on the material's mass-produced nature. There is no individuality, as there is in quality pieces, and the nature of the production creates a gap between producer and owner which helps to drain away meaning. A corollary of this, and one which similarly reduces the cultural content of the piece, is the lack of high craftsmanship and the use of lowly regarded materials, particularly plastic, which, after some vicissitudes of regard in the nineteenth and early twentieth century, settled down as the mass-production artefact material *par excellence*, and is, in popular esteem, more or less a synonym for rubbish, however unjust this may sometimes be. The implication is that those who collect this stuff are themselves trivial and trashy, possessed of neither moral, aesthetic nor intellectual sensibilities; low in every way.

Some of the spurious masterpieces share these characteristics. Garden gnomes and much gift ware are made of plastic and by the techniques of mass production. All of this material is made cynically with an eye to sales, not honourably with a view to high principle. Some of the spurious things, however – the fakes, the horribly stuffed and preserved human and animal remains, the 'pop' art – have been the subject of much anxious thought and craft skill. In much of this stuff there is an element of parody, of humanistic values perversely turned into copies begotten on the wrong side of the moral and aesthetic blanket. All this may be true, but it does not explain why this material, in contrast to the spurious artefact collections, sometimes strikes us as provocative and exciting, as in Roy Strong's word, sexy. The reason why it arouses us is because we don't always feel like being worshipful, even if it is at our shrine. Humans share a giggling, sniggering streak, which we can read variously as a shameful element in our baser natures, as a need to let off steam harmlessly – one of the fundamental things collecting is about in its social aspect – or as a significant comment upon the true nature of the world.

Viewed in this light, we can see the connection between much collecting and the post-modern world, in which values have disintegrated through an understanding of their brutal nature and their intrinsic lack of meaning, and cultural traditions wash together in a sea of relative values and pick-and-mix eclecticism. The city wall has become a loose heap of bricks, which anybody can arrange as he likes, and does, as a serious artistic statement in the great national art galleries of the world. The collectors of the spurious and the meretricious can say, this is what the world is really like, futile, graceless and muddled; this is how humans really are, stupid, posturing, self-deceiving, treacherous and nasty. Better to turn the back on a masterpiece tradition which tries to convince us that black is white, that meaning exists and we can be a part of it. Better to face the truth and create art which reflects its nonsense; better to collect chocolate penises (as many do) rather than Oriental rugs, since the penises were probably made in controlled conditions for a reasonable wage, not by children in sweatshops, and, in any case, are arguably truer to ourselves as we really are.

The paradoxes and contradictions inherent in this line of argument are, of course, the reason why most 'modern' or contemporary art (i.e. most art executed after about 1914) remains for most people inside the spurious quadrant. The problems are vividly demonstrated in the collection of bronzes known as the Piss Flower series, by Helen Chadwick, which were exhibited at a range of galleries, including the Liverpool Tate, during 1993. The genesis and form of the bronzes are described as

> Chadwick's way of making her mark on the snows of Northern Canada was to set out each day to a different spot in the area, where she and her partner would systematically urinate within the template of a flower which she had earlier designed. The resulting 'garden of flowers' are the casts made from these traces, into which liquid plaster was poured. When the plaster was set they were turned upright and shipped back to Britain, cast in bronze and then lacquered in a white cellulose enamel. These flowers have both male and female origins. The central stamen is female, contrary to our biological readings. The ground on which we stand shifts continually; Helen Chadwick has given us a new species. Equally important to her is that, as an artist, she was only partly in control and that at a significant point the body took over, making its own mark. She provides us with a record of the force of our bodies' action.
>
> (Tate Gallery Liverpool 1993)

Here we have bits of human evacuation preserved as artwork, entirely in tune with the subversive collections of false teeth and mangled taxidermy, where rejected effluvia is turned into significance. Here, also, are the genuinely interesting and beautiful physical shapes and relationships created when warm liquid meets frozen water; we are reminded of the undoubted fact in our unforgiving world that photographs of cancer cells or viruses can look as beautiful as pollen or snowflakes. The Piss Flowers have that erotic content which, in its infinite variety, hovers around all our responses to material culture. But were Chadwick and her collaborator pissed off and in deeply nihilistic mood when they undertook the work; or were they taking the piss from the rest of us who have been inveigled into considering their ironic pretensions seriously; or, are we all just pissing about, filling in time because to do anything else is a waste of time?

When we look at the collections of ordinary artefacts we see that, within the same emotional and philosophical climate, albeit much less self-consciously, they too are telling their own story. Here again the world of classic values is ignored, its relevance not even in question. Human meaning and sympathy are poured into these humble products, lifting them out of the ordinary and 'making something of them'. In an instinctive way people express this about their collections when they say 'It means a great deal to me.' They have *made* culture out of distance and heartlessness by offering their own sentiment, in all the meanings of that complicated word, by creating a little warmth and cheerfulness, shadowed as this must be by the sadness which accompanies all human happiness. In a cold world, brief and fleeting meanings, soon dispersed, are the best that can be hoped.

CONCLUSION

We can summarise the argument by saying that aesthetic, moral and epistemological values are a part of social mechanism, designed to help things go on being what they are: there is a depth to the politics of value and change which we will explore, but for the moment this can stand. Value and knowledge are seen, like most worthwhile things, to be double-edged because they both help to create cultural significance and make ideological statements.

In the European tradition (as in every other), objects are valued against traditions in the long term, which set parameters of value. This chapter has identified the key set of these, and used them as a framework for assessing the cultural significance traditionally allotted to the kinds of objects which are found in collections. The same criteria, embodying as they do the same mind-set, also give us a way of understanding how collected material from the worlds outside that of the European mainstream has been appropriated and integrated into ideological statement.

CHAPTER EIGHTEEN

COLLECTING THE OTHER, WITHIN AND WITHOUT

————— •◆• —————

However we may differ in our faiths or our politics . . . the pages of history, the regions of science . . . are both the common property of scholars, of Christians and of gentlemen.

Leicester and Midland Counties Journal, 23 June 1849

INTRODUCTION

Questions of identity have, one way and the other, run through much of the argument in this book. At its beginning I set forth the proposition, argued through Part Two and constituting the backdrop for Part Three, that a distinguishably European tradition, particularly important in relationship to the material world, defined many Western attitudes towards the accumulation of objects. This has much to do with a particular European mind-set, operating in the long term through a span of some three millennia of European history and helping to shape external and internal relationships. But, clearly, any self-conscious definition of 'self' with all that this implies can only be achieved in relation to a perceived 'Other', which is seen as different and (inevitably or otherwise is unclear), as inferior, unpleasant and dangerous.

Probably all human communities recognise themselves in relation to a cultural 'Other', although their mechanisms for doing this are very varied, and small-scale segmented societies, in particular, seem able to absorb 'Otherness' by ramifying systems of kin and material exchange links which avoid sharp-edged cut-off points. Historically speaking, the cultivation of such sharp edges has been a recurrent characteristic of the European past. Greeks saw themselves as intrinsically different to barbarians, the bearers of *Romanitas* as different to those who would not accept it, and Christians as distinct from the followers of the Prophet Mahomet. The same instincts come into play when, from about 1450 onwards, Europeans were forced to account, not for Middle and Far Eastern cultures with which they had been in contact time out of mind, but for wholly unexpected communities in the Americas, Africa and the Pacific.

It can be argued, with some persuasiveness, that although the need to make cultural distinction between 'them' and 'us' is common to all humans, in the European tradition it takes on a particular tone, and is, indeed, fundamental to the system, one of the structuring dichotomies which make the system what it is. As Said put it, in relation to the Orient, but in terms applicable to the whole non-Western world:

> Orientalism is never far from what Denys Hay has called the idea of Europe, a collective notion identifying 'us' Europeans as against all 'those' non-Europeans, and indeed it can be argued that the major component in European culture is precisely what made that culture hegemonic both in and outside Europe: the idea of European identity as a superior one in comparison with all the non-European peoples and cultures . . . Under the general heading of knowledge of the Orient, and within the umbrella of Western hegemony over the Orient during the period from the end of the eighteenth century, there emerged a complex Orient suitable for study in the academy, for display in the museum, for reconstruction in the colonial office, for theoretical illustration in anthropological, biological, linguistic, racial, and historical theses about mankind and the universe, for instances of economic and sociological theories of development, revolution, cultural personality, national or religious character.
>
> (Said 1978: 7–8)

Traditional gender images structure the relationship with the exotic. Hall draws attention to a painting of about 1600 by van der Staet (Hall and Gieben 1992: 303). Europe, in the person of Amerigo Vespucci, stands impressively draped in the clothes which mean civilisation, holding the symbol of authority, the banner of their Most Catholic Majesties of Spain; behind him his ships show that God is on the side of force. In front of him, in a hammock and naked, reclines a young woman, symbolising the New World about to be taken. Around her are exotic plants and animals, and in the background a cannibal feast is going forward. The points – ideological, sexual and economic – could scarcely be more clearly made. In such irresistible form was cast what Said has called 'the essence' of our views of Eastern promise and difference, 'the ineradicable distinction between Western superiority and Oriental inferiority' (1978: 42).

With this is linked the notion of an earthly paradise in which all live a simple, innocent life in a state of Nature where elaborate and punitive social organisation is unnecessary. The women are beautiful and naked, and sexuality is open and free. As Vespucci put it 'all lived according to Nature', and went naked and unashamed: 'the women . . . remained attractive after childbirth, were libidinous, and enlarged the penises of their lovers with magic potions' (Honour 1975: 56). This kind of thing formed the counterpoise to opposite ideas about primitive savages engaging in bloodstained and probably cannibalistic rites. They are all mirror images of each other, and their force comes from their capacity to feed sexual fantasy of several kinds, particularly the fantasies of Western males.

Markey (1985) has suggested that anthropology as an exploring discipline became necessary in order to account for all the human communities which were not merely being newly discovered, but which turned out to be organised in ways quite incomprehensible to Europeans, incomprehensible because, of course, they operated, by and large, within the totem/tabu framework which is normal to 'most people' but not to 'us'. This problem had not arisen in relationship to European neighbours in the Middle East, because, as it happened, they too worked through the less usual oath/ordeal perspective, and so appeared relatively 'normal' and permitted a simpler response.

Foster has suggested that the notion of the exotic Other should be accorded the status of one of Foucault's epistémes:

> the exotic is an *épistèmè*, a relatively fixed cultural problematic which becomes operational as an internalized *gestalt* and structures discursive activities pertaining to cultural difference; anthropologizing is but one such discursive activity. The exotic, much like the concept of culture itself, is a great zero, a place-holder about which is elaborated complex semantic systems and cross references defying the imagination of even the most far-out science fiction novelist.
>
> (Foster 1982: 21)

This follows Foucault's own view that 'to describe a . . . statement does not consist in analysing the relations between the author and what he says . . . but in determining what position can and must be occupied by any individual if he is to be the subject of [the statement]' (Foucault 1972: 95–6).

Our relationship with the past is similarly constituted in terms of the dichotomy between the 'Same' which sees an intelligibility and a kinship in the past, and the 'Other' which sees the past as essentially alien and unknowable. Fragmented and dislocated though the mass of collected material from the past may appear to be superficially, deeper acquaintance with it may suggest that the same conceptual skeleton sustains much of the infinitely various flesh. The guiding principle which animated many collectors over the last five centuries or so has been primarily to create a relationship with the past which is seen as real, reasonable and helpful. This is to say, using Ricoeur's language (1984; see Thomas 1990), that they have been collecting under the sign of the Same, itself one way of describing the fundamental European prescription that the world is intelligible through the processes of thought. The role of the Same supposes that there is a real and direct relationship between one set of events and the next so that history is not really a random set of occurrences but a living web of cause and effect in which the effects are not predestined but may, at least in part, be what we make them.

Through the application of this sort of model, not only do large structures of history become recognisable and intelligible, but so does the place of each of us within it. The past becomes reasonable and intelligible, and by drawing material from it in a reasonable and intelligible way, helpful trends can be reinforced or encouraged and progress made towards some perceived satisfactory working-out of the pattern.

If viewing the past under the rule of the Same glorifies the scheme of things, viewing it under the sign of the Other celebrates the opposite, whether knowingly or unknowingly. This is to embrace the notion that the past is indeed a foreign country and everything is different there. This is Foucault's attempt to get beyond 'the consoling play of recognitions' (1972: 88) in which material from the past make sense under the rubric of the same, and, as Thomas says:

> Such a history is based not on searching for similarities between past and present, but in the recovery of temporal distance. By recovering the *difference* of the past, such a history seeks to de-legitimise the present. In this way, the difference of the past becomes one of its most political characteristics. The prototype of such a history was Nietzsche's *Genealogy of Morals* (1969) which served as a model for Foucault's work on penal systems and sexuality. In each case the aim was to historicise the seeming universals of human condition by an act of contrast between past and present. All of the common-sense values dissolve before genealogical analysis – words don't keep their meanings, desires don't keep their meanings, desires don't keep their objectives, ideas don't keep their logic.
>
> (Thomas 1990: 20)

The upshot of this is that in historical interpretation of any kind, whether written or material, we are sure to move between the notions of history as the Same and the Other. The material available for collection comes to us from the Other, essentially different and distant, but we will turn it into sensible Sameness by interpreting it in the light of understood parameters. We will, in other words, incorporate it into a system by assuming that it is a part of that system, and really always has been so all the way along.

The Us : Them, Home : Exotic and Same past : Other past paradigm is linked with others which structure European consciousness – notably that of individual self-identity – all of which can only be made up through a sense of boundedness. This requires an awareness of historical development and an ability to compare and contrast other communities with one's own. So, as Rowlands has put it, 'boundedness requires a definition of 'otherness', an excluded category of the incomprehensible or the undesirable against which the certainty and familiarity of habitual and traditional action can constantly be reaffirmed' (Rowlands 1987: 2). Otherness becomes the place of the alien, the primitive and the unconscious, sharing 'common properties in their unpredictability, irrationality or uncontrollable nature in contrast to stable self identity being the product of belonging to bounded social units embedded in traditional ways of life' (Rowlands 1987: 2; see also Kaplan 1994). The categories of objectivity and subjectivity, largely shaped by this peculiarly Western experience, are constituted as direct opposites.

The structuring notion of the Other may have been chivvied into existence as a result of direct experience of communities which seemed obviously 'different', but it drew on a deep-rooted and characteristic preference to see reality in terms of distinctions like then : now and here : there. Together with the other developed consequences of this kind of thinking, it became part of the modernist mind-set through which Europeans understand the world. We may correspondingly see the world of European meanings as sustained by the pressures which boundedness produce. We can, not too fancifully, see the meaning system as rather like Saturn and its rings. The planet itself and the area immediately around it form a coherent whole, a system of meaning and value. The inner and outer rings, held in place by internal forces, circle around the planet, the outer-most ring representing the boundary of the system. The whole thing is held in place largely by the forces it itself generates as it moves through space, and it is the creation of a past which, in the final analysis, presumably involves the whole history of the universe, but which, in a more immedi-ate sense, is its own cosmic history and that of its near neighbours. The whole elaborate configuration is sustained by self-balancing pressures from the past and of the present and so remains poised. It is perhaps worth adding that not only is this a particularly European kind of value system, it is also a particularly European approach to self-analysis.

Time and space constitute the two axes through which we experience difference, and the point where they cross at any given moment represents the place where identity is constructed, both severally and collectively. But both time and distance are not flat categories, perceived as possessed of uniform cultural value throughout their span. Like Saturn's rings, together they bound the centre in a series of arcs, each of which represents an impor-tant and distinguishable stage in a progression of difference. To put it another way, European conscience as we have experienced it suggests a sequence of cut-off points in time and distance which are mutually sup-portive and together serve to define Europeans to themselves and structure their response to other people.

STRUCTURING THE OTHER

Notions of the distinction and difference which constitute the Other in its twin spatial and temporal guises can be plotted against axes of

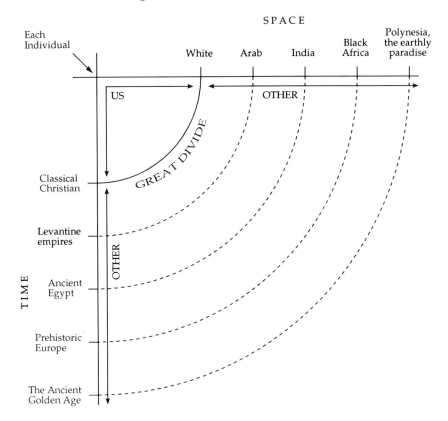

Figure 18.1 Notions of distinction and difference plotted against the axes of time and space to create sense of Us and Other

the two dimensions (Figure 18.1). This provides a crude sketch of the mind-set it represents but it serves to show how apparently separate appreciations actually reinforce each other. Although this scheme matches the actual progress of time and distance closely, it should be noted that it is intended to represent how a particular cast of mind sees distance, rather than a 'realistic' plot of what that distance is in the strictly factual sense.

In terms of space and time we can see, closest to the centre, a ramifying set of spatial distinctions which take their mark from a single individual: family, community, a rural or urban allegiance, northern or southern English and so on. The same distinctions have their temporal dimension through grandparents, community history and broader history. It is within this area, too, that the cultural differences which create class are constituted, with all the richness and dislocation which this implies. These distinctions extend spatially and temporally to take cognisance of those who speak a different European language, eat different food and belong to a different branch of Christianity. The sharpness of these internal distinctions should never be underrated, and, of course, they constitute the stuff of much historical and sociological discussion as well as much real life, but from the point of view of the Us : Other paradigm all these experiences constitute 'Us' in the sense that no matter how bitter and ferocious the differences may often be, the ferocity has the essential character of internal strife: not for nothing have the 1914–18 and 1939–45 conflicts been described as the First and Second European Civil Wars. As we shall see, however, this 'Us' is itself constituted by comparison with a range of internal 'Others' in a complex system of checks and balances.

Beyond this European world comes the great divide. In terms of the distance, the first, and in some ways the most significant, boundary comes with being white, for it is here that all whites, regardless of class and creed, unite. The temporal equivalent is the classical world with its Christian culmination, and the two together constitute the great cultural cleft: within is European and 'Us', beyond is exotic and 'Them'. The next point of distance, both in actual geography and communal consciousness is the Arab world, whose relative 'whiteness', acknowledged high culture and (as we have seen) relative familiarity give it this position. The past equivalent is probably the empires of Assyria and Babylon, who covered the same Levantine (always a loaded word) territory. Next along the axis of distance come India and the rest of the Far East, including China, and their equivalent in the past is perhaps Pharaonic Egypt. Next come 'primitive blacks', matched by prehistoric Europeans, all of whom are seen to be distanced by a shared low technological level and an inability to communicate through literacy. Finally, on the outer boundary come the variations of Eden, the necessary limits to complete the cosmological scheme.

Needless to say, a moment's scrutiny reveals these perceptions as crude stereotypes, which work by neglecting individual histories and internal distinctions and by suppressing unwelcome aspects of the relationships. All this is true but it is not the point: political perceptions have much more to do with wishes than they do with 'facts', and desires are more potent than objective suggestions. One further point should be made. The way in which we structure distance, and therefore the material collections which are a part of this structuring are, of course, themselves a part of the European past; other people's perceived otherness and distance becomes in due course part of that other 'otherness' of our own past. This thought must be constantly borne in mind during the discussions which follow.

The rest of this chapter will concentrate upon a discussion of Us and the Other Within, that is within that section of the plot which lies inside the great divide.

US AND THE OTHER WITHIN

The notion of 'Within' is, obviously, as complex as that of 'Without' (Figure 18.2). Although there is the great divide where Europe ends and the Other outside begins, within Europe itself there are distinctions which constitute Otherness, and one of these is structurally significant. In terms of the tradition of Western and Western-descended Europeans, there is an outer-European zone which in temporal terms is constituted by the medieval, perceived as 'Gothic' in the historical sense and 'unfree' in the political, and in spatial terms is occupied by Eastern Europe, seen as having emerged from medieval life only to fall under similar Communist unfree regimes.

We shall look first at the central individual core of Same and difference, or self and Other which collecting helps to create, and then at the zone of

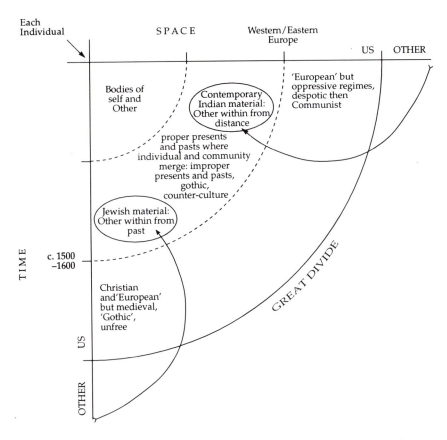

Figure 18.2 Notions of distinction and difference within Us which create cultural complexity

315

the Western European internal, within which the tradition of 'proper collecting' contrasts with that of 'improper' collecting of Gothic and popular culture. The European internal also holds elements traditionally perceived to be external within itself. These may be described as the alien within, and are most obviously represented by Jewish traditions and the lives of the non-Arabs, Turks and Indians, representing, respectively the Other from the axis of the past (Jewish traditions) and from the axis of spatial distance (non-Europeans).

BODIES POLITIC

Our own bodies are the primary mode in which we experience the world, and against which we form notions of normal and abnormal, or regular and freakish. The normal body becomes the microcosm of the world, and our bodies are metaphoric to the larger body of the universe. Notions of what constitutes normality are, of course cultural constructions like every other idea, and change in time and space just as ideas of beauty do, but this corporeal relationship to the idea of the norm seems to be the root reason why we are attracted to the bizarre and the peculiar, because since the normal and the abnormal define each other, it is only by gazing on the abnormal that we can appreciate our normality.

Within this grouping comes collected human material to do with abnormality or death, like Egyptian mummies, shrunken heads and other preserved pieces, and freakish animal material, either that which is naturally so (like two-headed lambs), or that which has been turned into unwholesome copies of human life by perverted taxidermy. Such material on public display is both now shocking and still hugely popular. In 1949, Sir John Forsdyke, the Director of the British Museum wrote:

> I doubt, for instance, if the principal popular attraction of the British Museum, the Egyptian mummies, would be tolerated by public opinion if it were proposed to introduce them now. I do not know when they were first on show, but their exhibition is probably related to the time when people were publicly hanged at the two ends of Oxford Street and Holborn, and corpses were common objects of respectable curiosity. The important consideration is: do these sensational exhibits induce people to take an interest in something better? I think not, but that on the contrary, they encourage them to hope for something worse. In the Mummy Room of the British Museum that hope is gratified by the body of a predynastic man, who crouches naked in the grave among his pots and pans. I do not think that many of the people who look at him give any thought to his historical significance. He would indeed attract far more attention than he does if the

story were generally known that he is not a predynastic Egyptian at all, but a Coptic dealer in antiquities who was killed and kippered and sold to the British Museum by an otherwise unsuccessful rival.

(quoted in Beard 1992: 1)

Forsdyke is probably right about the circumstance of the display of Egyptian mummies, but certainly wrong about the view taken of them by public opinion, both in 1949 and now. All this is the material culture of the horror film, but all the more ghoulish because it is real.

Public collections, which gratify our need for the mortal in a coarse-grained fashion, are matched by private collections which do similar work in a subtler and more directly personal sense. The Bones and Rusty Metal Objects Collector is a 26-year-old female art student whose collection includes nine large rusty nails, twelve miscellaneous rusty objects, six complete bones and twenty-three fragments and five works of art which embody similar collected pieces. A few years ago, the Collector had a medical experience which has left her mentally and emotionally scarred, but through her collecting and its translation into art she has begun to come to terms with what happened to her. For the Collector, her bones symbolise the decay of the body and the rusty metal the decay of machinery, both of which she feels are involved in her personal tragedy and that of the world at large. As she says, 'Life is very fragile and balanced but can fall apart so easily.' Rusty objects also represent dried blood, and she used them in her work like 'scabs protecting wounds'.

The central paradox of a collection like this is expressed in the Collector's words: 'Some people can see the beauty in the objects I collect, but others think I am a bit macabre when they see my work. I see it in their faces.' We can, it appears, only come to a sense of ourselves as functioning flesh and blood bodies by direct and tangible reference to material which is no longer ordinary living tissue. A number of theories have been developed to account for why all this sort of thing has a horrible fascination for us, all of which involve the idea of reference to normality.

Stewart (1984: 109) argues that these are not 'freaks of nature' but 'freaks of culture', through which the viewer is able to form an acceptable idea of the normal and the aberrant, and so confirm his reassuring view of himself as normal, healthy and (relatively) beautiful. Monte (1977) picks up Freud's idea of the conflict between the life-force and the death-wish, and suggests that this leads to seek out morbid material: our death-wish leads to intimations of mortality, but at the same time our life instinct is repelled by the idea. Humphrey (1984a) argues that we search out experiences which enable us to classify the world, and this search becomes pleasurable itself, leading to curiosity about something which fits into a known category ('lamb') but is in some glaring way different ('two-headed'). The perennially intriguing nature of theme and variation gains emotional force from the physical intimacy of the comparison. Blood and bones, in all their manifestations, are in every sense close to home, and we have no choice but to construct them into a scheme of things which can offer hard comfort.

COLLECTING THE PROPER WITHIN

Like collecting at the strictly bodily level, much collecting has also been directed towards creating proper and improper notions of what constitutes the relatively recent past which, in broad terms, makes the 'Within' for contemporary Europeans, that is, the period from about 1600 to the present day. In order to understand this better, we need to see what kinds of collecting have been brought to bear on the idea of the 'proper Us' past and present, and how 'improper' collecting works in tension with these to show us the Other Within.

All the collecting intended to demonstrate the past comes under the broad rubric of Romantic, and, as a matter of historical fact, collecting in this mode began in the last third of the eighteenth century, as the Romantic movement began to gather momentum. The effort to define the mental cast labelled 'Romantic' has reached the dimensions of an academic cottage industry, and all the complexity of arguments cannot be rehearsed here (see particularly Bloom and Trilling 1973; Clay 1981; Thorlby 1966; Shanks 1992). What is clear is that the Romantic spirit has given us clear collecting modes which draw on European history to give us our proper pasts, the collections which represent local history and difference, and those which represent national values and institutions through great men and great institutions.

From the Romantic movement's earliest beginnings in English letters, and conspicuously in Wordsworth's early poems like *The Old Cumberland Beggar*, first published in the *Lyrical Ballads* in 1798, romantic minds have paid attention to the ordinary and the particular, and to the attempt to record the fleeting moments of people's lives. Written rather larger, this comes to the desire to assert the peculiarities and particularities of local experience – provincial or parochial – and to find ways of catching and holding these which will assert their individual value. In collecting this was the emotional genesis of the major effort made throughout the nineteenth and early twentieth century to gather in the material culture of disappearing ways of life, and to assert their significance before it was too late.

The story of this kind of collecting in Scandinavia (Alexander 1983), in Wales (Stevens 1986), and Scotland (Cheape 1986) has often been told. Its intention was to dignify its subject, to recover the authenticity and therefore the value of the 'folk' ways of life which it recorded and which, in the romantic spirit, were considered to be essentially truthful and sincere. In this

individual : **community**

souvenir : relic

heirloom : heritage

Figure 18.3 Relationships between personal and communal material

way, the everyday artefacts of the people, and their own remembrances of times past, were turned into the genuine material of general history. Notions about simplicity and the eternal verities of family, land and seasons came to be one of the principal components of developing nationalism, and in this development the folk collections were significant.

Very similar points are made by the collections which relate to the 'great men' of the past. Here are all the enormous accumulations of material preserved because of their associative value, and presented as important for this reason. An historiography which believes in the truth of the relationship between past and present also tends to believe that individual interventions have been significant in turning the one into the other, and to see great men (and the odd great woman) as one of the primary explanatory narratives. The collection of Dickens material gathered by the Comte Alain de Suzannet is very typical (Slater 1975). Suzannet acquired material throughout his life. Twenty-one years after his death in 1950, his widow presented a substantial part of the collection to the Dickens House Museum, while the rest was sold at Sotheby's on 22 and 23 November 1971. What we see here is the translation of personal souvenirs into community relics, of family heirlooms into heritage as the heirloom of us all, partly as a result of – and partly to underpin, – the notion of 'greatness', in this case of Dickens as a novelist of genius who is in the great tradition (*pace* Leavis) of English and European writers (Figure 18.3). It is the transference from individual to community status which creates national shrines and material icons, and this happens when the individual's role comes to assume a universal role as point of reference.

One piece in the Suzannet Dickens collection makes these positions particularly clear. Slater's catalogue entry for Dickens's cigar case reads:

K.2 DICKENS CIGAR-CASE, leather, lined with watered silk, gilt rim, Dickens's monogram 'C.D.' on the front in raised gilt plaque on the reverse on which is engraved:
  'A Souvenir of Happy Memories
  Rustling above the dusty growth of years
  Come back green leaves of yesterday.
A Thought from Nicholas Nickleby Ch.49'
  With the case is an autographed letter (3 pages, 8vo, Gads Hill 22 June [1870] from Georgina Hogarth to Frank Beard

... I have the charge under Charles's Will of distributing among his dear friends the familiar objects in his study. First of all we think of you – & shall never forget you in association with him – in the memory of what you did for him at Preston – & still more in the remembrance of what we all went through together in those last hours – I send you a Cigar Case which was given to him before he went to America – It is a double one – & has an inscription which will make it valuable to you ...

The case was acquired by Maggs Bros. from Beard's nephew, Mr. Cass, and purchased from Maggs by the Comte de Suzannet in April 1930. Presented by the Comte de Suzannet to The Dickens House in 1933.

(Slater 1975: 160)

The case served as a souvenir for Dickens himself, from the moment when it was given to him, as the sentiment 'Come back green leaves of yesterday' makes clear. After Dickens's death it was given to his friend Frank Beard to serve as a personal memorial. This double piece of souvenir/heritage then passed on to the market to be purchased by Suzannet as first an item in an obsessive personal collection, and finally as a component of a national shrine. But this did not happen without a certain stage-management. Georgina Howarth was the sister of Dickens's wife Catherine, and after Charles and Catherine parted in 1858, Georgina stayed on as his housekeeper until his death in 1870. After his death Georgina not only distributed his intimate effects suitably, but also edited much of his correspondence and other remains in the interests of his reputation, probably eliminating references to his affair with Ellen Ternan: so his reputation as a great man and a great writer was established, and so both Suzannet and the Dickens House continue to preserve it.

Explanatory collecting of this kind drifts very close to a great theme of modernist Europe, that of the growth of the nation state, seen as a natural and progressive outcome of what had gone before. Nationalistic collections can and do take many forms, and their emotional significances have often been analysed. Here, as we have just seen, belong the collections of folk-life material, and here too, with provincial values running beside national ones, belong the collections of urban historical material, designed to explain the significance of mining communities or weaving towns in their own right and in their place in the scheme of things. But one particular kind of collection makes the significance of this sort of collecting especially clear, and is worth pausing over because it draws together so many of the threads discussed here: the collections of their own history held by the famous fighting regiments of the British Army.

The oldest British regiments have a particular niche in history. They were founded in the decades preceding 1700, and the three hundred years of their existence is therefore coterminous with the developed phase of modernism as this worked itself out through the particular progressive view of history associated with later capitalism and imperialist policies. Trade followed the flag and among the first flags were usually the colours of a British regiment of foot entrusted with the task of producing policy in the field. But regiments, in spite of multiple amalgamations and reorganisations down the years, are also families with long memories, and this *esprit de corps* is seen as an essential ingredient in their fighting powers. The resulting regimental collections have a character all their own, in which personal souvenir/heirloom material is also that of community relic and national heritage, in a curious amalgam of the apparently trivial and the overwhelmingly significant. Moreover, since the British regiments are territorially based, they are a point of intersection between national and 'folk' history, both rural and urban.

There are in total, some 173 such collections preserved in regimental museums up and down the country. The material on show ranges wildly from Victoria Crosses won at Ypres to sepia photographs of C. Company in cantonment at Felixstowe; from bugles dented as the regiment assaulted Delhi during the Indian Mutiny to trophies won by Major Goss in the Battalion clay-pigeon shooting competition. The collection of the King's Regiment (8th Foot), Liverpool is typical. The King's Regiment was formed originally in 1685, and its collection is now displayed in the National Museum on Merseyside. The proposal for a regimental museum was first made in *The Kingsman – The Journal of the King's Regiment, Liverpool* in June 1928. The writer had seen the Salle d'Honneur at the French Foreign Legion barracks at Sidé-Bel-Abbes and describes the room:

> the walls covered in battle flags captured in many lands . . . souvenirs of a dozen campaigns . . . photographs of heroes, medals etc. fill the spaces between the weapons; and how this is treated with great respect, having its own sentry. Here, the recruit receives his first lesson in esprit-de-corps.
>
> (*The Kingsman* June 1928: 62)

The writer wanted the King's Regiment collection to be displayed in order to preserve the image and identity of the Regiment and the honour, patriotism and nationalism of the Army as a whole.

The collection includes oil-paintings, particularly of events in the South African campaigns, dress featuring full-dress tunics, drums, the King's Colour of the 25th (Service) Battalion, a number of swords and captured weapons, and King Theebow's umbrella presented to Col. le Mesurier during the Burma Campaign (1885–87) when he handed the King over to the authorities in Madras. What we have here is genuinely significant national history broken down to its fundamental, personal level. It is intensely simplistic, which is no doubt why regimental museums are so popular with the visiting public, and the vivid immediacy of the story told merges with an unquestioning and highly selective style to produce a very powerful image.

It is obvious that the beauty of all this proper historical collecting from society's view is that cultural norms, aesthetic, emotional, moral, are continually re-produced. Moreover, this is disguised by the fact that collections are not, like most narratives about the past, couched in language, and so it looks as if the assertions of written texts are being matched and backed up by an independent source, the accumulated objects, as if, as Thomas says 'a pure, intelligible meaning is being expressed through the imperfect, distorted artifice of discourse, be it verbal or material' (1990: 19). In fact, of course, both stories are being created against the same paradigms, and, as Foucault puts it 'there is nothing absolutely primary because when all is said and done, underneath it all everything is already interpretation' (1972: 189). There is nothing outside the text, written or collected, for all are interpretations of reality.

COLLECTING THE IMPROPER

The Romantic mind was always interested in asserting the claims and realities of the darker side of human experience, as an area of the human personality which orthodox explanations choose to ignore, concentrating as they do upon the rational and the acceptable. This interest, which we may call Gothic, was not new, for traditional Christianity, to go no further, has always shown an intense awareness of wickedness, but the ascription to it of interest and value in its own right was novel.

Much material was accumulated under this rubric, but we sense that the collectors themselves often lost their nerve, and chose, more or less deliberately, to assemble the collection under some more presentable motif. The mid-nineteenth century developed a number of ideas which passed as scientific, like those associated with the name of Lambroso who believed that there was a measurable relationship between character and the dimensions of the human head and face. Collections were made of the death masks of those hanged in British prisons in furtherance of these claims: one such survived in Exeter, Devon, until the 1960s. The masks, made of greyish plaster of Paris and showing twisted faces without hair, were quite dreadful, and with them must always surely have been associated a more-than-scientific but rather pornographic fascination. And yet all this, the deaths themselves and how we feel about them are, undoubtedly, elements of genuine experience. Collections like this are in many ways the collective version of the way in which collections of freaks and abnormalities work for each of us as individuals. Just as they show us what physically normal animals and humans are like, so Gothic collections of this kind show us what mentally normal society should be like, and yet at the same time provide excuse for an enjoyable emotional *frisson*.

If Gothic collections provide an inverted commentary upon the normal, the collections of popular culture provide a similarly subversive commentary upon 'normal' culture. The same kinds of equivocation surround collections which strip the familiar away from things, treating the discarded or the disregarded as important in ways which tend to illuminate or subvert received significances. Hence are all the collections of 'ordinary things' with which individuals create their own meanings and assert their unique identities; here too, are the deliberate collections of carrier bags or burger cartons or cola tins, made to assert the cultural significance of things culture would prefer to ignore. This is an individualistic proceeding in which we make things as we wish, selectively choosing and rearranging so that a kind of significant personal continuity is stressed and a romantic, idiosyncratic wholeness and significance achieved. This is truly present-ing the past, treating the past as a gift tub whose presents, whatever their antecedents, are for use by each person in the present.

With this runs a desire, often very self-conscious, vocal and obstinate, to take up an attitude critical and suspicious of orthodoxy, which is seen as leaving a great deal of experience out of the reckoning. Orthodox systems of investigation and explanation are seen as fatally flawed, not just because they leave out some detail but because they are, of themselves, through their broadly progressive and complacent nature, incapable of giving a proper account of things; indeed, this mental frame supposes that such an account can never be given because the living mass of contradictions, muddles and unexpected consequences defines description, in the most literal sense.

Much collecting, of very different kinds, issues from this state of mind. The whole effort to collect what is usually called labour history – that is, the material culture of the toiling classes – belongs here, as part of the effort to get written into the story those uncomfortable aspects of it which orthodoxy might choose to gloss over. The same motives animate the desire to collect popular culture usually seen as the material side of ordinary life and its amusements: here belong the collections of football shirts and match programmes, packaging materials and early radios. All of this, with its desire to celebrate the lives of ordinary people is, from the point of view of 'high culture', collecting in the counter-culture, at one with the urge to wear nose studs or paint the face with team colours. Its effect is to enable those within and those without to recognise each other more easily.

COLLECTING THE ALIEN OTHER WITHIN

Material culture does not only create images which reflect and therefore explain the nature of inwardness within its own terms: it also creates images which support inwardness through comparisons with traditions which are within the system but seen, by the system itself, to be alien to it.

Historically, within Europe since at least the full Middle Ages, this role of the Other Within has been occupied by the Jewish communities distributed across Christendom. The immediately alien nature of traditional Jewish material culture, particularly that of religious material, has always seemed obvious. The shock of the Other has come across most vividly in the appearance of the Hebrew texts which appear on religious material: a language which is neither Latin or Greek, which has Oriental-looking wedge-shaped forms and which is read in what, by comparison with written European languages, is back to front.

This sense of alienation has had its impact upon collecting, as upon every other aspect of life. There have been moments in the broader intellectual history of Europe when Jewish material culture and traditions have been of general interest, notably during the seventeenth century when a fundamentalist Protestantism was interested in the Old Testament in the original language and esoteric practitioners were concerned with the traditions of the Cabbala, but generally interest in accumulating collections of Judaica was very limited, in contrast to the large quantities of Buddhist, Hindu and Islamic art collected by Europeans from outside Europe. It seems that non-Christian traditions were of interest providing they belonged safely (historically and geographically) with the exotic Other Beyond but not when they were interwoven with the fabric of things at home. Jewish material culture was written out of the European story until the middle of this century, just as the culture which it expressed was deemed obscurantist and anti-enlightenment.

The factors are, of course, a part of the historical sequence which led ultimately to events within Nazi Europe during the 1940s. Thereafter, collecting and the museums which show the collections are a part of the morally and emotionally complex processes of recording and remembering. Among other things, these collections remind us that intention as Marin says, 'makes a difference: one of the world's greatest collections of Judaica lies in Prague, amassed by the Nazis with the purpose of exhibiting the culture of what they intended to be an extinct race' (Marin 1994: 33). This collection is now in the State Jewish Museum, housed in a group of historic Prague synagogues and has become what Greenblatt describes as 'the resonant impure "memorial complex" that they are – - for resonance, like nostalgia, is impure, a hybrid forged in the barely acknowledged gaps, the causurae, between words such as *state*, *Jewish* and *Museum*' (Greenblatt 1991: 48).

Equally irresolvable issues surround the Holocaust Memorial Museum in Washington, which contains thousands of actual objects like pavingstones from the Warsaw ghetto and a railway boxcar from Treblinka (Gill 1993; Gourevitch 1994). There is already a substantial tourist industry centring on Holocaust sites in Poland (Kugelmass 1992), and opinion is divided about how the site of Auschwitz-Birkenau should be treated (Cesarani 1993). Collections of material which relates to the Holocaust will continue to be built up, in parallel with the developing availability of documentary records. The central paradox in all this is that the obligation to remember, which rests upon us all, inevitably carries with it the need to maintain a narrative of difference through which alone the material, at an historical level, is explicable.

Within contemporary Britain, the collections of material which relate to the cultures of the subcontinent of India follow what might be regarded as a well-worn path, in which the aim of the collector is to maintain or recover a sense of identity by the deliberate accumulation of what is regarded as characteristic cultural material. This is how the Indian woman collector who contributed to the People's Show 1992, collected dolls of India, mostly dressed in regional costumes. She makes the dolls' clothes herself, and regards this as a very important part of their character. She says: 'My favourites are the folk scenes or historical and traditional items. These articles depict a typical social and cultural mixture which can attract the public eye and enrich the community approach with further improvisations.' The collection is extremely important to her: 'Nothing could be more appealing to me than the collection which has been my dream since childhood. The importance goes on increasing by every additional development.' From the point of view of the collector, the style of this collection is much like that of very many collectors in Britain who gather dolls in Highland costume and similar pieces but from the angle of the viewer, it serves to underline cultural distinctions.

However hard some contemporary collectors and museums try to present the life of Indians in Britain or in India as 'normal', the end results have a curious tendency to belie their efforts. A few years ago an exhibition called *Vasna: An Indian Village* toured major venues in Britain. It aimed to show daily life in a typical Indian village as it is lived today, and did so through the medium of realistic reconstructions of houses and façades. It intended to mirror reality by creating juxtapositions like traditional handmade tools next to an ordinary blue metal British tool-box, and showing a bullock cart in the same context as a radio. But the overall effect was to create not a view of ordinary people, the friends and families of those settled in Britain, living ordinary lives, but a kind of Merrie India, of traditional timelessness.

There is perpetuated the sense of difference and distance, against which, as with the Dolls of India, contemporary British material can be contrasted and the 'normalities' of life and material design be reaffirmed. This rhetoric of difference is intended, in particular, to bolster Western notions of quality against what is perceived as the over-elaboration and tinsel-status of much Indian religious art, and its strange mingling of different design traditions, in contrast to the 'purer' forms of the West, and this in spite of the fact that much European popular religious art follows much the same path.

CONCLUSION

This chapter has established parameters of what for Europeans constitutes the Other, both as an attitude of mind and as concrete cultural forms in the world. It has considered how, within the European cultural system itself, culture forms are defined through a series of Inside : Outside relationships. In the next chapter we shall show that a very similar sequence characterises our notions of 'Us' and 'Them', in relation to space and the exotic or non-European cultures distributed around the world, and in relation to the pre-classical past, although here, of course, the Europeanness already defined constitutes the 'Us'. Meanwhile, there is a further important point to be made.

The discussion on the politics of value suggested that collected material is allotted value in relation to the grid which allows the qualities of authentic : spurious and masterpiece : ordinary (artefact) to be plotted against each other (Figure 16.4). Here, the canons of classical art give us authentic masterpieces, and the intellectual qualities of 'genuine' material give us 'authentic artefacts'. Kitsch pieces give us spurious masterpieces, and commercial goods, when they are turned into collections, give us spurious ordinary things. In the light of this, we can see that what the collections from the Other Within are doing is to mirror, or underpin, the values which the categories express. The qualities which the material from the ethnic minority communities represents contrasts with, and therefore confirms, notions about the proper forms of fine and applied art. The collections of the Jewish tradition, regarded as strange, obscurantist and expressed in a language which looks fundamentally 'Other', shadows the 'authentic artefact'. Equally, among the collected Other Within, the Gothic material shadows and supports the 'normal' and in so doing offers inauthentic masterpieces, while collected popular culture turns 'proper' commercial goods into the spurious ordinary of collections. In the same way, the 'good' and the 'bizarre' collections which define each person and his or her immediate family, give us similar supports above and below the horizontal line.

As we shall now see, this line of thought sheds considerable illumination on the ways in which collections have been assembled from the Beyond and the Before.

CHAPTER NINETEEN

THE OTHER BEYOND AND BEFORE

———— •◆• ————

It was the most marvellous stone in the world, for when you lifted one of the flakes you found the form of a sea-fish between the two pieces of stone . . . there was nothing lacking in its shape, eyes, bones or colour to make it seem otherwise than if it had been alive. The King gave me one of these stones.

Jean de Joinville *Life of Saint Louis*, written *c.* 1309
(Shaw 1963: 315)

I saw things which have been brought to the King from the new golden land: a sun all of gold a whole fathom broad, and a room of silver of the same size . . . and all kinds of wonderful objects of various uses . . . so precious that they have been valued at one hundred thousand gold florins.

Albrecht Dürer (Honour 1975: 28)

INTRODUCTION

On the other side of the great divide which separates the Europe from the Rest stand the exotic Other of the Beyond and the equally strange Other of the Before (Figure 19.1). It must be borne in mind we are here quite specifically concerned with objects from these Others and how they have been collected in ways which help to maintain the views which Europeans have taken of themselves in relation to Others. The following five sections of this chapter will examine the rationale behind the European collections of exotic material from outside Europe. The next section will pursue the notion of the past Other. The concluding section will draw together the threads of the discussion in this and the preceding chapter.

EXOTIC MATERIAL: SEEING THINGS

Clearly, the meanings attributed to collected exotic objects cannot be disentangled from the range of strategies which are used to construct the exotic, and these are easily listed – eyewitness accounts; novels, especially

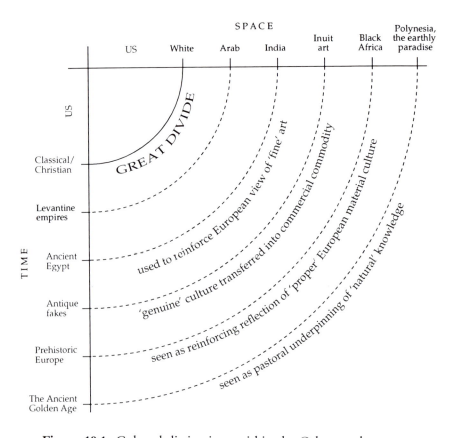

Figure 19.1 Cultural distinctions within the Other used to support those made within Us

by early popular novelists like H. Rider Haggard; films, especially again ancient popular films like *Sanders of the River*; anthropological writing and, perhaps especially, film; and contemporary journalism, including particularly television film. Collected objects share with all these narratives an essentially selective character, but they also possess, as all objects do, an intrinsic relationship to their original context which gives them their particular power. Much effort has been expended lately on disentangling the politics of anthropological (in the broadest sense) narratives like those just listed (e.g. O'Hanlon's excellent account of collecting in contemporary New Guinea, 1993; see also Sanjek 1993), but much less thought has been directed to the politics of exotic objects, and it is with this that we are concerned.

To enter a room in which exotic collections are stored may be, as Fenton said of the Pitt Rivers Museum:

Outdated
Though the cultural anthropological system be
The lonely and unpopular
Might find the landscapes of their childhood marked out
Here, in the chaotic piles of souvenirs

(Fenton 1983: 82)

But to people accustomed to such collections, the experience is as deeply familiar as memories of early days, and as the eye travels over the store-room shelves and racks and drawers, the viewer experiences a powerful yet relaxing feeling of comfort and reassurance. There are many reasons for this. Exotic collections tend to smell pleasantly of wood and natural oils. Their colours are predominantly browns and beiges brightened sometimes by paint and feathers, and their arresting shapes can be distinguished through the low-level lighting. All this is clearly a part of the collector's psychology, and has to do with the kind of identity-building which we have already discussed. But there is an additional and very significant reason for the familiarity of exotic collections, which is that, wherever they are, however large they are and however they were accumulated, the material in them is always pretty much the same.

This statement may need a little qualification in respect of very recent collections made in the field by professional anthropologists, but even these, despite admirable intentions to capture a broad range of material culture, tend to end up with very much the accustomed feel. An exotic collection which concerns any part of Africa invariably contains carved wooden figu-rines, drums, mankala game boards, stools and personal items like combs, pipes and snuffboxes. Prominent in African collections are Hausa cloth lengths, Masai spears with their impressive iron blades and butts, Ashanti stools, walking-sticks from the Cape carved with snakes, the black face masks from the women's societies in Sierra Leone, west coast gold weights cast in brass in the form of miniature figures and figurine groups, and 'fetish' figures from the Congo region. Their Pacific equivalents are intri-cately carved paddles from the Cook and Astral Islands, mushroom clubs from Fiji, lengths of tapa (bark) cloth from across a wide island range, greenstone pieces from New Zealand, carved canoe prows from the Solomons, ceremonial dress made with feathers and pearl shell from, especially, Hawaii and Tahiti, kava bowls (for serving a specially prepared drink) and carved clubs, bowls and equipment for consuming betel-nut from New Guinea.

From the Inuit come kayaks and the small bone parts of hunting equip-ment (but not the larger and more cumbersome wooden and hide parts), and, from the Western Inuit, carved bow drills and darts. From the Plains Indians anything bladed, feathered or beaded, and from the south-east, pottery. From the Amazon come blowpipes with their quivers fitted with (yes) tiny, poison-tipped darts, together with woven fibres, feather head-dresses and shrunken heads. From China come fabrics and embroideries, material said to have been taken from the Forbidden City, or the Summer Palace, executioners' swords, sheaths for the long fingernails of mandarins, and boxes of tiny shoes for bound female feet. From Japan come tea services and *samurai* equipment, and from India material relating to religious life.

Once collections are seen like this, two things become clear. Firstly, many of the individual items are exceedingly significant in original cultural terms; they represent important moments in the history of their community, usually the moments when Europeans arrived, and they are among the most powerful artistic and creative statements which the community has made. In practice, these two kinds of importance often come together, as the 1897 punitive expedition to Benin city and subsequent acquisition of bronze and ivory objects shows particularly vividly. Even those objects which do not embody particularly significant moments hold, of course, all the cultural meaning which all objects always hold. Secondly, as collections, that is, as cultural assemblages in their own right, what they tell us about their communities of origin, though very important, is outweighed by what they tell us about the communities of their collectors. Much of it may be 'primitive art', to use Sotheby's term, but most of it is not 'ethnography' in the sense of an attempt to create a sustained narrative of a particular group; unless, indeed, the group be that of the collectors themselves.

How this happens, and its consequences, have been the subject of much recent anthropological discussion (Clifford 1988; Clifford and Marcus 1986). We are coming to a clearer view of the Western agendas which are written into the construction of material narratives drawn from Western ideas of the exotic and how these support European notions of themselves. It has become obvious that the so-called 'scientific' collections of Pitt Rivers in his generation, or Boas or Younghusband in theirs, have served to create a superstructure of Western intellectual ideas as a cultural explanation of perceived differences. Cruder collections, made by government officials, missionaries and military men were reflections of aspirations towards cultural and ideological dominance, as analyses presented in Birmingham City Museum's Gallery 33 project have demonstrated (Peirson Jones 1992).

This, the operation of the cultural allegory, is now taken as given in anthropological circles, and needs no elaborate discussion here. But there is a deeper and even less conscious purpose which underlies cultural constructions, a second allegory which embraces and contains all that has already been said, but is not bounded by it. Material culture is collected from exotic communities not merely in order to support Western notions in a general sense, but also to underpin the European distinctions of quality and value, which we distinguished in Chapters 16 and 17. Exotic material, like European material, is collected in the four modes defined (in these chapters) in ways which shadow and underpin the material assumptions. So 'primitive' or non-European art forms part of the yardstick against which Western art is produced, 'airport art' helps in subtle ways to confirm our notions of kitsch; collected material culture from peoples who, particularly, play out European notions of 'natural' and 'uncivilised' underpin by contrast the system of knowledge and understanding which our own 'genuine' collections make manifest; and collections of exotic goods are used to vindicate the 'normality' and cultural appropriateness of European 'ordinary' or consumer goods, however much these may have a dubious or 'spurious' status where they are themselves treated as collections.

In order to develop this theme, I have chosen from the wealth of possible examples the material collected from four very different parts of the exotic world, which occupy four different points along the path from 'Us' to the ultimate 'Them'. These four accumulations also represent a chronological spread of how the exotic has been understood, beginning with the mid-eighteenth century and proceeding by way of the nineteenth to the present day, and so they help to illumine the temporal depth which attitudes to the exotic embody. The four chosen theatres are British India (mid-eighteenth century and onwards), Polynesia (essentially late eighteenth century), the Central Inuit (mid- to later nineteenth and early twentieth century), and Black Africa (later nineteenth and early twentieth century). Together they stage a complex play of distinction and reinforcement.

JEWELS FROM THE CROWN

Until the (relatively recent) advent of film and television, collected objects from the Indian subcontinent were the medium through which notions about Indian culture were transmitted to Europe, particularly, but not only, to Britain whose empire India became. This was done partly through the enormous number of souvenir collections which found their way into English homes between roughly 1750 and 1950 and partly through some major collections which were very influential in fixing ideas about the eastern Other.

In 1759 Robert Clive, whose colourful career established British power in India, wrote to the then Prime Minister, William Pitt the Elder, saying:

> I have made it pretty clear to you that there will be little or no difficulty in obtaining the absolute possession of these rich kingdoms: and this with the Mughal's own consent, on condition of paying him less than a fifth of the revenues thereof. Now I leave you to judge whether an income upwards of two million sterling, with the possession of three

provinces abounding in the most valuable productions of nature and of art be an object deserving the public attention; and whether it would be worth a nation's while ... would prove a source of immense wealth to the kingdom and might in time be appropriated in part as a fund towards diminishing the heavy load of debt under which we at present labour.

(Ashton 1988: 19)

The letter is transparent to the point of naïveté and shows how completely dazzled the British were by the wealth of the Indian empire displayed through the centuries-old accumulation of a craftsmanship heavy with precious metals, gemstones and ivory. The value of India, the notion of the subcontinent as inexhaustible possession, haunted the imagination of over two centuries of Englishmen, in the same way that 'the Indies' had taken root in the mind of Spain (Lach 1994). It is important to understand just how overwhelming the richness of India was to British Imperialists, and how, in response, mechanisms of cultural distinction had to be worked out in order for a sense of superiority to be maintained.

Clive himself accumulated a collection of Indian material which featured pictures, swords and textiles, objects chosen in typical nabob style for their opulence and curiosity value. The collection was inherited by his eldest son Edward (1758–1830), who also went out to India and was there at the time of the war against the Tipoo Sultan of Mysore, who was finally defeated by British forces (with some considerable difficulty) after the siege of Seringapatam (1799). A colonel wrote of the siege

> Nothing ... can have exceeded what was done on the night on the 4th. Scarcely a house in town left unplundered, and I understand that in camp jewels of the greatest value, bars of gold have been offered for sale by our soldiers.
>
> (National Library of Wales Clive Papers)

The division of the spoils included the breaking-up of Tipoo Sultan's magnificent jewelled throne, a large and spectacular piece of which was given to Clive as a gift from the British Army.

The magnificent objects from Tipoo Sultan's palace come round in a second figure of the dance of submission and dominance, when we realise that two ivory thrones, originally acquired by the British as spoils of war from Mysore, reappear a century later in the collection of George Curzon, Marquis Curzon of Kedleston and Viceroy of India from 1899 to 1905. The thrones are now at Kedleston Hall with the rest of Curzon's collection, which includes applied art and textiles, and memorials of the Delhi Coronation Durbar in 1903, one of the great imperial spectaculars. Curzon himself appreciated Indian craftsmanship for its own sake: he summoned Sir John Marshall out to India to act as his adviser on antiquities and he added substantial personal gifts to important monuments and collections (Rose 1969).

From the mid-eighteenth to the late nineteenth century, we can see in these proconsuls of empire how taste modulated from crude greed, relieved only by part-dazzled, part-baffled intimations of quality, to appreciation of Indian craftsmanship in its own right. The Great Exhibition of 1851, with its display of Indian artefacts, fanned, as Nicholson (1983) says, the flames of controversy between the orthodox exponents of design and the members of the new movement of radical designers. The orthodox view, presented by Ralph Wornum, said that the Indian exhibits showed 'an absence of glaring faults, but no feature of beauty' (1851: vi). In agreeing with this, the *Art Journal Catalogue of the Great Exhibition* included only one page of illustrations of Indian material in its extensive treatment of the exhibition. Nevertheless, Henry Cole and his radical colleagues set out to gather material which subsequently formed the nucleus of the Indian Collection at what became the Victoria and Albert Museum (Cole 1874). Their catalogue of 1853 referred to items in the metals section as showing how 'orientals always decorated their construction but never constructed decoration' (*Catalogue of the Museum of Ornamental Art* 1853) but Owen Jones' remarks in the *Catalogue*:

> contrasted Indian craftsmen (their strong cultural values and design principles) with their European counterparts who, in the search for novelty had 'no guiding principles in design and still less of unity in its application.'
>
> (Nicholson 1983: 27)

But the British tiger did not change its stripes, and throughout the history of the raj, no matter how enormously influential Indian design was upon the products of the West, particularly in the field of textiles and therefore in the everyday appearance of homes and women's dress, the structuring attitude was *comparative*. India's collected wealth provided a backdrop against which the British could stage their own play.

Ideas of collected Indian art and craftsmanship as part-trophy, part-referent, against which one's own cultural traditions may be placed, come into sharper focus when what the West had come, through the seventeenth century, to understand as 'high art' or 'fine art' becomes important. This sharpness took its keenest edge from the cultural fact that in India the production of art was inseparable from religious belief, as, of course, it had been through most of European history and so remained in the hands of many practitioners throughout the eighteenth and nineteenth centuries. In India, almost alone of the recently discovered exotic world, the Europeans found an ancient, complex and profound indigenous religious tradition, expressed in a huge body of written texts and in what were unmistakably architectural and artistic schools of similar depth and significance. This knowledge was not completely new; the West had had some notion of Indian traditions since at least the time of Alexander the Great in the fourth century BC and, interestingly, it has been argued that Indian teachers known to have been in Alexandria helped to shape what we know as Neoplatonic thinking. What it did require in modernist Europe was a response, and this came primarily in relation to works of Indian sculpture in stone and (generally on a much smaller scale) bronze.

Indian sculpture seems to have been first collected by Charles Stuart, known as 'Hindoo' Stuart, who served as a general in the East India Company Army from 1777 to his death in 1828. He took an enthusiastic interest in Indian temple sculpture, and appropriated fragments from ruined temples, much as his compatriots were doing throughout Greece and Asia Minor. Stuart came to acquire a fine collection, particularly of the Pala period, which eventually found its way into the collections of the British Museum in 1872. Stuart himself and a number of fellow officers in the Indian service, like Sir William Jones, founder of the Asiatic Society of Bengal in 1784, and Sir Charles Wilkins who in 1798 offered to curate the collection accumulated by the Asiatic Society and was eventually appointed its librarian, took an enlightened interest in Indian culture, a point Fisch makes:

> these men were not completely indoctrinated by narrow European, English and Christian values, but arrived with a remarkable openness towards what they found in the East, ready to accept different values and customs and to adopt a new style of life. What they were lacking was not so much education as indoctrination.
>
> (Fisch 1985: 35)

The Asiatic Society's collection was housed in the East India Company's building in Leadenhall Street, London, where the thrust of its collections were to demonstrate the commercial interests of the company and the natural history of India. The collection grew rapidly, and in 1808 received the famous musical tiger made for Tipoo Sultan, the contents of whose palace runs as a thread of continuity throughout all these collections.

This was not the only collection of Indian art on display in London. Nicholson quotes *The Times* of 9 January 1823 which gives an account of Indian material in the collection of the London Missionary Society that showed 'idols given up by their former worshippers for the folly and sin of idolatry' (1983: 26). This line sets the tone, glossed in a number of ways with the ideology of the day. Writing at about the same time, Hegel classified the incomprehensible 'horrible, repulsive, loathsome distortions' that he saw in Indian plastic art as representative of the earliest primitive 'symbolic' phase in the universal evolutionary development of art forms (Miller 1927: 189–220). Moreover, since in Hegel's view art expressed the innermost soul of a people, and therefore a specific kind of art could only spring from a particular kind of people, the ideological ring is closed.

In 1879 the South Kensington Museum (eventually to become the Victoria and Albert) accepted most of the old East India Company collection, and Sir George Birdwood was appointed Art Referee for the new Indian Section of the Museum. He continued to champion Indian decorative arts, but could describe Indian fine art rather differently: 'The monstrous shapes of the Puranic deities are unsuitable for the higher forms of artistic representation; and this is possibly why sculptures and painting are unknown, as fine arts, in India' (1880: 125). As late as 1910 he could describe a Javanese figure of Buddha displayed at the Royal Society of Art as:

> The senseless similitude, by its immemorial fixed pose, is nothing more than an uninspired brazen image, vacuously squinting down its nose to its thumbs, knees and toes. A boiled suet pudding would serve equally well as a symbol of passionate purity and serenity of soul.
>
> (Smith 1991: 21)

These remarks produced a response in form of a letter to *The Times* of 28 February 1910 signed by a roll-call of young artists:

> we the undersigned artists, critics and students of art . . . find in the best art of India a lofty and adequate expression of the religious emotion of the people and of their deepest thoughts on the subject of the divine. We recognise in the Buddha type of sacred figure one of the great artistic inspirations of the world.
>
> (Miller 1927: 270–3)

As Nicholson points out, much of the credit for this shift in attitudes must go to art historians Ernest Havell and Ananda Coomaraswamy, whose books questioned the use of European canons to judge Indian art. Havell advocated that the critic should 'place himself at an Indian point of view' (1911: vi) and see that in Indian art the intention of the artist was to realise a transcendental idea of inner vision, rather than to imitate nature, hence 'not to reveal beauty from nature but to reveal . . . the Noumenon within the phenomenon' (1911: 23). To Havell, therefore, Indian art was the visual embodiment of Indian philosophy. Ananda Coomaraswamy developed this idea by advocating that in Indian society, as in medieval Europe, 'Art is religion, religion art, not related but the same' (1934: 62). Thereafter change was achieved slowly throughout the rest of the twentieth century.

What was happening through the later eighteenth and nineteenth centuries, and to a certain extent on into the twentieth century, emerges very clearly. The collections of Indian applied craftswork could easily be reduced to the level of European commodity, where they contributed to the repertoire of decorative motifs available to producers attempting to woo customers in the market-place with designs sufficiently, but not dangerously, exotic. Indian fine art was different. Its explicit eroticism, stylisation and view of the human figure came close but not close enough to the canons of Western taste as these had been established first in the classical world and then in the fifteenth century. It therefore came to be used as contrasting paradigm against which Western art could be more securely established. The Western view of Indian art through the centuries of modernism served to reinforce that same Western view of its own traditional 'fine' artistic values.

MAKING A THING OF IT

Across the globe, European values have not only appropriated the native material culture, they have transformed it. Sometimes this has been done from without, as when indigenous traditions virtually disappear to be replaced wholesale by the products of Western technology, a phenomenon familiar in many parts of eastern and south-eastern Asia. Sometimes it has happened from within, as in the various cargo cults of the Pacific or the cross-appropriation (if 'appropriate' is the right word) of logos from commercial lager advertising used as symbols on fighting shields which O'Hanlon found among the Highlanders of New Guinea (O'Hanlon 1993). Sometimes it happens as a complex process of multiple responses in which the indigenous people are the junior, and the Western world the senior, partners, and from which comes that curious, but commercially viable, commentary on Western notions of value which we call 'tourist' or 'airport' art, and which has now achieved a wide scope and complexity of its own. As an example of this particular kind of interaction, we shall take the contemporary art produced by the Inuit of the Central Arctic, which richly illustrates the interplay of cultures.

The Central Arctic Inuit occupy the islands and mainland peninsulas west of the Davis Strait (between Greenland and Baffin Island), east of the Mackenzie River, north of the mouth of the Hudson Bay and northwards through the Arctic archipelago. Their traditional way of life is that of the classic hunting band, with a suite of material culture finely tuned to the tundra and its surrounding Arctic seas: seal-hunting gear including kayaks, snow gear including igloo-building equipment and sledges, sewing equipment and fur clothes, and a variety of stone pots and blades. These objects are mostly deeply familiar to the Western audience, partly because they are so much *sui generis* and partly because, when the Arctic was explored, firstly by the Royal Navy in the first half of the nineteenth century and then by some very famous anthropologists like Frans Boas (1964), and Knud Rasmussen (1929), their published reports and diaries made a major impact on the public of the day. Here, for the first time, Western readers saw drawings of Eskimos with their kayaks and igloos, and the pictures made an indelible impression, to become an instantly rec-ognisable part of the European iconography of the Other.

Archaeological study during the first half of the twentieth century revealed that in the past, the Central Arctic communities had possessed an important artistic tradition, known as the Dorset culture from its first recognition at Cape Dorset on south-west Baffin Island. Dorset traditions, which included improved seal-hunting gear, seem to emerge around 1000 BC and to have continued to around AD 1000 when they were transformed into an economy based on whale hunting and on larger villages known as the Thule culture. Dorset art is characterised by three-dimensional carving in the round, usually of walrus ivory but sometimes of wood, and of a size small enough to hold comfortably in the hand. Humans and bears are the favoured subjects, but sea mammals and other animals were also often carved. As in all art, form and content are inextricably interwoven, and the small size of the pieces does not detract from their great vitality; they exude intensity and power, whether the finished concept is realistic or highly stylised. Dorset carvings are relatively rare, and probably no more than a few hundred are known altogether. This, combined with the high technical qualities which they show and the clear sense they give of a coherent aesthetic tradition, suggests that Dorset art was not the product of widespread, general activity among the communities but rather was created by specialists, perhaps shamans, able to articulate concepts about their carvings and to pass their traditions on.

By the time Europeans arrived in the north, this tradition was in the distant past and had been forgotten. The local Thule culture populations seem to have been producing little or no carving beyond very basic soapstone pots for cooking and as oil-lamps. But in the years immediately following the end of the Second World War several important strands came together. By then the old hunting economy had largely collapsed and its place had been taken by the miserable conditions which always seem to succeed the erosion of a traditional way of life. More and more, people were becoming dependent upon store-bought goods, for the purchase of which they had no regular cash wage. By then, too, the Arctic had become a factor in the military strategy of the Western world, and its huge mineral resources an important part of the global economy. All this necessitated the creation of some thirty settlements throughout the north, where most of the population are now fixed, living permanently in wooden prefabricated houses supplied by the Canadian government and sustained by government welfare programmes.

These developments are the context of the outburst of modern Eskimo art, which was brought into being, almost single-handedly, by James Houston. In 1948 Houston, himself an artist who had been greatly impressed by what he knew of Dorset work, visited Eskimo settlements on the eastern side of Hudson Bay. He saw for himself how desperately they needed a livelihood, and he encouraged the people of Inoucdjouac, Cape Smith and Povungnituk to make more of their soapstone carving. Houston was surprised at the quality of the small animal, bird and human figurines which he collected. In 1948 several hundred were exhibited by the Canadian Handicrafts Guild in Montreal and sold very rapidly. The potential was obvious, and through Houston's efforts art centres were established, not only on the east Hudson Bay coast, but also at Cape Dorset, Lake Harbour and Repulse Bay, among others.

Eskimo art is marketed in the south through Canadian Arctic Producers (CAP), a private company set up with government backing, which acts as wholesaler. Genuine pieces usually carry the igloo official trade mark, and sometimes the artist has also scratched his or her signature on the base of the carving, either in Roman script or Eskimo syllabics (a script designed to cope with the many-syllabled Eskimo words). In 1967 the Canadian Eskimo Arts Council was formed so that advice could be offered on matters of artistic development and quality.

This has resulted in the creation of a large North American and Western European market for Eskimo pieces. Cape Dorset, the ancient centre in south-west Baffin Island produced the most prestigious of the early contemporary Eskimo sculptures, and among their work pieces like *Spirit*, a greenstone figure part-bear, part-fish and with a human face, carved by Kabubawakota, stand out as major achievements. But in settlements like Igloolik and Frobisher Bay, the visitor will be offered a variety of objects, many of which can be purchased relatively cheaply and chosen from an increasing range which includes not only carvings in stone and bone and prints, but also basketwork, jewellery and assorted knick-knacks constructed from oddments of fur and bone (Plate 13). The deliberately stimulated demand creates a backlash in the Eskimo communities, where sales of locally made handicrafts have become economically increasingly important.

What has happened among the Inuit is, of course, merely a particularly well-scripted example of what has happened across the non-Western world. Contemporary Inuit 'art' has only the most tenuous of links with the genuinely impressive ancient artistic inheritance of the Arctic. The new pieces, even the 'best' of them, bear no intrinsic relationship to Inuit culture romantically conceived; they are alien stock grafted on to the traditional root, without 'natural' function, and with the wrong designs, made in the wrong materials and in the wrong sizes. At an obvious level, the exploitative element is easy to pick out and condemn; the Western buyers who pay for poor designs, probably in the belief that they are acquiring quality goods, and the carvers who are reduced to producing routine, shoddily imagined pieces by the demands of the market. All this is to make the point that here we see former Inuit hunters drawn into the workings of global capitalistic supply and demand, to the detriment, be it noticed, not just of the Inuit, but of all concerned. The system can be seen as exploiting the Western buyers just as much (or almost as much) as it does the Inuit carvers.

Equally interesting is the specific way in which this Third World tourist

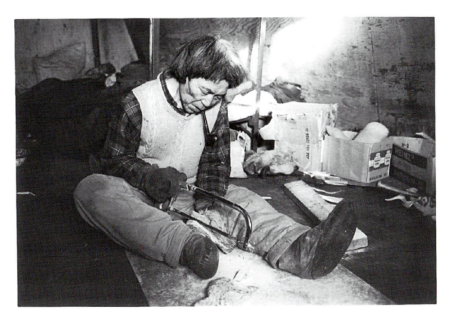

Plate 13 Contemporary Inuit carver roughing out a carving from the raw stone block, Frobisher Bay, Baffin Island. (photo: Canadian Government Photo Centre)

material is attuned to Western notions of quality and value in the object world. Inuit culture had a range of material culture which, as in all societies, carried its germane relationship to itself. But when this relationship and its material is turned by Western influence from living culture into reified commodity, the commodity which emerges belongs, in the terms which we are using here, generally within the spurious masterpiece class, and we see native culture perverted in commercial interests to become European kitsch. The legitimate culture of the Other is transformed into material which helps to sustain a particular element in the Western frame of reference.

NO NEW THINGS

Europe has a complex relationship with other people's objects (as, indeed, it does with its own). One characteristic, if unconscious, motive in the assembling of exotic material is to act as a kind of under-mirror to the normal commodity goods of Western civilisation in order to demonstrate the moral rightness, the ethical necessity, of these goods and the social practices which they inform. With this can be linked the notion of material acquired as moral victory, which itself celebrates the rightness of the European social system and the goods upon which it depends. Collections of material from black Africa particularly represent this facet of appropriation of the Other, and what I mean can be demonstrated through the collections of African material held by the Royal Ontario Museum, Canada, the subject of a recent exhibition and publications by Jeanne Cannizzo (1989, 1991), upon whose work I draw here.

When Cannizzo started work on the African Collection project at the museum, she found that 'The lack of any chronological depth, geographical concentration or ethnographic focus was immediately apparent' (Cannizzo 1991: 150). In other words, while the material objects themselves told little in the way of an 'anthropological' story, the rich historical documentation about their European collectors which accompanied them cast upon them a flood of light of a rather different kind. Among the most illuminating collections in this regard were those gathered by Revd Walter T. Currie, known as the Canadian Livingstone, who, as a Congregational church missionary, left for the Portuguese colony of Angola in 1886, and set up his mission at Chisamba among the Ovimbundu. Here he stayed for some twenty-five years, a period which also embraced a long journey into the interior through what is now Zaire, Malawi and Zambia to Lake Nyasa and back to Angola, in 1903.

Currie's vision, like Livingstone's was 'to replace "paganism" with Christianity, the slave trade with legitimate commerce, and "barbarous" customs with their own form of civilization' (Cannizzo 1991: 155). All this, of course, represented the main preoccupations of contemporary European culture and was implicit in the design of, and the use made by, the material culture which that society produced. One way and another, the material which Currie and his family acquired, and which was used back in Canada at missionary fund-gathering meetings in order to add realism and appeal to the missionary effort, was geared to underpinning the rightness of Western material culture.

Like all missionaries everywhere at the time, Currie insisted that his female converts wore full-body lengths of trade cloth, preferably converted into some semblance of European clothing, and surviving photographs show women at the Chisamba mission station about 1895 wearing the local version of the ubiquitous 'Mother Hubbards'. This is the material-culture equivalent of missionary position sex, and with it went efforts to turn the Ovimbundu women into 'home-makers'. This involved learning how to set tables with locally improvised versions of Western goods, and to wash dishes and clothes in tin baths. The Ovimbundu men were set to work in the carpentry shop and flour mill which Currie set up in the hope of encouraging legitimate commerce and civilised behaviour, so that white bread could be put on the Western-style tables, couples could sleep in wooden beds and huts could have doors to keep the neighbours out.

The people were encouraged to live in square – not the traditional round – houses, strung out in European rows, each occupied by a nuclear family. These changes, of course, brought about a social disruption which Currie probably never realised.

This approach to Ovimbundu culture structured the collecting of the material which survives in the Royal Ontario Museum. Some of the material represents the straightforward victory of one religious practitioner over another. Currie seems to have converted Chief Kanjundu when his Western medicine made more headway against the chief's bronchial asthma than indigenous medicine had done. In 1898 Kanjundu rejected polygamy, freed his domestic slaves and dismissed his traditional herbalists and diviners. Cannizzo suggests that the chief had sound economic reasons for this transaction. The Currie collection includes a set of three objects, a beaded charm, a medicine pouch and a rattle, which a chief, possibly Kanjundu, carried as protection against disease. The transference of this kind of thing to the missionary, and his exhibition of it at Canadian meetings, manifested in material terms the victory of Western notions.

A similar point is made by the many combs which Currie collected. The wooden combs and ivory hairpins were gathered by Currie without any distinction being made between ornamental and functional pieces, nor as to which were worn by men and which by women: most of the Canadian viewers may have thought that they were all women's pieces. They seem to have been collected in part as a way of demonstrating the potential for civilisation which the Ovimbundu possessed: since, the unspoken argument runs, these African primitives are instinctively so alive to proper habits that they dress their hair with pins and combs like ours, there is good in them which can be brought out. The same kind of argument may apply to the large numbers of local walking-sticks which many missionaries, including Currie, seem to have acquired, at a time when most European males of dignity and substance carried a cane.

Examples could be multiplied, from the Currie collection and from a huge range of material collected in Africa at much the same time. A serious effort, perceived in moral terms, was made to introduce into Africa a watered-down version of Western life, an effort which was not undertaken in quite the same way in most of the other 'exotic' parts of the world, and is probably a production of perceived peculiarly childlike and primitive simplicity of the African peoples. This involved making careful choices from among the local material culture of objects which could underpin Western material and social values, and helps to explain why so many collections from this period are so very similar, because the same kinds of things offered themselves to make the same points many times. African material culture was turned into a pale reflection of Western material culture because it could then be seen as underpinning the Western material and moral system, and exotic collections were brought home to demonstrate the point.

TOKENS OF PARADISE

Europeans, principally English and French, first confronted the Polynesian islands of the Pacific at a significant moment in the history of European development when the tide of enlightened rationalism was rising to its flood. Bougainville's voyage to the central Pacific took place in 1766–9. Cook's three voyages, in the course of which he visited most of the principal island groups, took place in 1768–71, 1772–5 and 1776–81. Unlike most voyages of exploration, Cook's, in particular, had from the beginning an explicit scientific purpose, although, naturally, this was accompanied by a desire to further national interests, the two together making a typical Enlightenment project. The first voyage was intended to observe the transit of Venus in order to further astronomical calculations, and the voyages carried artists like Weber so that a visual record could be kept, and scientists like Joseph Banks (Carter 1988; Whitehead 1971) and the Swede Solander, a student of Linnaeus, to observe the flora and fauna and collect specimens: curators still speak of Solander boxes, the special specimen boxes which were designed for, and used on, the trip.

The quantity of ethnographic material which duly arrived back in England was considerable (see Gathercole and Clarke 1979). Some went into the London curio market more or less immediately, and went through a number of public collections and sales, including that of Sir Ashton Lever (disposed of by lottery in 1786 and sold on in 1806) and that of William Bullock (sold up in 1819). Some remained in private hands and does to this day. Other pieces have found their way into a wide variety of museums (Kaeppler 1978, 1979). The flavour of the history of these collections is well conveyed by what happened to some of the Polynesian material now in Exeter City Museum.

The Exeter collection includes (among much else) a mourning dress from Tahiti, comprising a head-dress and breast piece both featuring pearl shell, a feather gorget, also from Tahiti, a staff from Easter Island, and eight clubs from Tonga (Plate 14). Annotated copies of what is known as the Leverian sale catalogue exist (that is, from the sale in 1806) and among the purchasers were a Revd T. Vaughan of Exeter, a Capt. Cook (alias Smith) of Wortham Manor House near Okehampton, a Mr Rowe who certainly bought on behalf of a Devon family (*Catalogue of Sale of Important Works of Art and Artefacts*, 16 March 1971, Bearnes Salerooms, Torquay) and William Bullock. The Accession Registers of Exeter City Museum record a long series of donations made to the museum by the Devon and Exeter Institution including their collection of material from the Pacific and the north-west coast. The *Western Luminary* for 28 September 1813, describes a sale of the White Horse Hotel, Lifton, of material which had until shortly before 1813 been in the possession of the Capt. Cook who had bought at the Leverian sale. The material sold at the White Horse included what is described as 'a

Plate 14 Mourning dress from Tahiti, comprising a head-dress made of feathers and pearl shells, a crescent-shaped breast piece mounted with pearl shells with a pearl shell pendant, and an apron made of tapa (bark) cloth and cut pieces of coconut shell. Donated to the City Museum, Exeter, by the Devon and Exeter Institution. (photo: Exeter City Museum)

dress made of the bark of trees ornamented with feathers and sharks' teeth, worn by the King of Otaheite [Tahiti] . . . with the priest's neck and head-dress who attended'.

These descriptions roughly fit the gorget and the mourning dress parts now in the Exeter collections, and since the Devon and Exeter Institution

343

was founded in 1813 with the avowed intention of establishing a museum, it seems likely that these two pieces, probably together with some others, were purchased at the White Horse sale for the new Institution. Equally, it may be that some of the pieces bought at the Leverian sale by Mr Rowe on behalf of the Devon family were eventually deposited in the Institution, and so came to the City Museum. The short *Account of the Origin and Progress of the Devon & Exeter Albert Memorial Museum* by G. T. Donisthorpe (1868) says 'at the sale in London of Mr Bullock's noted collection, Sir Thomas Acland made purchases amounting to several hundred pounds, and presented what he had thus acquired to the Institution'. A sad note is added to the effect that most of the specimens have been destroyed by insects, a few only remaining. There are then, three sources by which material from Cook's voyages may have reached the City Museum (Pearce 1973).

The collections of flora and fauna have similar histories. The bulk of Sir Joseph Banks' collection was bequeathed to the British Museum in 1820, but it is likely that other material collected by him remains elsewhere. Wigan Museum Service holds a collection of some 1,700 sea shells from the Indo-Pacific region, which were once housed in their own cabinet reliably dated to the later eighteenth century. The collection was donated to the museum in 1942 by G. H. Banks of Winstanley. Since Joseph was the last of the Revesby Abbey Banks, and the Winstanley Banks were their close relatives, it seems possible that some of Joseph's material ended up with the branch of the family and so passed to Wigan Museum .

Neither as ethnographic nor as exotic natural-history specimens were the Cook collections the first to come to Europe, but they stand in a particular position to the development of modernist thinking. The islands had seemed to those who had experienced them to embody all the delightful characteristics of the exotic Other, to be an earthly paradise of sun and sea where food grew naturally in abundance and the women were willing. In this timeless Eden, both nature and human society seemed to be in a state of nature from which universal inferences might be drawn, and a kind of rational, enlightened benchmark established to act as the positive measure against which other natural and human history might be set. Clearly, such a mark was crucial: rational positivism works by measurement and comparison, no matter how sophisticated this might become, and for this to operate there must be both a point of departure and a recognised standard.

From notions of the equation between physical evidence and positivist understanding comes the academic paradise of stability, predictability and the capacity to form explanatory theories, which have been characteristic of social anthropology since its tentative beginnings in the later eighteenth century and its subsequent developments. We are offered the idea of an 'essential culture', much like that of an 'essential individual', which can be documented, recorded and analysed. Broadly the same has been true of the natural sciences. These in their naïve modernist forms can be perceived as romantic, pastoral ideas, academic fantasies as irresistibly seductive as the islands whose collected materials did much to establish them.

This returns us to the concrete reality of the early Pacific collections, and their importance (see also Kirch and Sahlins 1992). The Cook ethnographic material, however sensationally some of it was appreciated (see Thomas 1994), is a point of departure for the investigations of human society. It is not for nothing that some of the anthropological work which has penetrated furthest into the broad stream of intellectual life was carried out in the Pacific region. Pitt Rivers used this material in his own collection to illustrate his Darwinian view of the development of geometrical design; Malinowski carried out key work in the area, and so did Margaret Mead. It is also worth noting that Polynesian society gave the West both the word and the notion of 'tabu', and, as we have already seen, social anthropology (and its younger relations in all the fields of social studies) developed as they have done largely in order to account for the very strange totem/tabu societies which early modern travellers encountered. In so doing, they helped, of course, to solidify and extend the competence of the West's own peculiarities.

The same is equally true of the natural-history material. The Banks Collection became a prime force in the stabilisation and elaboration of the Linnaean system. It showed that, because this system could be used successfully to classify and explain Pacific material, it was of universal application with the status of a fundamental explanatory narrative.

Neither then nor now, needless to say, were the Polynesian islands the natural paradise of academic imagination. Most of the island groups were possessed of particularly hierarchic societies in which position was determined by birth, chiefdoms of classic form. Cook himself was killed on a Hawaiian beach in 1778 either as a ritual sacrifice to the fertility gods as some modern anthropologists have thought, or, as Obeyesekere has recently argued (1992) as a result of his own increasingly erratic behaviour. Now, as David Lodge has put it, Hawaii has an interest of quite a different kind:

> 'Really?' said Bernard. 'I'd no idea that tourism came into anthropology.'
>
> 'Oh yes, it's a growth subject. We get lots of fee-paying students from overseas – that makes us popular with the admin boys. And there's bags of money available for research. Impact studies . . . Attractivity studies . . . Trad anthropologists look down their noses at us, of course, but they're just envious.'
>
> (1991: 60)

In other words, the meanings to be attached to all this material are as 'poly' as the islands from which it comes. Polynesian material is not the fundamental collecting statement which underpins the 'natural order' and the transparent values presumed to reside in the authentic artefact quarter of the plot (in which purely intellectual material values rest), because such positivist ideas cannot exist in such an essential way. What the Polynesian collections did, and to a certain extent still do, was to occupy a vacant space in the modernist mind-set, a vacancy which had to be filled if the modernist narrative was to proceed.

COLLECTING THE OTHER BEFORE

Now that analysis of the collected Other Beyond has shown the way in which these collections work, the collected Other Before can be discussed more briefly. The kinds of material that have come from the past and have been brought into collections are infinitely familiar to those who have spent time working with them. From the Middle East came religious objects, inscriptions and monumental art. Material collected from pre-Christian Egypt (Christian Egypt is scarcely collected at all) concentrates upon grave goods, especially ushabti figures and beadwork, and handsome red-fired and black-painted pottery of the pre-dynastic period, mummified remains and monumental masonry. Medieval material is not much represented in collecting, except for areas like the Nottingham alabasters and some of the elaborate ceramics. The nineteenth-century collectors had discovered the distant past of European prehistory, forming collections typically of flint tools, Bronze Age and Iron Age metalwork, and the contents of barrows. From the 1880s onwards collections of this early material have come from organised campaigns mounted to excavate and study particular monuments and expanses of landscape: the originators of such collections believe themselves to be operating within more substantial intellectual and technical parameters than those which animate many other collectors.

Such, very broadly, are the non-classical or pre-classical collections through which these pasts are represented throughout the European world, whether they are now within museums or remain in private hands. What is needed is a historiography proper to collections which will enable us to form a clearer idea of how and why this material accumulation, given its very spasmodic and fragmented nature, is a significant element in forming our ideas about the nature of the past. Such a historiography will need to shed light on the continuing relationship each generation has with the past. It will need to offer an overarching notion through which the intentions of those who have been accumulating the material are made intelligible, and it will need to relate this to the changes through which the same collection is seen to mean different times, and new kinds of collecting come to be followed.

Milton's famous description of Ancient Egyptian sculpture as 'the brutish gods of Nile' sets the tone for one major aspect of the way in which Egyptian culture has been viewed in Europe, and this over a term which spans mature modern times from their beginning in the mid-seventeenth century to around the middle of the twentieth century, a point which, as it happens, coincides with Egyptian independence and Western loss of control of the Suez Canal (1956).

During this time, for Western culture generally, the point about ancient Egyptian culture and art was that it was not Greek. Like India, Egypt was revealed as a seemingly inexhaustible source of rich things, often superb in their craftsmanship and in the use of difficult raw materials. Similarly, as archaeology revealed a literate society with its own recorded history, bureaucracy and professional army, it became unmistakably clear that this was a sophisticated society with its own character, and possessed of an exceptional staying power, which had enabled it to maintain its own development over some twenty-five centuries. The immense popular impact made by Carter's discovery of the intact tomb of Tutankhamun in 1922 really only added a demotic dimension to what scholars had long understood.

But in the West at large the applause was tempered by the kind of revulsion which Milton expressed. The statues, like that of Amenophis III's giant head and arm on display in the British Museum's lower Egyptian gallery, are on altogether too enormous a scale. The temples, similarly, are far too vast and diminishing. The pyramids, though perpetually fascinating, lack subtlety. The monumental art, whatever some of the paintings may show, is seen as inhuman, or indeed, a-human, and this is linked with two characteristically Egyptian, and apparently un-Greek, motifs – the existence of a centralised slave state, and an undue preoccupation with death. A slave state alone, the argument runs, could have produced these colossal monuments, and we hear the crack of the taskmasters' whips which runs through the presentation of Egyptian culture from Exodus to *Aida*. Equally, this is a society which devoted most of its wealth, and apparently all of its imagination, to death and the afterlife, perceived in materialistic terms as very much like that on earth. Spirituality took the form of magic, and it is no accident that much esoteric lore in the seventeenth, eighteenth and nineteenth centuries was given a vaguely Egyptian flavour, as is one clear strand in the horror-film industry.

This strong (if unreflecting) distaste is compounded by the character of collections of Egyptian material, particularly those collections of stolen objects made largely by purchase during the last two centuries or so. Faking, at all levels and in all ways, is a major problem in Egyptian antiquities, so much so that the study of any group of material tends to reveal unwelcome discoveries. This problem runs back as far as Milton's times (see Whitehouse 1989). Among the better-known instances of faking on a large scale, and one which deserves a full study, is that associated with the visit of the Prince of Wales to Egypt in 1869. The Prince was shown the site of excavations in the Thebes necropolis and presented with a number of mummies which were afterwards distributed among a range of British museums. There seems no doubt that this material was a put-up parcel from a number of sites and periods, all of which bear little relationship to each other, or to investigations at Thebes.

This is paralleled by another collection problem. Mummified remains, sometimes of humans (and quite often of individual hands or feet) and sometimes of animals (hawks, cats and crocodiles) were much cherished by nineteenth-century collectors. Unfortunately, a good deal of this material, whether genuine or fake, was not well treated in the original mummification process, and has often been poorly stored since then. The dismal result is a range of pieces which are beginning to decompose and about which relatively little can be done, but which, like so much Egyptian material, help to fill our mouths with the taste of mortality.

The cumulative result of this collecting history and the perceptions of which it is a part has been to create an image of Ancient Egypt and its art and culture which, like that of India, shadows the supposed qualities of Greekness, seen as essentially European, and therefore supports the classical canons of what constitutes both proper thought and good art.

If Egyptian sculpture helps to underpin the collections properly accounted within the authentic masterpiece quadrant, then Egyptian fakes, together with all other faked antiquities, are the 'past' material-culture equivalent of contemporary tourist art, like that produced among the Inuit. Fakes, like airport art, are not what they appear; they are sold as genuine experience but are essentially the products of our own culture, not the cultures of distance. Fakers have malicious intent. They operate, often, in the long term, rather like spy moles implanted within – and yet subverting – the apparent fabric of things. But, like tourist art, fakes rely to a considerable extent upon semi-conscious collusion between maker and buyer. One of the curious things about fakes is that, although they pass muster in their own generation, they are often transparent to the generations which follow. They reflect their own times' view of the past too well, fading into the kind of parody which airport art also sometimes shows, and both, by contrasting with 'genuine' collected material, support the spurious masterpiece category where the dubious and the doubtful reside.

The material from the deep past of European prehistory has the same significance as that of the deep distance of Black Africa: in both, the cultural distancing is so complete that they and their collected material culture can be safely used to underline the capacity for normality, as understood in the West, and so privilege this normality, which is represented in the contemporary Western world by the proper use of ordinary everyday things, which are admirable when so used but perverted into spurious artefacts when they are plucked out of context to be misused in ways which classic values cannot support. Prehistoric archaeology is the material-culture study *par excellence*, and every approach to understanding it has to be made through an appreciation of collected objects situated in a concrete landscape of space and the temporal continuum. This requires the expenditure of a great deal of thought about the nature of the collecting process, and its relationship to ancient societies, a cumulative deliberation which has given us most of what is now material-culture studies. It requires also, a meticulous reassemblage of material fragments, continuously worked over, classified and interpreted; and these two enterprises must be brought together in a marriage of theory and practice, the outcome of which, as most intelligent prehistorians now recognise, tells us relatively little about any 'real past', but a great deal about ourselves (Shanks 1992).

In an interesting analysis of the ways in which the material remains of the European Bronze Age have been successively interpreted, Morris distinguishes five interpretative models. These are the Celtic/heroic model, which relates the weapons and grave goods to the values of competitive individualism; the notion of autonomous development, which stresses local trajectories; the prestige goods system, which is essentially the heroic model brought up to socio-economic date; peer polity interaction of which Renfrew writes 'the intention is to develop a cross-cultural approach, with the hope of obtaining general insights' (Renfrew 1986: 180); and the new culture history which is interested in the exploration of symbolic ideologies (Morris 1988). All this shows that prehistory, as a study in general and like all studies but more obviously than many, works to reflect and uphold the intellectual status quo.

What is distinct about prehistory is how it does this. The underlying message attached to the pots and stone tools, weapons and necklaces is the fundamental importance of daily life as it is lived, and the significance attached to understanding it. Prehistoric studies assert the value of 'ordinary' material culture, such as every excavation yields often in bulk, as a way of underlining the value of ordinary daily life and its appropriate material base. There is a paradox inherent in this. Contemporary authentic material culture, when transposed into collections, offends the canons of classic good taste, but prehistoric and historic material culture, transposed into collections, becomes authentic material of knowledge, embodying intellectual values. This does not affect the present argument, but it does point the way to a further discussion about how old does 'history' have to be and what effect this has upon the processes of valuation. Meanwhile, the prehistoric material in our collections, particularly when it is on display in our museums, asserts the moral quality of the ordinary.

I argued earlier that the intellectual values expressed in the authentic artefact quadrant are underpinned by the human and natural material gathered in those newly discovered regions, particularly Polynesia, which their European discoverers could regard as the earthly paradise, the uncontaminated place where modernist values could find their 'natural' mirror image. To a certain extent, prehistoric material has served the same purpose, particularly when it, too, took on the character of a past golden age, the temporal equivalent of the distant paradise. The inhabitants of this mythic early Eden would show forth uncorrupted knowledge as do those of its distant ocean counterpart; in both, the animals and plants are ordered and named as the first step towards understanding.

CONCLUSION: DARK AND LIGHT TWINS

We must now pull together the threads of the analyses which have been the subject of this chapter and the previous one, through which we have pursued the notion that classic European parameters of value are maintained, in a range of ways, through the collections which have been compiled from material which represents what European consciousness designates as the 'Other' in its various incarnations. This Other has been seen as both Within where it faces its opposite, and Without, along the two axes of the Beyond, the geographical distant and exotic, and the Before, the temporally distant, and here Otherness works on a sliding scale of increasing difference. Nevertheless, everywhere it represents the force which keeps the right and proper in place.

'Right' and 'proper' is represented by the classic collections of the European world, particularly those of Greece and Rome, of the Renaissance and of the art and intellectual material which stands within this great tradition. This, of course, can only be sustained by various internal suppressions, quite apart from the fundamental notion it encompasses. Greece, quite as much as Egypt, was a slave society, and modernist Western historians found it necessary to treat Greek ideas about homosexuality with considerable reserve. We might say that the material-culture equivalent of this was a reluctance to embrace the notion that much Greek monumental art, far from always being pure and pristine marble, was often decorated with coloured paint. It was comfortable for the modernist West to see the ancient Greeks as making love, literally and figuratively, with great passion but perfect propriety.

How the Other is used to maintain these proprieties is demonstrated by the way the collected-material culture of the various Other relates to the parameters of classic value which the grid of authentic : spurious and masterpiece : artefact shows us. It is clear that, in a range of ways, the material from the Other underpins, or mirrors, or provides direct support, for the collections of classic value, so that their own natures are revealed. Moreover, this happens in a coherent fashion, so that across the board, in each stage of Otherness, there is an aspect of that Other which is being used to underpin classic European values. As Figure 19.2 shows, the collections which relate directly to self divide between the quadrants of the

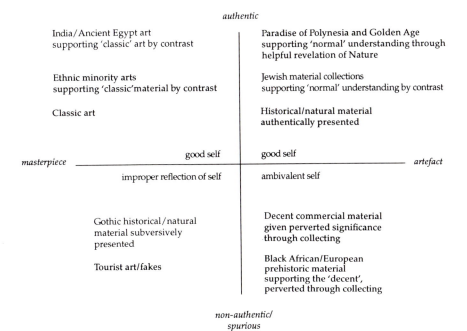

authentic

| India/Ancient Egypt art supporting 'classic' art by contrast | Paradise of Polynesia and Golden Age supporting 'normal' understanding through helpful revelation of Nature |

Figure 19.2 Relationships between Us and Other used to structure and support political valuations

grid; so, in the same way, do those of the Other within, while those of the distant in time and place pair off in relation to their degree of distance and find their places within the pattern. Viewed from this perspective, the collections from the world's cultural traditions represent, in European eyes, a coherent material cosmology or ideology in which the dark twins of the Other support and sustain the light twins of classic values.

The kinds of pasts and distances produced by object collections are obviously interlinked with those kinds produced by other sorts of narrative, particularly within documents and oral tradition, but they do not run exactly parallel: the kinds of things which people chose to accumulate from distance and past are capable of telling stories which are not quite like those which other narratives tell. As with all the other narratives, the compiler is selecting in order to create meaning: in the case of the collector, this means deciding what pieces to acquire and what to let go. But unlike other stories, the collected objects are themselves of the distance in a fundamental sense. They genuinely come from a genuine Other, as all material culture must do, and however much and however often they are reinterpreted, they retain this genuineness. They offer their own historiography in our way of constructing ourselves and our opposites.

CHAPTER TWENTY

COLLECTING THE SHAPE OF THINGS TO COME

—— ·◆· ——

Knock on yourself as upon a door and walk upon yourself as on a straight road. For if you walk on the road, it is impossible for you to go astray ... Open the door for yourself that you may know what is ... Whatever you will open for yourself, you will open.

The Gnostic Gospel of Truth, written *c.* 200 AD (Pagels 1982: 136)

The things that owe their existence exclusively to men nevertheless constantly condition their human mentors.

The Human Condition (Arendt 1958: 5)

INTRODUCTION

Collecting is intimately bound up with the processes through which material goods acquire (and sometimes lose) value. We have seen in the previous three chapters what criteria of value have emerged from the historical depth of collecting practice, and how these criteria, in part constructed and underwritten by collected material which come from outside, are perceived by the European collecting tradition as its own best practice. All value is therefore symbolic value: all societies need a material valuation range in order to function, and a modernist, materialistic, capitalist system, in particular, needs a symbolic system elaborate enough to work with all the consequent elaboration, of which it itself, of course, is a part. Modernist society, therefore, needs a range of parameters against which value can be created, and which are seen as legitimate because they are bound into social practice.

But in the modernist tradition, social practice has two distinct faces, that of the private and public or, as we have termed them in this book, that of poetics and practice (see Giddens 1991: 197). As Benn and Gaus have put it, the distinction 'between publicness and privateness is a practical one, part of the conceptual framework that organises action in a social environment' (Benn and Gaus 1983: 5). Changes in valuation arise as a result of perpetual interaction between these two domains. How things gain and lose value has been the subject of a good deal of recent discussion, much of it triggered off by Thompson's book *Rubbish Theory* (1979), which will also be drawn into this discussion. Appadurai (1986a) has discussed 'the social life of things', and Kopytoff the notion of object lives (1986). Carmen has discussed the issue in relation to the archaeological heritage, particularly where this has to do with heritage law (1990, 1994). This chapter will take the discussion of parameters of value further and relate them to how collecting operates in social practice.

RELATIVE VALUES

The discussion in the previous three chapters has suggested that traditional valuation sees collected objects as falling into one of four fairly well-marked categories, all of which have their qualities reinforced by the ways in which material which is not of the modernist European mainstream has been regarded and accumulated. It is possible to draw together the parameters of value in operation here with those which can be seen to work in the poetic sphere of collecting to give us a closer insight into the ways in which collected objects are valued.

The most important parameters of value are set out in Figure 20.1. Some are capable of relatively 'objective' assessment. The relative rarity of raw materials, for example, is not a topic which will attract much argument. Gold and gemstones really are fairly uncommon materials in earth's geology, although their 'rareness' is undoubtedly enhanced by manipulation of the markets. Marble, hardwoods, ivory and leather rate high in the score table of both rare and 'genuine' materials, particularly as purchasers become more aware of conservation issues. Plastic, on the other hand, although it has its own history of differing regards, is generally regarded as a 'low' material, because it can easily be made in quantity. The criterion of out-right rarity is also capable of being quantified: it is a fact that the world holds very few examples of the notorious Cape of Good Hope Triangular stamp. Similarly, the 'genuineness' of an object's associative value, the question of whether it did or did not belong to this or that historical character, is also a matter of the application of normal evidential criteria in the ordinary sense, although the outcome may well be inconclusive, and we may wish to argue about the relative importance of the character concerned. Similar arguments apply to notions about authenticity, reproduction and fake.

Levels of craftsmanship which the object is perceived to embody is another important parameter of value. We give importance to the degree and quality of the workmanship involved, and are able to separate this from criteria concerned with design and aesthetic value. We recognise quality work in, for example, some mid-Victorian artefacts which would still be deemed unpleasant on aesthetic grounds; similarly we lament the expenditure of craftsmanship on materials which do not seem worthy of it, like

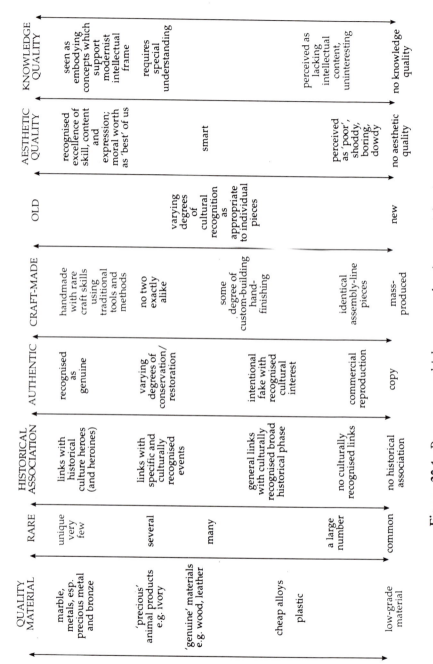

Figure 20.1 Parameters which create value in material culture

fine embroidery carried out on inferior fabrics. In the ability to recognise, and to agree about recognising, high-quality work as such we seem, curiously enough, to strike one of those very few areas where most of the world's cultures seem to agree: a nicely woven basket is a nicely woven basket the world over. This is presumably because we have embodied here some of the fundamentals of our human species, the ability to learn techniques and to co-ordinate hand and eye in the manipulation of raw material. Our hands and our eyeballs are such that this is possible, and our temperament such that we take pleasure in their skill. Mass production is at the opposite pole to handmade, and we traditionally rate such pieces lower in the scheme of things.

The plot thickens when the more subjective criteria are bought into the story. We privilege 'age' as against 'newness' in objects, counting something which has been around for some time as of more significance than something newly made. But how old is old? A range of relative answers can be given to this question depending upon taste and circumstance. Questions of aesthetic value in relation to 'ordinary' value, or intellectual value in relation to 'uninteresting', are even more difficult. All of these questions can only be answered at all, no matter how inadequately, by reference to 'classic values' or 'understood criteria', all of which depend upon narrative descriptions about the cultural authenticity of fidelity to 'best traditions', which is another way of saying that we attribute value to those things which make us feel comfortable.

A different kind of subjectivity is expressed through the criterion of 'how much this means to me', the degree of meaning being relative to the ways in which the collected object helps to establish and define individual identity along the lines discussed in Part Three. Here we touch again the crucial conjunction of public and private values, although we can see that the line between the two is fuzzy not sharp, because in real life how we judge the aesthetic or intellectual qualities of a piece will be influenced by what role it has played in our lives, and correspondingly, the sentimental value of a piece is likely, at least sometimes, to be enhanced if it is also 'important' in a more public sense. This double link, though complex, is very important in collecting of all kinds, because it is one of the ways in which collectors feel happy about their material. The emotional quality allotted to any piece by its owner, however, is impossible for anybody else to score.

In those aspects of value allotment which belong rather more to the public sphere, those individual objects score highest which score high against each of the criteria, regarded as an interdependent system (Figure 20.2). So, for example, we can draw up the multiple grid shown in the figure and score a range of pieces against it. The pieces have been chosen to bring out a range of results. Those objects which score highest in the largest number of the parameters, that is, which show a cluster of the spots in the

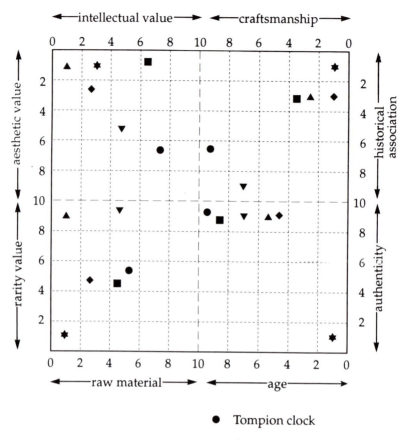

Figure 20.2 Multiple grid to show object scores against parameters of value

centre of the grid, will be those which are accounted the most valuable. We can see that the Tompion clock does best, that the 1930s motorcycle does next best, and that the plastic dinosaur comes in last. In large part, this cultural valuation is followed by market prices – the Tompion clock probably *would* fetch the most at auction, but the market-place match is not complete, because the next most valuable piece will be the Cape of Good Hope stamp, and in certain circumstances it might fetch more. This mismatch between culturally ascribed value and monetary value is some-thing which we shall pursue.

VIRTUAL REALITY

The description of value has a further and most significant dimension, and this resides in the responses which the object itself provokes. Clearly, objects derive their cultural potential from the histories of the ways in which they have been made, used and viewed, but, equally clearly, when a single individual responds to a piece he does so in relation to the con-crete object itself, which appears to him to demand a response by virtue of what it is, that is, its accumulated social meanings together with his own emotional response to it. What we see is a complex sequence of interactions between the individual and the object which changes both of them, alter-ing the life-history of each. This interaction is crucial and we can trace its passage in terms of both the collector and of the collected object.

The mutual dance in which the collector and the object of his gaze engages can best be understood in terms of response theory, which was originally developed by Wolfgang Iser (1974) in order to explain what happens when we read a page of text, but which translates very readily into the material world. Response theory rests on the idea that the viewer's response to an object is as significant as the object itself. We have, as it were, the text created by the object and its accumulating context, and the act of what Iser calls 'realisation' accomplished by the viewer, through the process which Roman Ingarden, a writer drawn upon by Iser, calls *Konkretisation*. The meaning of the object lies not wholly in the piece itself, and not wholly in its realisation by the collector, but somewhere between the two.

The Walsall collector who collects American World War II uniforms understands the history of the Second War and its material culture, and knows how this material has ebbed and flowed in popular esteem as inter-est in, and ideas about, American soldiers have changed between 1944 and 1994. But he also carries out his own realisation by bringing to the objects an emotional response which comes partly from his own imagination and partly from the way in which the GI uniforms work upon that imagina-tion. It is this interplay which creates meaning; but the precise moment of convergence is impossible to pinpoint, and so, as Iser says, 'must always remain virtual, as it is not to be identified either with the reality of the text or with the individual disposition of the reader' (Iser 1974: 274).

It is this 'virtuality' which gives objects their dynamic nature. As a collector views potential acquisitions, his creative urges run hot, his imagination is engaged and the dynamic process of interpretation and reinterpretation begins. The object activates the collector's own powers, and the product of this imaginative activity is in the virtual reality of the object, which endows it with present reality, with the reality which the collector gives it when he takes possession of it. This work of imaginative construction is immensely significant to collectors, because it is the fire out of which come the relations between objects which makes every collection more than just the sum of its parts. We habitually talk about forging links between disparate things in order to reveal hitherto obscure unities, and here we touch the heart of both the creative and the collecting process.

In this act, the dynamics of viewing are revealed. The potential meaning of any object is inexhaustible, but it is this very inexhaustibility which forces the collector to his decisions about what he thinks it means. When the Walsall collector looks at his service cap and coat ten years after their acquisition, they may seem different to him, either richer or more naïve and boring; in either case artefact is turned into experience. In one sense, it is the collector who has changed, and the artefacts are acting as mirrors of his developing personality. Many collectors report this kind of experience, and see themselves as 'growing out of' some of their collected pieces. In another sense, the object has had the effect of modifying the collector, so that he has come to feel differently about it, making him into a slightly different person to the one he was before. So we have the characteristically paradoxical situation in which the collector is forced by the object to reveal aspects of himself in order to enlarge himself by experiencing a reality which is different to the one he had experienced before. Herein lies the dialectical structure of collecting. The need to respond gives the chance both to bring out what is in the object and what is in ourselves. It is a dynamic and complex movement which unfolds as time passes, and in the act of interpretative imagination we give form to ourselves.

Viewed from the angle of the collected objects, what we see is a kind of material biography in which the objects' status changes, sometimes very dramatically, over the span of years through which they survive. How this works is well illustrated by the biography of what is now the Straw Collection.

THE HOUSE THAT WILLIAM BUILT

When William, last survivor of the Straw family, died in 1990, he bequeathed the contents of 7 Blyth Grove, Worksop, to the National Trust, and the Trust was able to purchase the house itself, and the house next door, 5 Blyth Grove (National Trust 1993). The importance of the whole property lies in the objects which have accumulated in the house since 1932, and which are still, and always have been, in their original positions and relationships.

7 Blyth Grove, the house of the Straw family from 1923, is a substantial semi-detached house built about 1906, and is a typical example of a well-to-do business man's house in a provincial town in the earlier part of this century. William Straw senior had been a successful grocer with a shop in Market Place, Worksop, which he opened in 1886, and was able to exploit the appetites of the developing local middle class for good-quality supplies and delicacies. In 1896 he married Florence Winks, whose father had the equally successful butcher's shop on the opposite side of the street. At first they lived above the shop, and then moved to Blyth Grove (which William bought for £767 2s 6d), where their three sons were born. William died suddenly in 1932, and Florence in 1939.

By 1939 William junior had already accumulated enough investments to live on, and was living a life of leisure in London: his diaries show that he frequently visited the National Gallery and the British Museum Reading Room, although he spent every weekend in Worksop. From 1939 William and his brother Walter settled down in the house, Walter cycling daily to the Market Place shop which he managed, and William staying at home to cook and clean. It was a routine which was to last for forty years.

The house had been redecorated in 1923. All the rooms were papered with the then fashionable Sanderson's patterned border designs, dado and picture rails were fitted and all the woodwork wood-grained and varnished. All of these fittings survive, together with the new lavatory in the bathroom and the new gas stove in the kitchen which William senior had put in. The stairs were covered in an Axminster carpet with an Egyptian design of flowering reeds and pectorals, very fashionable following the discovery of Tutankhamun's tomb in 1922. The death of their parents had been a shock to the three brothers, especially William, and soon after his final return home in 1939, he seems to have decided that the house and its contents would be kept as a shrine to both his parents, especially his mother.

William would not allow a radio, television, telephone or central heating in the house. In 1940 he drew up an inventory, on scraps of paper, in which he listed the contents of the ground floor down to every last tin and packet of food. Virtually everything still survives. The dining room possesses the suite which was a wedding present to William and Florence, together with William's pipes and tobacco pouch and, on the right of the fireplace, a calendar for 1932 decorated with a picture of two kittens. The sitting room, Florence's domain, is dominated by her handsome piano and her collection of china and glass ornaments, and has 1920 Sanderson's curtains and matching chair covers. The bedrooms still have their washstands and all the paraphernalia of the 1920s and 1930s: detachable collars and their collar boxes, collar studs and their boxes, trays for hairpins, and matching china ornaments for the dressing-table. Both bathroom and kitchen amply display the bleakness well known to those who can remember such apartments as they survived into the 1950s. The store cupboard holds ancient jars of Crosse & Blackwell salad cream and Fowler's pure cane Italian treacle.

Walter died in 1976, and William lived on in the house alone until illness drove him into hospital in 1985. He finally died five years later and the National Trust inherited his estate. He seems to have voiced his intention to do this as early as 1940, although he probably saw the contents of the house as a historical resource rather than as an exhibition, and we do not know to what extent he expected, or hoped, that the whole would stay together on site. The Trust were initially equally rather cautious, since houses like Blyth Grove were at that time well outside the normal scope of their work. However, in 1990 they embarked on a documentary survey and maintenance work, and decided to open the house to the public in 1993 on an appointment-only basis. The response, both from the visiting public and the international media has been overwhelming, and clearly the Straws' home has touched a sensitive nerve.

The history of the collection, and the way in which its nature has changed through time, reveals very clearly the dynamic relationship between collection, individual and the surrounding world of changing tastes and appreciations (Figure 20.3). The original group of furniture and fittings within the house was accumulated by Florence and William senior between 1923 and 1939. At the beginning of this period the objects were simple commercial pieces, acquired in the normal way, with cash from shops and suppliers, although some of the things, it is worth noting, had the status of gifts, particularly pieces like the family photographs and the wedding presents. As the 1930s proceeded, the whole ensemble gradually acquires that very characteristic flavour, which we have noticed before, and which is neither quite collection nor quite non-collection. The room contents are the focus of significant feelings, especially for Florence, for whom there are collections within collections, particularly her sitting-room ornaments, which operate in a way typical of women's accumulations. During this time, we can say, the material would score high on the parameter of sentiment, but come nowhere much on most of the other parameters, although making a reasonable showing in the craftsmanship ones. In terms of our earlier plot, the house contents would count within the lower right-hand quarter in its character of 'normal commercial artefact' (see Figure 17.1, p. 271).

In 1939, with Florence's death just as war was breaking out, the situation shifts, but only a little. Given the circumstances of the time, nobody would expect that any major changes would be put in hand, or that the two brothers would do other than carry on as they did. A Second World

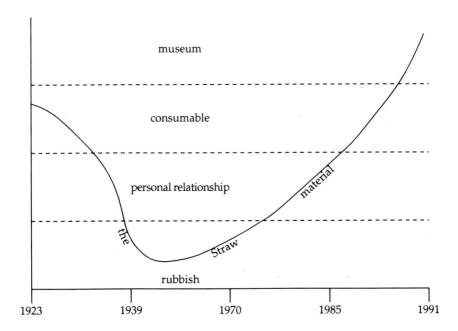

Figure 20.3 Dynamic between collection, individual and public taste: the Straw material

War ARP warden's helmet still survives in the lumber-room, and the iron railings and gate outside were requisitioned, in the normal way, for war material in 1943. William complained bitterly about this and, typically, made such detailed measurements before their removal that the Trust have been able to reinstate them as they were.

This detail is immensely significant. William, who although intelligent and active, seems to have been of a withdrawn disposition and whose mother was apparently the only woman in his life, had already developed the obsessive devotion to the house contents which was to be the dominant feature of the rest of his life. He seems to have endeavoured to put a public face on this obsession by undertaking various pieces of local historical research (one of which, incidentally, involved the recovery of a marble from the Arundel Collection from a local site) and by making records relating to the history of particular pieces in the house which had a bearing on local events. But, essentially, his relationship to the material was that private one between the collector and his collection, through which is shaped his family relationships and those with his peers in Worksop, his place in time and space, and so his world-view and his personal identity.

During this long period, up to perhaps the end of the 1970s, the material, in terms of its public appraisal would have continued to score fairly low on all except the private parameters. In terms of quadrant plot, it had fallen into the spurious artefact mode, which is to say that it had become good, ordinary commercial material perverted into a 'pseudo'-collection because its custodian was trying to appropriate to it a significance which his society was not prepared to allow. William's grip on ancient sauce bottles swings close to what is often seen as the pathology of collecting, where the habits of the miser grin through, and most of the things at this time would have been characterised, in varying degrees, as rubbish.

Gradually, however, taste changed and as 1930s material became more fashionable through the late 1970s and 1980s, so William's obsessions gradually became more publicly legitimate, and the house contents began correspondingly to take on more of the character of a genuine collection. This could not have happened without the intervention of households like William's, which kept such material long enough for it to become fashionable again as it gradually fed on to the market. From having been a pseudo-collection, the Blyth Grove material becomes semi-collection in the public sense, that is, a collection still in the lower half of the quadrant plot, but on the way up.

At William's death, he realised his long-term ambition of leaving the whole collection to the National Trust. The Trust, after wrestling with initial doubts, are approaching it as a unified collection to which is rightly applied all the normal and proper curatorial and communication professional expertise. The collection, now visibly established as such, scores high on enough of the parameters to demonstrate its importance – its material, especially, in so internally integrated a form, is rare, its craftsmanship is high, its associative value is of interest, and above all its intellectual value as a historical record is now extremely significant. The collection has moved into the top half of the plot where it is now seen as authentic artefactual material with an importance well within the European historiographical mainstream. Maybe already, some of its individual pieces may count as 'authentic masterpiece/fine art and craft' – the Sanderson fabrics, perhaps – and others may come to do so.

We can see that the Straw Collection has passed through a number of states, and survived two major crises; the first when Florence died and when, if William had not been the person he was, the collection might have been split up, and the second in 1985 when William died and the National Trust was required to take a difficult decision. Its history makes particularly clear the complex relationship between accumulated material, people and public value.

All collections and often individual objects within collecting, have this kind of history, and similar charts could be drawn up for all of them. Collections of casts of Greek and Roman sculpture, for example, present complex histories, and are now the subjects of great interest (Figure 20.4).

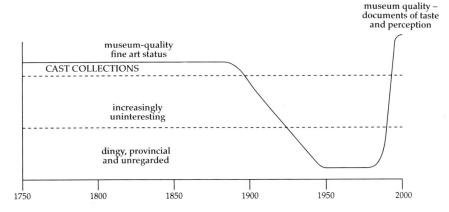

Figure 20.4 Dynamic between collection and public valuation: classical casts

Cast collections are held in many museums. The Trustees Academy in Edinburgh has a large group purchased from the Albacini firm of restorers and cast-makers in 1838 (Davies 1991). The Museum of Classical Archaeology, Cambridge, founded in 1884, contains well over five hundred casts taken from ancient Greek and Roman sculptures or, in some cases, casts from casts (Waldstein 1889; *Museum of Classical Archaeology Catalogue of Casts* 1986; Beard 1993). The Cast Gallery of the Ashmolean Museum has a similar collection (Heseltine 1990), so does the Victoria and Albert Museum in its Cast Gallery, and so too do regional museums like the Harris in Preston, Lancashire (Plate 15).

The notion of this kind of collection seems to begin in the eighteenth century following the accumulation of the big collections of marbles, like those of Arundel (Haynes 1975) in the seventeenth century, Townley (Cook 1977) and Ince Blundel (Southworth 1991) in the eighteenth century, and, of course, Elgin around the beginning of the nineteenth (Jenkins 1992). The casts, which were intended to provide education and training for artists as well as general edification, occupy a particular position in the scale of values right from the beginning, being at once recognised as copies, but at the same time accorded the same kind of prestige as genuine classical antiquities. We might see them as rather like the topographical prints which also became very fashionable in the early nineteenth century, in which the original drawing was made by a Turner or a David Cox, but the steel engraving done by a W. Willer or a George Cooke, lesser men unrecognised in the wider artistic scene. The published prints, usually in book form, were printed and sold, and came to have the same kind of relationship to the original as do the casts.

The cast collections held their 'fine art' status well during most of the nineteenth century but began steadily to lose place through the twentieth,

Plate 15 Casts of classical sculpture on show in the Ring Balcony of the Central Lantern, Harris Museum and Art Gallery, Preston, Lancashire, about 1900. (Reproduced by kind permission of the Harris Museum and Art Gallery, Preston)

and by the 1970s had lapsed into the spurious masterpiece class. By this time, too, the casts themselves were rather the worse for wear, and their dingy appearance matched their declining status. But as collection studies have begun to gather force, through the work in this area of scholars like Jenkins, Davies (1991), Penny (1991) and Beard, so the cast collections themselves now advance again to the status of important historical documents in the history of taste and perception, which construct their own legitimate view of the world. They have shifted upwards, not back into the 'fine art' quadrant, but into the neighbouring one of authentic historical material. It would be impossible to say whether this is a result of scholastic interest which turned to these casts, or whether the casts themselves inspired the new appraisal.

Some collections, like that of Sir William Burrell, the late-nineteenth-century Glaswegian shipping magnate, have simpler biographies, because the material within the Burrell collection has always belonged within the genuine masterpiece class, and so passed relatively smoothly from private collection to public collection. Some, like many of the natural-history collections, were always of the authentic artefact class, and passed similarly smoothly into museums. Others, like much historical and ethnographic material, often with extended personal connotations, have individual histories similar to that of the Straw Collection. Collections like that of the Sainsburys demonstrate how exotic material has passed from the categories of 'peculiar and unpleasant' to 'primitive art' and so to 'major world artistic tradition'. The same transition has been registered by many collectors of modern or 'pop' art on behalf of their material.

Many others, probably the great majority, through a range of biographical vicissitudes, fail to succeed and are sold up or thrown away. When we consider the holdings of the Walsall Eggcup collector or another collector's accumulation of milk bottles, we are made uneasy by our inherited ideas of what constitutes appropriateness. The eggcups have neither significant intellectual nor aesthetic quality, although they do possess the emotional force which has gone into them from their collecting. The shed full of milk bottles, no matter how lovingly tended, strikes us as aberrant, as the pathological, misconceived side of the human urge, but in fact, the difficulty seems to lie not so much in the surrounding emotional structure as the nature of the objects upon which this emotion is lavished. 'Appropriateness', we see, rests in the obscure area between the eye of the beholder and the extent to which his society will, or will not, agree with him about the qualities which he is willing to link to his possessions. Here society is less like a firm table-top and more like a trampoline, where each movement sets up responsive movements all over the surface and fresh configurations are for ever possible through which ideas of suitability and value change.

The relationship between society and the collector and his material is a complex one, which raises important questions about how 'real' or 'acceptable' meaning in objects is created, and so how possession of particular cherished material allows a collector to be a respected member of society or turns him into a peripheral oddity. This is another way of saying that we need to find a way of understanding the balance between our individual capacity to place one particular psychological value on objects and society's desire to assign to objects a stable valuation in the scheme of things. This returns us to the collector as social person. Any collector's objects, as they survive, have a fixed form and a definite factual history (however difficult this idea may be), without which they could not exist and we could not begin to understand them; but if collecting were to consist only of uninhibited speculation, uninterrupted by any 'realistic' constraints, the result would be a series of purely individual sequences with little relationship to each other, and meaningful only in terms of the collectors' personality, no matter how bizarre, idiosyncratic or simply ill-informed this may be.

If the collector cannot conjure up the emotional excitement which William felt, and which Iser (1974) has given us a way of appreciating, with all the claims to validity which this implies, he will lose interest in the material. But if his interpretation departs too far from contemporary norms, his community will lose interest in him. In one sense, the balance is held by the objects themselves, with their tangible and factual content, about which the community has a developing consensus view, and the collector's act of interpretation must take this consensus into account. In another sense, and one true of many collectors, the collector deliberately lives on a knife-edge of credibility. He acknowledges the reality of the factual consensus, but proceeds to erect on this an emotional superstructure upon which, by implication or directly, he invites community comment.

Both William and the people of Worksop (and elsewhere) agreed enough about the factual content of the family material to create a consensus, but here the significance of the collection begins, not ends; the collector is endeavouring, also, to create a community consensus about the imaginative content of his material. Many collectors fail in this, but many are succeeding, and so generally held ideas about value and interest are changing as a result. Naturally, in this, collectors are hindered, or abetted, by broader economic and social movements, but there is a real sense in which they are at the cutting edge of material change. Many collectors operate on the cusp of current norms, and society views them with a complicated smile. We need therefore to come to a further view of the relationship between collecting and society.

COLLECTING IN SOCIETY

It is customary to say that there is a dividing line between 'high' and 'low' culture, and that the divide follows more or less that fundamental division in European society between the educated upper and middle class at the top, and the lower or working classes at the bottom. An understanding of exploitation of the rest by the bourgeoisie of the West was a large part of the point of Marx's analysis of social practice, and in this he has been followed by virtually all social critics. Writers like Bourdieu (1984) suppose that cultural code, his *habitus*, is only available to those who have been educated to understand it, and a significant element in all post-structuralist commentary is the assumption that cultural mechanisms are necessarily a confidence trick employed to throw dust in the eyes of the lower orders, so creating a kind of Anti-Code of cultural subversion and deconstruction. Herbert Gans (1974) followed by Bayley (1991) and many others, has refined upon the notion of the fundamental divide to produce schemes which describe the cultural outlook of a range of perceived social classes, along the lines set out in Figure 20.5. This follows standard sociological practice of seeing the community divided into As (the educated professional classes), Bs (less well-educated business people), Cs (skilled and self-employed workers) and Ds (semi-skilled and unskilled workers), although it goes without saying that the complexity of the northern European and North

Highbrow culture

- possessed of 'cultural capital', i.e. grip on traditional, mainstream European culture
- expects discussion of conceptual (i.e. philosophical, psychological and social) issues
- interested in the notions of taste, discrimination and the possibilities of distinction
- interested in processes by which culture is created
- gladly accepts different levels and kinds of meaning
- interested in popular culture

Middlebrow culture

- possessed of some respect for traditional European culture
- prefers culture cast in traditionally accessible forms, i.e. figurative, narrative, unambiguous design
- anxious about questions of good taste
- uncomfortable with the revisions of meaning
- dislikes popular culture and regards taste as an expression of social position and possible upward mobility

Lowbrow culture

- prefers culture which relates directly to own area, family and immediate past
- little interest in abstract ideas; content much more important than form
- places most weight on personal preference to which notions of 'taste' do not greatly apply
- takes for granted idea that you can put whatever meaning you like on your own things
- regards popular culture as culture

Figure 20.5 Characteristics of highbrow, middlebrow and lowbrow culture

American social scene means that these distractions (and all like them) are drawn with a very broad brush.

Recent investigation into the visiting of heritage sites bears out these broad cultural distinctions (Merriman 1991). It has emerged that high-status people are interested in the global approach to world history, are more likely to belong to clubs with a heritage interest and visit more museums and other formal heritage sites. Low-status people are chiefly interested in their own family histories, are more likely to approach the past by way of metal-detecting rather than 'heritage' groups like museum friends and are less likely to visit museums. People's appreciation of the 'past' seems, in terms of social status, to be in line with the broad distinctions observable in their overall approach to taste and culture.

It would be going too far to say that collecting runs directly against this trend, but what we know of collecting suggests that the matter is, at the very least, more complex than this. The point has already been made that, regardless of class, women tend to collect like each other, and men like each other (see p. 208). This is not only a matter of the style of the collection, although style is a very important element in the whole. Women from any social background are likely to collect material from the commercial artefact class, and exactly the same collections of Snoopy T-shirts or pottery animals can crop up in every kind of home. The adults who collect genuine material, historical or natural historical, can come from anywhere, just as children seem to collect indiscriminately across the social classes. Subversive collections of inauthentic artefacts are similarly not class-bound. The collecting of most *objets d'art* is indeed the preserve of the well off, but even here it is not uncommon to find people from every walk of life with a passion for 1930s art deco ornaments, or 1950s Scandinavian-style 'contemporary' cutlery. Information from the Leicester Collecting Project makes it clear that every kind of collection, with the sole exception of the financially very expensive, can and does crop up in every kind of social background.

Moreover, what we know of the history of collecting suggests that this may always have been more true that we sometimes think. Thompson (1979: 324) quotes from the account of a northern hand-loom weaver who in the 1820s 'collected insects in company with other young men in the village. We formed a library . . . I believe I and a companion . . . collected twenty-two large boxes of insects'. At the same time, and in the same general area, the Earl of Derby was assembling the substantial natural-history collection which he left to Liverpool City in 1851. The scales are very different, but the cast of mind and the aspiration are exactly the same.

The classless simplicities of collecting must not be overdrawn, but it does seem as if here we touch on an area of human life where we all respond to the object world and its accumulative possibilities in the same ways, and where individual quirks of temperament are the determining factor in what an individual will and will not collect. Probably the reason why material culture works like this for all collectors regardless of social background (and perhaps potentially for *all* of us) is because, like our families, material goods are so very close to us. Just as we all, regardless of class, tend to feel the same kinds of things about our close family, for good or ill, so we tend to have the same sorts of relationships with the object world, with all the possibilities which it offers.

From the point of view of each individual, one of the most important possibilities which each object offers is that of becoming a gift. 'Gift' is a standard characteristic of much of the material within collections. Many such pieces are gifts in the most literal sense, of having been bought or acquired by one person in order to make a present to somebody else. This is, indeed, one of the chief ways in which collecting becomes embedded in family and social relationships. But the huge majority of collection pieces, in fact, have this status because they operate as gifts which the collector has given himself. Many collectors make this quite explicit: they use the language of gift-giving unselfconsciously to describe how they spend money on themselves, and how they view the outcome.

Gifts, as we saw at the beginning of this study, occupy a particular and deep-rooted role in European society, which as a characteristic of the long term still works with us. Gifts are sacred in their capacity to create and define relationships. Once an object becomes a gift, it crosses from the world of commercial transactions (even though it will usually be bought in the first place) and into that of personal reference. This is why we gift-wrap presents, why we normally scrape away any indications of price, and why we exchange them in ritual circumstances which come round annually (birthday, Christmas, end of holiday) or once in a lifetime to mark a rite of passage (wedding, Christening, coming-of-age, etc.). It is also why we do not part with gifts easily, and if we do, we feel upset or guilty. Gifts are not cash business, but socially embedded exchange, in which we follow the psychological patterns of our deep ancestors. Gift-giving is an important point where public and private meet, and where commodity is turned into culture, which is itself at the heart of the collecting process.

The idea that collecting, as a form of relationship to the material world for which 'gift' is a useful notion, is broadly common to us all across the social scene because we all hope that our private interests may become publicly acknowledged, is a helpful one. What seems to happen with collecting, is that a great many people collect deliberately neither in terms of Bourdieu's *habitus* code, with the educational capital that it requires and the social prestige that it brings (although of course *some* do), nor in terms of a kind of *anti-habitus* or deconstructionalist mode (although again *some* do), but somewhere between the two. Characteristically, a great many contemporary and past collections were made against material which was not at the time of collecting within the purview of 'high culture', or even 'medium culture', but which the collector hoped would soon become so. In philosophical terms we might describe this as the perpetual movement in which an aesthetic reasserts itself; historically we are seeing poachers perpetually becoming gamekeepers. In the cultural terms used here, material collected in the lower, ordinary and inauthentic half of the plot stands a chance of converting to the upper, 'fine' and authentic half; and in personal social terms, outsiders look to become insiders and to achieve the personal satisfaction and recognition which this means. Everybody, from every walk of life, hopes that their doubtfully regarded collection of today will rank as tomorrow's valued authentic.

This can be put into a significant European historical perspective. What may be the called 'the Romantic temper', with its stress on individual feeling and history and its links with the personal statement which all collecting embodies and from which change comes, is itself an abiding attribute of European society, just like the *habitus*. Like the *habitus* code of classic values, romantic deconstruction is a recurring explanatory narrative, albeit of an anti-kind.

It is possible to produce a very simple plot of some of the outstanding movements in European sense and sentiment, and, by organising these under the rules of Code and Anti-Code, to show how prevailing attitudes have bounced from one to the other over a very long period (Figure 20.6). Christianity as it began to crystallise in the second, third and fourth centuries AD was answered by the fragmentative individuality of the

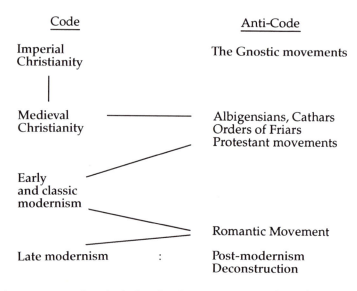

Figure 20.6 Historical sketch of progressive Code and Anti-Code attitudes

manifold movement we call Gnosticism, with its characteristic denial of the reality of historical process and its stress on the validity of individual experience (Pagels 1982). Catholic Christianity emerged victorious, until roughly 1200 AD, from which time it was faced with movements inside and outside the Church, like those associated with the various Orders of Friars, which again exalted the experience of the individual at the expense of authoritative explanation. The individual faculty reasserted itself in, particularly, the wilder shores of what we call Protestantism.

From the eventual religious wreckage emerged the overarching explanatory narratives of reason and all that went with it to make up early modernism, the classic statements of the Code which themselves draw on their cultural ancestors. But while the eighteenth century was directing itself to being reasonable, it was incubating the Romantic Movement (in the historical sense), for the very good reason that, if people are using reason as a method of understanding in one generation, they will turn the same reasoning on the idea of reason in the next, an enterprise which has had disconcerting results. Romanticism was more or less absorbed into late modernism as Wordsworth grew old and poets turned respectable, but meanwhile the narratives of modernism were soon to be deconstructed by the subversive thinkers, like Bourdieu and Baudrillard, who can be lumped under the post-modernist or post-structuralist label.

From the perspective lightly sketched in here we can see that post-structuralism is the current representative of a long-abiding attitude of mind. At the level of argument, the claims of Romantic deconstruction are exceedingly difficult to refute, and always have been, since the only answer to them is faith, described continually afresh in whatever may be the current contemporary diction. (We cheerfully say 'I have faith in human reason' and ignore the obvious contradiction.) But at the level of living, it is no use at all: Gnostics, Romantics and post-structuralists exist only in the movement of revaluation, even though their vision may be 'true'. They do not help us to bring up our children or make a home as best we can, and, on the whole, we *want* to do these things. Consequently, we veer back to live under the Code, with all its manifest contradictions and injustices.

All this has an important bearing on the narratives created by collecting, as, of course, it does on every other narrative. Some of the older material links up directly with the historical sketch offered above. The sixteenth- and seventeenth-century cabinets of curiosities were assembled in a spirit of dislocation from previous medieval and Catholic certainties: hence their close association with the theory and practice of magic, a doctrine of cosmic sameness which defied earthly connections. 'Curious' was a complimentary term as Furétière's *Dictionary* of 1690 makes clear:

When those who have a thirst for learning and desire to look at the

treasures of art and nature are described as having an Inquiring Mind
(curieux) it is meant as a compliment.

(quotation in Pomian 1990: 55)

But as a different notion of the Code asserted itself in the eighteenth century, curiosities lost prestige until, as part of the underside of Romanticism,
the word 'curious' was appropriated to mean 'pornographic'. It was not
until the narratives of late modernism emerged, themselves obliged to take
account of the destructiveness of post-modernism (or post-structuralism),
that we find an interest in these cabinets, converted now into origin
stories (Impey and Macgregor 1985), one of the best loved of the genres
of the Code, and into food for deconstructive fiction like *Foucault's
Pendulum* (Eco 1990).

Objects like Chartist banners may have been collected and preserved
as an act of latter-day Romantic defiance in the 1850s but they are now
considered 'significant', and the feelings we attach to them are rightly called
nostalgic but wrongly called romantic, for this is romanticism tamed, as
the truly Romantic struggles of the past suffer a sea change to become part
of today's story of corrections and consolations. Such pieces are turned
into narratives of the dignity of labour and the life of the working
man. So souvenirs are converted into history, and feeling becomes fact.
Other collections, many of the most recent, still have most of their
collected career before them. We may wonder if the kitsch collections of
china cats, and printed T-shirts now being collected, however unconsciously, as deconstructing gestures in the contemporary world, will shed
their cultural defiance to become historical documents in their own right
– perhaps they will.

Society, in other words, perpetually turns rude material gestures into
proper material rituals and material collected iconoclastically itself becomes
icon. The consequence is that collections made under the sign of romantic
difference which belong originally to the lower half of the chart of values
are perpetually moving round as time passes and the storytellers get
to work. Collecting acts out the continuing interrelationship between the
individual and the community, and, as time goes by, produces stories from
the past which are, rightly, satisfactory to all concerned. Gradually, and
in a very hit-and-miss fashion, romantic, individual and essential nihilist
collections achieve a community value and are absorbed into the explaining narratives.

The post-structuralist writers suggest not merely that all value is ideologically based, but that it has, at the end of the day, no value or meaning
at all, since it is fundamentally self-referential and self-serving. In a world
of relative values fixed points disappear, and anything can be what anybody wants it to be. But to put the matter like this seems to miss the point
at the level of human action. People seem instinctively to create meaning

with (among other things) what they collect, and from this standpoint the relationship which the collecting bears to received cultural traditions, Coded or otherwise, is less important than the fact of the imaginative leap to significance. Collecting is a legitimising process in which social change can be both encouraged and recorded for later encouragement. It can act as consolation and reconciliation by creating socially validated meaning from individual experience. The content of the Code changes, but the need for the Code does not, and hence the simultaneous feeling of momentous shift and perpetual similarity of which collecting habits are a universal part.

CONCLUSION

We have seen that the material which makes us collectors is allotted a symbolic value against a range of value-adding parameters which range from the relatively easy to gauge (outright rarity) to the highly subjective (aesthetic value) and personal (sentimental value). Valuation of material against these parameters can shift, and in consequence collections can move around the four quarters of the plot of values. The place where these movements happen lies within the relationship of the collector to his material, and of him to his larger society; and the collecting process, with its embedded gift character is one of the main ways in which the value of material comes to change. We have seen that this process of change has surprisingly little to do with the social or educational origins of the collector, and a great deal to do with the belief shared, in a greater or lesser degree by most collectors, that one day society will agree with their view of the importance of what they have. Collections may show the observer the discrepancy between private pastoral and public lust, but the collector hopes to convert both into validated legitimacy.

The history of the Straw collection, in particular, shows how this movement can work. It suggests that the notion of full public collection status (for which 'heritage' would be the contemporary term), consumable commodity, and rubbish represent important ideas in themselves, and important moments in the process of the collection. We need to come to a better idea of what these categories mean, how they link together and how the commodity market, in the broad sense, is involved with them, to produce the mechanism which gives the structure of value-change.

CHAPTER TWENTY-ONE

RELATING COLLECTIVE VALUES

——— •◆• ———

Get your new heirlooms here, ladies and gents.
　　Barker heard at car-boot sale, Market Harborough, June 1993

He grew rich as a Dust (rubbish) contractor – coal dust, vegetable dust, bone-dust, crockery dust – all manner of dust.
　　Our Mutual Friend (Charles Dickens 1865: Chapter 2)

INTRODUCTION: CONSUMING INTERESTS

To say that material changes value, and that collecting is one of the principal mechanisms, perhaps *the* principal mechanism, through which this happens, is to say that material can move from one of the quadrants of the plot to another, since these are the symbolic qualities through which our society creates value. The mechanism for this is that of market exchange, and therefore we need to explain further the relationship between the two. This relationship is far from simple, and, although all the dividing lines are blurred and themselves never still, we can see that each of the quadrants has a particular relationship to an aspect of market exchange (Figure 21.1).

The authentic masterpieces have their own exchange mechanism, and we call it the art market, which deals not only in fine art, but also in important applied art and antiques. Next to the art market stands the market of ordinary high-street shopping. Here normal goods are bought, for 'proper' consumption or for turning into collection, a consumption of a kind but one which transforms 'decent' goods into indecent (from the public point of view) collection. Below this 'ordinary' shopping stands the market where spurious collecting takes place; much of this, as we shall see, depends upon mutual exploitation and connivance between seller and purchaser. Above the art market stands the curious a-market of the authentic artefacts, the place where much intellectual property dwells.

The exchange mechanism has two further capacities. Overarching the 'top' end is the idea of the museum, the repository where the 'good' objects go in a kind of material heaven. Underarching the bottom end is the idea of rubbish into which old, tired and undervalued things drop. Although the system does not work so mechanistically as to give two mirroring

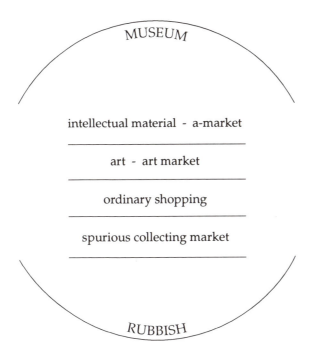

MUSEUM

intellectual material - a-market

art - art market

ordinary shopping

spurious collecting market

RUBBISH

Figure 21.1 Object valuation in relation to market exchange

images divided at the line between the art market and the commercial consumable market, there is a twin-like relationship between the ways in which
museums and rubbish work, the ways in which the two central legitimate
markets operate, and the ways in which the a-market and the spurious markets perform. The system is a dynamic one, and is capable of producing
change in material valuation, but before we explore this and analyse the
interrelationships of the component elements, we must consider the nature
of market value as such.

The market exchange system described here has historic depth, and is
a function – or is the determining character – of the development of complex
modernist European society. The critique of the system usually starts from
the assumption that demand and supply exist in a real or fixed relationship
to each other in which the buyer 'sees the commodity as a means of survival'
and the seller 'sees such necessities as a means for valorization' (Haug 1986:
15). So, for the consumer, the commodity becomes the fetishisation of use,
along traditional Marxist lines, and is linked in argument with the, presumed
bad, effects of capitalism which stifles human capacity:

> The transformation of the commodity relation into a thing of 'ghostly
> objectivity' cannot therefore content itself with the reduction of all
> objects for the gratification of human needs to commodities. It stamps its

imprint upon the whole consciousness of man; his qualities and abilities are no longer an organic part of his personality, they are things which he can 'own' or 'dispose of' like the various objects of the external world. And there is no natural form in which human relations can be cast, no way in which man can bring his physical and psychic 'qualities' into play without their being subjected increasingly to this reifying process.

(Lukàcs 1971: 100)

Adorno takes up the same point in his *Negative Dialectics*:

The [exchange] principle, the reduction of human labour to the abstract universal concept of average working hours, is fundamentally akin to the principle of identification. [Economic exchange] is the social model of the principle, and without the principle there would be no [exchange]; it is through [exchange] that nonidentical individuals and performances become commensurable and identical. The spread of the principle imposes on the whole world an obligation to become identical, to become total.

(Adorno 1973: 146)

Mass culture is seen as homogenisation, in which the standardisation of the product becomes a virtue and a selling-point.

In fact, of course, genuine human needs in the sense of strict survival are minimal, even in northern European climactic conditions, and do not begin to account for the exchange networks in which we all participate. 'Need' is almost entirely culturally determined, and ideas about 'use' and 'value' are mutual conspiracies with their roots deep in the European past. Given the truth of this, there should be more scope for freedom within capitalist economics than such economic criticism allows. One way of doing this is to home in on the most salient characteristic of modernist capitalism, its scope for mass production, and see this as an opportunity for the creation of fresh cultural meanings:

The technique of reproduction detaches the reproduced object from the domain of tradition. By making many reproductions it substitutes a plurality of copies for a unique existence. And in permitting the reproduction to meet the beholder or listener in his own particular situation, it reactivates the object reproduced. These two processes lead to a tremendous shattering of tradition which is the obverse of the contemporary crisis [fascism] and the renewal of mankind. Both processes are intimately connected with the contemporary mass movements. Their most powerful agent is the film. Its social significance, particularly in its most positive form is inconceivable without its destructive, cathartic aspect, that is, the liquidation of the traditional value of the cultural heritage.

(Benjamin 1969: 221)

Baudrillard sets this capacity to create new meaning in an absolute statement by maintaining that the relationship between exchange value and use value is the same as that between any signifier and signified, and that both kinds of meanings, the logic that is of inherited meaning, is the same as the logic of capitalism:

> In fact the use value of labor power does not exist any more than the use value of products or the autonomy of signified and referent. The same fiction reigns in the three orders of production, consumption, and signification. Exchange value is what makes the use value of products appear as its anthropological horizon. The exchange value of labor power is what makes its use value, the concrete origin and end of the act of labor, appear as its 'generic' alibi. This is the logic of signifiers which produces the 'evidence' of the 'reality' of the signified and the referent. In every way, exchange value makes concrete production, concrete consumption, and concrete signification appear only in distorted, abstract forms. But it foments the concrete as its ideological ectoplasm, its phantasm of origin and transcendence [*dépassement*]. In this sense need, use value, and the referent 'do not exist.' They are only concepts produced and projected into a generic dimension by the development of the very system of exchange value.
>
> (Baudrillard 1975: 30)

Like all such statements, these are fascinating to read but difficult to live; indeed, given that we *are* cultured animals whether we like it or not, probably *impossible* to live, in that in real life the loss of any system will be smartly replaced by another. Indeed, this is one way of reading what post-modernist economics seem to be about.

Armed with these thoughts, we can return to the nature of the multiple markets in material goods and their mutual relationships.

THE A-MARKET

Authentic material, as we have seen, consists of objects which are held to embody intellectual value, to add to the sum of understanding about ourselves and our world. Typically, this material includes archaeological material, that is, the physical remains of earlier communities, historical material, much the same but of later communities running up to the present day, and natural-history material, the collected flora and fauna of the world.

It is not true to say that material of this kind is wholly divorced from the market processes of sale and purchase and the approach to value which this embodies. There have been, for at least the last four centuries, shops and sales which specialise in natural-history material and the kind of antiquities, like Bronze Age metalwork, which are attractive objects but not in the fine or applied art class; and these outlets have not lacked for purchasers. Nevertheless, it is fair to say that a very large proportion of this material does not have any valuation within the market, and lacks the corresponding market framework. Movement of material takes place characteristically through complex sequences of swaps and specialised exchanges. These are usually face-to-face exchanges managed between two principals dealing directly with each other, in the style of the simplest exchange mechanism normally found among hunter/gatherer bands with nothing much in the way of central institutions, bands whom the natural-history collecting community much resemble.

The massed boxes of fragmented pottery, chipped stone and broken bones, which constitute the principal part of the collections derived from archaeological excavation, similarly play no part in any market-place. A great deal of social-history material belongs in the same category. Most of it, in fact, has not been offered on any market since it was first new (or good-quality second-hand) and has passed through a number of private hands until it reached major collection status. The same is true of the bulk of natural-history specimens. Some fossils or geological pieces (especially the pretty ones) undoubtedly have a market value, and so do some complete collections, like early herbaria. Similarly, mounted specimens can be successfully offered for sale. Nevertheless, the great majority of the huge weight of floral and faunal material in collections has no real value specimen by specimen, and, as united collections, would be extremely difficult to price up.

For these reasons, and allowing for a little exaggeration to make the point, I have called this area the a-market, meaning 'marketless', in the same way that amoral means without reference to morals. Market notions of value and commodity are to a surprising extent irrelevant to the material world of intellectual value. Aesthetic feeling may be free, but aesthetic feeling embodied in a material presence differs only in its degree of expensiveness. Appreciative knowledge is also free, but knowledge embodied in a shell or a flint is almost equally so. We are faced with the peculiar situation in which the European world of capitalist supply and demand finds itself unable to bring its principal intellectual material within its system.

This is the more surprising in that the same world has a clear idea of intellectual property in a different sense, witnessed by the very vigorous laws which are concerned with the patenting of designs, the copyrighting of published material and the defending of performance rights in music. The reasons for the difference seem to lie within the area discussed by Fuller (1991): since the European world is unwilling to admit that knowledge is specific to individuals, and their times and contexts, it follows that the material evidence which is inextricably bound up with this knowledge must also be depersonalised and demarketed.

THE ART MARKET: THE PROPERTY OF A GENTLEMAN

The art market is that market-place where 'authentic masterpieces' change hands for money. It is the place where pictures, sculptures and antiquities traditionally are bought and sold, and these have been joined over recent decades by 'primitive' art, that is, non-European work, by 'vintage' and 'veteran' pieces like motor cars, and by a range of contemporary installations. The key question, therefore, is the relationship of 'art' and 'market'. Does the art market sell 'art', or does it create 'art' by the act of selling? How does this relate to monetary value, which is, after all, at the heart of any sale, and how is it possible to sell 'high culture' which is what accredited masterpieces are reckoned to be? These are complex questions, and the art market is itself correspondingly complex, returning different answers in its different aspects. It shows at least four distinguishable faces to the world. We can see the major international auction houses, led by Christie's and Sotheby's, together with similar but smaller concerns. Linked with these are the dealers, headed by firms like Agnew's, which deal in old masters, and the London and provincial antique shops in their varying degrees of superiority. Parallel with the world of Agnew's runs that of contemporary art dealers who, broadly speaking, sell work by artists who are still alive. Finally, there are the craft workshops, in some ways the equivalent of the antique shops, which sell new material with masterpiece pretensions.

Most of the works sold at auction, particularly the pictures and antiquities, are sold to dealers who will then deal with their clients, and the ways in which pieces are presented in auction sales shows how value is authenticated in this world. On Wednesday 11 July 1990, at their London premises, Christie's held a sale entitled 'Fine Antiquities'. Among the pieces offered was Lot 258. The sale catalogue gave this lot a two-page spread comprising a full-page, full-colour photograph opposite several paragraphs of description. The piece was described as 'A Roman marble statue of Venus Euplaea' showing the largely nude goddess draped in a 'diaphanous dress' and resting her arm 'on her attribute of a rudder'. The statue, we are told, dates to the early second century AD, and is five feet in height. The next paragraph, headed 'PROVENANCE' tells us, in bold type, 'the collection of Baron Mayer Amschel de Rothschild, Mentmore House', and adds that the figure may have come originally from Gavin Hamilton's excavations at Ostia in 1775. This is backed up by a statement headed 'LITERATURE', which refers us to a privately printed Mentmore catalogue. We are given details of the condition, and references to similar pieces in the Louvre and in the Townley Collection (now in the British Museum). The suggested price for the Venus is from £60,000 to £80,000.

It is clear that the financial value is created at least as much by the importance of the collector and the reference to similar collections – with their attributes of depth, history and accumulated taste – as it is by the aesthetic qualities of the piece itself, because the collecting history offers a guarantee of authenticity linked with the prestige of scholar. The significance of all this is underlined by the use of a special art-historical diction, appreciated by the *cognoscenti*. In other words, the value of the piece has been greatly enhanced by the work everybody has agreed to put into it.

This, the traditional ambience of fine art auction, developed into a spectator sport when A. A. Taubman bought Sotheby's in 1983. He turned the most 'important' sales into television events which combined the gala atmosphere of a film première – famous names, black ties and jewels – with that of a game show with suspense, surprise contestants appearing enigmatically on the telephone, and a fabulous prize for the lucky winner, coupled with a chance to achieve the record books if the price was high enough. In retrospect, it is obvious that the picture auction has all the ingredients of spurious soap opera glamour, if well handled with the right advertising and previews around the globe. The 'quality' of the art, declared in the kind of pedigree just described, cleverly linked with the kind of promotion for which the world clearly has an appetite, serves to jack up the prices which the pictures fetch in ways which combine advantages to the auction houses, to the investors who hold art as hedges against inflation and to picture owners who may intend to resell.

The Bond Street and St James's dealers may not operate directly in this twopence-coloured world, but they profit by it. Thomas Agnew & Sons was founded in 1817 and has sold old masters to the carriage trade ever since. In establishments like these, old or less old, it is easy to forget that you are in a shop. The atmosphere is a combination of the museum (of the more reserved, scholarly kind) and the gentleman's club, of which many of the most famous are, of course, only a stone's throw away. The pictures are treated with *gravitas*, and in a particular tone of voice and expression heard otherwise only at the Victoria and Albert Museum. Clients are treated like personal friends and exhibitions are like private parties conducted with old-world formal charm. It would be a vulgar error to suppose that the tone has been deliberately contrived, but it is allowed to take on a life of its own in which art and commerce give each other nicely blended support.

The contemporary art galleries are a stark contrast. Here scholarship has no relevance and reputations are frequently bubbles. Speed is of the essence as novelty succeeds novelty, and the atmosphere is more that of a fashion house than a museum. Sales are largely to the glitterati of the international social scene, and depend upon an axis of artist, dealer and critic in which productions rise and fall. The debatable nature of much of this art and the problematic future of most of it is turned to advantage in a world which sells the sensation of operating on the frontiers of understanding and exploration.

The craft shops, of which the old Bernard Leach pottery is a good example, are different again. They are usually based outside London and other international cities, originally for reasons of expense and choice, so patrons must make a special pilgrimage, often when they are themselves on holiday. The craft objects are made on the spot and access to the process is part of the purchaser's fun. Prices here are hugely lower than elsewhere in the masterpiece market, and the audience correspondingly more private and middle class. The historical links of such establishments run back into the arts and crafts movement and a latter-day William Morris tone is perceptible in many of them. Authenticity and the design style associated with particular workers is the keynote of the attraction. Like all the other dealers across the art field, what is being sold is as much lifestyle as art.

The essential paradox of the art market in all its manifestations is the notion that 'high culture' – that is, work which is by definition honourable and sacred – can be the subject of commercial transactions conducted for profit and within the ethic of the market-place. However nicely disguised, the bald facts of gain and loss, of calculation and investment, show through. From the vision which sees 'high culture' as necessarily defined and fixed, this is frequently spoken of as prostitution in which the essentially honourable is degraded by the touch of money, but this may be a simplistic view of the matter. The role of the art market is, and historically has been since at least the sixteenth century, to enable us to understand what honourable culture is. The market acts as a complex and interlocking sequence of transactions in which real, tangible, possessable objects are exchanged for money which could have been used to buy something else, and this on the strength of tastes and opinions fostered by those to whom their peers are prepared to concede special expertise. Naturally, since we live in the real social world, all this is dyed with assorted aspirations and snobberies which have no necessary relationship to art works themselves, but this may matter less than we are sometimes tempted to think. The art market is a necessary mechanism which enables us to keep in touch with, and give expression to, our own abiding and changing senses of what things we believe to be important in one significant aspect of our material lives.

GATHERING THE ORDINARY

It is upon the area of ordinary consumables that most marketing and economic theory concentrates. Here is played out the complex dance of supply and demand which creates the commodities on offer in every high street. Prices will fluctuate, depending upon a large range of circumstances, but at any given moment each piece will have its recognised price which will form part of a network made up of other recognised prices.

The usual life-history for pieces purchased in ordinary shops is to undergo a period of use, after which they become worn out or consumed in some other way, and are then thrown away. But sometimes two kinds of events interrupt this flow. Ordinary objects may be deliberately turned into collections, in which case they become spurious artefacts to which individuals are attributing socially perverse values which the community may not share. Ordinary objects may, for some essentially irrational reason, survive. Partly worn saucepans, for example, in possession of their owner at death, escape the dustbin by moving through a house clearance sale. They become part of the world of rubbish, as does the collected ordinary in the eyes of the world, and, like all rubbish, take their chances of resurrection in the form of re-collecting.

These processes are now complicated by a clear effort on the part of sales concerns to turn shopping into a different kind of experience, in effect to turn commodity into a kind of culture through their selling expertise. In order, perhaps, to compensate for the kind of locally rooted experience shopping once offered, in direct interaction with shop assistants who would cut off, weigh and wrap the goods and handle the money exchange, shops now go out of their way to create a new contact with the goods. Special kinds of advertising stress the tradition behind the product, the cuisine of which it is a part, or its exotic nature, all of which harness notions of the Other to help create a cultural self. Special effects are mounted with stage lighting and music, and floor shows of various kinds.

Consumable goods are displayed as if they were in a museum, just as some museum displays become increasingly like department stores. The expanses of plate glass reflect each other, and the techniques of dressed dummies, modern-style life-size dioramas, and carefully casual settings are the same. 'Real objects', that is, authentic museum-grade pieces, find their way increasingly into shop displays, just as the material culture of the shop-window is coming into the museum, where a great deal has been learnt about lighting and positioning. The two now share the same kind of label: Willis quotes a museum-like label from a San Diego supermarket which read 'Cherimoya, prized by the Incas, now grown in Santa Barbara' (1991: 17).

The distinctions between the museum gallery, the museum shop and the store, particularly the kind of boutique which often calls itself a 'gallery', become unclear. The same designer labels or artefacts made in the Third World may easily appear in all three. Purchases from both museum and shop will be encouraged by advertising and dressed in commodity packaging: the carrier bags carrying the newish zebra-stripe logo of the Natural History Museum in South Kensington now rival those famously in green and gold of Harrods, its near neighbour.

The result of this is to blur traditional distinctions and allow the emergence of a new kind of immediate culture. The line between 'real' heritage and instant heritage wavers as pastiche begins to be an experience in its own right. It becomes possible to see consumable goods in a new and personally related light as fit vehicles for meaning and feeling, and so we see the deliberate transference of consumable into collectable.

CONSUMING COLLECTABLES

A large section of the consumables market is directed towards producing those spurious art works known as 'collectables', even though this word is also used in a more general sense. Here belongs much of the material labelled as kitsch, and most of that which the trade calls gift ware. These are produced by the normal commercial processes of manufacture and retail specially to satisfy our appetite for souvenir and bond-creating objects, for creating collections which will become part of the furnishing of our homes. They are the point of conjunction between a legitimate commercial desire to supply a demand, and the apparently consistent need of human individuals to turn consumable into culture by investing objects with emotional categories. It is this need, in turn, which offers opportunity for what can be seen as the exploitative side of this trade, its aspect of confidence trick.

The character of this consumption of collectables comes out very clearly when we consider the mail-order advertising of, mostly, ceramics aimed at this market, and this is worth analysing in some detail. A survey of the national press carried out between June 1993 and January 1994 showed that some forty-four of these items were offered for sale (Figure 21.2). The advertisements were expensive full-colour large-size or whole-page affairs, appearing in a wide range of newspapers which included particularly the Sunday magazine supplements of the *Daily Mail* and the regular issues of the *Radio Times*, one of the very few regular journals which is virtually classless.

The majority of the pieces on offer were figurines, ranging across Victorian dressed dolls, the Girl Evacuee, My First Tooth and Anne Boleyn. Cottages formed a distinct subset of this group. Plates came next, offering a Hawaiian undersea vision in the Discovery of Anahola, fantasy with

Plates	10
Figurines	22
Pseudo-antiques/Speciality pieces	8
Pieces intended for boys/men	4

Figure 21.2 Mail-order collectables advertised in the British national press between June 1993 and January 1994

Rainbow Valley of the Unicorn and animals in trousers with Foxwood Tales. Cottages and kittens are again recognisable subgroups. What may be called speciality pseudo-antiques are the final identifiable group, featuring teapots, the Spice Village with its cabinet of miniature houses each intended for a particular spice, thimbles and 'Fabergé' eggs. Again, a distinct group focus on the natural history with replica birds' eggs and bird images.

All of these pieces are marketed with collecting rhetoric and, although some are sold as one-offs to be associated (or not) with other objects as the owner chooses, a high proportion are sold as parts of sets which can be collected in their entirety, like the Gem Fairies, the Born to be Famous figurines, Foxwood Tales and Granny's Cottage. Similarly, the purchase sometimes includes various 'free' display stands for the group, like the domed display piece which comes with the thimbles, the whatnot which goes with the Limoges boxes, the glass and brass stand which accompanies the Fabergé eggs and the mahogany-finish wall cabinet for the replica birds' eggs.

The greater proportion of the pieces are marketed by a small number of companies, conspicuously by the Franklin Mint, Danbury Mint, Brooks and Bentley, Princeton Gallery and Bradford Exchange. They are doing big business. Each advertisement page in a colour supplement costs up to £18,000. Brooks and Bentley has about 86,000 customers on its books and produces between 60 and 80 new items a year, some in limited editions of about 10,000. The Franklin Mint does over 5,000 different items. The managing director of one of the big collectables companies estimates the annual turnover of the industry at more than £50 million a year in Great Britain alone (Jennings 1993).

Clearly, these companies know what they are doing. Their stock-in-trade is to give their products the gloss of 'genuine heritage', that is, to talk about them in language which creates an atmosphere of authenticity, of 'culture' in both senses, rather than commodity. This pseudo-heritage is achieved in a number of ways. Phrases like 'heirloom quality', 'hand-painted' and 'intricate detail' are freely scattered. One approach is by way of (perfectly genuine) technical quality. The Unicorn plate and many others are identified as of fine bisque porcelain or fine bone china, and as possessed on a 22 carat gold rim. Gold is the undeniable hallmark of quality in the popular mind, and there is clever use of technical language like 'bisque' which prospective buyers are unlikely to understand but will find impressive. One wonders just how cynical the reference to 'faux pearls' is in relation to the Victoria doll, and, in any case, in this world the use of a French word still carries echoes of ancient gentility and modern chic.

The advertisements are careful to give us the name of the artist, and sometimes, as with the Granny's Cottage plate, to tell us that it has been signed, in this case by Robert Hersey. Suspense, a plate which features a dewy-eyed girl child sitting up in bed with a boiled egg on a breakfast tray, accompanied by a cat and a dog, and saying her prayers, tells us that this is re-creating the Pears Victorian tradition: 'Thomas J. Barrett, the 19th century proprietor of Pear's soap . . . every year commissioned a famous artist to paint a portrait, which was then given away as a poster with "Pear's Annual . . . Suspense" by Charles Burton Barber was reproduced in the Pears Annual of 1894.' This is very clever. It assumes a level of artistic culture in the reader – the recollection that Millais' *Bubbles* has some connection with Pears soap – which flatters, while simultaneously endorsing the authenticity of what is on offer. It helps to confirm the mutual conspiracy between producer and purchaser. 'Suspense', like others, comes with a certificate of authenticity.

Various sorts of contemporary endorsements are on offer. Some have a link to well-known and much respected charities: the Dambusters plate to the RAF Benevolent Fund, Granma's Bonnet figure to the National Children's Home, and the Noble Birds set to the Royal Society for the Protection of Birds. Arthur, embellished with 'precious silver and 22 carat gold', with distinctive display base, is presented by the International Arthurian Society. The replica birds' eggs were 'developed in liaison with Colin Harrison – for 26 years curator of the British Museum's famous collection of almost one million eggs of birds of the world'. These insidious links connect the trade to the wider and mightily prestigious world of the great national institutions.

The recurrent themes in this art offer themselves very clearly. We are invited to endorse the more presentable Victorian values, particularly those to do with the family, and especially involving children. Nature is offered as an ideal, happy and majestic. A certain sort of history is included, notably that which looks back to the Second World War like the Dambusters and the Evacuees, events perhaps within the memory of those at whom the material is aimed. With these go the historical characters whom everybody has heard of, like King Arthur and Anne Boleyn. The accent is heavily upon a deeply nostalgic view of life, soppy, tacky, sentimental in the worst sense, carefully presented in a way calculated to create an impression of genuineness and authenticity.

Spurious heritage does not come cheap. Plates like Anahola and the various cottages sell at around £20.00. Figures like Little Sherlock cost £69.95, while the Goose Girl costs £145.00 and the dressed Boudoir doll £245.00. The figurine of Arthur, resplendent in gold and silver, will set the collector back a cool £495.00. Of course, the price is part of the act. The potential purchasers know that fine bisque embellished with precious metal will be expensive, because this is an important guarantee of its genuineness and therefore of its significance.

And who are these purchasers? Keith Yeo, Managing Director of Brooks and Bentley says:

Our customers are normally women, particularly working women, who have some money to spare. They buy from us out of convenience as much as anything else. They haven't got the time to go out and shop around for what they want so they appreciate the ease of mail order.

(Jennings 1993: 31)

While a few – a very few – of the items are aimed at men, like the replica vintage cars, the replica eggs and possibly the Dambusters plate, the great majority of these pieces are obviously and cleverly directed at a market composed of poorly educated, middle-aged women whose jobs give them a disposable income, and who wish to link themselves to the admired world of the 'heritage' past and of traditional moral values. These are in essence the same people who buy most of the gift ware on offer around the world.

If kitsch is taken, in accordance with its German origin from *kitschen* to mean 'put together sloppily', then these plates and figurines are not that in the material sense, for their level of production is far from negligible. Nor are they so in the cultural sense, because they represent a very carefully crafted product, which has both met and encouraged a market segment. What they are, in terms of classic taste, is essentially meretricious. They are the result of a complicity, a collusion between manufacturer and purchaser with intent to maintain a kind of conspiracy of value which operates as internal to itself. But this very internalism gives opportunity for the making of personal meaning.

RUBBISH: THINGS IN LOW PLACES

The zone at the bottom end of the system is that of rubbish; here collects all the material which loses normal market value and so sinks through the other categories. In some ways rubbish is the most interesting component of the system. The notion of 'rubbish', that is, of material to which no socially coherent value attaches, is more or less confined to modernist economic practice: in any pre-modernist world in past or present all objects have their recognised exchange value and will be integrated elements in a system of use which processes everything in endless cycles of construction and consumption. Unless and until contemporary complex market economies take the recycling of waste seriously, the production of rubbish will remain one of the material characteristics of European-style societies.

Apart from the rubbish and waste tips themselves, which are much worked over by collectors, the characteristic locations of rubbish are the house clearance auctions, the true junk shops, sometimes the charity shops, and various kinds of car-boot sales and the like. These venues give us an important insight into the relationship between rubbish and the market.

Unlike normal commercial undertakings, these sales activities are intermittent and spasmodic. They happen only occasionally, or only on certain days, or, like the junk and charity shops, they tend to have opening hours which do not correspond to those of the high-street shops. In the same way, they do not work against an established scale of prices. The principle of this kind of dealing (just like that in fine-art sales) is that the seller gets what he can and the purchaser gives what he must. Similarly, the purchaser has little or no redress if the object turns out not to be what he expected, for the chief adage here is not 'the customer is always right' but 'let the buyer beware'.

In all these senses, it can be said that rubbish is the zone below economic discourse as this is usually understood, just as museums represent the zone above. In another sense, it is the middle ground where objects which have had one kind of value have the opportunity of acquiring another kind of value and so start to move up out of the rubbish zone. It is the area of dirt and muddle where conversions can take place as warm feeling flows, bargains are discovered and hope of value created. Within the system as a whole, it is the important locus of change.

MUSEUMS: MATERIAL HEAVEN

Museums overarch the system of collections; they are the final, eternal resting-places of those collected objects which are deemed to be paradigms of their kind within the framework of value, as this is created through the dynamic of making meanings. The museum as institution is both at the apex of the system and at its crux because museums and their material provide the point of reference against which the rest of the collecting system can operate. This works in all modes of meaning – in practice, for the individual and as politics – because for all three the notion of enduring value is deeply significant.

Museums are the modernist heirs to the European tradition in the long term which has created an organically related sequence of holy repositories – deposition sites, temples, churches and royal treasuries – in which collected material of abiding community significance can be stored and (usually) displayed. These long-term links are made unmistakably and deliberately explicit in the iconography of the museum architecture which makes so clear a statement in the centres of most European cities. The first building created with the intention of housing a public museum was that for the Ashmolean, in Broad Street, Oxford, opened in 1683 (Plate 16). It is a building of relatively modest consequence, but with features, like the main entrance, which fall into line with the official architecture of the day.

By 1850 there were nearly 60 custom-built museums in Britain; by 1887 at least 240; and by 1928 over 500. Most of these were in buildings intended

Plate 16 Main entrance to building which originally housed the
Ashmolean Museum, Broad Street, Oxford. The three floors were
intended for the museum, lectures and a laboratory. The building now
houses the University Museum of the History of Science.
(photo: author)

to impress, and the notion of museum as home of the muses, as glorious
embodiment of the moral excellence of the state, and as monuments which
created a communal history by showing the present as the proper heir
of the past, came happily together in the taste for grand buildings in the
neo-classical and Greek revival styles. In Britain alone the number of such
buildings must run into hundreds, and one must stand for all the rest:
the Liverpool City Museum (now part of the National Museums on
Merseyside) was opened in William Brown Street in 1860 (Plate 17). It
forms part of a group of similar civic buildings which run up the hill crested
by the magnificence of the temple-like St George's Hall, the whole intended
as a latter-day Acropolis. Nor was the cathedral side of the tradition

Plate 17 Main entrance to central building of the National Museums on Merseyside (previously City of Liverpool Museum), William Brown Street, Liverpool. The building was designed in the neo-classical style and opened in 1860. (photo: Department of Museum Studies, University of Leicester)

neglected, and the neo-Gothic taste permitted a riot of carved animals and plants, which seemed like Darwin's theories translated into stone. Alfred Waterhouse's Natural History Museum at South Kensington (1881) had a group of terracotta animals which, at Professor Huxley's suggestion, included a statue of Adam to represent 'the greatest beast of all' (Plate 18).

The material housed in these grand gestures is that which has emerged through the system of value-making to be given the status of aesthetic or intellectual touchstone, against which similar material will be evaluated and either admitted to the shrine or turned away. The massed collections hold material which operates within all of these paradigms of Us and the Other previously discussed, in order to create the systems of distinction and

Plate 18 Main entrance to Natural History Museum, South Kensington, London, taken in 1976. (photo: Department of Museum Studies, University of Leicester)

comparison through which we construct ourselves. This is not merely a matter of representation or reflection; since, as we have seen, modernist knowledge is based in the notion of material evidence, following a mind-set deep in the European tradition, museum collections *are* knowledge and understanding, displayed in ways which makes knowledge manifest.

Since museums are overarching community manifestation of the sacred set-aside, an emotional response which we all share and which we all attribute to our individual collections, it follows that deposition in a museum, through which sacredness and significance are guaranteed, is the goal to which many collectors aspire for their material. As we have seen, museums offer individuals the hope of recognition and a kind of immortality: it is the individual's chance to join the great game. With this, however, goes a kind of ambivalence. Those who seek acceptance also court refusal, and the consequent strain fosters a certain love/hate relationship between established museums and private collectors, which finds expression in a wide variety of particular arrangements and relationships. All this has, of course, its political nature. An institution which chooses collected material for retention also excludes and, given the powerful social inheritance of this institution, the choices made will have their stabilising effect upon what are usually called establishment values, with their view of past and present quality.

This has sometimes been the subject of specific critique. When the Science Museum, London, mounted an exhibition on nuclear power and pressurised water reactors, an exhibition which was positive in tone, Levidow and Young suggested that the large sum of money put up by the UK Atomic Energy Authority not only largely paid for the exhibition but also gave it control over the exhibition's contents (1984). Similar, if less specific criticisms have in the past been levelled at the cultural choices museums make, which have worked to exclude working-class or popular culture, black history, women's art, and so on. With this go investigations into the position of museum staff, especially the curators who are seen to exercise crucial control over the collections (Dimaggio 1983) and through whose professional practice (Pearce 1992: 118–43) policies are made and implemented.

Particular issues of this kind, however, effectively evade the crux of the matter. Museum collections have a curious, unadmitted but necessary relationship to the workings of the multiple market and the values which it generates. In order for values to exist at all, and especially when social value is linked with financial value as it frequently (although by no means always) is, there must be a point of reference where the acknowledged 'good of its kind' can be used as a comparison against which other material can be judged. But, at the same time, it is necessary that this touchstone material is kept carefully separate from the workings of the market and so preserved from charges of corruption and special pleading which would fatally undermine the whole value system. The museum as cultural institution must be seen to make a space for itself different from the marketplace, in which 'pure' judgement can be exercised and a corpus of approved pieces built up; but, of course, the consecrated material is that which the market endorses.

This is the central paradox of the museum and its collections. The European tradition, particularly in its modernist and broadly capitalist manifestations, sees its command over knowledge in terms of the relationships between objects, as evidence of the operation of the natural world, as the mechanisms of technology, and as the 'authentic' in art and history, and generates concrete values accordingly. Museum collections display the visible proof of our physical mastery over time and space, and the understanding which this embodies, and clothe these proofs in the compelling magnificence of traditional museum iconography. So collections are separated from commodity, and this is the central reason why curators will not give valuations and enter into impassioned debate about the sale, or other disposal, of museum material, for to return the sacred to the world

Plate 19 Display from *The Curator's Egg* exhibition, put on at the Ashmolean Museum, Oxford, by Mary Beard and John Henderson, between December 1991 and May 1992. (photo: Mary Beard and John Henderson)

undermines the sacred nature of the whole. And yet, without notions of sacred authentication, the market could not function and whole interlocking system of valuation would founder. The role of museum collections in the whole system is to draw aside the skirts like the good woman of the modernist moral code and provide the still, small voice against which truth can be verified and judged.

But, like women and goodness, museums are also part of the dynamic inherent in the whole moving structure of valuation and collection-making. In part, this takes the form of self-scrutiny. The exhibition known as *The Curator's Egg*, mounted at the Ashmolean Museum in 1991–2 was an 'exploration within the museum's own culture and language: an exploration of the values, the claims to value, the legitimation of value, that the museum supports' (Beard and Henderson 1989: 8). It made its points by putting questions, often subversive questions, in place of traditional labels (Plate 19), and suggests that 'the museum is its own prize exhibit'. In part, it appears as the capacity to accept new kinds of collections – of popular culture, of avant-garde art and so on – and to absorb these into the canon. This is what we have been seeing over recent years, and it is to the nature of this dynamism that we must now turn.

CONCLUSION: COLLECTING TOGETHER THE SYSTEM

The dynamic of the system means that all the elements articulate in different ways to create collections which themselves produce value changes. Now that we have explored the characters of the individual elements, we need to see how this interactive dynamic comes about (Figure 21.3).

Once material bought in the course of ordinary high-street shopping – the chocolate wrappers, the children's toys, the pairs of earrings – is seen as part of a collection, it shares in the sacred set-aside character which is part of the emotional relationship between collected and collector. But at exactly the same moment in market terms, it becomes second-hand, and so starts the short slide into the bottom rubbish category. The same thing is true of those market pieces deliberately manufactured to belong within the collection framework, the gift ware and instant heritage which, as we have seen, are characteristic elements within the spurious masterpiece class. The same, broadly, is true of the other kind of spurious material – aircraft sick bags, poker-work direction signs stolen from pubs – which similarly in market-place terms drop into rubbish once they are detached from the contexts.

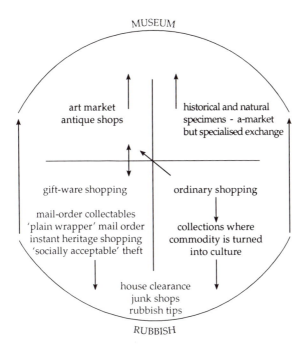

Figure 21.3 Dynamic interaction of collections, market and valuation

Within the rubbish zone are both those pieces already incorporated into collections of these kinds, and a vast array of objects which have not been collected but have dropped out of the market through the usual processes. These include the disposal of surplus or bankrupt stock or sale goods, and the mechanisms of use through which things gradually become so second-hand as to lose all discernible commercial value. Here is the happy hunting-ground for a very large number of collectors, who search for whatever material they are drawn towards, and gradually accumulate impressive groups of whatever their material urge encompasses.

Gradually, partly through the passing of time, partly as a result of the infectious enthusiasm and desperate desire of the collector, and partly from the revisionism which the sheer sight of the massed material compels, some (but not all) of this collected rubbish is re-evaluated. It begins to acquire virtue in terms of the parameters of value discussed in the previous chapter. Age is added to it; its associations become interesting; it strikes a spark with developing notions of taste; and it acquires the intellectual dignity of historical document. Successful collections become first amusing, then interesting, and finally important. They move from the mode of collection which flanks or frames the system into the artistic and intellectual categories at the top. The sequence, then, is consumable commodity – rubbish/ collection – durable museum material, and for collections each stage is marked not only by differing valuations but also by physical movement, from shop (or similar) to home, to institution.

Naturally, only a minute proportion of the available rubbish goes the whole of this route. Most material never finds its way into a collection, and most collections do not discover themselves in museums. Nevertheless, a large proportion of the collections taken into museums have traversed this path. Most collections in the broad social-history field have had this experience, and in so far as the contemporary collections of Franklin Mint plates or glass frogs or signs saying 'Gentlemen' will achieve museum status, they are likely to do so as historical material documenting the 1990s. The same is true of ceramic or metal which comes to be seen as embodying significant movements in the history of taste and design.

This broad movement downwards and then up does not exhaust the internal dynamic of the system. Not all material in the 'ordinary commercial class' drops down into rubbish. Good-quality furniture, for example, is bought to move into a house where it forms part of those furnishings which share in the collection character. It may survive a difficult period a generation or so later by retaining enough craftsmanship value to remain a desirable commodity, and so pass more or less directly into the art and antiques market and hence to museums. Some top-class furniture has enjoyed this kind of experience for the last three hundred years. Material within the art market itself can drop downwards, first into the spurious masterpiece category and then perhaps into rubbish. The work of the

Pre-Raphaelite painters was first admired, and then scorned, and the pictures drifted close to the spurious class. Since then they have again become much desired and hold an assured place in the museum zone. Much 'modern' or 'pop' art is bought and sold by dealers within the fine-art market world, but much of it, particularly after the passage of a few years, drops right through the system into the rubbish zone, from which it may or may not rise.

Material from the a-market of intellectual value seldom has the capacity to slip down into a commercial value of any kind. It can, however, slide directly into the rubbish class. This comes about particularly if it has been carelessly treated so that its internal categories are confused, its supporting documentation lost and its actual material badly damaged. A capacity to become rubbish may also be intrinsic in the collection itself because, although all collections are a part of the function of knowledge and have their niche in intellectual history, some do this much more powerfully than others, and some so feebly as to make a negligible statement. These distinctions are exceedingly difficult in theory, but happen quite easily in practice. Once such collections become rubbish, of course, they are available for re-collection, and the cycle starts again.

As we have seen, the two top categories of art and intellectual value have their own material. In the case of art, the market and the collection is much the same in that the great majority of art works only really existed within collections, and it is these collections which the market feeds. Intellectual value is more complex. Where it resides in natural-history specimens, it may have a similar relationship to a natural-history market, but this, as we have seen, is very small; most natural material is collected directly from the field. The same is true of archaeological material of the kind (flints and pottery) which cannot be treated as fine art. Historical material, however, is likely to have been collected from the rubbish zone.

This brings us to the final area of dynamic. It is from the artistic and intellectual categories that museums select their material. Many are called but few are chosen; the proportion, particularly of intellectually valuable collections which achieve immortality within an established museum institution, is exceedingly few. The perceived quality of the collection is the prime force in this, but all the usual confusions of personality, resource and sheer chance also play their role. While there is some movement of material within the museum zone, there is very little downwards back into the world. This has the effect, from the point of view of the market, of tying material up in dead hand for ever more. From the point of the system as a whole, it means that one artery within the system flow is blocked and material therefore accumulates in one place. From the point of view of the museums themselves, it becomes an urgent debate about accession and disposal policies. But from the angle of social meaning, the sanctity of museum collections is bound up with the significance of the institution and its place in the wider whole.

We see a system in perpetual internal movement, but marked by one resting-place. For much material (although, we should remember, not all) rubbish is the zone of transformation where collections are created and the unregarded detritus of commodity is turned into meaningful culture. At the other end, the museum zone is that of the transformed, the place of apotheosis where market values and cultural values become one. The dynamic in the system is created by the collecting process. Collections occupy the middle ground between one valuation and another; they are the mid-zone of leaving and becoming, from which change emerges. This is why they do not fit readily into the received wisdom which correlates class and perceived quality in the *habitus*-type of system proposed, among others, by Bourdieu. The collecting middle ground is a messy, chancy, exciting place, where all sorts of people play.

CHAPTER TWENTY-TWO

VESTED INTERESTS

—— •◆• ——

'If I find something I know I like, if I know I like certain clothes, then I know I'm that kind of person.'

Common Culture (Willis 1990: 89)

INTRODUCTION

This Part has tried to show that the social value which is placed upon a group of collected objects depends upon the operation of a particular cosmological view which is constructed from the standpoint of 'ourselves'. This brings into its lattice-work a series of value-creating parameters in which individual collected pieces participate, and positions the whole in time and space by using the Other before and beyond to underpin, or shadow, the resulting structure. This mode of creating value runs through our intellectual, aesthetic and historical appreciations, and bears a complex relationship to the market exchange of goods, in which broadly speaking financial values follow cultural values but with the marked exception of much intellectual property to which no (or negligible) monetary value is assigned.

What the workings of the market does is provide a necessary mechanism for the value system's dynamic. The different kinds of market, and the social qualities which are attached to them, make it possible for material to undergo a sea change in valuation, so that from the rubbish zone, into which many things drop, collections can emerge which meet the social parameters of value as time passes, and so move up the value scale. The crucial factor here, the value-adding factor to use contemporary language, is the passion and effort of the collector, who, by the persuasive powers of his collecting, achieves an assemblage which becomes meaningful. The value dynamic locks into long-term practice partly because it is from long-abiding *mentalités* that many of the parameters of value derive, and partly because, in order to function, it must provide from within itself an apparently independent touchstone of reference which is guaranteed by its traditional depth, the modernist version of which is the museum.

Speed in valuation change, coupled with intense market concentration, is nowhere more visible than in the world of designer fashion and clothes (Quick 1994; Hume 1993) and so we will consider the fate of a group of

Plate 20 Front of Cambridge Jean Company shop, Cambridge in 1994. The shop, which sells Levi jeans, has an interior fitted with rough wood stained dark brown, intended to simulate frontier conditions.
(photo: author)

Levi jeans in order to draw together the threads of this discussion in Part Four.

COLLECTING BY DESIGN

Levi jeans are currently on sale in the Cambridge shop known as the Cambridge Jean Company (Plate 20). The shop has been got up with rough wooden fittings, stained brown and in 'low-tech' design, intended to give the impression of a trading post on the old Western frontier as this institution has come to us by way of innumerable films. The trousers come in a number of models, and that known as the 501 makes the point very well. Much more conspicuous than the garment itself are the labels which are sewn on to its outside. One of these says 'Patented rivets for extra strength since 1873'. Another gives us 'The famous Levi-Strauss and Co. button, a symbol of quality since the 1860's'; and a third asks us to 'Look for the red tag on the right back pocket. Registered trade mark since 1936'. Finally, there is 'XX Exclusive XX all cotton denim, a Levi tradition since the 1870's'. The thrust of this sales pitch is obviously to create for

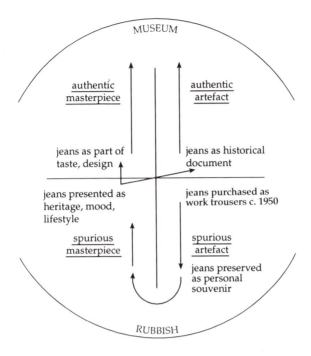

Figure 22.1 Structuring processes in relation to Levi-Strauss jeans

brand-new clothes a high enough score on the parameters of value, historical among others, to give them a cultural value which will mingle with, and reinforce, their commodity value, and so help Levis to win the commercial battle over the main rivals, Wrangler and Lee. What is interesting is why the commercial battle has taken this particular tone and how individual collectors relate to it (Figure 22.1) (Tredre 1993; Gilchrist and Manzotti 1993).

Around 1950 a pair of Levi-manufactured *serge de Nîmes*, indigo-dyed trousers could be purchased relatively cheaply as work trousers. In spite of all the mythology about French dockside slang and the sailors of Genoa (*Gênes* in French), the trousers seem not to have been called 'jeans' until the 1960s, but they already had the rivets and buttons to which the labels refer. In terms of the then valuations operating in the market-place, such trousers would have an extremely modest second-hand value, and once bought in the course of normal shopping would slip rapidly into the rubbish zone. They did, however, have very genuine hard-wearing qualities, with the result that over the years some acquired the patina of personal sentimental valuation which we frequently attach to everyday clothes that have become like a second skin. A small proportion of such material survived, commercially rubbish, but now endowed with the souvenir emotions which are spurious in terms of social value but significant in terms of personal value.

Meanwhile, in 1954 Marlon Brando had worn Levi's in *The Wild One* and James Dean had done the same in *Rebel Without a Cause* (1955). The jeans were capable of supporting the image of a cultural rebel precisely because they were work wear, and so they came to symbolise the anti-culture strain in popular culture which has been such a significant element in the post-modern world, with its emphasis on youth, which can demonstrate its unified and Outsider nature through what it chooses to wear. Jeans had acquired an anti-value of considerable cultural significance.

To this original anti-value, others were added. In 1938 Levi-Strauss had introduced the first jeans for women, in lightweight denim, called the 701 Lady Levis, and at the end of the 1950s Marilyn Monroe was photographed wearing a Lee Storm Biker jacket, first launched in 1933. Over forty years on, it is difficult to appreciate how outrageous and upsetting many found the sight of women in men's work trousers. The first stitches had given way in what was to become the unravelling of much visible gender difference, and jeans are still one of the normal foils for the women's post-punk combinations of Doc Marten-style boots and layered baggy shirts and jackets.

Many women now glean in the second-hand clothes market, buying used men's suits, jackets and raincoats which can be altered and combined with female clothes in ways which deconstruct traditional feminine styles. Jeans are a vehicle of deconstruction for both sexes. Tatters and patches are fashionable, and natural fraying is frequently aided by discreet snips. Jeans can be bought ready distressed which means that areas of dye have been bleached out and the cloth softened through industrial washing processes. The new anti-fashion seems likely to prescribe seams that show their stitching and raw edges on the outside, as designer Jean Colonna is doing, and Marks & Spencer is copying.

Distressing is a parody of heritage, and heritage is both a value and a selling-point. Levi-Strauss have turned their history into marketable heritage, but, it is important to remember, their history is, after its kind, perfectly genuine: the firm really does go back to 1855, it really has been manufacturing the same sort of garments ever since, and it really does have a genuine archive of styles and detailing. What is distinctive about the history is that it is now interesting and important, something which has been brought about partly through the passage of time, and partly through changes of tone.

The genuineness of their history is, of course, shot through with its own meretricious mythology. The cowboy image still crops up intermittently: the 1994 Levis commercial was set around a campfire in Monument Valley and showed Ethan Browne in a cowpoke hat accompanied by the suggestion of horse harness. Cowboys were always mostly urban fantasy and are now an outdated one, but it is interesting to see how the myth of the Other beyond, in this case the Wild West, is still appropriated to support the material culture of the insider. We might add that Levi-Strauss, by name so peculiarly well suited to structuralist analysis, are a Jewish firm in origin, like many in the clothing trade, and so show the traditional Other within supporting insider fantasy.

The jeans embody all these cultural commercial trends. Their identification as lifestyle, as at once heritage and anti-hero, avant-garde and anti-fashion, turns them into spurious masterpieces for which a particular kind of disestablishment value is developed. This is not solely the result of clever promotion; we concur in our own deception and dissemble our own understanding. The result is that the surviving 1950s jeans cease to be private history and become public interest. Very shortly they become authentic artefacts, historical documents laden with satisfactorily genuine information about the history of taste and design and of the relationship of this to post-modern social attitude. In due course, they will be treated as 'costume' in the high culture, high applied-art sense, and share some of the characteristics of the authentic masterpiece. By this time, they will have long since been taken into significant museum collections and will be on show with their peers in the Victoria and Albert Museum Costume Court.

CONCLUSION

The analysis of the 1950s jeans lays bare a number of significant points in the process through which the valuation which we place upon material is transformed. The jeans began as 'culture' in the anthropological sense, that is, as a genuine element in a coherent pattern of social life. They acquired the character of anti-culture in a different sense, anti-establishment, gender-bending, a moody intellectualism in alliance with demotic gesture. In due course, this anti-culture becomes culture, in every sense of the word. We see here a cycle of change which is very characteristic of much of the collecting process over recent centuries, and perhaps longer.

One important part in this process is the way in which commodity becomes culture: again, this has been especially significant over the past two, or perhaps three, centuries since the growth of mass production, but is discernible as a movement of 'inwardisation' in the long term. What I mean by this is the capacity of possessors to endow material with personal meaning, to take it into the inwardness of their lives and allow it to take on meaning which it previously did not have. This means both that collected objects survive physically – a crucial part of the process for material culture – and are opened up to the access of community feeling in which contact with old objects sparks off new feelings. These new feelings are neither quite the manipulation of the producers of goods, nor the imaginative effort of the possessors and viewers alone; they rest somewhere between, in a mutual conspiracy in which, in the end, the possessors and viewers often seem capable of creating the meanings they choose.

But one final important question remains. Given, as this Part has tried to show, that the value with which a collected group of objects is accredited arises in reference to a number of value parameters into which are woven a range of political references intended to help us construct ourselves, and given that the multiple market-place is the dynamic mechanism through which the valuation placed on individual pieces can change, do we see, or are we likely to see, structural change in the system itself, or just changes in the content of the structure? To put it concretely, may the main axes of spurious/authentic and masterpiece/artefact (with which we began) change, or merely the contents of the quadrants? And, must the system inevitably pivot around the twins of 'rubbish' and 'museum'?

It seems likely that in a strange way both are true. Notions of discrimination and distinction which give ideas about authenticity, historicity and comparative analysis, together with the conviction that these principles are rooted in the material world under our hands, seem to have shaped, and still shape, what has been the most influential mind-set the world has experienced, and they are unlikely to be abandoned. But, just as the tradition of modern France is to be revolutionary, theoretically an internal contradiction, so the European tradition is to be dynamic. The structure belongs within the long term, but as its content changes, these changes also alter the meanings given to the structural elements themselves: basic themes remain but are perpetually understood to reveal new tones and colours, as each generation grapples with them afresh.

PART V

COLLECTING IN THE EUROPEAN TRADITION

CHAPTER TWENTY-THREE

COLLECTING IN THE EUROPEAN TRADITION

——— •◆• ———

[Miss Mackenzie] leaned forward and kissed herself in the glass.
Miss Mackenzie (Anthony Trollope 1865: Chapter 9)

INTRODUCTION: BODIES OF EVIDENCE

The quotation from P. G. Wodehouse which this book started with touches on a number of themes with which this study has been concerned. In the story of Peters' conversion to collecting is the psychological aspect of the matter, encapsulated by the analyst's advice, with all its humour and obsession; there is the historical depth which gives respectability to collections of the antique, and the relationship with the Other, represented by the ancient Egyptian scarabs; there is the characteristic erotic note, for Peters will love his things with a love passing that of women; and Peters, although holding a European mind-set, is an American, reminding us that 'Europe' came to mean more than the inhabitants of one small land mass and now, in many important respects, means the world.

Underlying this local and specific example we can see all the discourses which characterise European modernism and the earlier traditions upon which modernism drew, a particular kind of relationship between the individual, other individuals and the world, a tradition (however muted at times) of dynamism and change, a particular mode of erotic feeling, and an economic system which depends upon the production and consumption of a continuing spiral of goods. In all of this there is a paramount belief in the essential and absolute power of reason and in the physical evidence with which, as a matter of necessity, reason is informed. The aggregate of this is a particular relationship with the material world in which people and ideas can be reified and objects, if not deified, at any rate humanified.

All these motifs of the cultural long term have gathered momentum, linked as they are with the mental structure characterised as the oath/ordeal paradigm with its preference for distinction and discrimination, and family structures which combine a certain freedom of opportunity with something of a tendency to concentrate access to resources in a relatively small number of persons. The result is a historiographical thread of the long term which shows us a continuing wish to gather material in special communal ways in a sequence which begins with barrows and hoards, progresses to temples and shrines, moves to churches and palaces, and so to the museum of the full modernist age. The material so gathered is reckoned as sacred, as treasure, as knowledge, and as the living relic of the mighty dead still working amongst us. At the same time, a parallel thread in the long term shows us the individual as accumulator, collecting material as an approach to self-realisation and to creating relationships with others.

The power of this European cultural narrative of the long term rests less in its 'historical reality' than in its standing as 'communal fiction'. It may be urged that the classic intellectual enquiry (that is, the European approach to understanding) which assumes that 'things' have a 'discoverable nature' carries within it the humanist fallacy which gives all humans a real identity, the sentimental fallacy which assumes that supposed fellow-feeling enables us to understand each other in past and present, and the material fallacy, which assumes that material objects have a meaning other than that which limited consensus has agreed for them. Whether this is reality or 'reality' is beside the point. The communal fallacy is powerful enough to create the extended meaning in historical depth which we can see, and of which the collecting process is a part. Efforts to show the same discontinuities in a single human social life fail for the same reasons. However the body of evidence is laid out, it seems clear that the European cultural grip on materiality is 'normal' to itself, but probably 'abnormal' viewed from any non-European perspective.

SACRED THINGS

At the heart of the collecting process is the notion of 'set-aside', a quality which is justly described as 'sacred' and which has both a private and a public aspect. It springs from the idea of sacred as this emerges in the early European languages, and which links with the oath/ordeal paradigm, itself the source of the notion of distinction and difference: set-aside sacred things are possible because not everything shares this character. Sacred collections are therefore capable of expressing distinction, and of creating relationships which define the response to the Other either of past or of distance, and they can do this in both individual and community terms.

For the community, the sacred collection is stored within its shrine, through its successive historical manifestations. Here it acts as the community's endorsements of its own value judgements about aesthetic, knowledge and history. The museum collection acts as the touchstone for that authenticity of physical evidence upon which, in the last resort, understanding rests. For the individual, his own personal collection does much the same, validating his judgement of his own life, and linking this to the broader judgements of the community as he may or may not wish to do. In both dimensions the collected objects both reflect our ideas about ourselves, and act with their own magical power to reinforce and enhance these ideas.

The notion of the collection as set-aside and sacred has considerable historical depth, which is, of course one of the reasons why it is possessed of such emotional power. The concept of the gift as a means of creating social relationships endowed with similar force helps us to understand the role of collecting within the whole social fabric. The notion of the honourable gift, like that of the poetic imperishable fame with which it is linked, has been identified as part of the view taken of individuals in society which is characteristic of the European mind-set in the long term. As, in Braudel's terms, the European long term moved into what it is useful to call a capitalist economy, itself a part of the cluster of attributes typical of modernism, so the basic of social cohesion became market exchange, not that of person-to-person gift-giving; what, in primitive linguistic terms we might call a shift from *methom* to *mizdo* (see p. 71). But the notion of the set-aside collection continued to embrace the emotional values connected with gifts.

At the community level, just as museums inherit earlier ideas about community treasure which can create relationships with the gods (that is, with our own most deeply held beliefs externally defined), so they also inherit the idea that to give material freely to museums is a meritorious act which conveys famous immortality; and the huge bulk of museum collections were indeed acquired as free donations. For individuals, their collections retain the character of gifts, goods which are embedded in feeling and action rather than commodities to be bought and sold. They often are linked with contemporary practices of embedded exchange at Christmas, birthday and holiday time, and in any case collectors characteristically view all their things as presents to themselves, however they are come by.

The essence of the gift/collection is its capacity both to embrace and encourage meaning which is seen to transcend that of daily occasions, and to help create the broader purposes into which daily life fits (or is made bearable). The emotional aspect of this is its sacred character; its economic equivalent is the complex workings of the market, particularly as this has developed, and with logarithmic scope, over firstly the last three centuries or so, and then over the last few decades. Collections rest at the top of the market, where they are lodged in museums (or aspire to them), and where, by definition, they are not for sale. Collections also rest (mostly) at the bottom among the rubbish, where collectors exercise choice and judgement and things are offered at 'give-away' prices. Between the two lie ordinary commodity market transactions. The complicated way in which these elements relate to each other has been traced in Chapter 21. The important point here is the capacity of the gift/collection to exist in parallel with, and in complex relationship to, ordinary exchange, and so its ability to create sacred cultural meaning perpetually afresh.

LOOK BUT NOT TOUCH

Together with notions of 'gift culture' and the sacred runs the theme of collecting as erotic experience. This is why the diction, especially the critical diction, of collecting is full of explicitly sexual words like 'fetish', 'voyeur', 'passion' and 'love', why the erotic element in our appreciation of the past is so significant, and why collecting and the sexual life share an overlapping language, so that we use metaphors drawn from each to describe the other and phrases like 'desirable', 'chasing', 'making' and 'keeping in the closet' crop up all the time. If collecting is a variety of religious experience, it is also a form of sexual experience (as the older literature insisted) reminding us again that the correspondence, or confusion, of these fields of feeling is normal across the human family.

If a relationship between sex and religion as the realm of the sacred seems to be something of a human norm, however, its identification with the material world of goods appears to be peculiarly European, and indeed to be part of the knot of traits which gives the European tradition its particular – and rather strange – cultural character. The European ideas of dichotomy between subject : object, or individual : world, produce a situation in which collections of material can become *alter egos*, both fields for the intellectual and aesthetic efforts at distinction and manipulation which we admire and parallel constructions of the self; they are at the same time separate from us as despised non-human materiality, and an essential part of our self-aware capacity to know and understand.

This parallels the European view of the feminine very closely. Deeply embedded in traditional European culture are notions of woman as thing to be pursued and possessed, woman as sacred to be revered, and between these two, woman as normal person to be lived with on terms which are capable (at least) of developing into something like equality. When we remember that this same triple image is operating within a society whose long-term predispositions also allow considerable freedom in marriage choice but link this with property notions which have always been capable of leaving many young men of the educated class poorly endowed, we can see that the emotional link between the need to accumulate things from the material world and the view of women will be complex but compelling.

Among many other things, the masculine need to make material statements explains why, as the surveys show, men's collections made in one mode and women generally in another, and why the male mode dominates our thinking to the extent that 'collecting' itself has tended to be defined within its terms, with the result that hitherto much female collecting has been unrecognised or has disappeared without trace. Not, of course, *all* female collecting: in a society with inbuilt gender ambivalence, as ours is, we would expect to find the occasional Kyniksa of Sparta dedicating a statue at Olympia or Kriemhilde inheriting the Nibelung treasure, or Renaissance princess collecting in the grand manner like Isabella d'Este, or English middle-class lady like Ethelred Benett achieving her significant collection of fossils: these women are not sports or peculiarities, they represent the other, albeit much smaller, facet of the same tradition, in all its characteristic complications.

As we saw in our discussion of the dinner party, look freely but do not touch is an odd but characteristically modernist way in which much of the interrelationship between the genders is organised, a tendency which seems to run deep in northern, although not southern, European life. Exactly the same motif of looking but not touching applies to those collections, the major collections enshrined in museums, which are held as touchstones of significance, references to validate evidential deduction and inference. Like virtuous women of good family in daily social life they are open to view, but may not be handled, except by special appointment in special back rooms, and through special arrangements with the (usually male) gate-keeping curator (and it can be so difficult to 'get at' material). The moral centres of museum collections and of femininity are clearly the same: endorsing market values while remaining apart from the market, and enabling the broadly capitalist modern economic discourse to proceed but pretending not to be by keeping the eyes closed while it all happens.

Within the material market-place complementary things are happening. Like the museum, and the collectors who mostly contribute to museum holdings, the market is operated largely by men. It is, however, addressed principally to women as consumers, since most shopping in the European world is done by women. Here we have women operating literally as 'women of the world', in their mode as mature, sensible (in every sense) people, on an equality with such male shoppers as they encounter and able to compare and contrast, bargain and decide. This has its underside. Choice is deliberately trammelled, and the market is manipulated in various exploitative ways. Moreover, the gift ware and collectable 'instant heritage' market particularly aimed at women operates as a cynical parody of 'sacred values', offering a spurious, illegitimate and essentially trivial under-version of 'real things'. Within this double perspective the role of women is, as always, ambivalent and difficult to sustain with material dignity.

Below the level of rational economic discourse, itself one of the great modernist fallacies, stands the zone of rubbish, the whores both female and male of the object world where everything is open to offers. This, as we have seen, is the characteristic zone of collecting (although not the only one) where old objects are reinterpreted and endowed with fresh meaning through the collecting process of imaginative selection. It is where changes of value come about, and hence changes of content within the valuation structure, and so changes in financial price and all other forms of expressing desirability.

The links across the system though which these changes happen, and their relationships to parameters of value – epistemological, aesthetic, historical – with their roots deep in European cultural norms, have already been traced. What we see here is how one metaphor, that characteristic European way of making meaning, shadows another, so that the collecting process is one with the metaphor through which gender is given meaning, and that through which market forces are able to operate.

EUROPE AND THE OTHER

Many of the characteristic modernist European metaphors of cultural practices – including that of collecting – are now global culture and practised in areas where they have wrought organic changes in the local cultural long term. The one which has not is that metaphor which has constructed the material – of natural and human history – from the exotic world into a pattern which underpins and sustains European cultural values, and the identification of gender which, as Thomas has shown (1994) lurked within the absorption by Europe of the newly discovered Other world in all kinds of ramifying ways.

Historically, the problem of coping with the human Other has been assessed (in Europe) in one of two ways: by a universalism which assumes shared human characteristics under the infinitely various appearance, and by a relativism which supposes no common essence but merely a series of local forms of behaviour, all of which are equally 'right' in their own time and place. Universalism arrives at a universal view of human nature which is somehow always that of the European consensus; indeed the notion of 'human nature' in this sense is itself a part of European culture. Universalism leads, therefore, to a condemnation of much Other culture as inhuman and to be suppressed. On the other hand, relativism condemns us to complete moral inertia since it gives us no way of condemning the slave trade or female clitoridectomy. In spite of arguments offered with great power and persuasiveness by writers like Todorov, a feasible middle ground between these two remains elusive, however welcome it would be.

Collections of the Other are now stranded in the gap between relativism and universalism. Historically, they were made between roughly 1500 and 1950 when a kind of universalism, often a very crude kind, prevailed, and so the material and natural culture could be collected in ways which demonstrated a Eurocentric universalism and its preferred content, as we have seen. These collections are now being reinterpreted in a relativist light as a (very flawed) approach to giving non-European peoples back their own cultural pasts. The dilemma remains.

THE SHAPES OF THINGS TO COME

The object of writing this book, among other things, was to treat collecting as a social phenomenon, which should be examined from the perspective of its own proper critique rather than as a loosely historical bundle of anecdote. Recent work (e.g. Elsner and Cardinal 1994) encourages the hope that this transformation in the field is indeed underway. Collecting studies, we may observe, are following a classic Kuhnian pattern: the realisation that the social character of knowledge and the integrity of its historical and emotional contexts is as important for our understanding as the content of knowledge as such; the developing application of this to our study of collections, where the character is seen to be at least as important as the content, coupled with an increasing understanding of the role of objects in European society as a whole; and the emergence of networks of individuals based mostly in museums and universities, but with strong links to the wider world of collectors, for whom this study is a speciality (see Figure 1.1, p. 5).

Within this investigative context, a range of projects beckon. We know all too little about the nature of collecting in the classical world, and yet this collecting was the model to which Renaissance, and therefore all subsequent, collecting referred. Recent work is gradually uncovering evidence for those feminine endings, the women collectors of later modernist times whose collections do not survive. The ways in which the Other of time and space has been created through material collecting form a field of enormous size and significance; so do the ways in which knowledge has been constructed through scientific collecting: all of these topics are beginning to seek and find their authors. The whole People's Show experience is a major phenomenon which needs to be written up at an appropriate level. The relationship between the world of amateur collectors and their clubs and the museum as institution, with all the power-broking which these words imply, asks for detailed exploration. The qualitative and quantitative investigations into collecting practice in Britain and the United States (especially Pearce's Leicester Contemporary Collecting Project and Belk's Odyssey Project) are being written up, and point the way to further enquiries, particularly, perhaps, a more broadly based discussion of the role of material culture in contemporary society. Gradually, as work progresses, broad models for collection studies will emerge for further development and modification as the study of theory and practice develops; but for a field of discipline not yet ten years old this list gives enough to be going on with.

COLLECTING OURSELVES

Collections are essentially a narrative of experience; as objects are a kind of material language, so the narratives into which they can be selected and organised are a kind of fiction, and it is no accident that both fiction and collection are a characteristically modernist European way of telling experience, with their formal and imaginative roots deep in cultural traditions of the long term. Like fiction, collections narrate world-views of knowledge and moral understanding in relation to the individual hero or heroine, family and society, the past and the exotic. Like fiction, too, their ways of creating the narrative flow are open to analysis, and prove to be not a reflection of the nature of things, but a social construct in which apparent sense is created from a range of possibilities and discontinuities. In the view they offer of the human condition, collections, like all narratives, are neither true nor false; they are trueish, that category offensive to European logic, and each has to be treated on its own terms to yield up what any particular narrator feels to be its significance.

Collecting holds the middle ground within the social system, between market and temple, where values are created out of rubbish. Collecting is capable of drawing out and strengthening our feelings of irony, melancholy, subversion and self-knowledge. Like all fictional narratives, it offers the scope to play games and experience magical transformations: we are all the heroes of our collections. The giftlike character of collected material gives it the capacity to turn commodity-turned-rubbish into internal cultural meaning, originally for one hopeful and imaginative collector and eventually, perhaps, for us all. This is why there is less contrast than usually supposed between 'classic' and post-modernist or contemporary collections: all have the chance of becoming 'classic' through the power of our individual and collective imaginations. It is also, I suspect, why the class-based differences which loom so large in most discussions of cultural life matter less in the collecting process. Almost all collectors, of whatever class allegiance, know they are operating in the dangerous middle, where both the snakes have their heads and the ladders their first rungs: they do this deliberately and glory in their foolhardiness. Their stories, like all stories, they make up as they go along.

This suggests that collecting has its strongly optimistic aspect. If the accumulative relationship to the material world is shaped by European inherited cultural practice, it is informed by the equally European poetic of self-expression, and offers, through the operation of politics, a chance to create changes in the way we view the visible and tangible world, with all the symbolic values this implies. People are not wholly determined by their pasts, and collecting is a gesture of self-assertion with a dynamic potential. It is also as intimate as our own homes. When Miss Mackenzie (in Trollope's novel quoted at the beginning of this chapter) kisses her own reflection in her bedroom mirror, she is asserting her essential self and its possibilities within the framework of her material life and its construction within the novel. When collectors acquire pieces they are asserting the same close kind of potential transformation within the fictional construction which we call social life; and who knows what may come of a kiss?

BIBLIOGRAPHY

———— •◆• ————

Abraham, K., 1927, *Selected Papers on Psychoanalysis*, Hogarth Press, London

Adorno, T., 1973, *Negative Dialectics*, Routledge & Kegan Paul, London

Alexander, M., 1966, *The Earliest English Poems*, Penguin Books, London

Alexander, E. P., 1983, 'Arthur Hazelius', *Museum Masters*: 241–75, Nashville

Alexander, J., and Pinsky, P. (eds), 1987, *Age of Chivalry*, Royal Academy of Arts, London

Alsop, J., 1982, *The Rare Art Traditions The History of Collecting and its Linked Phenomena*, Thames & Hudson, London

Altman, I., and Low, S. (eds), 1992, *Place Attachment*, Plenum Press, New York

Ames, K., and Martinez, K. (eds), 1992, *Material Culture of Gender/Gender of Material Culture*, University of Michigan Research Press, Ann Arbor

Appadurai, A., 1986a, 'Introduction: Commodities and the Politics of Value' in Appadurai, 1986b: 3–63

Appadurai, A. (ed.), 1986b, *The Social Life of Things*, Cambridge University Press

Arendt, H., 1958, *The Human Condition*, University of Chicago Press

Aristides, N., 1988, 'Calm and Uncollected', *American Scholar*, 57, 3: 327–36

Arnold, K., 1993, 'Mysterious Museums and Curious Curators', *Museums Journal*, 93, 4: 20–1

Ashton, S., 1988, *Colonialism in India*, British Library, London

Austin, E., 1993, 'Interview with Brick Collector', unpublished: personal communication

Baekeland, F., 1988, 'The Psychological Aspects of Art Collecting', *Psychiatry*, 44: 45–59

Bailey, D. R. S., 1978, *Cicero's Letters to his Friends*, Penguin Books, London

Baker, F., and Thomas, J. (eds), 1990, *Writing the Past in the Present*, St David's University College, Lampeter

Baker, R., 1992, 'Marilyn Monroe' in People's Show, 1992

Bann, S., 1988, '"Views of the Past" – Reflections on the Treatment of Historical Objects and Museums of History (1750–1850)' in Fyfe and Law, 1988: 39–64

Barasch, M., and Sandler, L. (eds), 1981, *Art, the Ape of Nature*, Harry N. Abrams, New York

Barley, M., and Hanson, R., 1968, *Christianity in Britain 300–700*, Leicester University Press

Baudrillard, J., 1968, *Le Système des objets*, Gallimard, Paris

Baudrillard, J., 1975, *The Mirror of Production*, Telos Press, St Louis

Baudrillard, J., 1981, *Towards a Critique of the Political Economy of the Sign*, Telos Press, St Louis

Baudrillard, J., 1983, *Simulations*, Semiotext, New York

Baudrillard, J., 1988, *Selected Writings*, Stanford University Press

Bayley, S., 1991, *Taste: The Secret Meaning of Things*, Faber & Faber, London

Bazin, G., 1967, *The Museum Age*, trans. J. Cahill, Wang and Wang, New York

Beard, M., 1993, 'Casts and Cast-Offs: The Origins of the Museum of Classical Archaeology', *Proceedings of the Cambridge Philological Society*, 39: 1–29

Beard, M., 1992, 'Souvenirs of Culture: Deciphering (in) the Museum', *Art History*, 15, 4: 505–32

Beard, M., and Henderson, J., 1989, 'Please Don't Touch the Ceiling': The Culture of Appropriation' in Pearce, 1994: 5–42

Beckenridge, J., 1959, 'The Numismatic Iconography of Justinian II', *Numismatic Notes and Monographs*, 144: 57–60

Beckett, H., 1986, 'Cognitive Developmental Theory in the Study of Adolescent Identity Development', in Wilkinson, 1986: 25–47

Beckwith, J., 1964, *Early Medieval Art*, Thames & Hudson, London

Beggan, J. K., 1991, 'Using What You Own to Get What You Need: The Role of Possessions in Satisfying Control Motivation' in Rudmin, 1991: 129–46

Behrman, S. N., 1952, *Duveen*, Random House, New York

Belk, R., 1988, 'Possessions and the Extended Self', *Journal of Consumer Research*, 15: 139–68

Belk, R., 1991a, 'The History and the Development of the Consumer Behaviour Odyssey', *Highways and Buyways*, Association for Consumer Research, Provo, Utah 1–12

Belk, R., 1991b, 'The Ineluctable Mysteries of Possessions' in Rudmin, 1991: 17–55

Belk, R., 1992 'Attachment to Possessions' in Altman and Low, 1992: 37–62

Belk, R., and Wallendorf, M., 1992, '*Of Mice and Men*: Gender Identity in Collecting' in Ames and Martinez, 1992: 1–18

Belk, R., Wallendorf, M., Sherry, J., Holbrook, M., and Roberts, M., 1988, 'Collectors and Collecting', *Advances in Consumer Research*, 1988: 548–53

Belk, R., Wallendorf, M., and Sherry, J., 1989, 'The Sacred and the Profane in Consumer Behaviour: Theodicy on the "Odyssey"', *Journal of Consumer Research*, 16: 1–38

Belk, R., Wallendorf, M., Sherry, J., and Holbrook, M., 1990, 'Collecting in a Consumer Culture', *Highways and Buyways*, Association for Consumer Research, Provo, Utah

Benjamin, W., 1969, *Illuminations*, Schocken, New York

Benn, S. I. and Gaus, G. F. (eds), 1983 *Public and Private in Social Life*, Croom Helm, London

Benthal, J., 1989, 'An Interview with Sir Robert and Lady Sainsbury', *Anthropology Today*, 5, 1: 2–5

Benveniste, E., 1969, *Le Vocabulaire des institutions indo-européennes*, 2 vols, Editions de Minuit, Paris

Berger, J., 1972, *Ways of Seeing*, BBC/Penguin Books, London

Bernheimer, R., 1956, 'Theatrum Mundi', *Art Bulletin*, 38: 225–47

Bintliff, J., (ed.), 1988, *Extracting Meaning from the Past*, Cambridge University Press

Bintliff, J., (ed.), 1991a, *The Annales School and Archaeology*, Leicester University Press

Bintliff, J., 1991b, 'The Contribution of an *Annaliste*/Structural History Approach to Archaeology' in Bintliff, 1991a: 1–33

Birdwood, G., 1880, *The Industrial Arts of India*, Black & Son, London

Blackburn, J., 1989, *Charles Waterton, Traveller and Conservationist*, Century Press, London

Blanchard, T., 1993, 'They Took a Shine to a Thousand Shoes', *Independent*, 12 June: 23

Bloch, M., 1965, *Feudal Society*, Routledge & Kegan Paul, London

Bloom, H., and Trilling, L. (eds), 1973, *Romantic Poetry and Prose*, Oxford University Press

Boas, F., 1964, *The Central Eskimo*, University of Nebraska Press, Lincoln

Bourdieu, P., 1977, *Outlines of a Theory of Practice*, Cambridge University Press

Bourdieu, P., 1984, *Distinction: A Social Critique of the Judgement of Taste*, trans. R. Nice, Harvard University Press, Cambridge, Mass.

Bradley, R., 1987, 'Stages in the Chronological Development of Hoards and Votive Deposits', *Proceedings of the Prehistoric Society*, 53: 351–62

Bradley, R., 1988, 'Hoarding, Recycling and the Consumption of Prehistoric Metalwork and Technological Change in Western Europe', *World Archaeology*, 20, 2: 249–60

Bradley, R., 1990, *The Passage of Arms: An Archaeological Analysis of Prehistoric Hoards and Votive Deposits*, Cambridge University Press

Braudel, F., 1973, *Capitalism and Material Life 1400–1800*, Weidenfeld & Nicolson, London

Braudel, F., 1981, *Civilization and Capitalism: 15th–18th Century*, 2 vols, Collins, London

Bray, W., 1981, 'Archaeological Humour: The Private Joke and the Public Image' in Evans *et al.*, 1981: 221–9

Brears, P., 1989, 'Ralph Thoresby, a Museum Visitor in Stuart England', *Journal of History of Collections*, 1, 2: 213–24

Brears, P., and Davies, S., 1989, *Treasures for the People*, Yorkshire and Humberside Museums Council, Leeds

Brooks, E., 1954, *Sir Hans Sloane*, Blatchworth Press, London

Burk, C. F., 1900, 'The Collecting Instinct', *Pedagogical Seminary*, 7: 179–207

Butt, J. (ed.), 1963, *The Poems of Alexander Pope*, Methuen, London

Bywater, I. (ed. and trans.), 1920, *Aristotle: On the Art of Poetry*, Oxford University Press

Cabonne, P., 1963, *The Great Collectors*, Cassell, London

Campbell, C., 1987, *The ·Romantic Ethic and the Spirit of Modern Consumerism*, Blackwell, Oxford

Campbell, L., 1991, 'Consumption: The New Wave of Research in the Humanities and Social Services' in Rudmin, 1991: 57–74

Canfora, L., 1990, *The Vanished Library: A Wonder of the Ancient World*, University of California Press, Berkeley

Cannizzo, J., 1989, *Into the Heart of Africa*, Royal Ontario Museum, Toronto

Cannizzo, J., 1991, 'Exhibiting Cultures: "Into the Heart of Africa"', *Visual Anthropology Review*, 7, 1: 150–60

Carmen, J., 1990, 'Commodities, Rubbish and Treasure: Valuing Archaeological Objects', *Archaeological Review from Cambridge*, 9, 2: 195–207

Carmen, J., 1994, 'The Importance of Things' in Cooper, *et al.*, 1994: 1–12

Carter, H., 1988, *Sir Joseph Banks*, British Museum (Natural History), London

Caruthers, A., 1983, *Bias in Museums*, Museums Professionals Group, *Transactions*, 22

Catalogue of the Museum of Ornamental Art, 1853, compiled at Marlborough House, London

Cesarani, D., 1993, 'Preserving a Death Camp', *Guardian*, 29 November: 1–5

Chandler, J., Davidson, A., and Harootian, H. (eds), 1993, *Questions of Evidence: Proof, Practice and Persuasion across the Disciplines*, University of Chicago Press

Chapman, G., 1940, *Beckford*, The Alden Press, Oxford

Chapman, W., 1991, 'Like a Game of Dominoes: Augustus Pitt Rivers and the Typological Museum Idea', in Pearce, 1991: 135–76

Chatwin, B., 1988, *Utz*, Jonathan Cape, London

Cheape, H., 1986, 'Dr. I. F. Grant (1887–1983): The Highland Folk Museum and a Bibliography of her Written Works', *Review of Scottish Culture*, 2: 113–25

Chevallier, R., 1991, *L'Artiste, le collectionneur et le faussaire: pour une sociologie del'art romain*, Armand Colin, Paris

Childe, V. G., 1958, *The Prehistory of European Society*, Penguin Books, London

Chisholm, R., 1966, *Theory of Knowledge*, Prentice Hall, New York

Chomsky, N., 1964, *Current Issues in Linguistic Theory*, Mouton, The Hague

Clay, J., 1981, *Romanticism*, Phaidon, London

Clifford, J., 1988, *The Predicament of Culture*, Harvard University Press, Cambridge, Mass.

Clifford, J., and Marcus, G. (eds), 1986, *Writing Culture: The Poetics and Politics of Ethnography*, University of California Press, Berkeley

Cohen, H. F., 1994, *The Scientific Revolution*, University of Chicago Press

Cole, H. H., 1874, *Catalogue of the Objects of Indian Art Exhibited in the South Kensington Museum*, London

Cole, H., 1884, (with Cole, A. and Cole, H.), *Fifty Years of Public Works*, 2 vols, George Bell and Sons, London

Coles, J., and Harding, A., 1979, *The Bronze Age in Europe*, Methuen, London

Colvin, H., 1985, *Calke Abbey, Derbyshire*, The National Trust/George Philip, London

Cook, B., 1977, 'The Townley Marbles in Westminster and Bloomsbury', *British Museum Yearbook*, 2: 34–78

Coomaraswamy, A., 1934, *The Transformation of Nature in Art*, Harvard University Press, Cambridge, Mass.

Cooper, M., Firth, A., and Wheatley, D. (eds), 1994, *Managing Archaeology*, Routledge, London

Cranstone, B., 1984, 'The Pitt Rivers Museum: Past, Present and Future', *Museum Ethnographers Group Newsletter*, 16: 1–8

Crosby, S. (ed.), 1981, *The Royal Abbey of Saint Denis in the Time of Abbot Suger (1122–1151)*, catalogue of exhibition held at The Cloisters, Metropolitan Museum of Art, New York

Crossland, R., 1959, 'Indo-European Origins: The Linguistic Evidence', *Past and Present*, 12: 16–46

Csikszentmihalyi, M., and Rochberg-Halton, E., 1981, *The Meaning of Things: Domestic Symbols and the Self*, Cambridge University Press

Cunliffe, B., 1978, *Iron Age Communities in Britain*, Routledge & Kegan Paul, London

Danet, B., and Katriel, K., 1989, 'No Two Alike: Play and Aesthetics in Collecting', *Play and Culture*, 2: 253–77

Davies, G., 1991, 'The Albacini Cast Collection: Character and Significance', *Journal of the History of Collections*, 3, 2: 145–66

Davis, H. W. C. (ed.), 1959, *Aristotle's Politics*, trans. B. Jowett, Oxford University Press

De la Mare, A., and Jessup, M., 1992, *Snowshill Manor*, National Trust Enterprises, London

De Rougemont, D., 1956, *Passion and Society*, Faber & Faber, London

Deetz, J., 1977, *In Small Things Forgotten*, Doubleday Natural History Press, Garden City, New York

Derrida, J., 1992, *Given Time*, trans. P. Kamuf, University of Chicago Press

Dimaggio, P., 1983, 'The American Art Museum Director as Professional: Results of a Survey', *Bullet*, June: 5–9

Dittmar, H., 1991, 'Meanings of Material Possessions as Reflections of Identity: Gender and Social-Material Position in Society', in Rudmin, 1991: 165–86

Douglas, M., 1966, *Purity and Danger: An Analysis of Concepts of Pollution and*

Taboo, Routledge & Kegan Paul, London

Douglas, M., and Isherwood, B., 1978, *The World of Goods: Towards an Anthropology of Consumption*, Allen Lane, London

Duncan, C., and Wallach, A., 1980, 'The Universal Survey Museum', *Art History*, 3, 4: 448–69

Durost, W., 1932, *Children's Collecting Activity Related to Social Factors*, Bureau of Publications, Teachers' College, Columbia University, New York

Eagleton, T., 1983, *Literary Theory: An Introduction*, Blackwell, Oxford

Eco, U., 1983, *The Name of the Rose*, Martin Secker and Warburg, London

Eco, U., 1990, *Foucault's Pendulum*, Pan Books, London

Edwards, L., 1992, 'Marilyn Monroe' in People's Show, 1992

Ellen, R., 1988, 'Fetishism', *Man*, 23: 213–35

Elsner, J., 1992, 'Pausanius: A Greek Pilgrim in the Roman World', *Past and Present*, 135: 3–29

Elsner, J., and Cardinal, R. (eds), 1994, *The Cultures of Collecting*, Reaktion Books, London

Evans, J., Cunliffe, B., and Renfrew, C., 1981, *Antiquity and Man*, Cambridge University Press

Fawcett, H. A., 1960, *The Fawcett Collection of Antiquities*, Bristol Museum Service

Fekete, J. (ed.), 1984, *The Structural Allegory: Reconstructive Encounters with the New French Thought*, Manchester University Press

Fenichel, O., 1945, *The Psychoanalytic Theory of Neurosis*, Norton, New York

Fenton, J., 1983, *The Memory of War and Children in Exile 1968–1984*, Penguin Books, London

Findlen, P., 1989, 'The Museum: Its Classical Entomology and its Renaissance Genealogy', *Journal of History of Collections*, 1: 59–78

Firchow, E., Grimstad, K., Hasselmo, N., and O'Neil, W., 1972, *Studies for Einar Haugen*, Mouton, Paris

Fisch, J., 1985, 'A Solitary Vindicator of the Hindus: The Life and Writings of General Charles Stuart, 1757/8–1828', *Journal of the Royal Asiatic Society*, 1: 34–49

Fontana, B. L., 1978, 'Artifacts of the Indians of the South-West' in Quimby, 1978: 75–108

Forsdyke, J., 1949, 'The Functions of a National Museum', in *Museums in Modern Life*, Royal Society of Arts, London: 1–11.

Foster, S., 1982, 'The Exotic as a Symbolic System', *Dialectical Anthropology*, 7: 21–30

Foucault, M., 1970, *The Order of Things*, Tavistock Press, London

Foucault, M., 1974, *The Archaeology of Knowledge*, Tavistock Press, London

Foucault, M., 1986, 'Texts/Contexts of Other Spaces', *Diacritics*, 16, 1: 22–7

Fox, R., and Lears, T. (eds), 1983, *The Culture of Consumption: Critical Essays in American History 1880–1980*, Pantheon Press, New York

Fraser, Sir J., 1957, *The Golden Bough*, 2 vols, Macmillan, London

Fraser, W., 1981, *The Coming of the Mass Market*, Macmillan, London

Freud, S., 1927, 'Essays on Sexuality' in *The Complete Psychological Works of Sigmund Freud*, standard edition, Hogarth Press, London

Freud, S., 1963, 'Character and Anal Eroticism' in Rieff, 1963: 1–25

Friedrich, P., 1966, 'Proto-Indo-European Kinship', *Ethnology*, 5: 1–36

Frith, S., 1981, *Sound Effects*, Pantheon Press, New York

Fuller, S., 1991, 'Studying the Proprietary Grounds of Knowledge' in Rudmin, 1991: 105–28

Furby, L., 1978, 'Sharing: Decisions and Moral Judgements about Letting Others

Use One's Possessions', *Political Psychology*, 2, 1: 30–42

Fyfe, G., and Law, J. (eds), 1988, *Picturing Power, Sociological Review Monograph* 35, Routledge, London

Galbraith, K., 1958, *The Affluent Society*, New American Library, New York

Gans, H. J., 1974, *Popular Culture and High Culture*, Macmillan, London

Gathercole, P., and Clarke, A., 1979, *Survey of Oceanian Collections in Museums in the United Kingdom and the Irish Republic*, UNESCO, London

Geary, P., 1986, 'Sacred Commodities: The Circulation of Medieval Relics' in Appadurai, 1986b: 169–91

Gebhard, P. H., 1969, 'Fetishism and Sadomasochism', *Science and Psychoanalysis*, 15: 71–80

Gibbons, S., 1956, *Cold Comfort Farm*, Penguin Books, London

Giddens, A., 1991, *Central Problems in Social Theory: Action, Structure and Contradiction in Social Analysis*, Macmillan, London

Gilchrist, W., and Manzotti, R., 1993, *Cult: A Visual History of Jeanswear – American Originals*, Sportswear International, London.

Gill, B., 1993, 'The Holocaust Museum: An Unquiet Sanctuary', *New Yorker*, 19 April: 107–9

Gilligan, C., 1982, *In a Different Voice: Psychological Theory and Women's Development*, Harvard University Press, Cambridge, Mass.

Gombrich, E., 1985, *Norm and Form: Studies in the Art of the Renaissance* 1, Phaidon Press, Oxford

Goody, J., 1959, 'Indo European Society', *Past and Present*, 16: 88–92

Goody, J., 1976, 'Inheritance, Property and Women: Some Comparative Considerations', in Goody *et al.*, 1976: 10–36

Goody, J., Thirsk, J., and Thompson, E. P. (eds), 1976, *Family and Inheritance, Rural Society in Western Europe 1200–1800*, Cambridge University Press

Goswamy, B., 1991, 'Another Past, Another Context: Exhibiting Indian Art Abroad' in Karp and Levine, 1991: 68–78

Gourevitch, P., 1994, 'In the Holocaust Theme Park', *Observer Magazine*, 30 Jan.

Graham-Dixon, P., 1990, 'Telling a Naked Truth', *Independent*, 27 November

Gray, H. St G., 1905, *A Memoir of Lieut.-General Pitt Rivers*, Pitt Rivers Museum, Oxford

Greenblatt, S., 1991, 'Resonance and Wonder' in Karp and Levine, 1991: 42–56

Greenhalgh, P., 1988, *Ephemeral Vistas*, Manchester University Press

Greig, S., 1964, 'Da Staten Innløste Hon-Skatten i 1834', *Viking*, 23: 102–22

Griemas, A. J., and Rastier, F., 1968, 'The Interaction of Semiotic Constraints', *French Yale Studies*, 41: 86–105

Griggs, B., 1981, 'The Woman Who Can't Stop Giving Away Fortunes', *Daily Mail*, 22 October

Grimm, J., 1899, *Deutsche Rechtsalterthümer*, vol. 4, 4th edition (revised A. Heusler and R. Hübner), Weicher, Leipzig

Guggenheim, P., 1979, *Out of this Century: Confessions of an Art Addict*, Blacks, London

Gutfleisch, B., and Menzhausen, J., 1989, 'How a Kunstkammer Should Be Formed', *Journal of History of Collections*, 1: 3–32

Hall, S. and Gieben, B. (eds), 1992, *Formations of Modernity*, Polity Press/Open University/Blackwell, Oxford and Cambridge

Hammersley, M., 1992, *What's Wrong with Ethnography?*, Routledge, London

Hamp, E., 1979, 'The North European Word for "Apple"', *Zeitschrift für Keltische Philologie*, 37: 158–66

Hancock, E., 1980, 'One of those Dreadful Combats – A Surviving Display from

William Bullock's London, 1807–1818', *Museums Journal*, 74, 4: 172–5

Harland, R., 1987, *Superstructuralism*, Methuen, London

Harris, R., 1986, *Selling Hitler*, Faber & Faber, London

Harvey, D., 1989, *The Condition of Post-Modernity*, Blackwell, Oxford

Hatto, A. (trans.), 1969, *The Nibelungenlied*, Penguin Books, London

Haug, W., 1986, *Critique of Commodity Aesthetics*, University of Minnesota Press, Minneapolis

Havell, E., 1911, *The Ideals of Indian Art*, Black & Son, London

Hawes, E., 1985, 'Artifacts, Myth and Identity in American History Museums', *International Committee for Museology Study Series*, 10: 135–9

Hawkes, T. G., 1977, *Structuralism and Semiotics*, Methuen, London

Haynes, P., 1975, *The Arundel Marbles*, Ashmolean Museum, Oxford

Herrmann, F., 1972, *The English as Collectors*, Chatto & Windus, London

Heseltine, A., 1990, 'Antique Amalgams', *Oxford Today*, 2, 2: 34–8

Hewitt, J. P., 1988, *Self and Society: A Symbolic Interactionist Social Psychology*, Allyn & Bacon, Boston, Mass.

Hillier, D., 1993, *Interview with Studio Pottery Collectors*, unpublished: personal communication

Hines, J., 1989, 'Ritual Hoarding in Migration-Period Scandinavia: A Review of Recent Interpretations', *Proceedings of the Prehistoric Society*, 55: 193–205

Hirsch, E., 1982, *The Concept of Identity*, Oxford University Press

Hirschfeld, G., 1916, *The Collection of Ancient Greek Inscriptions in the British Museum*, 4 vols, 1874–1916, Oxford University Press

Hodder, I., 1986, *Reading the Past*, Cambridge University Press

Hodder, I. (ed.), 1987, *Archaeology as Long Term History*, Cambridge University Press

Hodder, I. (ed.), 1991, *Archaeological Theory in Europe*, Routledge, London

Honour, H., 1975, *The New Golden Land: European Images of America from the Discoveries to the Present Time*, Pantheon Books, New York

Hooper-Greenhill, E., 1992, *Museums and the Shaping of Knowledge*, Routledge, London

Hubert, H., and Mauss, M., 1974, 'Magic, Technology and Science', in Tiryakian, 1974: 237–41

Hüllen, W., 1990, 'Reality, the Museum, and the Catalogue: A Semiotic Interpretation of Early German Texts of Museology', *Semiotica*, 80, 314: 265–75

Hulme, P., 1986, *Colonial Encounters: Europe and the Native Caribbean 1492–1797*, Methuen, London

Hume, M., 1993, 'McQueen's Theatre of Cruelty', *Independent*, 21 October: 29

Humphrey, N., 1984a, 'The Illusion of Beauty', in Humphrey, 1984b: 121–37

Humphrey, N. (ed.), 1984b, *Consciousness Regained*, Oxford University Press

Hunter, M., 1985, 'The Cabinet Institutionalized: The Royal Society's "Repository" and its Background' in Impey and Macgregor, 1985: 159–173

Hutcheon, L., 1980, *Narcissistic Narrative: The Metafictional Paradox*, Methuen, London

Impey, O., and Macgregor, A. (eds), 1985, *The Origins of Museums*, Oxford University Press

Innes, M., 1972, *A Family Affair*, Penguin Books, London

Iser, W., 1974, *The Implied Reader: Patterns of Communication in Prose Fiction from Bunyan to Beckett*, trans. C. Macksey and R. Macksey, Johns Hopkins Press, Baltimore

Jackson, L., 1991, *The Poverty of Structuralism: Literature and Structuralist Theory*,

Longman, London

James, H., 1963, *The Spoils of Poynton*, Penguin Books, London

James, W., 1890, *The Principles of Psychology*, 1 vol., Henry Holt, New York

Jameson, F., 1981, *The Political Unconscious: Narrative as Socially Symbolic Act*, Cornell University Press, Ithaca

Jameson, F., 1984, 'Postmodernism, or the Cultural Logic of Late Capitalism', *New Left Review*, 146: 52–92

Jameson, F., 1989, 'Introduction' to D. Kellner, *Critical Theory, Marxism and Modernity*, Polity Press, Cambridge

Jameson, F., 1991, *Postmodernism: on the Cultural Logic of Late Capitalism*, Verso Books, London

Jenkins, I., 1992, *Archaeologists and Aesthetes*, British Museum Publications, London

Jennings, C., 1993, 'Fever Kitsch', *Independent* magazine, 256, 7 August: 30–2

Johnson, J. de M., 1914, 'Antinoë and its Papyri, Excavation by the Graeco-Roman Branch, 1913–14', *Journal of Egyptian Archaeology*, 1, 3: 168–81

Joline, A., 1902, *Meditations of an Autograph Collector*, Harper, New York

Jones, E., 1950, 'Anal-Erotic character traits' in *Papers on Psycho-Analysis*, 5th ed., Baillière, Tindall and Cox, London.

Jones, M., 1990, *Fake? The Art of Deception*, British Museum Publications, London

Jones, Sir W., 1786, 'On the Hindus', Third Anniversary discourse, reprinted in *The Collected Works of Sir Williams Jones III*, 1807, John Stockdale, London

Kaeppler, A., 1978, '*Artificial Curiosities' Being an Exposition of Native Manufactures Collected on the Three Pacific Voyages of Captain James Cook*, Bishop Museum Special Publication 66, Bishop Museum, Honolulu

Kaeppler, A., 1979, 'Tracing the History of the Hawaiian Cook Voyage Artefacts in the Museum of Mankind', *British Museum Yearbook*, 3: 167–86

Kapferer, B. (ed.), 1976, *Transactions and Meaning: Directions in the Anthropology of Exchange and Symbolic Behaviour*, Institute for the Study of Human Values, Philadelphia

Kaplan, F. (ed.), 1994, *Museums and the Making of 'Ourselves'*, Leicester University Press

Karp, I., and Levine, S. (eds), 1991, *Exhibiting Cultures: the Poetics and Politics of Museum Display*, Smithsonian Institution Press, Washington

Karp, I., Kreamer, C., and Lavine, S. (eds), 1992, *Museums and Communities: The Politics of Public Culture*, Smithsonian Institution Press, Washington

Kassarjian, H. H., 1982, 'Consumer Psychology', *American Review of Psychology* 33, 619–49

Kaufmann, T., 1979, 'Remarks on the collection of Rudolf II:' the *Kunstkammer* as a form of *Representation*', *Art Journal*, 38: 22–8

Kavanagh, G., 1990, *History Curatorship*, Leicester University Press

Kavanagh, G. (ed.), 1991, *Museum Languages: Objects and Texts*, Leicester University Press

Kellie, A., 1983, *Strathpeffer Doll Museum: A Catalogue and the Story of the Angela Kellie Collection of Dolls and Toys*, Strathpeffer Museum

Kent, J., and Painter, K., 1977, *Wealth of the Roman World AD 300–700*, British Museum Publications, London

Ketton-Cremer, R. W., 1957, 'The treasure of Oxnead', in *Norfolk Assembly*, Faber & Faber, London: 212–22

Kiernan, V. G., 1976, 'Private Property in History', in Goody *et al.*, 1976: 361–98

King, E., 1985–6, 'The Cream of the Dross: Collecting Glasgow's Present for the Future', *Social History Curators Group Journal*, 13: 4–11

Kinsella, T., 1969, *The Tain*, Oxford University Press

Kirch, P., and Sahlins, M., 1992, *Anahulu: The Anthropology of History in the Kingdom of Hawaii*, University of Chicago Press

Kopytoff, I., 1986, 'The Cultural Biography of Things: Commoditization as Process', in Appadurai, 1986b: 64–91

Kremer, R. A., 1992, 'Meaningful Materialism: Collectors' Relationship to their Objects', unpublished Ph.D. thesis, University of British Columbia, Canada

Kugelmass, J., 1992, 'The Rites of the Tribe: American Jewish Tourism in Poland', in Karp *et al.*, 1992: 382–427

Kuhn, T., 1970, *The Structure of Scientific Revolutions*, University of Chicago Press

Lach, D. F., 1994, *Asia in the Making of Europe*, 2 vols, University of Chicago Press

Lattimore, R. (ed.), 1970, *Aristophanes: The Frogs*, New American Library, New York

Leach, E., 1977, 'A View from the Bridge', in Spriggs, 1977: 170–3

Leach, E., 1982, *Social Anthropology*, W. Collins & Sons, Glasgow

Lehmann, K., 1945, 'A Roman Poet Visits a Museum', *Hesperia*, 14: 259–69

Lerner, B., 1961, 'Auditory and Visual Thresholds for the Perception of Words of Anal Connotation', doctoral thesis, Ferkauf Graduate School of Education, Yeshiva University, New York

Levi, P., 1971, *Pausanius: Guide to Greece*, 2 vols, Penguin Books, London

Levidow, L., and Young, B., 1984, 'Exhibiting Nuclear Power: the Science Museum Cover-up' in *No Clear Reason: Nuclear Power Politics*, ed. Radical Science Collective, Radical Science 14: 53–79

Levy, J., 1982, *Social and Religious Organization in Bronze Age Denmark*, British Archaeological Reports International Series 124

Liverpool Museums, 1971, 'The Blue China Craze', *Museum Piece*, November: 1

Lockyer, R., 1981, *Buckingham, The Life and Political Career of George Villiers, First Duke of Buckingham 1592–1628*, Macmillan, London

Lodge, D., 1991, *Paradise News*, Secker & Warburg, London

Lukàcs, G., 1971, *History and Class Consciousness*, Massachusetts Institute of Technology Press, Cambridge, Mass.

Lurie, A., 1986, *The War Between the Tates*, Abacus, London

Lurie, A., 1991, *Not in Front of the Grown Ups*, Sphere Books, London

Lutz, R. (ed.), 1986, *Advances in Consumer Research*, 13, Association for Consumer Research, Provo, Utah

Macfarlane, A., 1978, *The Origins of English Individualism: The Family, Property and Social Transition*, Blackwell, Oxford

Macgregor, A. (ed.), 1983, *Tradescant's Rarities*, Oxford University Press

Macgregor, A., 1985, 'The Cabinet of Curiosities in Seventeenth-Century Britain', in Impey and Macgregor, 1985: 147–58

Macgregor, A., 1989, 'A Magazine of all Manner of Inventions', *Journal of History of Collections*, 1, 2: 207–12

Mackenzie, L., 1993, *Angela Kellie and her Dolls*, unpublished

McKendrick, N., Brewer, J., and Plumb, J. H., 1982, *The Birth of a Consumer Society: The Commercialization of Eighteenth Century England*, Europa Publications, London

Mango, C., 1963, 'Antique Statuary and the Byzantine Beholder', *Dumbarton Oaks Papers*, 17: 53–76

Mango, C., Vickers, M., and Francis, E., 1992, 'The Palace of Lausus at Constantinople and its Collection of Ancient Statues', *Journal of the History of Collections*, 4, 1: 89–98

Mansfield Museum, 1992, *History of the Collections: Information Sheet*, Mansfield

Museum

Marcuse, H., 1964, *One-Dimensional Man*, Beacon Press, Boston

Marin, J., 1994, 'Keeping the Faith', *Museums Journal*, 92, 4: 33–4

Markey, T., 1972, 'Germanic Terms for Temple and Cult', in Firchow *et al.*, 1972: 364–78

Markey, T., 1985, 'The Totemic Typology', *Quaderni di Semantica*, 6, 1: 175–94

Markey, T. L., 1990, 'Gift, Payment and Reward Revisited', in Markey and Greppin, 1990: 346–62

Markey, T. L., and Greppin, J. A., (eds), 1990, *When Worlds Collide: Indo-Europeans and Pre-Indo Europeans*, Karoma, Ann Arbor, Mich.

Marriott, M. 1976, 'Hindu Transactions Diversity without Dualism' in Kapferer, 1976: 109–42

Marx, K., 1971, *Capital: A Critique of the Political Economy*, trans. S. Moore and E. Aveling, Progress Publishers, Moscow.

Mason, R., 1981, *Conspicuous Consumption: A Study of Exceptional Consumer Behaviour*, Gower Press, Farnborough

Mauss, M., 1925, 'Essai sur le don, forme primitive de l'échange', *Année Sociologique New Series*, 1: 30–186

Mayo, E., 1984, 'Contemporary Collecting', *History News*, 39, 2: 8–11

Mehta, R., and Belk, R., 1991, 'Artifacts, Identity and Transition: Favorite Possessions of Indians and Indian Immigrants to the United States', *Journal of Consumer Research*, 17: 398–411

Meillet, A., 1907, 'Notes', *Journal Asiatique*, 10, 10: 143–59

Merriman, N., 1991, *Beyond the Glass Case: The Past, the Heritage and the Public in Britain*, Leicester University Press

Miller, D., 1987, *Material Culture and Mass Consumption*, Blackwell, Oxford

Miller, M., 1981, *The Bon Marché: Bourgeois Culture and the Department Store*, Europa Publications, London

Miller, P., 1927, *Much Maligned Monsters: History of European Reactions to Indian Art*, Oxford University Press

Monte, C. F., 1977, *Beneath the Mask: An Introduction to Theories of Personality*, Holt, Reinhart & Winston, London

Morgan, C., 1991, *Athletes and Oracles: The Transformation of Olympia and Delphi in the Eighth Century BC*, Cambridge University Press

Morris, M., 1988, 'Changing Perceptions of the Past: The Bronze Age – A Case Study' in Bintliff, 1988: 69–85

Morris, W., 1962, *Volsunga Saga*, Macmillan, New York

Muesterberger, W., 1994, *An Unruly Passion: Psychological Perspectives*, Princeton University Press, New Jersey

Mukerji, C., 1983, *From Graven Images: Patterns of Modern Materialism*, Columbia University Press, New York

Mullen, C., 1991, 'The People's Show', *Visual Sociology Review*, 6, 1: 47–9

Murray, G., 1920, 'Preface' in Bywater, 1920: 3–20

Murray, M., 1962, *The Witch Cult in Western Europe*, Oxford University Press

National Museums of Denmark, 1991, *Museum Europa: Presentation of the Exhibition*, National Museums of Denmark, Copenhagen

National Museum of History, 1990, *The Exhibition of Ancient Chinese Trade Ceramic*, Beijing, Republic of China

National Trust, 1989, *Calke Abbey*, National Trust, London

National Trust, 1993, *Mr Straw's House, Nottinghamshire*, National Trust, London

Nicholson, J., 1983, 'Tinsel, Terracotta or Tantric: Representing Indian Reality in

Museums' in Caruthers, 1983: 26–31

Nietzsche, F., 1969, *On the Genealogy of Morals and Ecce Homo*, Vintage Books, New York

Obeyesekere, G., 1992, *The Apotheosis of Captain Cook: European Myth–Making in the Pacific*, Princeton University Press, New Jersey

O'Hanlon, M., 1993, *Paradise: A Brief Ethnography of an Exhibition*, British Museum Publications, London

Olmi, G., 1985, 'Science–honour–metaphor: Italian Cabinets of the Sixteenth and Seventeenth Centuries' in Impey and Macgregor, 1985: 5–16

Olmsted, A. D., 1988, *Collectors and Collecting*, paper presented at the Popular Culture Association annual meeting, New Orleans, quoted in Belk *et al.*, 1990: 50

Olmsted, A. D., 1991, 'Collecting: Leisure, Investment or Obsession?' in Rudmin, 1991: 287–306

Opie, R., 1988, *Sweet Memories*, Pavilion Books, London

Pagels, E., 1982, *The Gnostic Gospels*, Penguin Books, London

Panofsky-Soergel, G. (ed.), 1979, *Abbot Suger: On the Abbey Church of St Denis and its Art Treasures*, 2nd edn, Princeton University Press, New Jersey

Pearce, S. M., 1973, *Arts of Polynesia*, Exeter Museums Publication 72, Royal Albert Memorial Museum, Exeter

Pearce, S. M., 1983, *The Bronze Age Metalwork of South Western Britain*, 2 vols, British Archaeological Reports, Oxford

Pearce, S. (ed.), 1989, *Museum Studies in Material Culture*, Leicester University Press

Pearce, S. (ed.), 1991, *Museum Economics and the Community*, New Research in Museum Studies, 2 vols, Athlone Press, London

Pearce, S., 1992, *Museums, Objects and Collections*, Leicester University Press

Pearce, S. (ed.), 1994, *Museums and the Appropriation of Culture*, Athlone Press, London

Pearce, S., forthcoming 1996, *The Leicester Project: Collecting in Contemporary Britain*, Leicester University Press

Peirson Jones, J., 1992, 'The Colonial Legacy and the Community: The Gallery 33 Project' in Karp *et al.*, 1992: 221–61

Penny, N., 1991, 'Chantrey, Westmacott and Casts After the Antique', *Journal of the History of Collections*, 3, 2: 255–64

People's Show, 1990, Material held in Museum and Art Gallery, Walsall

People's Show, 1992, *Collections by Local People*, Museum and Art Gallery, Walsall, not paginated

Piggott, S., 1976, *Ruins in a Landscape: Essays in Antiquarianism*, Edinburgh University Press

Polanyi, K., 1957, *Trade and Markets in Early Empires*, Chicago University Press

Polomé, E. (ed.), 1982, *The Indo-Europeans in the Fourth and Third Millennia*, Karoma, Ann Arbor, Mich.

Pomian, K., 1990, *Collectors and Curiosities, Paris and Venice, 1500–1800*, trans. E. Wiles-Portier, Polity Press, Cambridge

Poster, M. (ed.), 1988, *Jean Baudrillard: Selected Writings*, Polity Press, Oxford

Price, D., 1989, 'John Woodward and a Surviving British Geological Collection of the Early Eighteenth Century', *Journal of History of Collections*, 1: 79–85

Pyrah, B., 1988, *The History of the Yorkshire Museum and its Geological Collections*, North Yorkshire County Council, York

Quick, H., 1994, 'Beauty and the Beastly', *Guardian*, 10 March: 14–15

Quimby, I. M., 1978, *Material Culture and the Study of American Life*, Winterthur

Museum, Norton and Co., New York

Radford, C. A. R., 1968, 'The Archaeological Background on the Continent' in Barley and Hanson, 1968: 19–36

Rasmussen, K., 1929, *Intellectual Culture of the Iglulik Eskimos*, report of the Fifth Thule Expedition, 1921–4, 7, 1. Cryldendalske Boghandel, Copenhagen

Rélibien, M., 1706, *Histoire de l'abbaye royale de Saint-Denis en France*, Paris

Renfrew, C., 1984, *Approaches to Social Archaeology*, Edinburgh University Press

Renfrew, C., 1986, 'Introduction' in Renfrew and Cherry, 1986: 1–18

Renfrew, C., 1987, *Archaeology and Language: The Puzzle of Indo-European Origins*, Jonathan Cape, London

Renfrew, C., and Cherry, J. (eds), 1986, *Peer Polity Interaction and Socio-Political Change*, Cambridge University Press

Ricoeur, P., 1984, *The Reality of the Historical Past*, Marquette University Press, Milwaukee

Rieff, R. (ed.), 1963, *Character and Culture*, Collier, New York

Riegl, A., 1982, 'The Modern Cult of Monuments: Its Character and its Origin', trans. K. Forster and D. Ghirardo, *Oppositions*, 25

Rigby, D., and Rigby, E., 1944, *Lock, Stock and Barrel: The Story of Collecting*, J. P. Lippincott, Philadelphia

Rinehart, M., 1981, 'A Document for the Studiolo of Francesco I' in Barasch and Sandler, 1981: 14–27

Ripley, D., 1970, *The Sacred Grove: Essays on Museums*, Victor Gollancz, London

Roberts, J. M., 1985, *The Triumph of the West*, BBC Books, London

Rorty, R., 1979, *Philosophy and the Mirror of Nature*, Princeton University Press

Rose, K., 1969, *Superior Person: A Portrait of Curzon and his Circle in Late Victorian England*, Camelot Press, London

Rowlands, M., 1987, 'Centre and Periphery: A Review of a Concept' in Rowlands *et al.*, 1987: 1–11

Rowlands, M., Larsen, M., and Kristiansen, K. (eds), 1987, *Centre and Periphery in the Ancient World*, Cambridge University Press

Royal Pavilion, 1991, *The Royal Pavilion at Brighton: Summary Catalogue of the Furniture and Furnishings*, Royal Pavilion/Borough Council, Brighton

Rudmin, F. W. (ed.), 1991, *To Have Possessions: A Handbook on Ownership and Property*, special issue of *Journal of Social Behaviour and Personality*, 6, 6

Rudwick, M. J. S., 1972, *The Meaning of Fossils: Episodes in the History of Palaeontology*, Macdonald & Co., London

Russell, B., 1917, *Mysticism and Logic*, Barnes & Noble, New York

Said, E., 1978, *Orientalism: Western Concepts of the Orient*, Penguin Books, London

Sainsbury, R. (ed.), 1978, *Sainsbury Centre for the Visual Arts – The Robert and Lisa Sainsbury Collection*, University of East Anglia, Norwich

Sanjek, R., 1993, 'Anthropology's Hidden Colonialism', *Anthropology Today*, 9, 2: 13–18

Sargent, T. O., 1988, 'Fetishism', *Journal of Social Work and Human Sexuality*, 7, 1: 27–42

Schama, S., 1987, *The Embarrassment of Riches: An Interpretation of Dutch Culture in the Golden Age*, Knopf, New York

Schubart, H., 1972, *Die Funde der alteren Bronzezeit in Mecklenburg*, Karl Wacholz Neumünster

Schultz, E., 1990, 'Notes on the History of Collecting and of Museums in the Light of Selected Literature of the Sixteenth to the Eighteenth Century', *Journal of the History of Collections*, 2, 2: 205–18

Searle, J. R., 1983, *Intentionality. An Essay in the Philosophy of Mind*, Cambridge University Press

Searle, J. R., 1992, *The Rediscovery of the Mind*, Massachusetts Institute of Technology, Boston

Shanks, M., 1992, 'Archaeological Experiences and a Critical Romanticism', *Proceedings of Nordic Theoretical Archaeological Group*, 1–34

Shanks, M., and Tilley, C., 1987, *Re-Constructing Archaeology*, Cambridge University Press

Shapin, S., 1994, *A Social History of Truth: Civility and Science in Seventeenth Century England*, University of Chicago Press

Shaw, M. (trans.), 1963, *Chronicles of the Crusades*, Penguin Books, London

Shoemaker, S., and Swinburne, R., 1984, *Personal Identity*, Blackwell, Oxford

Simmel, G., 1950, *The Sociology of Georg Simmel*, trans. K. Wolff, Free Press, Glencoe, Illinois

Slater, M. (ed.), 1975, *Catalogue of Suzanne's Charles Dickens Collection*, The Trustees of the Dickens House Museum/Sotheby Parke Bernet, London and New York

Smith, A., 1937, *The Wealth of Nations*, Modern Library, New York

Smith, V. A., 1991, *A History of Fine Art in India and Ceylon*, Oxford University Press

Snodgrass, A., 1980, *Archaic Greece: The Age of Experiment*, Dent, London

Solomon, M., 1986, 'Deep-Seated Materialism: The Case of Levi's 501 Jeans' in Lutz, 1986: 520–1

Solomon, M., and Assael, H., 1988, 'The Forest or the Trees? A Gestalt Approach to Symbolic Communication' in Umiker-Sebeok and Levy, 1988: 189–218

Sontag, S., 1979, *On Photography*, Penguin Books, London

Southern, R., 1959, *The Making of the Middle Ages*, Hutchinson, London

Southworth, E., 1991, 'The Ince Blundell Collection: Collecting Behaviour in the Eighteenth Century', *Journal of the History of Collections*, 3, 2: 219–34

Spamer, E., Bogan, A., and Torrens, H., 1989, 'Recovery of the Ethelred Benett Collection of Fossils', *Proceedings of the Academy of Natural Sciences of Philadelphia*, 141: 115–80

Speakman, C., 1982, *Adam Sedgwick*, Broad Oak Press/Geological Society of London/Trinity College, Cambridge

Spriggs, M. (ed.), 1977, *Archaeology and Anthropology: Areas of Mutual Interest*, BAR Supplementary Series 19, British Archaeological Reports, Oxford

Stenton, F. M., 1955, *Anglo-Saxon England*, Oxford University Press

Stevens, C., 1986, *Writers of Wales: Iorwerth C. Peate*, Cardiff University Press

Stewart, S., 1984, *On Longing: Narratives of the Miniature, the Gigantic, the Souvenir, the Collection*, Johns Hopkins Press, Baltimore

Strabo, 1949, *The Geography of Strabo*, trans. H. L. Jones, Loeb Classical Library, William Heinemann, London

Strong, D. (ed.), 1973a, *Archaeological Theory and Practice: Essays Presented to W. E. Grimes*, Routledge & Kegan Paul, London

Strong, D., 1973b, 'Roman Museums' in Strong, 1973a: 247–64

Swann, J., 1969, 'Shoes Concealed in Buildings', *Northampton Museums and Art Gallery Journal*, December: 8–21

Swinburne, R., 1984, 'Personal Identity: A Materialist's Account' in Shoemaker and Swinburne, 1984: 67–132

Taborsky, E., 1982, 'The Sociostructural Role of the Museum', *International Journal of Museum Management and Curatorship*, 1: 339–45

Taborsky, E., 1985, 'Syntax and Society', *Canadian Review of Sociology and Anthropology*, 22, 1: 80–92

Tait, H., and Gere, C., 1978, *The Jeweller's Art: An Introduction to the Hull Grundy Gift to the British Museum*, British Museum Publications, London

Tate Gallery, Liverpool, 1993, *Elective Affinities*, Tate Gallery, Liverpool

Thieme, P., 1953, 'Die Heimat der indogermanischen Gemeinsprache', *Abhandlungen der Geistes und Sozialwissenschaftlichen*, Akademie der Wissenschaft und der Literatur, Wiesbaden: 535–610

Thirsk, J., 1976, 'The European debate on customs of inheritance 1500–1700' in Goody *et al.*, 1976: 177–91

Thirsk, J., 1979, *Economic Policy and Projects*, Oxford University Press

Thomas, C., 1981, *Christianity in Roman Britain to AD 500*, Batsford, London

Thomas, J., 1990, 'Same, Other Analogue: Writing the Past' in Baker and Thomas, 1990: 18–23

Thomas, N., 1994, 'Licensed Curiosity: Cook's Pacific Voyages' in Elsner and Cardinal, 1994: 116–36

Thomas, N. L., 1982, 'Dr Hugh Fawcett: Obituary', *The Times*, 15 January, London

Thompson, E. P., 1979, *The Making of the English Working Class*, Penguin Books, London

Thompson, M., 1979, *Rubbish Theory*, Oxford University Press

Thorlby, A., (ed.), 1966, *The Romantic Movement*, Longman, London

Tiryakian, E. A. (ed.), 1974, *On the Margin of the Visible: Sociology, the Esoteric and the Occult*, John Wiley & Sons, New York

Torbrügge, W., 1971, 'Vor und Frühgeschichtliche Flussfunde', *Bericht der Römisch–Germanischen Kommission*: 1–146

Tredre, R., 1993, 'Denim's Big Three Get Back in the Saddle', *Independent*, 31 July: 35

Ucko, P., 1969 'Penis Sheaths: A Comparative Study'. *Proceedings of the Royal Anthropological Institute*, 2: 27–67.

Umiker-Sebeok J., and Levy, Sidney (eds), 1988, *Marketing and Semiotics: New Directions in the Study of Signs for Sale*, Indiana University Press, Bloomington

Vaidyanathan, T., 1989, 'Authority and Identity in India', *Daedalus*, 118: 147–69

Van den Bogaard, J., and Wiegman, O., 1991, 'Property Crime Victimization: The Effectiveness of Police Services for Victims of Residential Burglary' in Rudmin, 1991: 329–62

Veblen, T., 1899, *The Theory of the Leisure Class*, Macmillan, New York

Vestergaard, E., 1987, 'The Perpetual Reconstruction of the Past' in Hodder, 1987: 63–7

Waddle, B., 1993, *The Black Museum*, Little, Brown, London

Wade, C. P., 1945, *Haphazard Notes*, National Trust, Cheltenham

Waldstein, C., 1889, *Catalogue of Casts in the Museum of Classical Archaeology*, Cambridge

Wallace, M., 1993, 'Interview with Toy Collector', unpublished: personal communication

Wallerstein, I., 1974, *The Modern World-System*, 1 vol., Academic Press, New York

Warrington, J., 1964, *Aristotle: Prior and Posterior Analytics*, Dent, London

Watkins, C., 1982, 'Aspects of Indo-European Poetics' in Polomé, 1982: 104–20

Wenley, R., 1991, 'Robert Paston and the Yarmouth Collection', *Norfolk Archaeology*, 41: 113–44

Whitaker, J., 1912, *Jottings of a Naturalist*, W. Black, London

Whitehead, P., 1969, 'Zoological Specimens from Captain Cook's Voyages' *Journal of Society of Natural History Bibliography*, 5, 3: 161–201

Whitehead, P., 1971, 'Museums in the History of Zoology', *Museums Journal*, 70, 4: 155–60

Whitehouse, H., 1989, 'Egyptology in the Seventeenth Century. The case of the Bodleian Shabti', *Journal of the History of Collections*, 1, 2: 187–96

Whitley, M. T., 1929, 'Children's Interest in Collecting', *Journal of Educational Psychology*, 20: 249–61

Wilkinson, J. (ed.), 1986, *Feminist Social Psychology: Developing Theory and Practice*, Open University Press, Milton Keynes

Williams, N, 1989, *The Breaking and Remaking of the Portland Vase*, British Museum Publications, London

Williams, R., 1982, *Dream Worlds: Mass Consumption in Late Nineteenth-Century France*, University of California Press, Berkeley

Willis, P., 1990, *Common Culture*, Open University Press, Milton Keynes

Willis, S., 1991, *A Primer for Daily Life*, Routledge, London

Wilson, A. N., 1983, *The Sweets of Pimlico*, Penguin Books, London

Wilson, E., and Taylor, L., 1989, *Through the Looking Glass*, BBC Books, London

Witty, P., 1931, 'Sex differences: Collecting Interests', *Journal of Educational Psychology*, 22: 221–8

Wodehouse, P. G., 1967, *Something Fresh*, Random House, London

Woolf, V., 1978, *Between the Acts*, Granada Publishing, London

Wornum, R., 1851, 'The Exhibition as a Lesson in Taste', *Art Journal Illustrated Catalogue*, London

Wotters, C., 1961, *The Cloud of Unknowing*, Penguin Books, London

Wright, D. (ed. and trans.), 1953, *Beowulf*, Penguin Books, London

Yamaguchi, M., 1991, 'The Poetics of Exhibition in Japanese Culture' in Karp and Levine, 1991: 57–67

Yates, F. A., 1966, *The Art of Memory*, Routledge & Kegan Paul, London

INDEX